A Hill on Which to Die is a story of faith, c
a layman as devoted to Christ and to the Bible
Thank you, Judge Paul Pressler, for setting the _

W. A. Criswell, Pastor ~~~~~~~~
First Baptist Church, Dallas, Texas

My friend, Judge Paul Pressler, served with distinction in the Texas Judiciary.
I am most grateful for his contributions to Texas jurisprudence.

John L. Hill
Former Chief Justice of the Texas Supreme Court
Former Attorney General of the State of Texas

Reading this fascinating book will convince you that God began preparing
his servant Paul Pressler early in his youth to be the principal architect of the
amazing return of the largest denomination in America to its conservative principles. This book reveals many inside details of the most imporant religious event
of the 20th century. I found the book captivating reading! Anyone concerned
about the work of God in our generation should read this book!

Tim LaHaye
Author, Minister

Judge Paul Pressler has written a fascinating book which describes a courageous battle for truth and integrity and which makes one appreciate the contribution of principled leaders serving the Southern Baptist Convention. This is an
important book that shows the way to return to the ideals of religion and morality that have made America great.

Edwin Meese III
Former Attorney General of the United States

Factual! Compelling! *A Hill on Which to Die* is a real page-turner for any
who want the truth and an inside view of the conservative resurgence in the
Southern Baptist Convention. No one can better tell the story than Paul Pressler.
Southern Baptists owe an incredible debt to this man.

Adrian Rogers, Pastor
Bellevue Baptist Church, Cordova, Tennessee

I am very happy that the correct account has been told of President Bush's
offer to appoint Judge Paul Pressler to be Director of the Office of Government
Ethics. This appropriately clears the record.

Chase Untermeyer
Director of White House Personnel under President George Bush

CONTENTS

𝒫REFACE

Why would a person give up personal comfort and ease to become involved in a distasteful and bitter conflict that would impact his entire life? Some people have difficulty accepting the fact that a person might simply have convictions which are so strong that he or she must stand for them. I truly believe that Jesus Christ is "the way, the truth, and the life" and that "no man cometh unto the Father, but by" Him (John 14:6). Believing this, I had no option but to stand for what I know to be the truth. If you love a person, you must tell that person what you know to be true and what has meant everything to you. Not to share and not to make sure others have a chance to know the truth would be an unloving act of callous disregard. In order that individuals might understand how I came to my convictions and to know who I am in relationship to the Southern Baptist Convention movement to restore biblical fidelity, I write this book.

Some people might ask, "Why should another book on the Southern Baptist Convention be written? Many already exist." This book is not a definitive or completely chronological history. It is not an analytical work but my personal observations and the telling, as forthrightly as I possibly can, of why I felt that God had me do what I did and how I saw events unfolding in the convention. It is my story. It gives my background and contains my own personal reactions and observations, as they arise from my heart. You will find facts not before published. However, the events recorded here are accurate.

The notoriety which has come my way is not what I sought, envisioned, or desired. I signed on to help for what I hoped would be a short period. I thought that once we raised questions about the theological problems in our institutions, those in positions of authority would be willing to listen, others would lead, and the issues would be solved. We tried to discuss the issues personally with those in authority before corrective action began, but they rebuffed us. We believed that by having a conservative elected president of the convention, those in authority would then start listening to our concerns. I was not prepared for the onslaught directed against us by those vested with power within the convention.

History might not deal charitably with the conservative movement because so many of those who write history are not sympathetic with our goals and purposes. Since becoming involved in this controversy and having reviewed media accounts, I have become suspicious concerning the facts and the personalities of others who have been involved in historical movements in previous times. I know now, more than ever, that I see events and people through the opinions and prejudices of those who are writing about them. This I regret.

The excessive questioning of the motives of those of us who were involved in the conservative movement has distressed me. If the Lord tarries, it may interest those who might study the Southern Baptist Convention years from now to know what was really in the heart and mind of one of the participants. For this reason, I have written this book—not only to shed light on events that have not previously been explored in print but also to give my personal perspective.

Now that the controversy is essentially over, perhaps some people will try to understand what happened. This is not an argument for victory but an explanation of why a course correction had to occur and why, at great sacrifice, the battle had to be waged.

Terms are often confusing. Therefore, let me explain how I am using certain words. I use the word *liberal* to describe a belief that the original text of the Bible can or does contain errors or mistakes. I use the word *conservative* to describe a belief that the original text of the Bible was written by God in such a way that it is free from error or mistakes. A liberal is a person who holds to a liberal belief as it regards the Bible. Frequently I refer to an individual member of the liberal group as a "moderate," believing that a *moderate* is a person who protects the teaching of liberal theology regardless of his or her personal theology. A *conservative* is a person who holds to a conservative belief as it regards the Bible.

I refer to individuals throughout the book either by giving their full names and titles or by calling them by their first names. After a proper introduction of a person, I generally refer to a person in the manner in which I would address the individual to his or her face. If I call a person by his or her first name, I so refer to that person here. If I call that individual by a title, I do the same in this book.

Various examples are given related to matters being discussed. It has been hard to select which events to use. Space does not allow all to be reported. A reader should not assume that there is not additional substantiation. There is.

Frequently when we discussed a matter, Adrian Rogers would ask, "Is this a hill on which to die?" He was inquiring as to whether this really was an important enough issue upon which to expend energy and effort. By such an analysis we avoided extraneous matters.

Conservatives worked together because we believed that the restoration of the Southern Baptist Convention to a position of standing upon the complete trustworthiness of God's Word was a hill on which to die. We were willing to make personal sacrifices because we believed this. We believed that many people who could have been won to Jesus Christ would be eternally lost if liberal theology destroyed the Southern Baptist Convention as a force for evangelism and missions. This conviction made the cause truly "a hill on which to die." Countless millions will be brought to Christ because our institutions are being returned to the faith once delivered to the saints based on the authority of God's Word. A greater hill on which to die has never existed for a follower of our Savior.

This book is dedicated to the most wonderful wife and children anyone ever had. Nancy, Jean, Anne, and Paul carried much of the load as my time, which should have been more available to them, was used for the work of the convention. They never complained and were as dedicated to the goals as I. To them goes any credit that should occur from a human point of view. Their constant love and support enabled me to proceed.

January 1, 1999

$\mathcal{M}$Y HERITAGE

The preacher spoke faithfully at the associational meeting. His message was not for the reserved or fainthearted. He proclaimed:

> When false teachers are among us, . . . should we not, the united Baptists, cleave to our union, repel invasion, put down this hideous error, and drive away this monster of evil origin from the purity of the sanctuary? . . . we exhort you to your duty, but yet, we beseech you to do it with meekness and mildness if you can, but forcibly if you must; mark such as walk disorderly, reclaim them if you can, but when you cannot, put such away from you.

Despite the familiar ring of these words, they were not uttered during the recent Southern Baptist Convention controversy but almost 150 years before it began. My great-great-great grandfather, John Leigh Townes, preached this message in the September 1834 meeting of the Muscle Shoals Baptist Association in northern Alabama. The false teachers to which he referred were not the ones who denied the truth of the Word of God but rather the Campbellites, who were confusing some Baptists.

His words remind me that I am a product of the people and events who came before me and influenced my life. Thus, the story of my life begins with my spiritual and physical forebears. The streams that flow into the great river that has helped form me spiritually are not fresh or new. They are centuries old and run very deep. Multiple generations before me have laid groundwork that would eventually define me as a Christian, a Baptist, and a conservative. They would serve as role models for me as an active layman in Baptist life.

As early as in fourteenth-century Germany, my paternal grandfather's branch of the family laid some crucial roots for my Christian heritage. In 1395 my ancestor, Johann Bressler, royal secretary to King Wenzel of Bohemia, left Breslau, Germany, and moved to Neumark, in the state of Silesia. The family was called Bressler since it came from Breslau. The name Pressler is an English adaptation of Bressler, the German *b* being the same as the English *p*. About 1630 his descendant and my ancestor, Johann Pressler, and his cousin

Christopher left Silesia. Christopher went to Wittenberg to become a professor of law at the great university in this center of Lutheran learning. My ancestor Johann went to Strausburg, which was also a Protestant area. It was because of their strong Lutheran convictions that they moved from Silesia, which remained Roman Catholic, into areas which were Protestant.

These convictions continued to influence for yet two more centuries, into the family of his descendant and my direct ancestor, Charles William Pressler (Karl Wilhelm in German). Charles William, the youngest of ten children of August Nathaniel Jacob Pressler and his wife, Marie Christine Hermann, lost his mother when he was seven years old and was reared by an older sibling, Hermann Pressler, a Lutheran minister and head of the Lutheran school in Eislaben, Germany (where Martin Luther had lived and died). Charles became the first Pressler to settle in Texas. He migrated there from Germany in 1845.

His brother Hermann, as president of the Lutheran school, made pro-democracy statements and was put on trial for treason for those remarks. Charles returned to Germany for the trial. When it became obvious that Hermann was about to be convicted, the family escaped to Texas. Hermann became a Lutheran minister in New Orleans and died in the yellow fever epidemic of 1863.

Meanwhile, Charles settled in Austin, Texas, where he ultimately joined an Episcopal church. He named one of his sons Herman Paul Pressler, after the brother who reared him and after another brother, Paul. As Herman Paul Pressler III, I am Charles's great grandson. The original Herman Paul, son of Charles, was also the first Baptist in this Pressler family. He joined First Baptist Church of Austin about 1904 after he married Veannis Maddox, and he remained a member of that church until his death in 1937.

While my roots extend in my paternal grandfather's family to pre-Martin Luther Germany, my Baptist roots are deep ones with the Maddoxes, the family of my paternal grandmother.

The family that eventually would produce Veannis Maddox moved to Elk River in Fayette County, Tennessee, before 1800. The Maddoxes were not educated people, but they evidently were devout members of a Baptist church in that area. Their son, Nicholas, learned to speak Cherokee from the Indians who lived there. When the Cherokee Indians were moved from Alabama and Tennessee to the Oklahoma Territory in the event known as the "Trail of Tears," Nicholas became a scout on the trail. He moved to what is now Grayson County, Texas, and built his homestead at Indian Springs. He was active in a Baptist church in Grayson County, served on the first county Commissioner's Court of Fannin County, which then embraced Grayson County, and was the grandfather of my grandmother, Veannis Maddox Pressler, who married Herman Paul Pressler.

Veannis Maddox accepted Jesus Christ as Savior in a revival meeting in First Baptist Church of Austin in 1894 and was a member of that church until her death in 1975—eighty-one years a member of the same church. She taught Sunday School in the primary department for more than fifty years. As a child, I frequently visited my grandparents, accompanied them to Sunday School, and heard my grandmother teach. In her class were many students who eventuall became prominent in Texas Baptist life as well as in social, business, and political events in Texas.

Two other individuals who were my progenitors made their crucial connection with the Baptist faith quite unexpectedly (probably from their perspective but certainly not from God's). My great-great grandfather, Eggleston Dick Townes, wrote the following about his parents:

> My father Rev. John L. Townes was born in Amelia County, Virginia in 1784 . . . . He was married in 1806 to my mother who was P. S. Eggleston of Amelia County, Virginia . . . . In 1815 his wife who had been raised a high church Episcopalian attended a protracted meeting held in the neighborhood at Grub Hill Church, by a Brother Dabbs. She went to the event at first just to "see and be seen." As she entered the door the minister was reading his text. In a very solemn and impressive manner he read, "Marvel not that I say to you, ye must be born again." She was startled, [for she] had always thought herself as good as she could be. She was convicted of sin and attending the meeting through the week was converted and baptized the next Sabbath. To join the Baptist church was looked on in those days, and particularly by her friends and relatives, as quite disgraceful. The Maj. (her husband) was highly incensed. But his wife being a high-minded woman of good practical sense and deep piety with it patiently and at length argued that if he would study the Scripture with her, particularly the New Testament, and help her examine the questions of spiritual regeneration and immersion baptism, that if she was wrong she would leave the church. The Maj. was a skeptic, but after reading the New Testament, he became a believer and soon a converted sinner, and was happily converted and [was] baptized in 1816. Of course after investigating the New Testament, he too joined the Baptist church and very soon felt the Divine call to preach the gospel to perishing sinners, who like he had been blind and ignorant of the great plan of salvation through a crucified and ascended Savior. Indeed his first sermon was at the water the day he was baptized. Many of the lawyers were there and several became prominent Christians, dating their conviction of sin and acceptance of salvation from his exhortation and baptism.

It was Rev. John L. Townes' quotation that begins this chapter.

John Leigh Townes served as pastor in northern Alabama and southern Tennessee and with his first cousin, William Leigh, helped in the founding of the town of Leighton, Alabama. He was pastor of the First Baptist churches of Courtland, Florence, and of Moulton, among other pastorates he held in northern Alabama.

His son, Eggleston Dick Townes, was chancellor (judge) in northern Alabama. In 1854 Dick Townes resigned this position and moved to Manor, Texas, with his family and a group of relatives and friends. He served as the first moderator of the Austin Baptist Association and was active in Texas Baptist life. His son, John Charles Townes, who was a district judge and later dean of law at the University of Texas for many years (the law school building there is named for him), was also very active in Texas Baptist life. He was Sunday School director at First Baptist Church of Austin and later led the organization of University Baptist Church in Austin, where he taught a large Sunday School class for many years. He was vice president of the Baptist General Convention of Texas.

His son, my maternal grandfather, Edgar Eggleston Townes, was the lawyer who wrote the original charter of the Humble Oil and Refining Company (which later merged into Exxon) and was general counsel of that company from 1917 to 1943. In 1904, he married my grandmother, Mary Elsie Garrett, in Brenham, Texas. He was an outstanding Baptist layman, serving as a deacon in his church and on the Baylor University trustee board for many years. I remember as a child accompanying my grandfather to listen to him preach. Later I drove him to preaching assignments so I could spend extra time with him.

Through my grandfather, Edgar Eggleston Townes, I also have a connection with the Huguenots, the legendary French group who fled France in search of religious freedom. In 1667 Suzanne Rochet, who would be the great-great-great-great-great grandmother of E. E. Townes, was born in Sedan, France. Her parents, Jean Rochet and Marie Trufel Rochet, were Huguenots. When the Edict of Nantes, which gave Protestants civil and religious rights, was revoked by Louis XIV in 1685, two of their daughters fled France because of their faith in the Lord Jesus Christ. In the confusion of the flight, their little sister, Suzanne, was left behind. Her father remained in France, and after the Catholic authorities prepared to put Suzanne in a Roman Catholic convent, he managed to have her smuggled out of France on a ship in a large barrel marked "Merchandise." All correspondence between the father and sisters referred in code to Suzanne as "the little nightcap" that was left behind.

On July 13, 1692, she married Abraham Michaux, who, with his family, had also fled from Sedan, France. He was the great-grandson of Rev. Nicholas

Severin, pastor of a refugee Huguenot church in Ludweiler, Germany. Ultimately Abraham and Suzanne Michaux immigrated to Virginia around 1702. In 1744 he died in Goochland County, Virginia, leaving a will which read in part as follows:

> First and principally, I commend my soul unto the hands of Almighty God, hoping through the merit, death, and passion of my Savior, Jesus Christ, to have full and free pardon and forgiveness of all my sins and to inherit everlasting life and my body I commend to the earth to be decently buried.

Baptist roots once again extend back generations in my maternal grandmother's family—the Garretts—as well. Before the American Revolution, Edward Garrett (born 1733) and his wife, Ann Owsley Garrett, moved from Virginia to South Carolina. Some family records indicate that they were Tories. On January 5, 1883, my great-grandfather wrote concerning him as follows: "During the Revolutionary War he was a Tory, thinking it a crime to rebel against the king. His descendants have not been very proud of his record as a Tory, but it shows a conservatism that has passed down to his posterity."

Records show that the Garrett family gave the land for the Warrior Creek Baptist Church in Laurens County, South Carolina, before 1800. The graves of many Garretts are found in the churchyard on the land they gave.

A grandson of the Edward Garretts—Hosea Garrett, born in 1800—was a Baptist preacher. His daughter, Nancy, married her first cousin, O. H. P. Garrett, who had come to Texas in the 1830s. He had returned home to marry. Hosea Garrett went with his new son-in-law and daughter to Chappell Hill, Texas, as a Baptist missionary. Hosea Garrett was much opposed to a charismatic movement that seems to have been under way in South Carolina at that time. This movement used prayer cloths and the laying on of hands. This was one of the reasons he left South Carolina for Texas.

When Hosea arrived in Texas, he founded the Providence Baptist Church of Chappell Hill, Texas, in the early 1840s. He was a leading pastor in Texas, served as chairman of the Baylor University board of trustees for thirty-eight out of its first forty years of existence, and was a major contributor to Baylor. In *A History of Texas Baptists* by J. M. Carroll, on pages 202-203, appears this paragraph:

> It is probably an unquestionable fact that Hosea Garrett was the greatest single friend that old Baylor at Independence ever had. From the day of its founding to the time of its removal from Independence, Garrett was the one single, continuous friend . . . Garrett worked for Baylor continuously for over forty years, and was officially connected with it. Nearly every year of that time he was President of the Board of Trustees. For twenty consecutive years he

missed only one meeting of the Board. For ten consecutive years he served as her agent without any pay, and in addition, during Baylor's life at Independence, he probably gave to it more money than any single other individual.

He preached the convention sermon in 1855 and was elected president of the Baptist State Convention in 1860 and also was second vice president of the Southern Baptist Convention. He was very close to other Texas Baptist leaders. A letter addressed to Garrett from Brother H. C. McIntyre on December 31, 1873 states as follows:

> Our mutual friend and brother Judge Baylor died yesterday (at) one o'clock. His dying request (was) that you should perform the funeral service . . . I purchased his coffin last night and Carter will be after it this morning. He will be buried on the college grounds in Independence. Can't say at what time 'til Carter gets here.

Hosea Garrett was killed at the age of eighty-eight when he was thrown from a horse.

His son-in-law (also his nephew), O. H. P. Garrett, was secretary of the Baptist State Convention from 1859–61 and 1869–85. He was corresponding secretary in 1867. After the Baptist General Convention of Texas was formed, he was secretary of this convention in 1886.

O. H. P. Garrett's son, Christopher Columbus Garrett, was also active in Texas Baptist work. He served as district judge and then the first chief justice of the First Court of Appeals from 1892 to 1905. He and his wife read books in Greek and Latin. Their daughter, Mary Elsie Garrett, married Edgar Eggleston Townes in 1904. They were my maternal grandparents.

An early Baylor University supporter; an early leader of the BGCT; Baptist pastors in Virginia, Texas, South Carolina, Alabama, and Tennessee; longtime Texas Baptist Sunday School teachers; outstanding Baptist laymen; Baylor trustee board members; those who suffered for their faith in Europe during the early days of the Reformation—all these forebears of mine made lasting imprints in my life as a Christian and in Baptist life in this country for decades before my birth.

I agree with the psalmist who wrote, "The lines are fallen unto me in pleasant places; yea, I have a goodly heritage" (Ps. 16:6).

$\mathcal{T}$HE CONTENTED, CURIOUS YEARS

Family togetherness, church activities, a comfortable lifestyle, contentment, and an appreciation for and curiosity about a world beyond my immediate boundaries marked my early years in Houston, Texas.

My father was a lawyer, very hardworking and very successful. He moved from the legal department of the Humble Oil and Refining Company into general management and was vice president and director of Exxon USA after Humble was merged into it. He was president of the Houston Bar Association and, among other things, gave tremendously of his time on a volunteer basis to the Texas Medical Center. He served as chairman of its management committee and chairman of the board of Texas Children's Hospital.

My mother spent many hours giving of herself in community activities, as well. She was president of the Junior League of Houston, the Houston Heritage Society, the River Oaks Garden Club, and the Houston Bar Auxiliary, and has been active in many other worthwhile organizations. Despite her community involvement, my mother managed with good live-in help to provide for me and my younger brother, Townes Garrett Pressler. We were surrounded with love.

In spite of my parents' busy lives, they always found time for my brother and me. They were available for the little things and were involved in supporting us in our daily lives. Both my parents read extensively and were excellent marksmen, both with rifles and shotguns. As a family, we particularly enjoyed bird hunting and spent much time together in duck blinds and around stock ponds where doves came to water. In addition, we took many wonderful family trips. My family members loved me and supported me, giving me a firm foundation for life. They are the ones I have sought to emulate.

Since my brother was five years younger than I, we had different friends but were close. When I was at Princeton University, he attended prep school at Lawrenceville, just ten minutes away. Because both of us were in New Jersey, this allowed us times together. When I was in law school at the University of Texas, he was an undergraduate there. He is now a successful petroleum engineer in Houston, and we live in the same neighborhood. He and his wife Bette have three children and presently seven grandchildren, all of whom are close to us and our children and grandchildren. Townes and Bette are both active in community activities.

From my earliest days, I remember attending Sunday School and church at Houston's South Main Baptist, where my parents married in 1928. My grandfather Townes was one of the leading Sunday School teachers and deacons of South Main, and my grandmother taught Sunday School and was active in all phases of church life. They were the model Christian family. I was very close to them and did many things with them. They had a profound influence on my life. They were the most genuine and outstanding Christian couple I have ever known. We held the same values and had the same motivations and priorities. I was so blessed to have had them as a second set of loving parents.

I remember sitting in the church and hearing my pastor, Dr. E. Hermond Westmoreland, preach. Ernest Loessner was our education director, and D. K. Harrell led the youth. I admired, loved, and appreciated our Baptist leaders.

Because the Texas heat was so severe and no air conditioning existed, many families, including ours, moved away from Houston for the summer. Therefore, some of my earliest memories relate to the summers that we spent in the Adirondack Mountains in upstate New York. My grandfather and grandmother Townes owned a home on a hill near Elizabethtown, New York, where my Uncle Chris, who was born blind, his wife, my mother, and an aunt brought their children each year until World War II started. I never began or finished a year of school on time, since we moved up in May and returned in September.

We had a main guest house on our part of the hill, with five bedrooms for the family and two rooms for servants' quarters. There was also a guest house. My grandmother would motor up with the cook, the maid, and the chauffeur, while the gardener lived year-round in the village near our summer home. The men of the family moved to the country outside Houston and stayed on a farm of my grandfather's near Humble, Texas—an area which is now the El Dorado Country Club.

For a small child, the days in Elizabethtown were wonderful, with no poisonous snakes and a large area of mountain beauty over which I could wander. I had my cousins to play with, and adults were always available. We loved riding around in the seven-passenger Lincoln touring car, with Uncle Chris playing the harmonica. As we rode, we sang hymns and old-time songs. The highlight of the summer was when my father arrived and spent a couple of weeks with the family.

Several adults who summered there also were particularly kind to me. We swam in the pool at the home of the Lambs. Mr. Lamb was an architect who was instrumental in building the Empire State Building. Judge Augustus Hand's family had a home on the main street of town. He and his brother, Judge Learned Hand, were especially friendly toward me. I remember one afternoon in particular when I, as an eight- or nine-year-old boy, spent a couple of hours talking with the Judges Hand in the library of their home. Just below us on the hill was the home of the Campe family from New York City. Mrs. Campe's brother was Nate Leipzig, who spent most of the summers with them. He was a magician. I know now that he was one of our nation's greatest magicians, but I knew him as a friend who entertained me in a delightful way. He made a coin walk over his fingers through muscle control and did other things which charmed me.

My grandparents located in Elizabethtown because Mr. and Mrs. Wayman Adams had an artist studio and art school there. My grandfather's sister and Mrs. Adams were brought up together. Mr. Adams was world-renowned as an artist and painted my mother and me along with other members of the family. I knew him as my friend who told wonderful jokes. I still remember some of them. As a young boy I was greatly blessed by my adult friends.

Only one thing bothered me about those summers in Elizabethtown—the Baptist church there closed for the summer. Combined services were held with the other denominations. This seemed very strange to me, as I could not understand people not having tremendous spiritual needs in the summertime as well as in the winter.

When I was ten years old, I came to know Jesus Christ as my personal Savior. This occurred during a revival meeting at South Main Baptist Church. I was sitting about six rows back in the middle section of the church. The preacher talked about what being a genuine Christian involved. I realized that I had never disbelieved the gospel; I had always accepted the facts of the gospel, just as I had accepted the other facts of history, but I had never recognized that *I* was a sinner and that Jesus Christ shed His blood to pay the price for *my* sins. As I sat in the pew, I bowed my head, accepted Him as Savior and Lord, and Jesus Christ came into my heart.

Although our family was very close and loving, a cloud hung over our family's church attendance because of a sin that my father saw occur during his young adulthood. My father made a profession of faith in the First Baptist Church of Austin, Texas, in March 1916, and was baptized the following June 18 at age thirteen. His father was a deacon, and his family vacationed and picnicked frequently with the pastor, his family, and several other families from the church. Six years later, the pastor ran off with a woman from the church.

This event affected the remainder of my father's life. He never again trusted pastors and regularly commented that pastors were hypocrites. He attended

Sunday School regularly but rarely attended worship. His mother, my grand-mother Pressler, also rarely attended the worship services of her church even though she taught in the primary department for more than fifty years in First Baptist Church of Austin, Texas. The rest of my father's family members were also greatly affected by this pastor's sin.

A couple of years after I became a Christian and the Lord was making a real difference in my life, I overhead my father say to my mother one night, "I told you when we were married that we should have gone and joined the Episcopal church. Paul never would have heard of any of this business about being saved over there." That greatly disturbed me because it clearly revealed my father's atti-tude and the struggle he had with Baptist pastors because of the sin of one.

My father died in 1995. For more than seventy years, the sin committed by the pastor of his youth affected his life and that of his whole family. I am grate-ful that he really trusted the Lord when he was a young man. This trust was espe-cially evident in the last months of his life.

My father's attitude about ministers created a particular hurdle for my church attendance in my youth. On Sunday mornings, I rode to Sunday School with my parents and stayed for church with my grandfather and grandmother Townes, since my parents returned home after Sunday School. Because I desired to attend Training Union on Sunday nights, I rode with Dr. and Mrs. John Henry Wootters, who lived two houses from us. After I obtained my driver's license at age fourteen, I was told I could use the car if I had a date or wanted to go to the country club for the Sunday evening dance but not if I wanted to go to church. If the Wootters were not in town, I would ride the bus to church.

I knew Jesus Christ had saved me. I knew that He was real. The hurdle that I had to jump to attend church merely strengthened my resolve to be faithful to Him. The ease of doing something other than attending church merely made me more determined to go, because I saw it as a barrier that Satan was putting before me. Perhaps opposition to my Christian faith at an early age was training that the Lord was giving me for future trials that were to come.

An important part of my spiritual growth occurred on a ranch named Hazy Hills, where my family began retreating for the summer after World War II began and we could no longer travel to the Adirondacks. Hazy Hills was a ranch which my grandfather Townes owned at Dripping Springs, in the Texas hill country near Austin. We went there several times during the year in addition to our summer stays. My parents, grandparents, brother, and I rode horseback for hours over those rugged limestone hills, along the beautiful creeks, and through the fields. I herded sheep and goats with the ranch hands. I often rode off by myself on my horse, stopping by a sparkling stream and reading my Bible. We had an old pump organ in the ranch house. I have precious memories of our standing around that old organ as my grandmother played the great old gospel hymns while we sang. Hazy Hills still belongs to the family.

God taught me a valuable lesson one weekend at the ranch. Each time we left the main ranch house, it was cleaned so the next group of my grandparents' family could find it in good shape when they came to use it. One Sunday afternoon, as our family prepared to return to Houston, I got ready first, went to the main room of the ranch house, turned on the radio, and listened to Dr. Charles E. Fuller on "The Old-Fashioned Revival Hour."

Dr. Fuller was preaching from Romans 8:28 and was putting the emphasis on the word *all* in the Scripture that says, "All things work together for good to them that love God." I thought it was silly for him to emphasize *all* since so many irrelevant things occur in life. As a teenager who always wanted to test everything, I got up out of my chair, walked a few steps over to the hearth of the fireplace, picked up a broom, put it down, returned to my seat, and said to myself, "Now what difference did that make? Nobody else will ever know whether I picked up that broom or not."

I then looked back at the fireplace. When I had picked up the boom, I had dislodged a stinging scorpion, a small and pain-inducing central Texas creature, from its hiding place in the broom. It needed to be killed to prevent injury to someone using the house. I got some newspaper, swatted it to death, cleaned up the mess, and went to the garbage can to deposit the newspaper I had used. The garbage can was empty. The ranch foreman had already hauled the trash away for burning.

I decided that I couldn't leave the mess in the garbage can, so I got some matches and walked down the hill to the barbecue pit and burned the paper. I made sure all of the sparks were out. I then went up the hill to the ranch house and was washing my hands at the kitchen sink. The window by the sink looked down the hill, and through it, I could see that the side of the hill was on fire. Evidently a spark from the barbecue pit had escaped.

Several members of our family fought the fire for a couple of hours. With the help of ranch hands, we were able to save two outbuildings which the flames almost reached. When the fire was out, I realized the chain of events that led up to the fire. Now when I teach from Romans 8:28, I emphasize *all*, even as Dr. Fuller so firmly imprinted on my mind that day.

CHAPTER 3

$\mathcal{A}$WAY FROM HOME

When I was sixteen, my family and I decided I would go away to prep school at Phillips Exeter Academy in Exeter, New Hampshire. Several of my friends were already attending there, and I was eager to go. My parents believed that the education I was receiving in Houston was not challenging enough for me. The move to Exeter was a chance to learn and to see a great deal more of the country. I have always enjoyed studying and the opportunities of learning.

I will never forget my first trip to Exeter. I flew with some friends in a private plane to New York City. Once there, they dropped me off at the Waldorf Astoria Hotel. When the cab pulled away from the curb, I realized that a month after my sixteenth birthday, I was all alone in New York City with enough money in my pocket to do whatever I wanted, and I no longer had family supervision. I am glad my relationship with Jesus Christ was sufficiently strong for God to have worked in my life—keeping me from doing something I would later regret. Although I was surrounded by temptation in that large, worldly city, and elsewhere on the East Coast, I experienced a period of spiritual victory rather than a period of defeat.

The next morning, I took a taxi from the Waldorf to Grand Central Station and traveled by train to Exeter. No one there "talked right." They all had Yankee accents, and it was a very dismal day for a Texas teenager. The train was late arriving in Exeter, and I was "fussed at" for being tardy. When I arrived in my room, I hoped to find good companionship and someone with whom I could talk. My roommate, however, was from Guatemala City and spoke very little English.

After an early breakfast the next morning, I went to the First Baptist Church, which was not quite two blocks from my dormitory. With youthful exuberance I burst into the pastor's office and announced, "I am Paul Pressler. I am from Houston, Texas. I was saved when I was ten. I am going to be here for two years, and I will want to be part of this church." My pastor-to-be, a seminary graduate, looked at me and said, "I don't know what you people from the South mean when you say somebody has been saved."

13

So, two thousand miles from home, at sixteen years of age, I had the privilege of explaining to my pastor-to-be what I believed the Bible taught about salvation. He was a gracious man, but theologically, things were very different. His lovely wife was from North Carolina and was one of the sweetest, nicest persons I have ever known. In many ways, she seemed to share the loneliness of being a Southerner up North, and I think maybe she also shared some of the loneliness of experiencing a different style of preaching and a different theology.

At that time no Sunday School existed in First Baptist Church of Exeter for persons over twelve years of age. The only way I could attend Sunday School was to organize a class and teach it myself, so that's what I did. Each Sunday we averaged about twenty of my schoolmates. Many of them had backgrounds that had never enabled them to hear the gospel. About fifteen to twenty years after I graduated, I received a letter from one of the young men who had been in the class. He had graduated from Rice University in Houston and then moved to Arizona. He told me that he had heard the gospel for the first time in that Sunday School class and that it had bothered him for those many, intervening years. He wanted me to know that he and his wife had just trusted Jesus Christ as personal Savior. I was grateful to know of some fruit from this Bible study. For me to teach the Bible to my contemporaries when I was only sixteen was a challenging but excellent experience.

During the summer, the Baptist church in Exeter held combined services with the Methodists and the Congregationalists, with a rotation of pastors as speakers. Some meetings were also held with the Unitarians. I did not then understand what Unitarianism was, but now I do, and the services with them confirmed some of the things that I barely realized then.

Exeter, of course, had its many diversions. I visited friends at Wellesley College, as well as other friends from Texas who were in New England and enjoyed an active social life. I was also highly interested in debate and politics and participated in various political groups on campus.

Jonathan Daniels, a leading North Carolina Democrat who later married Margaret Truman, the daughter of former President Harry S Truman, spoke to one of our political societies. Afterwards, I told him I had heard that the Baptist churches in North Carolina were becoming liberal theologically and asked him if this were true. He replied that he was unsure, but that if they were, he believed most North Carolinians would stop being Baptists and would join the Assemblies of God, independent Bible churches, or other such churches since the people of North Carolina were conservative. This conversation occurred in the late 1940s.

Although the Exeter experience was good in many ways, it was a wilderness experience spiritually. In this period, I was cut off from the props that had supported me, such as a good church, a supportive family, and a kind environment. These were replaced with attacks on the gospel. The school's Bible teacher taught six or seven students, and I felt that the only reason the school conducted Bible classes at that time was that the school's founder, John Phillips, believed and directed that the Bible should always be taught. A godly man founded Exeter, but when I attended the school, it was not what John Phillips intended for it to be spiritually.

During those days, I felt very much alone. Only a few activities, other than my personal devotional life, helped me spiritually. I attended a Jack Wyrtzen Word of Life Rally in Boston. I went with a small group of very fundamentalist people from the Advent Christian Church in Exeter. I sometimes attended church there, since that was the only church that had services on Sunday night. Also, since we were not allowed to have radios in our rooms at Exeter, I slipped down to the commons room early Sunday mornings and listened to "The Old-Fashioned Revival Hour" with Dr. Charles E. Fuller. His teaching was a tremendous blessing to me.

Most important was that these circumstances drove me to the Word of God for myself, and I found out how wonderful it was for a believer to go to God through His Word and not have to rely on any externals. My personal relationship with the Lord through prayer and through the study of His Word was sufficient to sustain and develop me spiritually. Exeter was, therefore, a good experience for me.

Graduation from Exeter was an excellent occasion. Of course, my parents attended, as did the parents of most of my friends. We went to Wentworth-by-the Sea, New Hampshire, a marvelous hotel near Portsmouth, to celebrate this event. With us was Paul Glenn, my roommate, and his family from Sharon, Pennsylvania. I had spent both of my spring vacations in Sharon with Paul, and we had become close friends. Later Paul became prominent in the investment business. He asked me to give him $10,000 to invest in the commodity market, but my father said that I should not do it under any conditions because it was so risky. Paul ultimately made millions of dollars with the $10,000 he put into the commodity market, and I missed out. The Lord knows what is best for us.

At the time we went to Wentworth-by-the-Sea for my graduation celebration, the 1948 National Governors' Conference was being held there. We saw Texas Governor and Mrs. Beauford Jester and met their daughters. Their daughter, Joanne, later married Tom Berry, an attorney in Houston, and the Berrys are two of our very good friends. My brother took a picture of Gov. Thomas E.

Dewey of New York and Gov. Earl Warren of California having dinner together. This was just a couple of months before the Republican National Convention, at which Dewey chose Warren to be his running mate. The disastrous election of 1948 for the Republican Party, in which Dewey and Warren lost to Truman and Barkley, ensued. In that chance encounter at Wentworth-by-the-Sea, my brother perhaps photographed, and we observed, the formation of the Republican ticket that year.

I had always planned to attend college at the University of Texas. However, all the other members of a group of eight to ten students who had become close friends through debate and public affairs planned to

High school graduation picture of Paul Pressler

go to Princeton. This group convinced me at least to apply to Princeton. When I was accepted, they convinced me to go with them. I decided I would attend Princeton for only a year or two and then transfer to the University of Texas. Hazy Hills, the ranch my grandparents owned, was just twenty miles from campus. I hoped to live on the ranch a great deal of the time, ride horseback, and commute to classes. Reason prevailed, and I accepted my admission to Princeton and remained there for the entire four years.

The Princeton experience was also unsettling in many ways. I knew a little bit of history—that Harvard was founded in 1636 to train young men in the Word of God and to prepare them to be missionaries to the Indians. Fifty years later, Yale was founded to train young men in the Word of God, to prepare them to be missionaries to the Indians, and to combat the theological liberalism at Harvard. In 1746 Princeton was founded to train young men in the Word of God, to prepare them to be missionaries to the Indians, and to combat the theological liberalism at Harvard and at Yale. I thought I was attending a Christian school. I did not realize that Princeton also had become theologically liberal.

Arriving at Princeton was a rude awakening for me. The first week I was on campus, I went to hear the assistant dean of the chapel speaking on the topic,

"The Bible: What It Is and What It Is Not." In essence, he said that a person should not expect a message from God when he or she reads the Bible. He said that the Bible represents humanity's reaching up to conceive the idea of God. He said a person can tell by the beauty of the language and the thought content how high man has reached.

As I recall, he advised that when a reader arrives at a passage such as the Sermon on the Mount or 1 Corinthians 13, these obviously represent good moral and ethical thoughts, and a person should accept them. When a reader arrives at a passage such as "without shedding of blood is no remission" (Heb. 9:22), or "I am the way, the truth, and the life: no man cometh unto the Father, but by me" (John 14:6), that is obviously the culture coming through, so the reader should disregard it. I was offended at this cafeteria-style approach to the Scripture and wondered what I had stumbled into. This caused me to consider returning home and attending the University of Texas after all. I am grateful that God did not allow me to do that because of the learning experiences I had in the East.

Early in my freshman year, I was invited to the home of Dr. Aldridge, the dean of the Princeton University chapel, for a Bible study. I knocked on the door a little early, because I was eager to attend. Dean Aldridge met me at the door. He said, "Mrs. Aldridge and I are having our cocktails on the terrace. Won't you come and join us?" I had not expected a preacher or Christian leader to be consuming alcohol. This showed me again that this spiritual environment was very different from the one from which I had come.

Religion class at Princeton was a different experience, also. Against the advice of some of my Christian friends, I took a couple of religion courses. I wanted to see firsthand what Princeton was teaching, and I was not impressed. The first day in one religion class, the professor drew on the board a map of Palestine. He showed how the trade routes between Europe, Asia, Africa, and the Middle East went through the area. He said that "the Hebrew scriptures" said that if the Jewish people had been religious and followed "their God," they never would have been invaded but would have lived quietly and peacefully. Considering the fact of where these people were located and the trade routes, he asked how many of us thought that they would not have been invaded just because of what the Bible said.

Three or four of us held up our hands. With his hands on his hips, the professor said our answers represented the most stupid display of blind, ignorant faith he had ever seen. He adjured us that we needed to grow up now that we had come to Princeton. He lectured that the only reason that this statement was in the Bible was that the religious leaders in Israel put it in there so they could exercise more control over the people.

I was highly offended by these and other similar remarks that were constantly made in religion class. These instructors operated from the premise that Scripture was the work of men and not of God. Perhaps it was a good thing for me to be exposed to radical liberal theology rather than to have liberalism subtly taught in its incipient form. This way I could recognize it for what it was and see how far liberalism would go when its presuppositions were accepted.

An incident in another class clearly showed the training and thinking of the religion department. The professor stated that Jesus never claimed to be an exclusive way to God. I held up my hand and asked what he thought about Jesus' saying, "I am the way, the truth, and the life: no man cometh unto the Father, but by me." The religion professor asked me, "Where is that?" I replied, "John 14:6." The professor answered, "Oh, John—John is a most unreliable source," and then went on with his lecture.

I was privileged to know various people from Union Theological Seminary and Riverside Church in New York City. There I also saw the essence of liberal theology. One evening, after graduation from Princeton, I was invited to the apartment of a Union professor, Dr. John C. Bennett, who later became president of the seminary. His son, John M. Bennett, who had attended Exeter, although later than I had, was there. Included for dinner were Rene D. Tillich, who also attended Exeter after I did, and Chris Niebuhr (even though he now doesn't remember it). Their fathers were Paul Tillich and Reinhold Niebuhr, well-known leaders of neo-orthodox theology.

I had been witnessing to an Exeter friend who was brought up in the Riverside Church in New York City and had no understanding of the doctrine of the substitutionary atonement—the fact that the Lord Jesus Christ died as our substitute to pay the price for our sins. This friend was at a particularly vulnerable point in his life, since his brother had just committed suicide. I had assisted this family when they were notified of the death. Since they lived in New York City and had no car, I agreed to drive them to Exeter to claim the body and to make funeral arrangements. I also cut my Navy leave time short at Christmas so I could stay with them during part of the Christmas vacation, at their request. It was a family much in need of Christlike love and compassion at this time.

Based on some of our earlier discussions, this friend, who was with me at the dinner with Dr. Bennett, began asking questions of our host. He asked Dr. Bennett if he believed in the inspiration of Scripture, and the professor replied that he believed the Scripture was inspired even as Dante was inspired when he wrote his *Divine Comedy,* as Milton was inspired when he wrote *Paradise Lost,* and as Beethoven was inspired when he wrote his Fifth Symphony.

Then my friend asked him if he believed in the resurrection of Christ. The professor said that if people asked him, he would tell them that he believed in the resurrection of Christ, but he certainly didn't believe the body came out of the tomb. Dr. Bennett said that when he used the term "the resurrection of Christ," he was saying that he believed that the Spirit of Jesus lives on.

My friend then asked him about the virgin birth. We were told that "nobody here" would believe that. However, Dr. Bennett did say that if anybody was trying to pin him down, he would reply in the affirmative, although he didn't believe in the virgin birth literally. He said that when he used the term "virgin birth," he meant that he believed that the conception of Jesus was a "beautiful idea." (I have yet to figure out that remark.) Through the use of a new definition of Christian terms, the gospel was being denied. The professor was using our vocabulary but not our dictionary. At least he was honest enough to explain to our group what he meant. My mind has frequently returned to that time when I sat in that apartment at Union Seminary and listened to what a president-to-be of that seminary had to say about crucial matters of theology.

During my freshman year at Princeton, Ralph Langley, who later became an influential Southern Baptist pastor in Texas and Alabama, and his wife Grace, and James Leo Garrett, who later became a renowned professor at two of our theological seminaries (Southern in Louisville and Southwestern in Fort Worth), and his wife Myrta Ann were at Princeton Seminary. I had the privilege of having their friendship and participating in many activities with them. Ralph wanted to hear Presbyterian preachers like George Buttrick and John Sutherland Bonnell in New York City, so I accompanied him to hear these men. I remember Ralph's being very impressed with their style, but my feeling was that they had very little to say. Although I valued Ralph's friendship very much, we differed.

I will never forget one Sunday when we were driving to church and passed the university tennis courts, where some students were playing tennis. Ralph stopped the car, got out, and yelled to the students, "What do you mean, playing tennis today? Don't you know it's Sunday?" I was very embarrassed, since that was not my style. Later on, I came to theorize that this action probably represented Ralph's conservative background coming through during the time more liberal men like Buttrick and Bonnell were beginning to influence him.

During my freshman year, I joined the Princeton Baptist Church, which was a couple of miles from town. It was an American Baptist church, and some lovely, gracious Christian people were members of it. The Garretts and the

Langleys, as well as others, frequently drove me to church, since Princeton students were not allowed to have cars. No Baptist Sunday evening services were held in Princeton except at the First Baptist Church of Princeton, which was an African-American church. I attended there regularly on Sunday nights. The Garretts, the Langleys, and I were the only regular white attendees. This was in 1948–49, before the school integration decision of *Brown v. Board of Education* and long before the movement toward integration had become strong.

Attending a predominantly African-American church would not be an unusual thing for a person to do now, but it was then. Although the members of the church were gracious, I could not persuade my friends to attend with me. I had no outreach, although I deeply appreciated the Christian fellowship there.

During the fall of my sophomore year, it became obvious that if we were to have any testimony for Jesus Christ to students through a worship service, we must have our own services on campus. From the dean of the chapel's office, I obtained the list of Baptist students and began contacting them. We found some who were interested in starting a Baptist group. Also, I had been attending a group called the Princeton Evangelical Fellowship (PEF) which, although not strong in number, was mighty in spirit. It was an outstanding group, led by Donald Fullerton, an independent missionary to India who had to return to the United States after health problems developed.

Mr. Fullerton had sufficient income to support himself and, as a Princeton graduate of 1913, he had a deep concern for a presentation of the gospel on the campus. He taught Bible studies on Sunday afternoons and Thursday nights. Sometimes one other person and I were the only people present, but God used Mr. Fullerton profoundly as he taught me to love and study the Word of God, even as those in my university classes and in the official religious establishment of Princeton attacked its validity and reliability.

Mr. Fullerton sympathized with our organizing the Baptist group, although he did not participate in it. He gave us a list of names of Baptist pastors in New Jersey who could serve as an advisory board. We therefore organized the Baptist Students of Princeton in the fall of 1949 and received the university's approval as a student organization. The First Baptist Church of Hackensack, New Jersey, extended an arm of its church to Princeton, and more than twenty of us joined it.

This was when an understanding called the Comity Agreement was in effect between the leadership of the Southern and American Baptist conventions. The understanding was that neither Southern Baptists nor American (Northern) Baptists would develop churches in the areas of the other's strength. We had wanted a Southern Baptist church to sponsor us which would allow us to join it. After attempting this, we found that we could not be recognized as a Southern Baptist group, since New Jersey was American Baptist territory and Southern Baptists were not willing at that time to break the Comity Agreement. Therefore, to give doctrinal stability we created an advisory board consisting of some Conservative and some General Association of Regular Baptist churches.

Dr. Joseph Stowell Sr., whose son Joseph Stowell Jr. is now president of Moody Bible Institute in Chicago, was pastor of First Baptist Church of Hackensack, New Jersey, the church we joined. He was a gracious man and did a great deal to help the work at Princeton. The advisory council of six or eight pastors met periodically and encouraged the students. We held our worship services in Murray-Dodge Hall, which was set aside for student religious groups to use. The Jewish group and ours were the main ones to use it for regular worship services.

A couple of years after we had been organized, one of the Baptist students went to request use of Murray-Dodge for Sunday morning and evening services for the following school year and to be sure it was reserved for us. The woman in charge did not know the student and remarked that she was glad his group was first because the school had been trying to find a way to get rid of those conservative Baptists. When she asked what group his was, he replied, "The Baptist Students of Princeton." She became very quiet and proceeded to make the assignment. This, among other things, demonstrated the underlying current of opposition. The liberal establishment of the campus did not want us because we were a conservative group.

We conducted the first revival that had been held on the Princeton campus for more than one hundred years. It was preached by Dr. Harold Fickett, then pastor of the First Baptist Church of Galveston, Texas. Ralph Langley preached a later revival in April 1951. Both revivals had good results, and God blessed in a wonderful way.

An interesting thing occurred when the *Baptist Student* magazine published by our Sunday School Board asked me to write an article about our Princeton experiences. The article was entitled "It Happened at Princeton" (April 1952, pp. 6–8). My original draft of the article was extensively changed before it was printed. I had referred to what I believed was the theological liberalism at Princeton, in the American Baptist Convention, and in the eastern part of the United States, with the need to ensure doctrinal soundness for the Baptist group at Princeton. All this was deleted from the article. I had naively not realized to what degree the article would be edited.

We broadcast the services of the Baptist Students of Princeton over the Princeton University radio station. One of the persons who trusted the Lord through the group was the technician who helped with the broadcast for the station. The Princeton Evangelical Fellowship also grew. The early days of isolation had turned into days of great fruitfulness and fellowship. In those three years after the Baptist Students of Princeton was formed, we saw more than one hundred Princeton students come to know Jesus Christ as personal Savior through it and the PEF. Many students from the nearby Westminster Choir College participated also. When I graduated from Princeton in 1952, I felt good about the ministry that had been started and was being maintained there.

One interesting side note is that everyone who joined the First Baptist Church of Hackensack, New Jersey, had to subscribe to its articles of faith. Among those who served as pastor of the Baptist Students of Princeton, and joined First Baptist of Hackensack in order to do so, were Cecil Sherman, later a prominent Baptist

Officers of the Baptist Students of Princeton, October, 1951. (Left to right) top row: Don Albarez, Nelson Peters, Paul Pressler, Dan Blalock; bottom row: Ted Martin, Ramsey Michaaels and Bill van der Hoeven

pastor; Jim McClendon, later a Baptist theology professor; and Jim Langley, later executive director of the District of Columbia Baptist Convention. All of these told the deacons of the church that they subscribed to the statement of faith of First Baptist, Hackensack. Some of its provisions were as follows:

I. Of the Scriptures

We believe that the Holy Bible was written by men supernaturally inspired; that it has truth without any admixture of error for its matter; and therefore is, and shall remain to the end of the age, the only complete and final revelation of the will of God to man; the true center of Christian union and the supreme standard by which all human conduct, creeds, and opinions should be tried.

(Explanatory)

1. By "the Holy Bible," we mean that collection of sixty-six books, from Genesis to Revelation, which, as originally written, does not contain and convey the word of God but IS the very Word of God.

2. By "Inspiration" we mean that the books of the Bible were written by holy men of old, as they were moved by the Holy Spirit, in such a definite way that their writings were supernaturally inspired, free from error, as no other writings have ever been or ever will be inspired.

Having listened to Cecil Sherman in later years and knowing he was one of the top leaders of the moderate cause in the Southern Baptist Convention controversy and later led the breakaway group, the Cooperative Baptist Fellowship (CBF), I have wondered whether he actually believed what he signed and told the deacons he believed, or whether he misrepresented himself. If he changed, I wondered when and what caused him to change, since he later took up a cause that is counter to this statement. Events such as this have convinced me that statements of faith cannot be, in and of themselves, a solution to doctrinal problems.

At graduation I was among the students who won the Potts Bible Prize, a privately endowed, university-administered prize. It was awarded, under the provision of its donor, to those who scored highest in an exam concerning the content of Scripture. The winner was to receive theological books. I asked for certain books by authors such as John Bunyan, who wrote *Pilgrim's Progress;* Dr. W. T. Connor, a well-known Baptist theologian and seminary professor, and others.

The religion department responded by saying these authors were unacceptable because they were not in accord with the thinking of the religion department at Princeton. So much for the liberals' liberalism! They wouldn't even allow me to be awarded books that were not liberal in thought. After some correspondence and appealing the matter above the religion department, they acquiesced and said they would allow me to obtain some conservative books for their historical value.

The narrow-mindedness of the liberal mind was very striking to me. Liberals at Princeton did all they could to stamp out conservative, Bible-believing Christianity through actions against the Baptist group and the PEF, through the ridiculing of our faith in class, and through seeking to deny me any conservative books through the award which I had rightfully won. Today's theological liberalism is not liberal in the sense of being open-minded. It is an aggressive, proselytizing doctrine which attacks biblical theology.

While I was at Princeton, my family and I helped in the organization of River Oaks Baptist Church in Houston. My grandfather Townes was the first moderator. We felt that a need existed for a Southern Baptist church in the River Oaks area, which was an affluent section and was then on the western edge of Houston. My family and I were all charter members, although I was there only for the summers. I moved my letter home each summer because I wanted to identify thoroughly with this new church. However, problems did arise. Some people who were fairly liberal decided that this was an opportunity to have a liberal Baptist church in Houston, and they joined the new church.

The pulpit committee interviewed Dr. Sankey Blanton, who had been president of Crozier Theological Seminary, a liberal American (formerly Northern) Baptist seminary. They asked him to be our pastor. The church vote on whether to call him was very close, but the chairman of the pulpit committee informed him that he was elected by "a substantial majority." When we found out what the chairman told Dr. Blanton, my grandfather, as moderator, wired Dr. Blanton and told him that out of fairness to him, he should know what the actual vote was. He spelled it out. After Dr. Blanton knew the extent of the opposition to his becoming pastor, he declined to accept. I had encouraged my grandfather to send the telegram. This saved River Oaks Baptist Church at that time from becoming a citadel of liberal Baptist thought in Houston.

CHAPTER 4

𝒜 FORK IN THE ROAD

When I graduated from Princeton in 1952, the Navy ROTC commissioned me as an ensign. My first assignment was six months at the Navy Supply Corps School at Bayonne, New Jersey. Since the officers had no Bible study, I organized one for them and their wives. The study met one night a week. Some twenty to thirty persons attended each week for the six months we were there. During my service in Bayonne and my subsequent duty in central Pennsylvania, I returned each weekend Princeton was in session to teach a Sunday School class for the Baptist Students of Princeton.

In Pennsylvania, I lived in Harrisburg and commuted eleven miles to the Naval Supply Depot at Mechanicsburg. I attended the First Baptist Church of Harrisburg for a while when Princeton was on vacation, but I found that this church was extremely liberal. I had been asked to teach a Monday night Bible study there and started teaching the first chapter of John. I emphasized such topics as the preexistence of Christ and the incarnation. The pastor, who formerly was a Southern Baptist, heard me and removed me from teaching. He said I was too fundamentalist to be teaching at First Baptist of Harrisburg. I observed that the church was dying as conservative theology was being eliminated.

Since I went to Princeton most weekends and kept my membership there, I was not a member of a church in Harrisburg. I did attend Grace Brethren Church on Wednesday nights, and some of the young people asked me to start teaching weeknight Bible studies. I conducted these on Monday, Tuesday, and Thursday nights for various high schools. Several students in these studies came to know Jesus Christ as personal Savior. Teaching these three nights a week, driving on Friday afternoons to Princeton, teaching Sunday School there, and then returning to Harrisburg on Sundays to be ready to go to the base on Mondays involved a fairly rigorous schedule, but I was grateful for the opportunities which the Lord had opened for me.

When I was stationed in Pennsylvania, I began to feel that a Christian was wrong to spend any money other than for absolute necessities. I saved every penny I possibly could, kept a notebook of every cent I spent, and balanced books at the end of the month. When I could not account for as much as three or four dollars during a month, I felt very bad about it. As a result of this, I was living on about half of my salary as a Navy ensign. I found that this excessive concern about the expenditure of money and preoccupation about doing things the least expensive way possible added a very unattractive and ungracious element to my personality.

Through this I learned that a Christian must be gracious in the manner in which he or she lives and not be so negative that people are repelled. I did not want to do anything, through my behavior or my words, that would keep me from reaching other people for Jesus Christ. It was a great learning experience. Subsequently, I have tried not to be extravagant but to recognize that a Christian does need to live in such a way as to have an attractive and positive lifestyle. We need to be good stewards as well as good examples in every way.

One of the issues I faced while I was in military service was where and how God would have me spend the rest of my life. Two paths appealed to me, and I was not sure which direction God was leading. One was to become a lawyer. That was the tradition of my family, as I would be a sixth-generation attorney. Many of my ancestors had been both lawyers and lay preachers, and I was interested in law and public affairs. For Christmas when I was twelve years old, my father and grandfather gave me a law book that was written by my great-grandfather, Judge John C. Townes, when he was dean of law at the University of Texas. The inscription that my grandfather wrote was as follows:

Dear Paul:

Your great-grandfather was the author of this book. I, your grandfather, as a typist, wrote the manuscript copy from which the printer printed the first edition. Your father is presenting the book to you. Four generations linked together by a book.

Your great-grandfather was the most nearly perfect Christian gentleman I have ever known.

As a lawyer, he was a philosopher making practical application to human affairs of the fundamental principle of right, justice, and equity as embodied in what we call Law. To him, the Law was not a set of technical rules whereby the calculating could trap the unwary, but the composite of principles of right providing for the orderly conduct of society for the maximum and equal protection of the rights and liberties of all.

He will long be remembered for his life, his example, and his teachings. We have in him a high standard to live up to.

Lovingly your grandfather,
E. E. Townes

I also felt led toward the ministry. I had a real interest in reaching people for Christ. I believe very strongly that since Jesus Christ is who He claimed to be, nothing else in the world except our relationship with Him and winning other people to Him makes any difference for eternity. The most important thing for me in life was proclaiming His truth. The question was: Was I called to do it as a lawyer or as a pastor? For some periods of time, I would feel called one way; at others I felt called to the other.

I took a leave from the Navy in 1953 and went home to tell my parents that I was headed for seminary and not to law school. Through the years, I had dreaded announcing this to them, because I knew of the tears, the heartache, and the difficulties in the family that this would cause. After I made my announcement, followed by great discussion, my parents told me they loved me and would support me in anything I did. I started making plans to attend Southwestern Seminary.

However, when I returned to the Navy base, I never again felt a call into the ministry. For the first time I had an overwhelming conviction, which never wavered, that God was calling me to be a lawyer. I think, in retrospect, that what the Lord wanted me to do was to be willing to tell my family that God was first in my life and that His will was more important than their plans for me. I think He wanted me to be willing to tell them that I would follow God's will and not theirs. Through the years, many testings of this have occurred, and the message has had to be reiterated. Nevertheless, God clearly resolved this issue for me. I was to be a layman, but as such, I was to witness for my Savior.

In the Northeast I had seen the advanced stages of liberalism. I did not see it in its early stages. An analogy says when a frog is placed in cold water and the heat is turned up, the frog will allow itself to be boiled to death because the change is so gradual that it does not notice. However, it will immediately jump out if it is placed in water which is already hot. Likewise, I think many people have succumbed to theological liberalism because it was introduced to them gradually, and they have not realized its problems. I saw churches in New England that were dying and closed because of liberalism.

One Sunday our pastor at First Baptist of Exeter read a letter from another church in New Hampshire stating that it was withdrawing from the American Baptist Convention and joining the Conservative Baptist Convention. He and the other members of the congregation expressed distress over this action. I wondered why the fellowship should be broken.

Then I reflected on the fact that our church had held joint meetings with the Unitarians, our not having Sunday School for persons over twelve years of age, the declining attendance of our church, and other such matters. I saw an atmosphere which was not conducive to the presentation of the gospel. Biblical Christianity was then minimally presented in New England, so I was alerted to what theological liberalism would do. Later I saw classmates at Princeton who arrived with strong moral and spiritual convictions but who became confused intellectually by those in the religion department. Then after becoming confused theologically, they lost their moral convictions. They would begin doing things that they had never before considered.

Liberalism was a warning to me; I was anxious to get home. I considered theological liberalism an infection that was limited to the northeastern part of the country, and I longed to return to the solid, Bible-teaching ministry of Southern Baptists, where I thought everything was right and no problems existed except in some areas of North Carolina. This was my spirit when I returned home. I still have the following letter which I wrote to the *Baptist Standard,* the Texas state Baptist newspaper, about modernism, which was synonymous with liberalism at that time. Although the *Baptist Standard* never published or acknowledged this letter, it shows clearly what my concerns were then.

Navy Supply Depot
Mechanicsburg, PA
February 6, 1953

Dear Sir,

I was very happy to receive my issue of the *Baptist Standard* this week. For the past months I have been traveling with the Navy and have not been located in a place where I could regularly receive a subscription. It was good to read of the work of Texas Baptists again.

I was especially interested in the article entitled, "What Is Modernism?" by Clyde J. Hurst in the January 29, 1953, issue. I enjoyed it very much and thought it was very excellent until I reached the last paragraph in which he states, "the Fundamentalist-Modernist controversy is now a matter of history" and seems to conclude that the Modernist brand of infidelity has been eliminated. With all due respect, I must take violent exception to this view or any idea which would lull Bible believing Christians into less diligence in coping with modern-day apostasy.

I was raised in Houston and came to know Christ as my Savior under the ministry of Dr. E. H. Westmoreland of the South Main Baptist Church of that city. My forebears have been active in Southern Baptist work since the organization of the convention. I hold the same general theological position as is held by all the Baptist leaders in Texas whom I have known. The millennial question has never been of great concern to me and I have close Christian friends who are "a-mils," "pre-mils," and degrees of both. With this background, I have been profoundly shocked by the tremendous strength of Modernism in the Eastern section of our country where I have been in school and have served in the Navy for the last seven years.

While at prep school in New Hampshire, I served on the Portsmouth Baptist Association Youth Council and knew most of the pastors in the area. A large number of them did not believe that there was any such thing as salvation except it be by moral refinement. To many of them the Bible was nothing more than a record of man's searching for God. They contended that it was an outstanding record of man's searching, but not that it was God's revelation of Himself.

Then I went to Princeton University in New Jersey where the religion (department) teaches that the Bible contains many mistakes and laughs at the idea of salvation. These religious authorities have referred to the doctrine of substitutionary atonement using Dr. Fosdick's term "slaughter house religion." I believe that the Bible teaches that Christ died on the cross to pay the price of our sins and that if a person does not accept Him as their Savior, they have no hope in eternity. Thus these men deny what I consider to be the basis of Christianity.

Three years ago, with Southern Baptist leadership, we organized a Baptist Student group on the Princeton University campus. Its three pastors, Rev. Dale Larew, Rev. James McClendon, and Rev. James Langley, have all been graduates of Southwestern Seminary and were at the time of their pastorates taking courses at the Princeton Seminary. Rev. Ralph Langley, now of the University Baptist Church of Coral Gables, Florida, and Harold Fickett of the First Baptist Church in Galveston have been the speakers for our revival campaigns. The group has been bitterly attacked by the moderates in the University area but nevertheless has been blessed of the Lord. The average attendance is well above the total number of Baptist students in the University.

My work on the Princeton University campus has enabled me to meet boys from Baptist churches and churches of other denominations from all over the country. A great number of these have never heard the Gospel except in ridicule. Several boys from Modernist Baptist churches have been saved at school. In most instances their home churches have attacked the group and the Bible way of salvation and have tried to wreck the faith of these new converts. (God is faithful and they have not been able to, I am grateful to say.)

As specific instances of the scene of Modernism, let me but cite some of my experiences during the first five weeks of 1953. On Saturday, January 3, 1953, I was visiting a friend in New York City and was, as his guest, asked out to dinner at the home of Dr. John Bennett, a professor at Union Theological Seminary. I avoided any argument and did not express my theological views to him. However, in the course of the evening he spoke of errors in the Bible, said that he believed very few of the Bible miracles could have happened, said that "nobody at Union would believe in the virgin birth," and that they did not believe in the bodily resurrection there. My friend, a member of the Riverside Baptist Church in New York City, told me later that this was also the position of the ministers of his church.

Most of these people will use the language of Christians on many points but tell you perfectly frankly that they mean entirely different things when you ask them personally. For example, many will say they believe about the resurrection. When you asked them what they believe about the resurrection, they will say that they do not believe in the bodily resurrection at all but are referring to the fact that Jesus' ideas and teachings didn't really stay in the grave with Him, but that they live on in the minds and hearts of men.

I am working with the young people's group at First Baptist Church in Harrisburg, Pa., while stationed here in the Navy. The assistant pastor of the church is a student at the Crozier Theological Seminary at Chester, Penn. His home was originally in North Carolina and last Sunday he candidated for a Southern Baptist Church in Virginia. On Sunday, January 18, 1953, I had my first opportunity to visit with him. When I discovered he was from North Carolina, I asked him if he knew my pastor's brother-in-law, Dr. Ralph Herrin of the First Baptist Church in Winston-Salem, North Carolina. I had heard Dr. Herrin preach in South Main Church when last home on leave. The assistant pastor replied in most derogatory terms saying that Dr. Herrin was a "narrow dogmatist." He also criticized the Training Union Study Course Book, *What Baptists Believe,* by Wallace which we were using in the young people's group as outdated, dogmatic, and too fundamental. This assistant pastor referred to some pastors in North Carolina and Virginia who are avowed Modernists as the hope of the Southern Baptist Convention. He also has tried to have the Christian Education Committee of the church remove me from working with the young people. This they have refused to do.

Last Sunday, February 1, 1953, while Princeton was on vacation (since graduation last June and while in the Navy I have been in the vicinity and able to return each Sunday to continue to teach a Sunday School class) I visited a friend of mine from school to whom we had been witnessing. Over the Christmas holidays he had told his pastor about our witness to him. When I went to church with him last Sunday, the Second Baptist Church of Wilmington, Delaware, the pastor, a Mr. Baker, preached about the "awful doctrine of substitutionary atonement" and said that no intelligent person could believe in such a "terrible thing." He said that it was "dreadful" to teach "anything like that" to young people.

These experiences can be multiplied many times from my own limited experience. I cite them to bring out the absolute folly of thinking for a minute that Modernism is dead and is not at work subverting the work of the Gospel. A great disservice is done when people are lulled to sleep and are not alerted to the danger. To provide the remedy, we must know that the disease exists and how to effectively handle the remedy—the Gospel of the saving power of our Lord Jesus Christ.

It is my earnest prayer that you will alert those who believe God's Word and love Him to the danger of modernism which confronts us today so that we can all be more effective witnesses to His glory.

Sincerely yours in Christ,
H. Paul Pressler III
Ensign (SC) USNR

When I was released from active duty in the Navy, my roommate from Princeton my last two years, Ted Martin (who was then halfway through Dallas Theological Seminary) and I went to Europe and the Holy Land. We visited twenty-nine countries on four continents in three and one-half months. We were with a group for only about one month of the time and that was mainly while we were in Egypt and the Holy Land. An uneasy truce existed in the Middle East at that time. The Jews had obtained independence only six years before (in 1948), and many exciting things were occurring.

I remember looking at the roster of those who were to be on the tour with us. About ten to fifteen ladies were designated as "Miss." Ted and I were very excited about that. Much to our chagrin, we found out that all of the "Misses" were at least thirty to forty years our elders. We did have one very close "girl friend" on the trip—Miss Emma Adams, a descendant of the Presidents Adams and a resident of Cincinnati, Ohio. Miss Adams was in her eighties, and she, Ted, and I were inseparable.

Ted and I did numerous exciting things, such as climbing the Great Pyramid in Egypt at midday while the others had their lunch. In Athens we stayed at the Grande Bretagne (Great Britain) Hotel, which was on the square in front of the presidential palace. There we listened to Archbishop Makarios address a unity (enosis) rally for Cyprus and Greece. Then the 100,000 participants marched against the Grande Bretagne Hotel as an expression against British imperialism. We were on the front sidewalk where the police were fighting the demonstrators

Paul Pressler, with city of Jerusalem in background. August 1954

just a few yards in front of us. When one of the police officers escorted us out of the area, we went to the roof and watched the rest of the battle from there. We were stoned in Jericho and chased with pitchforks near the Syrian border. Both acts were by Arabs, who thought we were taking pictures of things that would denigrate the Arabs' positions.

The trip was most meaningful because we could see the places where the Lord Jesus Christ had walked. It brought to life, as it has for so many others, biblical events and helped us realize the actual literal historicity of the life of the Lord Jesus in a more vital way. We saw the reforestation programs of the Israelis. We saw the land that had been misused for so many centuries beginning to come back to life, and we realized that God was fulfilling prophecy by restoring the Jews to Israel in the last days. This was a wonderful blessing in my life.

CHAPTER 5

COMING HOME

I returned home from Europe the day before law school began at the University of Texas. I was looking forward to being in Austin. It had always been another home for me because of significant roots there. The Townes family had settled at Manor, Texas, only a few miles from Austin, in 1854. The Pressler family had been in Austin since 1852, and the Maddox family had arrived there in the late 1800s. One of my Maddox great uncles had served as mayor of Austin. My grandmother had lived on the corner of Rio Grande and 10th streets since about 1900. My grandparents located at that spot because they wanted to live out from town. Of course, as anyone who is familiar with Austin knows, that location is now near the center of town.

I lived near the University of Texas Law School and was in the first class to use, for all three years, the new law school building, named Townes Hall after my great-grandfather. Law school was interesting and challenging, and those were three very profitable years for me educationally. Spiritually, I encountered things that I never anticipated.

The first Sunday I was in Austin, I attended University Baptist Church. My great-grandfather, Judge John C. Townes, led the organization of that church. For many years he taught a large Bible class there. The Baptist Bible Chair at the University of Texas was named for him. My father was in the last Torts class that Judge Townes taught in law school. When Judge Townes died, my father attended his funeral, and he remembered seeing my mother's family arrive at University Baptist Church for the service, although my mother was away in Virginia at Randolph-Macon Woman's College. I was interested in attending University Baptist because of family tradition. Dr. Blake Smith was the pastor. I did not realize that Dr. Smith was known for his liberal position on Scripture. The first or second week I was there, I was elected a discussion leader for one of the groups in Training Union, but I was removed when the BSU director and Dr. Smith learned about the conservative theological position that I held.

After several weeks I realized I would not have a ministry there, so I went downtown to attend First Baptist Church. Part of the Townes family had been in that church beginning in 1858. My grandmother Pressler joined in 1894, and my grandfather Pressler joined a few years later. I was anxious to fellowship in a place where my family had been very much a part of the church. Dr. Carlyle Marney was pastor, and as I listened to him preach, I was distressed to hear the same type of theology that I had heard in places up North. This type of preaching certainly contradicted the things that I believed. One of my liberal Methodist friends at law school quipped that he heard things were going so well down at First Baptist that "they are passing out ashtrays instead of Bibles on Wednesday night." Of course, this was a joke and not true, but it indicated the reputation the church was gaining in some parts of Austin.

After several weeks at First Baptist, I decided this was not the church for me, so I joined Hyde Park Baptist. There I found everything I had been looking for in a church. Dr. Lory Hildreth was pastor. Brother Hildreth preached the gospel with great fervor and great conviction. Harry Piland was the educational director. We became close friends. I taught Sunday School under him and felt very much at home. People were being won to a saving knowledge of Jesus Christ, and it was a very happy atmosphere.

The then-new church building, on the corner of 39th and Speedway streets in Austin, had just been completed. No seats existed in the balcony as yet, and the church was just beginning to grow. Even though practically no university students were attending at that time, I was happy. I served as evangelism director of the BSU and told others about Hyde Park. Eventually the number of students began to grow, and the church developed a tremendous student ministry. I had the privilege of teaching freshman boys in Sunday School there all three years I attended law school. Each year about fifty boys were in my class.

I was concerned because the same theological tendencies and trends that I observed in the Northeast were fully advanced in the two churches that had been so instrumental in my family's history in Austin. However, I knew that Southern Baptists were conservative and that somebody else surely would ultimately do something to correct such problems.

One of the highlights of my three years in Austin was Saturday lunch, which my grandmother Pressler hosted for all the family who were nearby. She always had a good cook, and Saturday lunch was the meal of the week. We were also invited any time we wanted to stop by. My grandmother Pressler, whom we called Nanna, prepared for meals as in the old days. Nanna always had twice as much food as the number of people who were expected to attend. She sent the extra food home with her hired help, which was then referred to as "totin' privileges." If we dropped by at the last minute with two or three friends, we knew that an ample supply of food existed. Nanna had a gong, which she rang to summon everybody to dinner. Saturday lunch consisted of fried chicken, rice, milk gravy, and big, fluffy biscuits with lots of strawberry jam. It was my favorite meal.

About halfway through law school, I began to contemplate what I would do after I graduated. My father advised that it might be good for me to work for the district attorney's office or the attorney general's office in order to lift myself above the crowd of those graduating from law school. I decided on another course that would have the same effect: I ran for the state legislature. This was before large counties had single-member districts. Harris County, with a population of well over one million at that time, had eight state representatives, all of whom ran from the whole county at large. I told my father of my interest, and he said, "Well, that is the dumbest thing I have ever heard. If you run, you will get beaten badly, and there is just no way you can ever be elected."

He cited some of my disadvantages, among them the following: (1) My grandfather and he had been active in conservative politics, and the winds were not blowing conservatively in 1956 in Texas; (2) he and my grandfather had both been associated with a big oil company (Humble and Standard Oil of New Jersey), and I would be attacked for that; (3) I had been in Texas for only two out of the last ten years. I had not developed my own circle of friends and therefore could be considered as coming from the outside; (4) I did not drink alcohol and would not be able to mix and mingle appropriately with the people who were in leadership.

After a long discussion, in which he aired these views, my father finally said, "Well, I think the best thing in the world for you to do is to run. You'll be badly beaten, and then it will get politics out of your system." That was all the encouragement I needed.

A friend of mine, Jim Yancy, an outstanding state representative, decided to run for another office and had told this to one of my close friends. The day Jim announced that he was not running for reelection, I announced my candidacy for his position. Five other people—four lawyers and one businessman—also entered that race. I came home Memorial Day weekend to begin a campaign of only eight weeks before the Democratic Primary on July 28, 1956. Contributions came in very well. I received less than $7,500 for my campaign, and that was exactly what I spent. This was a small amount to spend in a countywide race in Harris County in the 1950s.

The campaign was built around young friends of mine. They were from the group with whom I was brought up and from a lot of young people I had known through Christian activities. The *Houston Post* ran an article entitled "Unique Campaign Backs Pressler's Candidacy." It listed the names and showed a picture of the young people who were helping in my campaign. Since six candidates were in the race, no one singled me out for attacks. All three Houston newspapers interviewed me. I was the only candidate for the legislature that year in any of the eight races who received the endorsement of all three Houston papers.

I campaigned ceaselessly and was pleased with the way things developed. Letters signed by Jim Langley, James McClendon, James Leo Garrett, Joseph M. Stowell, Lory Hildreth, and E. Hermond Westmoreland were copied and sent to many Baptists in the county. I was gratified to have the support of many outstanding Christians.

One Sunday I spoke at a church in the eastern part of the county, sharing my testimony and not talking about politics. Afterwards a woman in the church introduced herself, saying her husband was the head of a certain labor union that had just attacked me, but she wanted me to know that I would carry her household three-to-one. She and her two voting-age children were voting for me. She said that if her husband ever knew, she thought it would break up the family. Such statements as this and the help from Christian friends encouraged me.

From the first returns, the outcome looked very good. I received 52 percent of the vote against 17 percent for the next-highest opponent and 48 percent for my five opponents combined. Margaret Davis, writer for *The Houston Press*, editorialized as follows:

> The most brilliant feat was by a conservative newcomer, young Paul Pressler, member of a wealthy and prominent family, who got a majority over five opponents to be elected without a runoff in Position 6. If Mr. Pressler isn't the only Phillips-Exeter-Princeton cum laude member of the House, he won't have a lot of company.

A woman ran against me as a Republican, but I returned to law school and did not campaign at all for the general election. Those were the days when Republicans were not strong in Texas. I was elected in November by an almost three-to-one majority. The Texas legislature had no Republican members at that time.

Representing well over a million people in the legislature was quite an awesome experience for a twenty-six-year-old. The legislative session began in January 1957. I had one semester of law school left and needed only six hours to graduate. I earned three of these hours through a course in legislation. The professor and I had an agreement. I would attend the class as frequently as possible and share with the class what actually was going on behind the scenes in the legislature, and he would not be strict in taking my attendance. By taking an office practice course, I was able to crowd most of my law school work into the first part of the semester before the legislative session became intense. I also continued teaching my Sunday School class at Hyde Park.

This was an interesting and full spring. During the summer and fall, the governor called three special sessions of the legislature. It kept me from getting down to practice law until after the legislative sessions were completely over late in the year.

Working in the legislature was extremely interesting. I enjoyed observing the inner workings of politics. For instance, the chairman of a committee on which I served came by one day and asked how I felt about a certain bill. I replied, "I am very strongly opposed to it." He said, "That's what I thought. I am naming you chairman of the subcommittee to study it. You are going to be pretty busy this session, aren't you?" I said, "I'm going to be so busy I don't know how my subcommittee is going to meet." He answered, "We understand each other." And that was the end of the bill's consideration for that session of the legislature.

Waggoner Carr, the speaker of the House, was a gracious, fine gentleman and led the House well. From time to time, various members had breakfast with him in the speaker's chambers. Waggoner always called on me or someone else to lead in prayer before we began our meal. In many ways a strong Christian influence existed in the legislature. The governor, Price Daniel, did not drink and created a very good atmosphere in Austin. Price was a leading Baptist layman, and his private actions conformed to his public image.

Price Daniel served as governor of Texas, chief justice of the Texas Supreme Court, and United States senator—the highest offices in each of the branches of Texas government. I admired him, and we were good friends. Several years after he retired from politics, we attended a reception together. He saw me across the room and came directly to see me. He spoke quickly with great zeal. He told me about being in Dallas with a group from Campus Crusade for Christ and about presenting the gospel in street witnessing. He told me he had led someone to accept Jesus Christ as his personal Savior. Price said, "It was the most wonderful experience of my life." What a tremendous statement from a great man who had received so many secular honors!

I saw him again not too long before he died. He expressed great concern for me, saying that the "Baylor people" were out to "destroy" me and urged me to be careful. (Price was a prominent graduate of Baylor University, whose leaders later attacked me during the denominational controversy.) I expressed appreciation for his concern but told him the cause that I was engaged in was so important, the individual cost to my reputation could not be considered.

Again, I observed the inner workings of politics when I authored a bill entitled "The Uniform Gift of Stock to Minors Act," which was something I believed would be very good for investing and estate planning. The bill passed through the House by a vote of 122 to 9. A certain senator had asked my permission to carry the bill in the Senate. One day my friend, Searcy Bracewell, who was senator from Harris County and a fine Baptist layman, came to see me and told me that the lieutenant governor, Ben Ramsey, was mad at the senator who was carrying my bill and that Ben was not going to let that senator pass another bill that session. Searcy suggested that I do something if I wanted to see it passed.

One day, right after lunch, I went to see the lieutenant governor. In Texas at this time, the lieutenant governor was thought to be more powerful than the governor. Since Ben was out of his office, I saw his secretary, who was a good friend of mine, and said, "Just tell Ben that I stopped by to see him about House Bill 375." I explained to her that my bill was being presented by the out-of-favor senator. That occurred about 1:28 P.M. I went back to my desk. Before 2:00 P.M. the senator who was carrying the bill came to me and told me that my bill had just been passed. The lieutenant governor had returned from lunch, called the Senate to order, called my bill up immediately, and it passed 28 to 0.

Even though I know my visit to the lieutenant governor's office was the reason for the bill's quick passage, I dutifully thanked the senator profusely, letting him feel as though he had gotten it through.

Various state agencies and institutions were always entertaining the legislators. An event I considered humorous occurred when the president of the University of Houston invited the legislators for a Sunday night dinner/dance at one of the country clubs in Houston. I politely refused. He then asked what Sunday night I could attend. I told him that I attended church on Sunday night and didn't go out on Sunday night otherwise. He and his office were very much taken aback and planned a special dinner party for me one night during the week.

About twenty-five of us in the House were young and conservative. Several of us were strong Christians, and we worked together on a great deal of legislation. I think we made a real impact on the state. Many of these people have continued to be my close friends through the years, and some have risen to high political office. My entry years into politics laid a strong foundation for my life thereafter.

CHAPTER 6

*G*OD'S DIRECTION: CHICAGO

Immediately after graduating from the University of Texas Law School in June 1957, I took a job with a small law firm because the firm would allow me to run for reelection. However, I found myself not being able to learn to practice law. The demands on me as a legislator were so great that I had difficulty getting into the books and learning the basic principles of legal practice.

I knew I had to make a major decision. Either I had to go full-time into politics, or I had to step back, catch my breath, and learn to be a lawyer so I would have a profession to fall back on if I were defeated for election. I chose the latter course. I saw many people in public office who knew nothing other than politics. They had neither the financial resources nor the acumen to pursue other areas if they failed in political office. Therefore, they felt great pressure on themselves to vote in a way that pleased their constituency so they could be reelected.

In the next election a vacant senate seat from my county was to come open. Many people asked me to consider running for it and offered their support. Another representative, Bob Baker, had already decided to run for it. He had a constitutional amendment proposed to raise the minimum age for a state senator from twenty-five to thirty years of age. This would have precluded my running, since I would not have been thirty by the time this term began.

It just so happened that I was on the constitutional amendments committee of the House. When the amendment came before the committee, I proposed an amendment to it which provided that the new age requirement would not go into effect for another two years after it was adopted. This would have delayed its effectiveness until after I was thirty. My amendment was easily approved. The next day Bob Baker came to my desk, slammed down the report of the committee action on my desk, and said, "I read your announcement for the senate." I said, "Now, Bob, why do you say that?" He walked away. I was keeping my options open, although I never intended to run.

I prayed the matter through and promised the Lord that I would stay out of politics until I could say to the voters, "You will be doing me a financial favor to retire me." Then I would be perfectly free to vote my own convictions and not

39

worry about the consequences. Far too many people in politics are not in that position.

After the special legislative sessions were called in the fall of 1957, I resigned from the small law firm and began interviewing. Judge James A. Elkins offered me a job with his Houston firm, Vinson & Elkins—which was then known as Vinson, Elkins, Weems, and Searls—and I accepted.

Judge Elkins was a person of very short interviews. The first time I went in to see him, we exchanged the customary greetings. He then said he liked what I had been doing in the legislature. I replied, "Yes, sir, but it is time for me to really learn how to practice law." He said, "That's right. You need to get out of politics." I responded, "Yes, sir, I am willing to do it. I want to practice law, and I wondered whether you would be interested in my working for you." He looked me in the eye and said, "You have a wonderful mother, pretty good father, much better mother than father—tell him I said so. I will talk to you in a couple of weeks." In three minutes my job interview was over.

About two weeks later his secretary called and asked me to come see Judge Elkins. I walked in, and he said, "I want you to start on January 1. Your salary will be $500 a month. Do you have any questions?" I had a couple of other job offers at the time, and I really hadn't decided to take the Vinson & Elkins offer if it was given, but in the presence of such a commanding personality, I said, "Yes, sir." I would come to work on the first of January.

I had two other notable meetings with Judge Elkins. He had to approve any marriage by members of the firm. When Nancy and I were engaged, I brought her to Houston from Chicago to meet him. In her exuberance, Nancy blurted out, "Oh, Judge Elkins, I just love you for sending Paul to Chicago, because I never would have met him if he hadn't been there, and you're just so wonderful to do that." People usually didn't speak to Judge Elkins so directly and informally, and he was not accustomed to having someone else lead the conversation, particularly not a young woman who was to marry one of his attorneys. He was very much enchanted with Nancy and appreciated her until the day he died. He approved the marriage. That meeting also lasted about five minutes.

Another time, I had a chance to get to know his personality in a different way than most people saw him. When my grandfather died in 1962, among his effects was a copy of the University of Texas yearbook, *The Alcalde,* from about 1901 when Judge Elkins had been the editor. I had heard that Judge Elkins was looking for a copy of that particular yearbook, so my grandmother told me to take it to him.

I went down and gave it to the receptionist in the hall on the second floor of the bank where the Judge had his office. I told her what I was bringing, and she said, "No, don't leave that here. I think you had better see Mrs. Paris (the Judge's secretary)." I saw Mrs. Paris, told her the story, and turned to leave. She said, "Wait just a minute. I think you need to see the Judge." So, I went in, although I had clients arriving to see me in about ten minutes. After I presented him *The Alcalde* and turned to leave, he said, "Boy, where are you going?" (He often called his young lawyers "Boy.") I replied, "Well, I'm sure you are busy, Judge, and I didn't want to disturb you." He said, "Come here and sit down."

In the next hour I made two or three unsuccessful efforts to leave as a most sentimental, kind, thoughtful man went through every picture in the book, relived events, and told stories to me. This was the true Judge Elkins behind the brusque exterior that he maintained.

After I accepted the job, I returned to Austin to the legislature. One day a legislative page summoned me, saying, "Judge Elkins of Houston is on the phone." I wondered what in the world I had done to cause Judge Elkins to call me. The Judge's words to me were, "Boy, how would you like to go to Chicago?" I had never been to Chicago. I didn't know what Chicago was like, and I didn't know why he was asking me if I wanted to go there. I asked, "You mean temporarily, on a trip, Judge?" He said, "No, no. We have an office up there. We do work for Pure Oil Company, and I want you to be assigned to that office for two or three years."

What could I say? I responded, "Well, whatever you want, sir." He said, "Your salary will be increased by 50 percent for the cost-of-living increase." This raised my salary to $750 a month, or $9,000 a year. This was an unheard-of sum for a beginning young lawyer in 1958.

Going to Chicago was certainly not what I had planned. I had looked forward to settling down in Houston after having been gone for more than eleven years, but that was not to be. The Judge knew how to get me out of politics. He had wanted me to resign from the legislature immediately. This would have caused the expense of a special election, for which the winner would not have actually served in the legislature because no more special legislative sessions would occur before the person's term was up. I won that argument and did not have to resign. Even though he sent me to Chicago to break me from politics, it had other results also and opened up an entirely different direction for my life.

Settling in Chicago in midwinter, I began to get acclimated to the office, where I replaced W. Randolph Smith effective January 1, 1958. Randy and I roomed together for a couple of months after his family moved back to Houston to get settled in school while Randy was breaking me in. Randy's father had been a bishop of the United Methodist Church in the Houston area, and the fellowship with Randy was a rich and rewarding experience. I was grateful for that time and for having a very sincere and dedicated Christian lawyer as the person who introduced me to the practice of law.

Chicago was very difficult. Days were cold, nights were long, and friends were few. Four of the other five lawyers in the Chicago office were married, and all were older than I. I did not have any ready group of friends. It was one of the loneliest times of my life. I had a few friends at Wheaton College, and my first dating opportunities in the Chicago area were there.

The Chicago office was created in the 1930s because the general counsel of Pure Oil Company once had approved some transactions after a great deal of pressure from the management. These transactions were illegal, and some of the management of Pure ended up in jail. The firm decided it would be best to hire independent counsel so that undue pressure no longer would be placed on the legal department. The situation worked very well. I enjoyed getting to know the people at Pure and have had lasting friendships with some of them.

On the first Sunday in Illinois, I attended the Evanston Baptist Church, a struggling Southern Baptist congregation that was about to close its doors. This was the only Southern Baptist church on the North Shore area where I lived. The North Shore was where the other Vinson & Elkins lawyers lived; to live in some other area of town, where I might have found another church to attend, would have been unacceptable to the Judge. (None of the Judge's lawyers ever did anything unacceptable to the Judge.)

This church had low attendance, rented property near Northwestern University, and was not reaching the affluent or educated people of Evanston and the North Shore. Most people attending were those who were economically disadvantaged and struggling. It was not a church that had a great deal of attraction to the community, and many questions arose as to whether it would survive. I spent the spring teaching Sunday School, organizing a Baptist Student Union for Northwestern University students, and generally pouring myself into our little church.

From the religious activities office I obtained a list of the Baptist students at Northwestern. They were not numerous, but we organized a Sunday School class for them. Entertainer Anita Bryant was one of these students, but she was so busy with appearances, having been selected as Miss Oklahoma and being a top contender in the Miss America competition, that she was not present on many weekends. The church grew somewhat. The pastor, Bill Kunst, was sincere, hardworking, and really loved the Lord. Later, some people from the community who could give stability to the church were attracted to it.

During the summer, I met Tex Randolph, son of one of the lawyers in the Vinson & Elkins office. Tex had returned home from college and was part of a group of Christian young people on the Chicago North Shore. I started attending their weekly Bible study. This opened a completely new world to me. I now had many friends college age and older who were fine Christians. It was truly a happy situation.

During the summer I began hearing about a young lady who was instrumental in starting this summer Bible study. Her name was Nancy Avery. She had just graduated from Smith College in Massachusetts and was spending the summer in Europe with her parents and two brothers. As a "coincidence," her brother Cam was incoming president of the Baptist Students of Princeton, which I had started. He and his family were Presbyterians. (The Princeton group had broadened denominationally after I left.) I had communicated by mail with Cam on numerous occasions, and we planned to get together as soon as he returned to Chicago. I first knew that he had a sister when I heard about her leadership in the Bible study.

In August I received a telephone call from Margaret Kerwin. I had met her through my Houston friend, Francita Stuart, with whom she had gone to Wellesley. Margaret and I had done a number of fun things in Chicago soon after I had arrived. She called and said her family had purchased tickets to a Seven College (which included Smith and Wellesley) tennis match benefit. She asked if I would be her date and help host a dinner party for ten or twelve people that evening before the match.

I checked and found that I had agreed to speak at Wheaton Bible Church that night. My rule was never to change a Christian speaking engagement for a secular engagement, but Margaret said she was in real trouble, needed help, and asked if I would please consider it. The people at the church said it would work out much better for them if I would trade places with next month's speaker and let him speak on the night when I had the conflict. That left me free to accept Margaret's invitation.

The day before the party Margaret called and said she had the flu but would still give the dinner party in her apartment. She asked that I be responsible for taking the group to the benefit and acting as host. Of course, I agreed. This meant that I had an extra seat next to me at the tennis matches, which were being held in the gymnasium of New Trier High School in Winnetka. During the intermission, as I visited with Tex Randolph, Cam Avery came up to speak with Tex, and Tex introduced me to Cam.

Just four days earlier, Cam and his brother and sister had returned from Europe. I was supposed to have lunch with him two days later, and he was to return to Princeton the morning after our lunch. I would not have met him until our lunch if it had not been for the casual meeting at the benefit. For the remainder of the matches, Cam sat in Margaret's seat next to me. At the end of the match, I asked him if he would like to go get some ice cream. He invited me to come to his house since he was taking his sister home. That evening, September 9, 1958, in the lobby of the gymnasium of New Trier High School, from where she had graduated four years earlier, Nancy Avery and I met through her brother Cam.

We had a delightful evening at the Avery home. The ice cream scoop which we used that night was presented to us at the rehearsal dinner when Nancy and I married less than six months later. I knew from the start that she was someone in whom I was very, very interested. She possessed all the charm, attractiveness, intelligence, Christian virtues, and consecration for which I had been looking for many, many years. I soon realized that I was very much in love with her.

The next meeting we had was three days later. I volunteered to help her find a job. She wanted to work in Chicago and to sign a lease on an apartment with five other friends who had just graduated from college. I knew that International Students, Inc. was looking for a secretary, so I arranged for Nancy, an ISI staff member, and me to have lunch together at Marshall Field's. The job did not work out, but my purpose was accomplished in becoming better acquainted with Nancy.

The first real date we had was the next night when we went to see the stage play, *Mame*. In the play soon after Mame met Beauregard, she went to his South Carolina plantation to meet her Southern in-laws-to-be. Nancy and I were engaged nine weeks later, and soon she was on her way to spend Thanksgiving on our Texas ranch and to meet her Southern in-laws-to-be. We never recommended our example to our daughters or to the young people we have counseled, but we knew it was right and according to the Lord's will for us.

As Nancy and I discussed theology, we were amazed to discover how similar our beliefs were. She told me I was the first Baptist she had met who believed the Bible was completely true. All of her exposure to Baptists had been with liberal American (formerly Northern) Baptists. Nancy was exposed to the same neoorthodoxy and liberal theology at Smith that I had experienced at Princeton. To stay true to the Scriptures, she met daily her freshman year with another Christian for prayer and Bible study. During their four years, the two of them started other Bible studies on campus. During her senior year she attended a conference at Union Seminary in New York City from February 14 to 16, 1958, and heard firsthand the liberal teaching of the seminary professors which I had experienced a few years previously.

I proposed to her and she accepted on Thursday night, November 6, 1958. On the following Saturday morning, I went to see her father at his office. He knew why I was visiting him. Her father was then and for many years the managing partner of Sidley and Austin, the largest law firm in Chicago. This firm was local counsel for Pure Oil Company, while Vinson & Elkins was its general counsel. When I met with Nancy's father that morning, he was very nervous. Never before or after have I seen him this way. He always knew how to negotiate every situation and moved in the most important circles with ease. I think I dealt with this particular situation better than he did. Because he loved his daughter so much, he did not know what questions to ask, so I volunteered information. It was an interesting experience, and I had complete peace and confidence.

I found out later that before I arrived at his office, he had called the Griffith Lawhon family in Houston to check me out. This was another example of how many mutual friends and connections my family and Nancy's family had. The Lawhons and my family had been friends for generations. When they were in Chicago with Vinson & Elkins, they were close friends of the Averys, went to the same church, and the wives were in a "sewing club" together. When Nancy's father reached Mrs. Lawhon, he asked her questions about me. Mrs. Lawhon asked why, and he told her. She laughed and told him that I had been in Houston two weeks before and had gone out with her daughter Virginia.

The Avery and Pressler families are amazingly similar. Our fathers were both successful lawyers and community leaders, and both mothers were active in the same types of clubs and community organizations. Both families were close and loving and did things together. Originating from the same type of background resulted in few adjustment problems in our marriage.

Nancy is close to her brothers as well as to her parents. Her father and both brothers are graduates of Princeton University, and her mother is a graduate of Smith College. Her brother, Cameron Scott Avery, is two years younger than she. He graduated from Harvard Law School and is now managing partner of a large Chicago law firm. Her other brother, Richard Manchester Avery, is five years younger than she. He graduated from Fuller Theological Seminary in Pasadena, California, spent a year on the mission field, and is now pastor of a Presbyterian church in Spokane, Washington. Her brothers have five children between them. We enjoy our times with them.

I passed muster with the Averys, and Nancy and I were married less than four months later. The wedding was at First Presbyterian Church in Evanston, which had been the Avery family church for several generations. The wedding was performed on February 28, 1959, by its pastor, Harold Walker, and by Lloyd Ogilvie, who was then pastor of a new Presbyterian church meeting in a school in Winnetka, Illinois, which the Averys had joined. Lloyd, who was later pastor of Hollywood Presbyterian Church, is well known for his writings and TV ministry. He now is chaplain of the United States Senate. Nancy's family and their friends provided us with lovely wedding festivities. Almost one hundred out-of-town guests attended. The John Nuveens hosted the wedding-day luncheon in their home.

Nancy and Paul Pressler cutting their cake at wedding reception, February 28, 1959

We honeymooned on St. John's in the Virgin Islands and in Puerto Rico, and then settled down to married life three blocks from the Northwestern University campus, where we could better minister to the students and I could easily take the elevated train to the city.

Nancy was a volunteer with Young Life and also helped lead the high school youth group at Winnetka Presbyterian Church. I taught Sunday School and Training Union for the college students at the Evanston Baptist Church as well as being BSU director for Northwestern. Instead of dropping anything, each of us adopted the other's schedule, and we did everything together.

Soon after we were married, Nancy was baptized at the Evanston Baptist Church. She had attended a liberal American Baptist church some of the time she was at Smith because it was less offensive than the alternatives. However, she believed what traditional Baptists believed. She was concerned about the direction of the Presbyterian denomination with its relationship to the National Council of Churches and other liberal organizations. She said she was glad to become a Baptist, but since she had lived a couple of towns away from her church when she was growing up, she wanted to be sure that when we moved back to Houston, we would live close to our church. That was little enough of a concession for me to make.

Nancy's parents were very close to Dr. Donald Gray Barnhouse, a great Bible teacher and Presbyterian leader. I did not realize how much Nancy's parents were concerned about her becoming a Baptist until the first time I was introduced to Dr. Barnhouse. He held my hand in his massive ones, looked me square in the eye, and said, "Oh, yes, this is the son-in-law who used to be a Baptist, isn't it?" He knew full well that Nancy had left the Presbyterian denomination and become a Baptist, but this was his way of expressing himself strongly to me about the matter. Dr. Barnhouse was a great saint of God, and I was grateful for this delightful contact with him.

We loved our work as volunteer directors for the Northwestern University BSU, which I had started. We took the students on several retreats, taught Bible studies, and frequently entertained the students in our apartment. As newlyweds, we felt very fulfilled. We had an outlet for ministry and were establishing a solid Christian home together. During that time, Dr. Bill Bright came to Evanston to get Campus Crusade for Christ started in the area. Nancy and I had become friends with Bill and his wife, Vonette. I had been active in Campus Crusade when I was at the University of Texas Law School from 1954 to 1957, and Nancy had met the Brights at a Forest Home Bible Conference in California in 1957.

Back in those days, Nancy and I did not have the money to pay for Bill to stay in a hotel room, and Campus Crusade could not afford one, so Bill slept on our sofa-bed for several days while he tried to get things under way for Campus Crusade in the Chicago area.

While I was in Chicago, some friends were starting the Christian Legal Society, and I was asked to serve on its board of directors. I was glad to see this national organization getting under way. It is very successful today. I had been active in the Christian Business Men's Committee since 1956 and had the privilege of going with its leader, the father of Bill Gothard, and others to Winona Lake, Indiana, where I spoke in the Billy Sunday Tabernacle. This was broadcast over WMBI radio station. Life was full and active for us in Illinois.

CHAPTER 7

$\mathcal{S}$EEDS OF DISSENSION

In May 1960, Ben Harper, for many years head of the Chicago division of Vinson & Elkins, called me into his office. He was an outstanding lawyer, a gracious and wonderful boss, and was well respected by everyone. He told me that my job was completed and that, after two and one-half years, I was being transferred back to Houston, effective June 1, 1960. I went home and told Nancy. Tears flowed, because this was happening very suddenly, and she had not thought of leaving her family to go to Houston so soon. We had known this would eventually occur, but we had not known when. We were settled in the Chicago area and involved in many activities. Pulling up roots was difficult.

The Evanston Baptist Church had grown and stabilized. I had helped with the legal work involved in buying its property on Crawford Avenue in Skokie (an adjacent town), and the name was changed to the Crawford Avenue Baptist Church. I felt that the situation there was established in such a way that our leaving would not hurt. (Unfortunately, some years later, the church called a liberal pastor, and it died and disbanded.) With real reluctance, we left Nancy's family to move to Houston. I, of course, was pleased because I actually would be living in Houston for the first time since I left for prep school, fourteen years earlier.

When we arrived in Houston, we moved into my parents' house. They planned to travel to Europe with Nancy's parents for the first part of the summer, and they were very happy to have us stay with them as long as we wanted.

We arrived on a Saturday. On Monday morning, Ann Elkins Flaten, Judge Elkins's granddaughter, called Nancy and asked her to go to a Bible study with her. Nancy was delighted. That Bible study continues today, and the women in it have been some of her closest friends. Nancy's biggest adjustment to the South was realizing that the generosity, openness, and friendliness were genuine and real. She immediately fit in, and everybody loved her.

In the heat of the summer, for three months, Nancy looked at houses. She probably looked at more than six hundred homes before we found the one in which we thought we would live for the rest of our lives. We did live there for the next thirty-three years.

It was expected that we would join River Oaks Baptist Church in Houston, since I was a charter member and my parents and grandparents were members there. We visited it several times. However, we were not tremendously excited about joining that particular church. Although my family had ties there and I was fond of many of the people, I had committed to Nancy that we would join a church close to our home. We found a suitable home less than a mile from the new, proposed location of Second Baptist Church. As soon as we bought the house, after praying about it, we felt led to join Second.

We had visited South Main because it was the church in which I grew up, but we were not pleased with the ministry it then had. We enjoyed First Baptist as much as Second, but at that time, First Baptist was still downtown, with no plans to move to the west side of the city. After the first of September 1960, we began to participate actively at Second Baptist Church, wanting to put down deep roots since we knew we probably would be in Houston for the rest of our lives.

Both of us immediately began teaching in the college department at Second Baptist and saw tremendous response. Several Baylor medical students attended. We had a good time working with them, as well as with students from Rice University, the University of Houston, and Texas Women's University School of Nursing. The directors of the college department were Johnny and Eula Mae Baugh, and we immediately became friends with them. Almost every Sunday night after church, the four of us, the pastor and his wife, and some others had fellowship together. I was asked to serve on the board of trustees for Second Baptist School, and enjoyed doing that for a number of years. When I was twenty-nine I had been asked to be a deacon at Evanston Baptist Church, but before I was ordained, I was transferred back to Houston. Second Baptist Church asked me to be a deacon, and I was ordained there when I was thirty-two.

Although we were good friends with the leaders of the church, we began to notice several things. It appeared to us that a close-knit group of a few people, including the Baughs, ran the church. It was obvious that anything this group wanted was done, and that these people spent a great deal of time, money, and effort for the ministry of the church and to make sure the church was conducted the way they wanted. It also became clear to us that Dr. James Riley, the pastor, was not the deep Bible preacher we desired. He had a good delivery, and he used beautiful, flowery phrases, but after a period of time, we began to feel that we had heard all he had to say, and that we were not being fed. This bothered us very much. However, Nancy and I continued to be active in the church and said nothing about this matter except to each other.

A major event then occurred in Southern Baptist life. Dr. Ralph Elliott, a professor at Midwestern Baptist Theological Seminary in Kansas City, Missouri, wrote a book, *The Message of Genesis,* published in 1961 by Broadman Press, a division of the Sunday School Board. In this book he said the following:

> In other words, one must come to the place that he sees the parabolic and symbolic nature of much of the Old Testament Scriptures. Genesis is to be understood in this light. It is not science. In the material attributed to J and P, the early writers were in no way trying to give a scientific or literal explanation. These stories are what Alan Richardson called parables—"parables of nature and man in order to convey deep religious insight" (page 15).
>
> The particular problem of chapter 5 is the longevity of the antediluvians. Various theories have been suggested, and it is impossible to be absolutely definite about any approach. It is difficult to believe that they actually lived as long as stated . . . In all probability, the Priestly writer simply exaggerated the ages in order to show the glory of an ancient civilization. Mesopotamian and Babylonian stories leading to the depiction of the Flood have a similar ten antediluvians with exceedingly long ages, often thousands of years older than any of the men mentioned in Genesis 5. The long ages of P are then an exaggerated literary medium for the purpose of expressing the view that sin brings degeneration (pages 58–59).
>
> Perhaps before any detailed statement of evidence has been presented, it already has been surmised that the present writer maintains the historicity of the patriarchal narratives, although it is impossible to deny the fact that sometimes the material may have been "legendized" just a bit and perhaps heightened as a means of intensifying the dominant characteristics in the patriarch's life. But where heightening has occurred, it is perhaps more valuable than historical fact in that it reveals the soul and pulse of a people who are certain that they live and move under the domination of God (page 79).
>
> Apparently, Abram first went to Melchizedek, a comrade who had joined him in battle, to divide some of the spoils. That some religious understanding was involved did not appear until Melchizedek introduced it. *El Elyon* means "highest God." In the Ras Shama text Baal is referred to as the *Al'iyan* (highest God) and he is also called the possessor of all things, a phrase used here in verse 19. This recognizes Baal as the supreme deity in the Canaanite pantheon. It would appear, then, that in verse 19, Melchizedek was blessing Abram by Baal, whom Melchizedek considered to be the highest god of the city-state of Salem. Thus, Melchizedek was extending blessings for, and receiving tithes in behalf of his *El Elyon,* to be equated with Baal. Out of courtesy, Abram did not object

to giving Melchizedek and his god what Melchizedek deemed to be his share of the booty, but that was as far as he was willing to go (pages 115–116).

This disturbed me deeply. I could not understand how anyone who believed the Bible was completely true could write this. Scripture says that Melchizedek was a priest of the most high God (Gen. 14:18; Heb. 7:1), not of Baal. This represented the same type of neoorthodoxy which I had seen in the Northeast and in Austin at University Baptist and First Baptist churches. It was particularly disturbing because the author was at one of the Southern Baptist seminaries teaching young men to be preachers. I told Nancy that our denomination surely would rise up as one and deal with this problem. "They are not going to allow it to continue," I said. I was shocked when an attempt to push the matter under the rug occurred. For some time nothing was done, and the problem was not dealt with. I talked to our pastor, James Riley, about this, and he told me not to worry about it because everything would be taken care of. Then I found out that James was speaking in support of Ralph Elliott. I was shocked to learn this after what James had told me.

Dr. Charles Trentham, a Southern Baptist minister who in later years was President Jimmy Carter's pastor at First Baptist Church of Washington D.C., led a revival at Second Baptist Church. The headline of an article about it in the religion section of the *Houston Chronicle* said, "Elliott Supporter to Speak at Second Baptist." This greatly bothered me because it positioned our church in support of liberal teaching in one of our Southern Baptist seminaries.

During an evening service on Sunday night before Dr. Trentham spoke, James Riley called the church into a business meeting to elect messengers to the upcoming Southern Baptist Convention annual meeting. When the discussion of electing messengers came up, I moved that we ask our messengers to express our deep concern about Ralph Elliott's teaching at Midwestern and that our messengers do all they could to see that he was dismissed. I know now that it was not proper to instruct our messengers, but I made this motion when I was a novice in convention matters. It arose out of my frustration and my wanting to do something. The surprising thing was that about 40 to 45 percent of the church members voting to elect messengers supported my motion.

I remember James shaking his head and Dr. Trentham putting his head in his hands when the matter came up for discussion. They were concerned. I was concerned. I did not realize what this would lead to in the future. My relationship with Second Baptist Church and its leadership went downhill from there. Little did I realize how greatly this matter would impact the rest of my life.

Nancy and I had become increasingly concerned about the way decisions at Second Baptist were being made. When the Elliott episode occurred, it caused us to realize that Second had serious problems. We studied the church's record and saw that under the pastorate of James Riley, a tremendous decline in attendance in Sunday School and in the preaching services had occurred. We were close to the Riley children and liked the whole family personally, but we felt a real need for revival in the congregation.

After the incident at the business meeting, Johnny and Eula Mae Baugh invited Nancy and me to Sunday lunch. Johnny was a Houston businessman who later in life made a great deal of money through Sysco, the restaurant supply business. We had a two-hundred-year tradition of having Sunday lunch as a family, but Nancy and I broke it on that occasion and went with the Baughs. I believed Johnny realized that my concern was genuine. When he suggested at lunch that a committee be set up at Second Baptist to study the Elliott matter, I thought that was a great idea. I presumed I would be asked to serve on the committee, and it would provide an opportunity to investigate some of our concerns. I thought this committee would consist of a group of people who would get together and find out the truth.

Now, after knowing the way some Baptists have done things, I realize that certain committees are set up just in order to keep people quiet. Having a committee to make a study allows some people to say that something is being done about a matter and, therefore, will keep persons not serving on the committee from complaining.

Johnny delayed a long time in making his motion to the deacons to set up the committee. After I talked to him several times and reminded him about his commitment, he wrote a letter to the chairman of the deacons and requested that the committee be created. In his letter he emphasized several times that it was to be a committee to help and support our seminaries. He said nothing about its being a committee to find out the facts about liberalism. It seemed to me that after our luncheon, Johnny had second thoughts himself, or perhaps took the matter to the pastor. Some people must have thought a danger existed in having a committee that would truly investigate.

This change in what I considered the purpose of the committee to be indicated to me that probably some authentic problems existed. The chairman of deacons was to appoint the committee. Bernard Green, my good friend of many years and an outstanding Christian, made the appointments. I was shocked to learn that most of those appointed were individuals who could be counted on not to rock the boat and not to reveal anything that would embarrass any seminary. I was not appointed to the committee.

The committee was appointed at the end of Bernard's term as chairman. At the last meeting where he presided, he announced its membership. At the next meeting Durward Anderson was to become deacon chairman. His wife had made some of my first baby clothes, and our families had been close friends for years. I explained the whole situation to Mr. Anderson. He told me that H. A. Nystrom, a fine person who had been named to the committee, was unable to serve and had resigned. One of Mr. Anderson's first acts as chairman was to appoint me to the committee as Mr. Nystrom's replacement. After that time my relationship with Johnny Baugh was never the same. What started as a genuine Christian friendship had been broken.

The committee met for approximately a year and a half. Several seminary presidents, Dr. Ray Summers of Baylor's religion department, and others appeared before the committee. Some who were interviewed answered questions in vague terms with ambiguous words which did not completely reveal the situation. By asking questions designed to elicit clear responses, I embarrassed some members of the committee. I was frequently reminded that the committee was to be helpful and not to create problems.

Finally, one of Johnny Baugh's closest friends, Gilbert Turner, said he thought that it was time to wrap up the study and offered to write the committee's report to the deacons. I agreed; he could write the majority report, and I would write the minority report, both of which would be submitted to the deacons. In response to Gilbert's objections to this idea, we decided that each committee member would write an individual report and all would be presented together. My report was different from the others. Mine was fifty pages, duplicated, submitted to the committee, and placed on the chair of each deacon who attended the meeting. This caused a great deal of comment.

My report, now entitled "Report to Second Baptist's Deacons" (contained in Appendix A), began to be circulated. I finally had five thousand copies printed, after I received requests. This widespread distribution appeared to upset the leadership at Second. The copies that I printed showed that the report was one I made to the deacons of Second Baptist Church of Houston. Second was, therefore, involved. Had the committee worked together to study the facts and make a joint report, I would not have acted so independently.

I had alienated the establishment of Second Baptist. J. Hal Machet was named the new director of the college department, having replaced Johnny and Eula Mae Baugh. Jeannette Clift, the actress who is now Jeannette Clift George, and Gerald Coley, an attorney now deceased, together with Nancy and me were the four teachers in the department. Reliable sources told me that several meetings were held in the church offices, and a letter was very carefully drafted for Hal's signature, dated August 24, 1967. The letter read as follows: "Please excuse me for the letter approach, but I am leaving for Glorieta and will not be back until September 1, 1967." It stated that other teachers would replace the four of us, but if we wished, we could stay and "help with the visitation program, contact prospects and absentees."

Several times since then, Jeannette and I have introduced each other at speaking engagements by referring to the fact that the only time we were ever fired from teaching Sunday School was the time that we were fired together. What had happened appeared obvious to me. I believe the damage control was to remove "unsafe people" from leadership. Authority was exerted to remove anything that could cause trouble or create dissension.

CHAPTER 8

$\mathcal{A}$T THE CAFE DU MONDE

Because of my report regarding the Elliott matter, some people in key positions in the Southern Baptist Convention knew about my concerns. One day I received a telephone call from Leonard Holloway, who was development director at New Orleans Baptist Theological Seminary. He wanted to visit with me about making a contribution to the seminary's endowment fund.

I met with him but told him that because of my own experience in seeing institutions like Princeton, Smith, Harvard, Yale, and Exeter take the money that God's people had given and use it to undermine the very principles that had motivated their founding, I was concerned about giving to any endowment fund. I asked him how he could ensure that any money that I gave or raised for a New Orleans Seminary endowment would not ultimately be used to undermine the gospel.

He could give me no assurances other than his belief that the Southern Baptist Convention would control it. He believed that the convention was in good shape. By then, I had seen the way committees were set up to control people. I had seen that when some seminary officials spoke, they sometimes used ambiguous words which could mislead their hearers. I knew too much about the Elliott matter and the dealings at Second Baptist Church to be reassured.

I began to think and pray about the matter and consulted with close Christian friends, some of whom were in the estate-planning field. We got together for a luncheon. Among those involved were Carloss Morris, a lawyer and principal of Stewart Title Company; John Heard, of Vinson & Elkins; Carroll Karkalits, an official at a chemical company (he later was a member of the Southern Seminary board of trustees); H. Harold Tate, a school teacher; Orrien Smith and Sam Oliphant, both businessmen; and several others.

We decided that the only way we could ensure that our money would be safe was to give it to an endowment fund created as an independent foundation. The fund would be used for the benefit of the institution so long—but only so long—as, in the opinion of a self-perpetuating board of trustees of the foundation, the school was adhering to a basic doctrinal statement which was set forth in the articles creating the foundation. Thus, we created the Evangelical

Christian Education Foundation (ECEF) and began raising funds to help New Orleans Seminary.

The creation of the ECEF gave me my first encounter with Baptist state editors. The District of Columbia state paper blasted us. It said that we were trying to buy New Orleans Seminary and attacked both the seminary for accepting and us for giving gifts from a foundation with strings attached. Others joined the chorus of denunciation. We were shocked! All we were trying to do was to make sure that the money we gave was used for the purposes for which we gave it. How could that be bad? This encounter was a foretaste of what was to occur later.

Besides giving to the endowment, the funds were to be used for scholarships. One of the early recipients of a scholarship was Richard Land, now president of the Ethics and Religious Liberty Commission of the Southern Baptist Convention. Other students also received assistance based on applications they submitted. Ultimately, after granting many thousands of dollars in scholarships, the ECEF became less active. The remaining funds were placed at New Orleans Seminary as part of its endowment fund but were subject to being returned to us without interest if the ECEF trustees ever decided that New Orleans Seminary had departed from its biblical foundation. Such determination was never made, and the ECEF was dissolved in December 1992. President Landrum Leavell wrote a most gracious letter accepting the irrevocable grant given to the endowment of New Orleans Baptist Theological Seminary.

Additional developments grew out of the deacons' committee at Second Baptist and my involvement in the Elliott matter. Dr. H. Leo Eddleman, then president of New Orleans Seminary, asked Nancy and me to visit the seminary to become better acquainted with it and to attend a layman's conference. We drove to New Orleans with Harold and Pauline Tate. Harold was a fellow trustee of the ECEF and was then a math teacher at Lamar High School in Houston. Now in retirement, he and Pauline have a ministry called Sonlight, which makes Christian radio tapes for distribution throughout the United States.

We had a delightful trip. While there, we met Dr. and Mrs. Eddleman and Dr. and Mrs. Clark Pinnock for lunch at the famous Antoine's Restaurant in the French Quarter. We had a beneficial luncheon and enjoyed greatly getting to know the Eddlemans and Pinnocks. In the late 1960s Clark caused a minor wave in the SBC with his stand for the inerrancy of the Scriptures, but when the inerrancy controversy began in earnest in 1979, Clark had moved on to a non-Southern Baptist school.

The layman's conference was interesting. Dr. Ray Robbins, a professor at New Orleans Seminary, led one class. He talked about how salvation was like having a container full of water that had rocks in it. He said salvation was comparable to taking out the rocks, which represented sin, so that more water could be added. He said the water represented the grace of God. Innocently, Nancy asked him if he were talking about the experiential aspect of salvation and not the judicial aspect. He replied that he was not sure that salvation had a judicial aspect. He then began speaking on another matter. Nancy stopped him again. She clearly had caught him leaving out the substitutionary atonement (the fact that the Lord Jesus Christ paid the price for our sins with His blood by His death on the cross).

In just a few minutes, one of the laymen who was president of a railroad was pounding on his desk, asking whether Dr. Robbins was trying to tell him that the blood of Jesus Christ is not the answer to the sin problem and the blood of Jesus didn't pay the price for his sins. The whole thing turned into a very distasteful situation because of a flippant answer by a New Orleans professor who thought he could get away with it, knowing the original questioner (Nancy) was a homemaker and was not seminary-educated. This gave us a great deal of insight into what was occurring at the seminary, even when it had an outstanding president.

Dr. Eddleman was a true man of God. He tried diligently to bring conservative scholars to New Orleans Seminary and to help solidify the conservative base of that school. However, some people who taught on the seminary faculty were in the moderate, pro-Ralph Elliott group. Dr. Eddleman never had the complete support of his board of trustees, and therefore, could not accomplish his purposes. He later retired from New Orleans Seminary a very disappointed man.

Another significant event occurred on this trip. Some weeks before leaving for New Orleans, I talked with Bill Price, another deacon at Second Baptist Church. Bill is a person in whom I have great confidence and with whom I now serve as a deacon at Houston's First Baptist Church. Bill asked me if I had ever heard of Paige Patterson. I told him that I had not. By reading the report I made to the Second Baptist deacons, he concluded that Paige (who was a student at New Orleans Baptist Seminary) and I thought alike. Bill had known Paige in Beaumont, where his father, Dr. T. A. Patterson, was his pastor. He described how Paige, even as a youngster, was faithful in witnessing for our Lord Jesus Christ and his adherence to the truthfulness of God's Word. Bill believed that Paige and I had the same interests and same drive and that we were concerned about the same things.

One night about 10 or 11 o'clock, after the layman's conference ended, Nancy and I went to the seminary apartment where Paige and his wife, Dorothy, lived. We knocked on the door, and I said, "Paige, we are Nancy and Paul Pressler. Bill Price said that we should get to know each other." They were working diligently on papers for their seminary classes, but Paige said, "Well, if Bill Price says we ought to get together, we'll just take a break and get acquainted." The four of us went to the Cafe du Monde in the French Quarter and had coffee, hot chocolate, and beignets until past midnight in early March 1967.

Others have reported that the Cafe du Monde that night was the scene of scheming and plotting to take over the Southern Baptist Convention. This simply is not true. The conversation was between four individuals who had a mutual interest in reaching people for the Lord Jesus Christ. We shared our hearts with each other. It was also a time for ones who had experienced liberalism in the Southern Baptist Convention to share their mutual concerns about the effect this was having on the proclamation of the gospel. It was a time when two young couples enjoyed being with each other—fellowshipping and getting acquainted. I was greatly encouraged to find that Dorothy and Paige had the same concerns as we did. It was ironic that meeting Paige Patterson was another result of the committee that Johnny Baugh set up at Second Baptist. If it had not been for my committee report, Bill Price would not have known about my concerns.

Through the years, Dorothy and Paige and Nancy and I have stayed in close contact. After graduating from seminary, Paige was called as pastor of First Baptist Church in Fayetteville, Arkansas. He kindly asked me to preach for him several times in the fall when a good football game was scheduled. Paige, a person whom I have admired and appreciated since we first met, has one of the greatest intellects I have ever known. He is a profound thinker who has a great heart for reaching individuals for Jesus Christ. However, he is not all seriousness. He has a delightful, teasing personality. Paige became one of my closest friends. At first, this friendship revolved more around presenting the gospel and good fellowship than it did with working through the structures of the Southern Baptist Convention.

CHAPTER 9

*Y*OUNG PEOPLE ALL AROUND US

Another by-product of our being excluded at Second Baptist was that Dr. Ed Blum, a friend who was then pastor of Bethel Independent Presbyterian Church—a newly formed, small, struggling congregation in Houston—approached me about a task. He said the church had no one working with young people. He asked if I would consider helping him train someone to get a youth group started at Bethel.

At Second Baptist, besides our work in the college department, we had also led the high school Training Union, but after we were dismissed as Sunday School teachers, we were dismissed from Training Union leadership, as well. One Sunday afternoon about 4 o'clock, we received a call that someone else would be taking over for us at 6 o'clock that evening!

Since we no longer had a teaching ministry at Second Baptist, I saw Bethel as an opportunity which God had given us. I had begun preaching rather frequently as a pulpit supply in Baptist churches throughout the Houston area, as well as teaching a series of Sunday School classes at several Baptist churches and at St. Luke's Methodist, St. Paul Presbyterian, St. Andrew's Presbyterian, and several other churches of different denominations. The idea of helping start the youth group at Bethel appealed to us, and Nancy and I could do this together. After praying, we accepted.

Bethel only had four prospects for its youth group. All were children of members. We began working with them and realized the tremendous opportunity. This was in the 1960s, a time in our country when youth were disturbed and society seemed to be coming apart. Values were being undermined by the hippie and liberal culture.

Many churches were merely serving punch and cookies and providing fun and games to their young people instead of introducing them to the meat of the gospel. We felt that God was leading us to do something revolutionary in trying to get the gospel to these youth. Bethel gave us complete freedom, and we taught deep theology and enjoyed recreational times with the young people. The group grew fairly rapidly, and before long we were averaging twenty or thirty high schoolers.

61

One of the leaders in the Bethel youth group, Bob Borden, was killed in a tragic car accident. His death was a catalyst that caused many young people to become serious about their faith. They began looking at things from an eternal and not a temporal perspective. They began to be concerned about the lostness of their friends and about reaching other people for Jesus Christ. The youth group and other Bible studies began to expand immediately. Although we had others who helped us, no one emerged who was able to take over the youth group, so we continued for sixteen years. By the time we gave it up in February 1979, we averaged about 135 each week and saw 50 or 60 young people annually trust Jesus Christ as personal Savior. Many of these have served or are serving the Lord in full-time ministries, and most are witnessing lay men and women today.

Nancy and I believe that the capacity and interest of young people are frequently underrated. Our regular schedule on Sunday night was to sing with guitars for twenty-five minutes, have announcements for five minutes, and conduct a Bible study for half an hour. Several times we even gave tests to the young people to see what they were retaining. This led us to prepare printed topical studies so our youth could study at home. This greatly increased their retention.

Most of the salvation decisions in this group occurred on retreats which we conducted several times a year. We had messy games such as throwing pies, watermelon football, and tug-of-wars across the creek, as well as times of deep Bible study in large and small groups. On one retreat, astronaut Jack Lousma was our speaker. While speaking, he looked up and saw a satellite passing overhead. He departed from his regular message to talk about space and having been there. The young people were impressed by his faith in the Lord Jesus Christ and in the Word of God. Those who accepted the Lord were discipled. An older believer was coupled with a new believer for a one-on-one study, and this was most effective. These pairs met once a week for a year, and by that time, the one who had been a new believer was ready to take on leadership. At times we had more than one hundred young people in this discipleship program.

In 1962 we met a young man named Andy Seidel, who was a cadet at West Point. When Andy was home on summer leave, he wanted to participate in a Bible study. Nancy and I invited him and eight of his friends to come to our home on the following Tuesday. The next week twenty-three boys attended. We then went coed, and for the thirteen weeks of each summer for about eleven years, we had one hundred or more high school and college students in our home for a Bible study. We had a general session and then broke up into smaller groups that were led by outstanding Bible teachers. Andy dated his future wife, Gail Norris, at the Bible study, and they served as missionaries in Europe. We saw many people come to know Jesus Christ as personal Savior through this Bible study also. The Bible studies we led worked together and complemented each other.

At that time I was vice president of the Houston Princeton Alumni Association and was also on its local admissions screening committee. Several students I met through the committee later became active in our Bible studies. One of these was Richard Land, who was mentioned earlier as a recipient of an ECEF scholarship to New Orleans Seminary and who later became president of the Ethics and Religious Liberty Commission of the SBC. Richard had a real heart for the Lord, and we became very close friends.

He attended Princeton University and worked with us in our summer Bible studies. After Richard graduated from New Orleans Seminary, our Bethel youth group helped support him while he was a student at Oxford in England. In order to raise money for his support, we had "Slave Days," in which students would hire out and individuals would make contributions to the youth group in order to compensate for their help. We also held spaghetti dinners, walks, and other fund-raising activities to support Richard and other projects of the youth group. Whenever we had a spaghetti dinner, we had a gospel presentation along with it because we had many young people who had trusted Jesus Christ as personal Savior but whose parents were not Christians. Many parents also eventually trusted the Lord.

Other activities in which I was involved during this period included serving as vice president of the Exeter Alumni Association and performing the legal work for KHCB-FM, a new Houston-based Christian radio station, which went on the air on March 9, 1962. Since then, we have purchased an AM station which broadcasts in Spanish, Mandarin, and Vietnamese. This language broadcasting has been one of my dreams. KHCB now owns a network of stations across Texas. I presently serve as chairman of the board of trustees of KHCB and as director of the National Religious Broadcasters.

Hal Guffey, a friend whom I had met at an Officers' Christian Union Bible Conference in 1953, became head of International Students, Inc. (ISI). ISI uses friendship evangelism to reach internationals with the gospel while they are in the United States. In 1969 Hal asked me to join his board of directors, and I agreed. In the early 1970s ISI purchased Star Ranch in Colorado Springs from Young Life and moved its operations to Colorado. Our youth group volunteered to clean up the grounds and paint and repair the buildings. Nancy and I took our three children, along with a couple of other adults, and chaperoned about one hundred young people each year for seven or eight summers. We went by bus to Colorado and held a two-week work camp and Bible conference. On each trip we saw several students accept Jesus Christ as personal Lord and Savior.

We were working with many young people who had very little church background. Once when we were leaving on the bus, one of the very active young people came up to me and said, "I have a friend with me. He has to go to Colorado. Don't ask any questions, but it is absolutely essential that he go."

I broke my rule about advance payment and agreed, and we took him. The young man, whose hair was down to his waist, did not look like someone who was headed for a Bible conference. I later learned that he was a member of a gang, had been having an affair with the gang leader's girlfriend, and that the gang leader was going to have him killed. He had to get out of town. Even before our bus got to Colorado, the young man trusted the Lord. He is now a successful businessman, a vibrant Christian, and active in a Southern Baptist church. This was the type of young person with whom we often worked, along with others from traditional backgrounds who had not been in trouble.

After the Sunday night Bible study, we went to someone's home for refreshments, singing, testimonies, and sharing. The young people thus became participants and developed a concern for others. Many in our group had enough affluence to know that material items such as money, travel, cars, and clothes did not satisfy.

Another event that was very successful with our young people was the Boys' Retreat, which we held each spring at our ranch near Dripping Springs, Texas. Approximately one hundred teenagers and college students attended each year, and many came to know Jesus Christ. Again, we did not have the typical young people one might find in a traditional church setting. Once, after I caught two boys with drugs, I went to the parents of both of them. Neither set of parents were Christians. One family developed strong support for their son, and eventually the whole family became Christians. In the other situation, the mother berated me for accusing her son of doing such a thing. The last time I heard, that boy's life was a mess, and he was addicted to drugs.

While these church-related activities were occurring, our lives had other aspects, as well. We were delighted to be in Houston with my family. Arriving in June 1960 gave us time with my grandparents before my grandfather Townes died in January 1962. He was one of the most consistent Christian gentlemen I have ever known and was a tremendous inspiration and blessing to me. His death from a stroke was a great shock, and we were glad to be with my grandmother and other family members when this loss occurred.

After returning to Houston, my first assignment at Vinson & Elkins was basically in oil and gas and then in estate planning. At first I worked under a person whose goals and purposes in life were far different from mine, and it was quite unpleasant. Later I was asked to work for Sidney S. McClendon Jr., who was a true gentleman and an outstanding lawyer. The privilege of practicing under him was one that I deeply appreciated. Things went well at Vinson & Elkins, but I did not see a real future for me there because the firm demanded the unreserved dedication of each of its lawyers. I had so many other interests in which I was engaged and which I considered even more important.

Nancy and I had three and one-half wonderful years together before our children began arriving. Our first child, Jean Townes Pressler, was born on November 24, 1962. Anne Lyle Pressler was born on February 11, 1965, and then our son, Herman Paul Pressler IV, was born on April 23, 1966. We were proud parents, and we were thrilled to have three such wonderful children. They all attended Second Baptist School. The children were very blessed by the association with the young people in the youth group Bible studies who were older and whom they could use as role models. Each of our children clearly trusted Jesus Christ as personal Savior before the age of five.

When Jean was five months old, we discovered she was born without a hip socket (as was Nancy). Since this caused her to be in splints or a full-body cast until she was eighteen months old, we hired a wonderful young woman from Honduras, Leonor Ferrera, to help Nancy. Leonor did not speak English, so we spoke Spanish in the home while she was with us from 1963 to 1969. We knew that Jean really understood the gospel when, at four years of age, she was explaining in Spanish to Leonor about how to be saved. She had heard the way of salvation only in English but had been able to translate the concept into Spanish accurately and knowledgeably.

Many humorous things happened while we were rearing our children. One incident occurred when Anne was three and Jean five. Anne had misbehaved, and we had her sit in a chair as a means of discipline. She was crying, and Jean came over to her, put her arms around her, and said, "That's all right, honey. Jesus has taken all of our punishment for us." Obviously, that was not a correct application of the gospel, but at least Jean was thinking in spiritual concepts.

Our children could not have had better grandparents. The grandparents on both sides of the family loved them, entertained them, and provided them with many opportunities. Nancy and I were very blessed because we had such good, loving help with the children.

We frequently traveled back and forth to Chicago. Nancy's parents told us that any time we wanted to visit them, they would pay for the transportation. We took them up on their offer as frequently as possible. They were believers and active in a Presbyterian church.

Life in those days was full. Besides church activities, Nancy was active in the Junior League, Bible Study Fellowship, and several other organizations. We were occupied with our children, and much demand was on me at the office. Life was complicated, but we felt good about what God was doing in our lives.

A crucial time occurred for me one day when I was delivering a report to David Searls, a named partner in Vinson, Elkins, Weems and Searls. My report should have required only about ten to fifteen minutes, but every few minutes, a call to Mr. Searls from some corporation president, governor, senator, or some other prominent person interrupted our conversation. Because of the interruptions, I spent a couple of hours giving the report. I looked at Mr. Searls and saw a man who was trapped by his own success and who had a look of desperation in his eyes. He was so fine, so successful, and so outstanding that he was in constant demand.

I went home that night and told Nancy that I had seen the epitome of success in the path along which I was headed, and I really did not want to follow it. (Not many years after that, Mr. Searls died of a heart attack.) We began prayerfully considering the professional direction that I should take.

The activities in the youth group and with our own children were taking up more and more time, and we were seeing more and more results in helping bring people to the Lord. I did not believe that I could lay aside the work God had called me to do simply in order to make more money.

CHAPTER 10

$\mathcal{A}$ CHANGE IN DIRECTION

I was sitting in my office on a Monday in October 1969 when Wilmer Hunt, judge of the 133rd Judicial District Court in Harris County, phoned me. It was a call that would change my life. In his court, I had pending a case in which a brother and sister, both of whom were single physicians and almost forty years of age, had petitioned to adopt a child. They had located the baby through their practice and wanted to have a child to whom they could leave their considerable wealth and continue their name.

I had previously discussed the matter with Judge Hunt. He called to tell me that he wanted me to put in writing our discussion on the matter. He said it would be best to act now because before the sixty-day waiting period for hearing the adoption had run its course, he would no longer be judge of that court. I asked him what he meant. He told me that nobody knew it, but he had decided to retire and had planned to announce it within the next few days. I sat at my desk stunned by Judge Hunt's announcement.

In Texas, judges are elected in a partisan election. No district judge has a district which is composed of less than an entire county. When the legislature creates a new district or appellate judgeship, or a judge dies or resigns while in office, the governor of Texas appoints a replacement. Just weeks earlier I had attended the swearing-in ceremony of four friends of mine who were becoming judges. As I returned from the ceremony, I thought about how fulfilling it would be to serve as a judge. I discussed this with Nancy, and she said she supported me if I wanted to pursue this interest. This occurred soon after I had given my report to Mr. Searls and became so discouraged about the direction I could see my life headed. After the call from Judge Hunt, I telephoned Nancy, and we prayed together. She said that if I was interested in pursuing appointment to this bench, she was fully behind it.

I then needed to see three people who were typically very difficult to reach. The first was my father, who was always very busy. Nevertheless, I was able to get through immediately to him to discuss the situation. He said he thought this was a serious mistake, since it would reduce my earning power appreciably, but if this was what I wanted to do, he was agreeable. Then I went to see Mr. Searls, who had always been my friend and mentor. Surprisingly, I got in to see him immediately. Mr. Searls' reaction was the same as that of my father. I then needed to see Raybourne Thompson, who was the managing partner of the law firm. Instead of having to wait for days, as was frequently the case, I was able to walk right into his office. Within less than forty-five minutes, I had contacted Nancy and the three others with whom I needed to talk before I could undertake seeking appointment for this judgeship.

When I was with Raybourne, he asked me whom I knew in the Texas governor's office. I told him that Bob Bullock, a friend of mine in the legislature, was working for the governor, Preston Smith, but I didn't know what position he held. (Bob later served several high elective offices, including that of lieutenant governor of Texas.) Raybourne told me to call Bob and find out from him who was in charge of the governor's appointments. I was able to connect with Bob immediately and learned that he, in fact, was the one.

When I told Bob that Wilmer Hunt was about to retire and that I was interested in an appointment to the position, he replied that this was news to him as well as to others in Austin. He said to his knowledge, no others had spoken for the position because no one knew it was to be vacant. Bob told me that if I wanted this judgeship, I would have his support. Then he gave me a list of eight people in Houston who were the governor's key supporters. He suggested I call some of them, asking that they contact the governor on my behalf.

The first on the list was my cousin, Paul Barnhart, who was very close to Governor Smith. In fact, soon after the gubernatorial election, I had flown to Dallas with Paul in his plane. We pulled up next to the plane on which the governor-elect had just arrived. We were all headed for the same political meeting. Paul turned to Preston and said, "Preston, you know my cousin, Paul Pressler, don't you?" Preston looked at me and replied, "Yes, I certainly do know John Hill's Harris County campaign manager." (John Hill had been one of Preston's opponents in the primary for the governor's race.) Preston then proceeded to talk to Paul but not to me.

Preston Smith had been my friend when we were in the legislature. In the House, I sat next to Doc Blanchard, who was state representative from Lubbock while Preston was state senator from there. When Doc was not at his desk and Preston wanted something done, I frequently did it for him. Preston was a great person and a very capable legislator. I would have gladly supported him for governor. However, John Hill, who was an outstanding lawyer, was also in the race. I had served with him on the local Young Life board, and he had asked me to be his Harris County campaign manager. Since John had asked me, I agreed to do it. With John and Preston running, I had two close friends in the race, but John had received my commitment of support first. Preston was not pleased about my backing John, who later served as attorney general of Texas and chief justice of the Texas Supreme Court.

I began contacting the others on the list. They were people whom I also knew. The whole chain of events regarding this appointment began happening on Monday afternoon. By Wednesday, five of the eight had already called the governor, and the governor told the last one that I should make an appointment to see him. I did and was in his office on Friday morning at 10 o'clock. By that time, seven of the eight had contacted the governor on my behalf, and the remaining one was in Europe. Key among those helping me were my cousin, Paul Barnhart, and oil men Pat Rutherford and Charles Alcorn.

I walked into the governor's office at the appointed time. We both stood. He did not ask me to be seated. We exchanged a few pleasantries, and then Preston looked me in the eye and told me he owed me nothing. He took about five or ten minutes to dress me up one side and down the other for supporting John Hill instead of him in the governor's race. Finally, he asked me directly, "Paul, why did you support John instead of me?" I replied, "Governor, both of you were close friends, and John asked me, and you didn't." The governor of Texas lifted his head sharply, looked at me, and asked, "Well, what will happen in the future if another of your close friends asks you to support him in a race against me?" I answered, "Governor, I will never have a closer friend than the one who appoints me district judge." Preston began to laugh, and he said, "OK, we will work this out." That was the end of my interview with the governor.

About a month later, after Wilmer Hunt had announced his resignation, everything seemed to be going smoothly, but I found out that Judge Hunt had delayed his announcement in order to allow a friend of his, Judge Pete Solito, then a domestic relations court judge, to muster support to get the appointment. By moving in quickly and decisively I had messed up their plans. Pete and Judge Hunt had been very active together in the Knights of Columbus. Pete had strong support, and he moved to put pressure on the governor as quickly as possible.

A great deal of pressure came from Jim Kronzer, a prominent attorney in Houston, and other plaintiff's lawyers who felt that because I was with a large defense firm and because my family had been active in conservative politics, I could not be fair to everyone. (Later, a friend told me that he heard Jim tell a group that he had been wrong on that one and that I had been a judge who had been fair to everyone.) Also the presiding judge of the administrative district, Max Rogers, was strongly backing Pete and was pushing Tommy Lichtenstein to replace Pete. I was glad the governor listened to his friends who were also my friends.

The governor called and asked me if I would consider taking a domestic relations court bench. I knew what he wanted. It was to promote Pete Solito to the vacant district judgeship and then to put me on the domestic relations bench. I said, "Governor, there is no way I could sit there and listen to all the fights between individuals in domestic relations matters every day. I am sorry, but I just couldn't serve in that capacity." He said, "All right, that's fine. I couldn't do it either, but I just thought I would try." A few weeks later my appointment came through.

Hoping to scare off opposition in the next election, I waited several days to take the bench in order to arrange a large swearing-in ceremony. That took place on January 14, 1970, and six to seven hundred people attended. Prominent political leaders from across the spectrum were in the front rows. The strategy worked, and the filing deadline for the next election passed without anyone running against me. I was safely in office as judge for the two remaining years of Judge Hunt's term of office.

I had not been a trial lawyer and had never argued a case in court, so becoming a judge so suddenly was a rather awesome experience. I had a wonderful clerk, Mrs. Merle Brown, and a most thoughtful and loyal bailiff, Ernie Gessner. My outstanding court reporter, Art Richardson, is still a close friend. With this excellent staff I inherited from Judge Hunt, things were much easier than they otherwise would have been. Merle arranged the first case for me with the help of Mrs. Lena Ferguson, the docket clerk. It was a workmen's compensation case. I will never forget getting on the bench and saying, "Gentlemen, proceed," and

Robing of Judge Paul Pressler by father, after being sworn in as District Judge

not having the foggiest idea of what would happen next. Both lawyers were gentlemen and had some understanding of my predicament. They tried my first case beautifully with very little interference from me. It was easy for me to pick up the routine after that.

Fortunately, as a trial judge, I could adjourn the court if I didn't know something and go look up the matter. In the early days of my trial experience, I had expert friends on both sides of the bar (some plaintiffs' and some defendants' attorneys) whom I could call and ask a question in abstract without divulging the specific matter at hand. If all of them gave me the same answer, I knew it was right. If they gave me different answers, I had to dig in the books more. I was grateful for my experience as a trial judge. If I remember correctly, in those nine years, only fourteen of the cases that I tried were reversed. Since I averaged about forty jury trials and almost one thousand other dispositions every year for the nine years that I was on the trial bench, I was pleased with my record.

Those were interesting days in Harris County on the civil district bench. Judges Bill Holland, John Snell, and Lewis Dickson dominated in the civil district judge meetings. They were all strong personalities and believed that they and not the lawyers should have complete control in their court. I was the new kid on the block. I kept my mouth shut and was as noncontroversial as I could possibly be. I have watched with pleasure the civil trial judiciary move into a position of more benevolent concern for those who are litigating in their court.

A few years later, Judge Ed Coulson, one of my close friends and one of the most gracious, capable, and kind people ever to sit on the bench in Harris County, came into my office. He told me that Governor Smith had called because a vacancy was about to occur on the Fourteenth Court of Appeals. Preston said that either Ed or I could have it and directed Ed to meet with me and decide which one of us would take it. It seemed to me that Ed really wanted it. I was not as experienced as a district judge as he was, and I insisted that he take it. He did. Therefore, I passed up my first opportunity to go on the appellate court.

I never let the governor regret that he had appointed me to the bench. Not only did I work diligently, but I was always available to meet with him whenever he came to town and to help him in every way possible. I still stay in communication with him. Through his appointment of me as judge, Preston Smith changed my life. Because of the schedule I kept as a judge and the difference in demands on my time from being a full-time lawyer, I was able to accomplish some of the goals and purposes which I had outside of my profession. This appointment opened the doors for me to become more heavily involved in Christian activities.

Some people might say that my finding out about the availability of the judgeship, being able immediately to see all the people with whom I had to clear the matter, knowing Bob Bullock, knowing all the people on his list, and getting ahead of the other one who was prepared to move into the position were all merely coincidences, but I do not believe that. I believe that God works in our lives and prepares the way. I am most grateful that He gave me a position from which I could be involved in what really mattered to me.

Being in the judiciary opened other opportunities for studying and learning. In the summer of 1970, after being reelected without opposition, I was required to attend the National College of State Trial Judges in Reno, Nevada. Nancy and the children went with me, and we spent a delightful month in the West as I further prepared to be a trial judge.

Years later, after more Southerners turned from being Democrats to being Republicans, people asked me why I ran as a Democrat. I would answer that my family and I had always been Democrats. When I was elected to the legislature, no Republicans served there, and when I became a judge in 1970, the state had practically no Republican judges. My convictions had always been conservative, but like the rest of my family, I had expressed my conservative convictions through the Democratic Party, believing that some hope for the party still existed. In 1988 I abandoned this hope and became a Republican.

Only in 1976 did I have opposition for reelection. About fifteen minutes before the deadline, I went to Democratic headquarters to see if anyone had filed against me. No one filed until about five minutes before the time expired. Then M. W. Plummer, a local attorney, did.

The story circulated that Plummer wanted to file against the newest judge, who was Presley Werlein, and that he got Paul Pressler and Presley Werlein confused and filed in the wrong race. I am not sure that is an accurate story. At that time I was under consideration for a federal judgeship, and another man who was a friend of M. W. Plummer wanted the same appointment. I had always thought that the man who wanted the judgeship was a friend of mine also. As soon as Plummer filed against me, I called this man and told him what had happened. He replied, "You don't say," in a way that made me think that he had knowledge of what I was telling him and knew a great deal more about it than he would admit. He responded that he would check into it and get back to me in a few days. I never heard anything from him about the race except to see his name appear among the supporters of my opponent.

I think Plummer's running against me (and forcing me to campaign) was this other man's way of trying to keep me from being involved in seeking a federal judgeship and clearing the way for himself. President Jimmy Carter later appointed the man who was Plummer's friend to a federal judgeship, but he was never confirmed because of severe opposition.

The vote in the Democratic primary in 1976 was anticipated to be about 50 percent minority, which was significant since my opponent was African-American. I had held court in Spanish and anticipated the support of the Latin American community. In fact, a Hispanic leader told me that I had his community's support and invited me to one of the main Hispanic functions. When I arrived, I found out that the community leaders had at the last minute switched their support to my opponent. Coordination between the minority groups occurred in the primary. My race was part of their working out a coalition. However, I had the support of some wonderful African-American leaders, including Beulah Shepherd, Gladys Goffney, Cecil Bush, and several others who were true friends.

I believe that two African-American leaders quietly kept the campaign from becoming destructive and helped me in their community. They were congressmen-to-be Mickey Leland and Craig Washington. When Mickey first ran for the legislature, I was judge in the case involving whether he was eligible to run because of the location of his residence. As in other such cases, I determined that it was a question for the voters to decide and that a person should not be excluded from running on a technicality when reasonable doubt existed about the facts. Craig, who represented Mickey in the case, later became state senator and then took Mickey's place in Congress when Mickey was killed in a plane crash. Craig and Mickey knew that I was fair, and that is why I believe they helped me in the race.

I received a substantial portion of the minority vote and won 60 to 40. My friends, including many from the youth group, were my strength and rallied to my support. My campaign budget was easily met, and the volunteer staff was extremely helpful. I had the overwhelming support of the legal and business community.

Two years later, the legislature expanded both the First and the Fourteenth Courts of Appeals from three to six judges. Both courts had jurisdiction over a fourteen-county area, including Harris County (Houston). Then-Governor Dolph Briscoe made the appointments for these six open positions. By then, I had more than eight and one-half years' experience on the trial bench. I had seen lawyers use all their techniques. I knew what would happen next in the courtroom, and I felt I needed more of a challenge. Nancy and I discussed it and prayed about it. We then decided that I was ready to move on and that seeking such an opportunity was the thing to do.

I did not know how to go about it, so I called my friend Joe Reynolds, whom I knew was close to the governor, to research the matter. I told him what I wanted and asked him how to go about getting the appointment. As it turned out, the governor had asked Joe to determine who should be the nominees. (Joe later replaced me as a member of the Executive Committee of the Southern Baptist Convention.) He said, "Paul, I am so delighted that you are interested. You can have it. I'll tell Dolph that you are going to get one of those appointments. All you need to do is make three or four courtesy calls."

He gave me the names of the individuals I should see and said he would call and tell them I was coming to see them. (Although he told me to visit them as a matter of courtesy, he assured me that I definitely had the appointment.) Nothing had ever been easier in my life. I made the courtesy calls, and that was it.

Dolph Briscoe had defeated Preston Smith for governor and had succeeded him in office. In that race, as I had promised, I supported Preston. However, Dolph did not hold it against me. Two governors in a row, neither of whom I had supported when they were first elected, appointed me to leading judicial positions. I am very grateful to them. Dolph and I became close friends, and we have stayed in touch through the years. As an aside, I find it interesting to realize that I have known every person who has been governor of Texas since 1917. Of course, I did not know all of them while they were governor but met and knew each personally at some time in their life.

I was sworn in as one of the six justices on the Fourteenth Court of Appeals on December 1, 1978. The appellate court functioned quite differently from the state district court where I had served. The lower court required its judge to be present to hear motions and evidence five days a week, basically from 9:00 A.M. to 5:00 P.M. On the court of appeals, the judges review the records of cases which have been tried, read the legal briefs submitted by the parties, and then after hearing oral arguments, write opinions stating whether the case had been properly decided in the court below, dealing with the points of law which had been raised on appeal. The Fourteenth Court of Appeals was later expanded to nine judges, with three judges sitting on a panel. Only twice each week did the three judges on a panel meet together. Once was to discuss the cases to be submitted and to rule on motions and the other time to hear the oral arguments on the cases. The rest of the time each judge worked on his own schedule.

When I first went on the appeals court, it had only civil jurisdiction. A constitutional amendment soon added criminal cases. I enjoyed the work but had to concentrate and study a great deal. As I learned the job, it became easier to manage, and my office hours were not as exact and demanding as they had been on the trial bench. It was not that I worked any less or spent any fewer hours, but the time was spent on my schedule. I did not have to punch a clock from 9 to 5. I am a night person, and Nancy and I developed a schedule in which we would work each night until almost midnight, and I would not go into the office until 9:00 or 9:30 each morning. No other job that I know of would have paid me a living wage, given me standing in the community, and provided me the flexibility of schedule that would allow me to be involved in the Southern Baptist Convention and in other Christian work in the manner in which I was. I fully believe that God put me in that position—just six months before the conservative movement in the Southern Baptist Convention moved into public view.

CHAPTER 11

GETTING INVOLVED

Another result of my writing the report to the Second Baptist Church deacons was a call I received from Rev. William "Bill" Powell, the leader of a new group called the Baptist Faith and Message Fellowship. When the Elliott controversy first started in the early 1960s, I had corresponded with Rev. Gerald Primm, Dr. Calvin Capps, and Dr. M. O. Owens, pastors in North Carolina. They had helped organize a conservative group concerned specifically about the Elliott matter and generally about liberalism in the Southern Baptist Convention. This correspondence had been brief, and I had not followed up on it. I had not heard of the Baptist Faith and Message Fellowship, which they helped organize, and was surprised to get the call from Bill Powell.

Bill, whom I had known casually, had been director of missions for the Chicago Baptist Association when I lived there. He then went to the Home Mission Board (now combined into the North American Mission Board). At great personal sacrifice, he left the security of the Home Mission Board to direct the struggling Baptist Faith and Message Fellowship.

Bill said he wanted to travel to Houston to see me. He did, and I was glad to meet with him. He looked through the records that I had kept on liberalism in the SBC and said he believed I was the only one he had ever met who had as many files on the matter as he did. Bill wanted to enlist me to work with him in the Baptist Faith and Message Fellowship. I was reluctant to do this because things were going too well in unrelated areas of my life. I felt sure that other people would take care of the problems in the convention. I had worried very much about the Elliott controversy, but I felt that it was an atypical situation. I believed that ultimately the system would take care of it. I knew that the vast majority of Southern Baptists were Bible-believing, conservative people. I could not conceive of a situation in which the denominational leadership would ignore its members and their theology. I was too comfortable and did not want to participate.

Bill asked me to speak to a meeting in Birmingham, Alabama, in November 1975. Nancy, the children, and I decided that going there and on to Atlanta would be a good way to take our family vacation. We drove to Birmingham, I spoke, and then we proceeded to visit some relatives and sites where my family had previously lived. I was pleased with the people I met in Birmingham and with a great many things about the meeting, but it did not seem that this group reached out to mainstream Southern Baptists or that it would be very effective in creating change. I withheld my full support. Later, Bill asked me to speak at First Baptist Church of Lenoir City, Tennessee. Although it was supposed to be a regional meeting, only a small group attended.

One of the most important discussions I ever had concerning the Southern Baptist Convention occurred on that drive from Lenoir City to Atlanta. Bill Powell described to me the way the Southern Baptist system operated. He explained the power of the SBC president. Bill was a careful reader and a real student. He left no stone unturned in his research. It was not my independent research that showed the way the convention could be turned around; it was Bill's. I was not impressed with the type of meetings Bill was conducting, but I was impressed that he had put his finger on the real solution to the problem of creeping liberalism in the SBC.

Here is how it works: The convention president appoints the Committee on Committees in "conference with the vice-presidents," according to Section 21 of the SBC By-Laws. "Conference" was not defined. Therefore it was assumed that the president had the right to exercise this power to appoint the committee and then share what he had done (or was going to do) with the vice presidents and consider their suggestions. We also assumed that the president had no obligation to follow their suggestions. We thus adopted a very narrow interpretation of "conference." There was never any official definition.

Had I been planning strategy for the liberals, I would have asked the SBC Executive Committee to define the term while the liberals still had absolute control of the Executive Committee. Had any official definition of conference existed that gave an equal voice to each of the vice presidents along with the president, the conservative movement could have been stopped. The liberal-backed candidates frequently won vice-presidential elections after 1979, though conservatives won the presidency. I was surprised that the liberals did not seize upon this strategy.

The convention does not vote to approve the Committee on Committees. It is appointed by the president and then meets and nominates the Committee on Boards (now the Committee on Nominations). The convention votes on whether or not to approve or amend the report of the nominees for the Committee on Boards. At the following SBC annual meeting, the Committee on Boards then brings a report nominating all those who should be elected to serve on the boards, agencies, and commissions of the convention.

Each entity of the convention is governed by a board elected by the convention for a term of three, four, or five years. Each person elected to a board which has a four- or five-year term is eligible for two terms. Thus, the rotation of trustees is very slow. Vacancies occur when a trustee's term ends or by a trustee's death, resignation, or his or her moving from the area from which he or she was elected as a trustee. Accordingly, the process can take as long as ten years to replace all of the trustees on a seminary board. (See SBC organizational chart.)

We now knew how to solve the problems we saw in the convention. Previously, conservative activities had not been effectively directed. Conservatives had been able to win all the battles, but we kept losing the war because we did not understand how the system operated. When a plan of action was developed to use the system and elect conservative trustees, our institutions could be returned to the principles that had made them great. To change the trustees would mean changing the institutions. Conservative trustees would hire a conservative president, who would then hire conservative professors and administrators.

That day I realized the far-reaching importance of what Bill Powell had discovered and taught me. I was so elated that I could not wait until I arrived home to tell Nancy but called her and said, "I think this is one of the most important days of my life. I now understand how the convention works and how it can be turned around!"

When Bill asked me to join the board of directors of the Baptist Faith and Message Fellowship, I did so with reluctance and reserve. I attended two meetings in Atlanta. Then the group asked me to serve as chairman of its board. I responded that I would consider doing it but never did. At that time the Baptist Faith and Message Fellowship was more than $20,000 in debt. A member had told Bill that he would help him financially but failed to do so. I worked with others to raise the money and pay off the debt. It was done with Bill's agreement that we would incur no further debts without the approval of the group's executive committee.

Very shortly after the debt was retired, I learned that Bill bought a computer and other supplies which, although needed, were not budgeted or approved. He had done so without following the proper procedure, and we were again in debt—this time by more than $14,000. This and other similar instances caused me grave concern, and I knew that I could not work with the Baptist Faith and Message Fellowship under Bill's leadership.

Some of Bill's methods also discouraged me. I believe strongly that when a person seeks to clarify a position, he or she should be given a full opportunity to do so. At times Bill seemed to try to extract a statement from a person and not

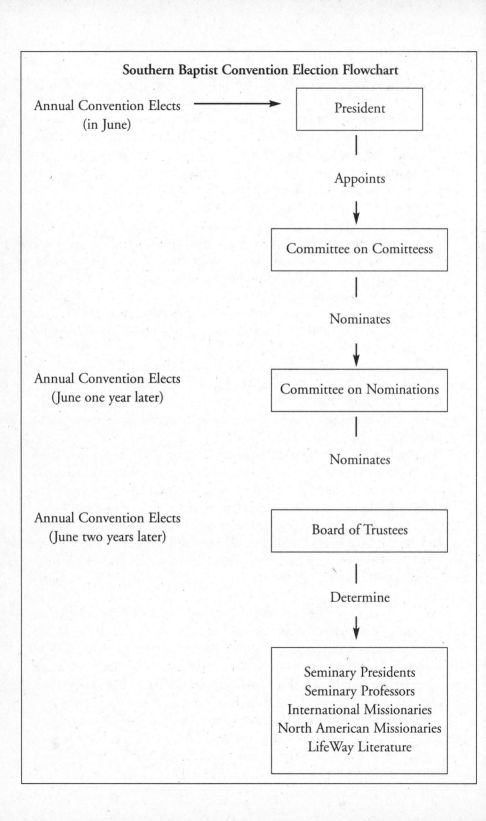

Southern Baptist Convention Election Flowchart

Annual Convention Elects
(in June) → President

Appoints

Committee on Comitteess

Nominates

Annual Convention Elects
(June one year later)   Committee on Nominations

Nominates

Annual Convention Elects
(June two years later)   Board of Trustees

Determine

Seminary Presidents
Seminary Professors
International Missionaries
North American Missionaries
LifeWay Literature

let the person clarify it. I could understand Bill's frustration because I have heard people say things and then deny what they said. I saw people who were constantly denying the plain meaning of what they had previously said. When Bill wrote his book, *SBC Answers and Questions,* I knew that I could not continue working with him. I felt the book was poorly written, inflammatory in tone, and unfair to some people. It was very sad to have this book represent the conservative movement.

However, the conservative movement owes a tremendous debt to Bill Powell. Without his diligence, his research, and his tenacity, the movement never would have gotten under way. Bill gave up his security at the Home Mission Board in order to pursue his dream of returning our institutions to their biblical roots. Bill loved the Lord, he loved God's truth, and he gave of himself unreservedly to see God's will done. However, as in many other cases, the one who starts a movement is not always the one who sees it to its completion. All of us can become battle-weary and battle-worn. Bill had been fighting the battle for a long time and had many scars.

One of my real regrets is that Bill Powell did not see the triumph of the movement which he initially led. Bill contracted Alzheimer's disease and never knew of the great victories. Only in heaven does he know what his sacrifice accomplished. I believe that his problems with finances and treatment of those on the other side were the result of the onset of Alzheimer's. I do not hold Bill responsible for what his poor health caused. No one realized he had this problem when he was in the early stages of the disease. In retrospect, he cannot be blamed.

After turning away from the Baptist Faith and Message Fellowship, I rested on the hope that others would take care of the situation and that I would not have to become personally involved. Unfortunately, this did not happen. In 1977 five young people who had been in the youth group which Nancy and I had led were freshmen at Baylor University in Waco, Texas. They called me one day and said that they were confused about what to believe and wanted me to visit them in Waco. They said that the things we taught them and the things that the Bible says were different from the things that their Baylor religion professors were teaching them. They wanted me to see their textbooks, hear what they were being taught in class, and help them know the truth. A few days later, I sat down with these students in a restaurant on the banks of the Brazos River. Together we reviewed their textbooks.

These students were being taught the same higher critical approach which I had seen at Princeton. This approach denied the complete accuracy of the Word of God. These young people who had been saved through our Bible studies were confused and were now in danger of being destroyed in their Christian witness. I was concerned that young people I had helped come to know the Lord and whom I had helped to build up in the faith were being harmed by teaching in an institution supported by the SBC Cooperative Program of giving. I felt discouraged.

Driving back to Houston that night from Waco, I promised God I would not sit back any longer. I would work to see our convention turned around, and I was determined to see it restored to teaching that the Bible is truly God's Word. That night I began to climb that hill on which to die because young people I loved and had nurtured were being undermined in their faith. I knew the problems had to be rectified.

That evening at Baylor brought back memories of the things I had heard at Princeton and at Exeter. I remembered the spiritual wasteland in New England that had been caused by others' failure to maintain their Christian testimony. Through the years many people have been hurt in their Christian faith because of the influence of Exeter, Princeton, and other such institutions. I no longer could sit back and let our Baptist institutions go the same way. I felt a burden, and I knew God required me to do something. I had no idea what lay ahead. I just knew God was beckoning me onward.

CHAPTER 12

MEETING THE RIGHT PASTORS

After I returned from Waco, I called my friend, Paige Patterson. From time to time Paige and I had discussed the situation in the convention. Although some people have alleged that from the first night Paige and I met, we devised a plan "to control" the SBC, we did not. Until this time we had expressed to each other general concern about the situation, but we had no plan of action to carry out our concerns or even a commitment to do anything. Paige had not been involved in the Baptist Faith and Message Fellowship. He had recently become president of the Criswell Bible College at First Baptist Church of Dallas and had moved to Texas from Arkansas. After the visit with the Baylor students, I called Paige because I always valued his judgment. I told him that I was really upset, I knew something had to be done, and I was willing now to do it. He asked if I were serious, and I replied, "Yes."

He gave me a plan of action. He said that if I were to pursue this, several things needed to occur. First of all, I had to meet some key people because I was unknown. He gave me the names of several pastors whom he believed I should meet. He said I should explain to them the way the system worked and how a turnaround could be accomplished. He also said that I had to find someone who is known to the Southern Baptist Convention establishment to work with me. I asked, "Who can that be?" He answered, "Well, let's pray about that matter."

I started traveling to meet the people on Paige's list. Dr. Jerry Vines, who was then the pastor of Dauphin Way Baptist Church in Mobile, Alabama, was conducting a revival for Dr. Homer Lindsay Jr. at First Baptist Church of Jacksonville, Florida (the church where he later became copastor with Dr. Lindsay). I made an appointment, went to Jacksonville, and met with the two of them together for a couple of hours. They were amazed to hear the way the system operated. They believed the convention could not be turned around, but they said if the others would help, they would also.

I called Adrian Rogers and, as with the others, I just said, "I am Paul Pressler. I am a judge in Houston, Texas. I am concerned about the direction of our convention, and I would like to come visit you, if you could spare me an hour of your time." In each case, the person said he was willing to talk to me. I went to

Memphis and spent a wonderful time with Adrian. He, likewise, said he didn't believe it would work, but he would help if the others would agree to do so.

I called Bailey Smith, then the pastor of First Southern Baptist Church in Del City, Oklahoma. At that time he was preaching a revival in Tulsa and commuting from his home. I arrived at the airport in Oklahoma City in midafternoon on Monday, February 27, 1978. He picked me up there, and we talked all the way to Tulsa, where he preached the revival, and talked all the way back. He immediately understood the issues and the possibilities. He was ready to help and has been supportive and self-sacrificing in his help through the years.

I was supposed to fly from Oklahoma City to Phoenix, Arizona, where I had a luncheon appointment with Richard Jackson, pastor of North Phoenix Baptist Church. When I arrived in Tulsa, I received a message from Richard telling me not to make the trip. I had already purchased non-refundable tickets, based on Richard's agreement for us to get together. I tried to call him but could not make connections. Later I heard that he told some people that he had done some checking on me after I had called. Based on the checking, he apparently determined that I was a Presbyterian, not a Baptist. (I have never been a member of any church except a Baptist church, even when I was working with Bethel, which was an independent Bible church.) I have always believed that Richard's information about this originated with someone at Second Baptist in Houston, because he had been a prospect of the church's pulpit committee after James Riley resigned as pastor.

Two others on Paige's list were well-known to me. Jimmy Draper had worked diligently to help me in my election to the legislature in 1956. John Bisagno was my pastor. I did not need to make the trips to visit them.

After I returned and told Paige about the visits, I mentioned his original suggestion about having a colaborer. I asked him whom he considered to be someone known by the bureaucracy who would be willing to join me in getting involved with this cause. Paige suggested, "How about me?" I was overjoyed! Thus was born the new movement for doctrinal stability in the nation's largest Protestant denominational body, the Southern Baptist Convention. This movement was not something that had been plotted and planned for a long time, although many people had a burning desire in their hearts to correct the liberal direction into which we were drifting. The Baylor event motivated us and brought us all together. The stage was now set.

CHAPTER 13

*O*UR SON

During the time I became increasingly involved with SBC matters, our family was also experiencing a deep, personal crisis that would impact us seriously in the years ahead. On Sunday night, January 16, 1977, as I taught the youth group Bible study at Bethel, I saw one of my friends moving down the center aisle of the room toward me. He told me to get someone else to continue teaching the Bible study so I could talk with Nancy on the phone right away. I could not imagine what had happened. Since the first of December our ten-year-old son, Paul, had experienced headaches and had become increasingly listless, but I could not imagine anything so serious as to warrant interrupting the Bible study. When I had left home for church that night, Paul had certainly not appeared to be in a crisis situation.

When I got to the phone, I learned that Paul had gone into a seizure and a coma and had been rushed to a nearby hospital. I left immediately. When I arrived and saw him, Paul was unable to recognize me. He was convulsing, and doctors could not get the seizures under control. My parents were leaving for South America. They detoured to the hospital, where the doctor told them that this situation with Paul would probably continue for an extended period of time. He encouraged them to go on their trip, as they could do nothing for him at the moment.

Paul then was transferred to Houston's renowned Methodist Hospital. Long days and longer nights ensued. The doctors told us that they did not know whether Paul would live through this dangerous situation. Even if he did, they did not know whether he would have any thinking or reasoning ability left. We did not know what would happen to our only son. Before he became ill, his pediatrician had told us that he was one of the brightest children she had ever seen. He had been energetic, alert, and a most giving Christian boy. To see Paul lie there helplessly in intensive care under heavy medication to try to keep him from convulsing was difficult.

In the corridors outside the intensive care unit, and through her tears, Nancy told me, "Darling, just remember that God has a plan for Paul and will give him the ability to accomplish everything in this world that He wants him

85

to accomplish." That was it. No more precious words were ever spoken by one spouse to another. No more succinct capsulizing of our faith as believers could possibly have been made. Paul was in God's hands. His life was under God's direction. We firmly believed Romans 8:28: "And we know that all things work together for good to them that love God, to them who are the called according to his purpose."

Our goals and aspirations for our children are not necessarily God's. He has an entirely different set of priorities. God's desire is not necessarily that a person be successful in the matters of this world but rather that the person be faithful in his testimony for Jesus Christ and in his relationship with God. We must live in such a way that through observing our relationship with God, other people are led to Christ.

After January 1977, the seizures and difficulties continued. Several times Paul appeared as though he was going to die. For a period of seven years he grew worse and worse. The seizures always seemed to be the worst when something highly significant was happening in the convention. In 1979, just two and one-half years after the seizures began, when attacks were being made on me from the floor of that legendary SBC meeting in Houston, Paul was in the skyboxes crying because of his severe headaches. This was where my attention was focused during those dramatic moments in our convention when the power base began to shift from liberals to conservatives. Anybody who thinks that I could have had the composure to direct what was happening on the floor of the meeting—as some have charged—simply does not know the situation.

A couple of years after Paul became ill, he asked me if anyone had become a Christian because of his sickness. I told him about a Buddhist student from Thailand who had trusted the Lord because he observed how our family was able to deal with the tragedy. Paul smiled and said, "Well, it's all been worth it, hasn't it?" I wept for joy at the spiritual maturity of my then twelve-year-old son.

Several major incidents in Paul's life occurred in 1984, around the highly significant time when I was being elected to the SBC Executive Committee. My wife's parents had their fiftieth wedding anniversary in October of that year, but we celebrated with them in May and December when the family could be together. Nancy's parents invited us to come to Illinois on May 31 for a large anniversary party and then go to a private resort club in Wisconsin the following week.

We were sitting in their living room the evening of June 1 when Paul's eyesight began to fail. (He had temporarily lost his eyesight a couple of times previously.) The doctors had told us that if Paul had another attack on his optic nerve, he might become permanently blind. Nancy always traveled with steroids in her possession, so after contacting the doctors in Houston, she gave him a large dose to try to stem the tide of what was happening to his eyes.

I left early the next morning to return to Houston with Paul and rush him to the hospital there. I insisted that Nancy and the girls go on to Wisconsin with her family. She could then relieve me before I left for the SBC meeting in Kansas City on June 10. We believed that it was highly important for me to attend this meeting, if at all possible, because of the Executive Committee nomination.

I spent the week before the SBC meeting living in the hospital with Paul. His condition seemed to be worsening. At this point he could not button his shirt, shave himself, or speak a whole sentence. We were told that within a few months, he might be bedridden, incapable of caring for himself, and probably blind. Our burden was incredible. Nancy returned, and Paul came home from the hospital on June 9. I left on Sunday, June 10, for Kansas City with our daughter Jean, while our daughter Anne stayed in Houston with Nancy and Paul.

On Monday morning, as I was leaving my hotel, I received word to call Nancy at the hospital. Early that morning Paul had started a seizure which could not be controlled, and he was in serious condition. Nancy insisted that I stay at the SBC meeting until Wednesday afternoon, since she believed that I was where God wanted me to be. It was a very emotional and trying time, not knowing whether I would ever see my son alive again, or, if he lived, whether his eyes could ever see me.

After the SBC meeting was over, Paul improved somewhat, and we decided to go to Colorado Springs, where we went every summer as a family. While in Colorado, as I was discussing a convention matter over the telephone with Jim Bolton, a deacon at First Baptist Church in Dallas and a trustee of Southwestern Seminary, he gave me some information he thought could help us with Paul's case. Jim told me that an employee of his had a son who had been diagnosed as having multiple sclerosis and that he had gone to an osteopath in Bedford, Texas. The boy was well now.

One doctor had already diagnosed our son as having multiple sclerosis, although we had never heard of a case of MS in a ten-year-old. We made an appointment with Dr. Steven Cordas, the Bedford osteopath, so we could stop and see him on our way home from Colorado. It was one of the most remarkable doctor's appointments we had ever had.

Although our expenses had been financially draining, we were blessed with excellent insurance. Because we lived in Houston, with its outstanding medical facilities, and because of my father's role as president of the Texas Medical Center and chairman of the board of directors of Texas Children's Hospital, we had the best doctors in the world available to us. However, we spent only $75 for the appointment with Dr. Cordas to hear some of the most important information we ever received regarding Paul's case.

Dr. Cordas told us that Paul appeared to be mercury toxic. He ran some tests and said he felt sure Paul did not have classic MS, but he advised us to determine when the amalgam silver fillings (which contain mercury) that Paul had in his teeth were put in.

Nancy keeps the most meticulous records I have ever seen. I was sitting at my desk at the court when she called to tell me she had just found the pertinent dental records from 1976. They showed that the two silver fillings—the only two that Paul had—had been put in his teeth only two days before he started to have pain in his extremities and headaches. We also became aware that the swine flu vaccine, given Paul on November 19, 1976, approximately two weeks before the amalgam fillings, was in a mercury preservative. We believe this was an important link, whereby the mercury in the silver fillings of his teeth worked with the mercury in the swine flu shot to create the problem.

Later tests confirmed that Paul was highly allergic to mercury and other heavy metals. We had the silver fillings removed. The dentist who extracted them said that if the fillings were relevant to Paul's case, we could expect him to get along very poorly for the next week or two because the mercury would be released into his system. After that, we should expect a dramatic, immediate improvement.

For the next ten days, Paul was in very bad shape with seizures and headaches. On the tenth day, he had a partial seizure after which he went to sleep, but after about two hours came bounding out of his room in a way he had not for the previous seven years. He said, "Let's do some studying." With the removal of the fillings, Paul was a different boy. Three months later, for Christmas 1984, Nancy's parents concluded celebrating their fiftieth anniversary by taking their whole family to Arosa, Switzerland. Paul was able to go and ski the easy slopes under close supervision!

Despite many ups and downs, we have seen marked improvement since 1984. Paul's blood studies have showed vast improvement. When we showed the various studies to a neurologist who was unsympathetic to the heavy metal toxicity theory, he stated that this change in the blood work would be typical for a person recovering from multiple sclerosis. The truth of the matter is, people do not recover from multiple sclerosis. Our lead doctors have begun to see the correlation between the mercury and Paul's condition. None now believe he has classic MS.

Pressler family skiing in Swiss Alps, December 1984

We do not yet know the final result of Paul's condition. He is certainly not well. While the mercury was in his body for seven years, it did great damage. He still has seizures and memory loss. He still has an irregular EEG and has a number of problems, but God is gracious. Paul's eyesight is back to normal, which the doctors doubted would ever happen. He graduated from a high school for children with learning disabilities. At Houston Baptist University, he was even able to take non-academic courses, including art and physical education. We are extremely grateful for that fine Christian institution, where Paul was welcomed graciously. He sings in the church choir, helps with a Saturday morning bread ministry, works as an artist in a community for functionally disabled adults, and has a productive, though protected, life.

The toll on us as parents continues to be wearing. It is difficult living in a situation where we never know when the next emergency will occur. Often when we make plans, Paul's problems flare up. Since he continues to have seizures, we need to have someone with him at all times. Nancy and I have difficulty ever relaxing completely, since we are always anticipating a problem. Many people who have criticized me because of my SBC involvement do not know the personal strain under which I operated.

Paul's sickness has constantly reminded us that God is in control and that many things are far more important than scholastic or materialistic attainment. Paul Pressler IV will likely never be able to follow in the footsteps of his family members who have served as lawyers, judges, clergy, or in high-profile public roles. However, his situation has reminded us that our relationship with Jesus Christ and recognizing His control over the things of this world are far more important than are any of these human achievements. I regularly recall the statement Nancy made to me in 1977 in that hospital corridor: God "will give him the ability to accomplish everything in this world that He wants him to accomplish." This puts all things in perspective.

Whatever happens to our son, he is in God's hands. Paul knows Jesus as personal Savior, and his eternal destiny is secure. Christ has given us the responsibility and privilege of having the most precious son in the world, one who is very special and one who keeps reminding us that Jesus Christ should be paramount in our lives. It is conformity to God's will and being under His control and under His power, and not the world's ambitions, that matters most.

CHAPTER 14

LEARNING THE ROPES

I'm always amazed when I think of how my involvement with the annual meetings of the Southern Baptist Convention has evolved over the years. Just eleven short years before the conservatives' first victory at the 1979 SBC, I was a total novice in the convention. The first SBC meeting I attended was in Houston in 1968. I was not a messenger. I merely went to hear the messages. I was impressed with the Pastors' Conference and some of the things that occurred at the SBC meeting, but I was there merely as an observer.

When the SBC met in Dallas in 1974, I again went for a few days to hear the preaching. I was a messenger from Second Baptist Church, but I was so naive that I did not know much about any of the presidential candidates. On the first ballot, I voted for Cliff Brannon of Longview. I reasoned that because he was an evangelist, he must believe that the Word of God was true. The runoff was between Dr. Kenneth Chafin, pastor of South Main Baptist Church in Houston, and Dr. Jaroy Weber, pastor of First Baptist Church in Lubbock, Texas. I hadn't heard of Dr. Weber, but I knew Ken's ministry at South Main and was not pleased. I voted for Dr. Weber. As it turned out, I believe I made the right choice, but it was not a choice based on knowledge. Through the years, many messengers must have voted in the same way.

Bill Powell encouraged me to go with him to the 1977 convention meeting in Kansas City. I left at the end of the youth group Bible conference/work camp in Colorado and went to Kansas City. I was overwhelmed with the number of people who attended. I was there solely as an observer. We stayed at a motel far away from the meeting site, and I felt very isolated from what was transpiring.

In 1978, as I was becoming more interested, I asked to be a messenger. Second Baptist was not sending its full contingent of messengers, but when the matter was raised in the business meeting, Eula Mae Baugh made a strong speech against me, claiming I had not been supportive of the pastor. She asked that I not be elected a messenger. I was not present at the meeting, but friends told me that I lost this election in a very close vote.

Although again only an observer, I learned some valuable lessons. It was understood that the so-called leaders of the SBC were getting ready to promote

Bill Self, a pastor in Atlanta, as the presidential candidate to succeed Jimmy Allen in 1979. According to their plan, Bill was to be nominated for first vice president as a stepping-stone to the presidency. Singer Anita Bryant, a former Miss America participant, came to the meeting to sing for the Pastors' Conference and surprised conservatives with her agreement to be nominated. It was known that she had taken a very godly stand against the homosexual movement in Miami and suffered greatly because of it. The question was whether she should run for first or second vice president. Bill Self, a moderate, had said that he was not going to run against Anita Bryant, so it was decided that she should run for first vice-president and keep Bill from setting himself up as the next presidential candidate of the SBC establishment.

She lost, however, by a two-to-one margin. The nominating speech for her opponent seized on the reluctance of some conservatives to have a woman "one heart-beat away from the presidency" of the SBC. She was attacked as an inexperienced outsider. The moderates, most of whom advocated women's ordination, were not above fanning emotions against a woman's leadership when it suited their purposes. That's what they did against Anita. Had she been nominated for second vice-president, she may have won. Bill Self was elected second vice president, thus advancing his presidential ambition for the next year in Houston. However, he was not in nearly as strong a position as he would have been as first vice president.

One of the reasons Anita agreed to run for vice-president was that she hoped to have some input on the selection of trustees through the nomination of the Committee on Committees. She shared our concerns about the SBC direction. Nancy and I had first met Anita when she was a student at Northwestern University, where we were volunteer BSU directors. We have always admired her greatly.

$\mathcal{M}$ARCHING TO ZION

The issue over which the conservatives and liberals have parted ways in the SBC is, and always has been, the nature of Scripture—not an interpretation of Scripture, but what Scripture *is*. We were concerned about the fact that some professors in our institutions ridiculed and mocked students who held to the inerrancy of Scripture. We were concerned because conservative, traditional Baptist beliefs were not adequately presented in some of our institutions. If the individuals in authority had been willing to listen to our legitimate and genuine concerns, we never would have worked to change the direction of the convention.

Year after year, our efforts failed as we attempted to reason with the group in charge. Therefore, we saw that no other way existed to effect change except to get the establishment's attention by electing a conservative SBC president and setting the wheels of change in motion. Thus, we began to prepare for the watershed 1979 Southern Baptist Convention meeting in Houston.

As I mentioned earlier, God opened the door for me to participate in changing the convention by altering my personal work situation. I had been appointed to the court of appeals and took office in December 1978. Before then, I could not have spent time traveling on convention matters. On the appellate court, I worked on my own time schedule as I researched, wrote, and published opinions. Only the oral arguments one day a week necessitated my physical presence in court, and I needed to be there a second day when we would discuss the cases with the other judges.

After I visited the leading conservative pastors and they expressed their willingness to cooperate, other things needed to be done to get the conservative movement under way. At the 1978 SBC meeting, while having breakfast in Atlanta with Jerry Vines, he asked me a highly significant question. "Paul," he asked, "are you going to minister to 250 high-school students or 13 million Southern Baptists?"

I understood what he was saying: as long as I had a youth group Bible study outside of a Southern Baptist church, I would not have the credibility to work with Southern Baptists, although my membership had always been in a Baptist church. I realized that I needed to give up working with the young people who had been very close to my heart. We had seen so many trust the Lord and grow in their faith in the Lord Jesus Christ. Concern for these young people and the fact that some of them were then being ridiculed as they went off to our Baptist institutions had motivated my participation in the first place. To give up working with them was difficult.

At no time in my life have I ever been happier in God's work than when I was with that youth group. Many times during the years of the controversy, with all of the conflicts and antagonisms swirling around me, I wished that I could simply return to the days where I was leading those Bible studies for 130 high-school students on Sunday nights as well as other adult Bible studies out of public view. Such was not to be the case, however. God had put a deep conviction in my heart concerning the convention. In February 1979, Nancy and I resigned from the youth group we had led for sixteen years.

It also became necessary to travel to communicate the message. The message was simple and a homiletically correct three-pointer: first, we have a problem. That could be illustrated in the writings of seminary and college professors in our Baptist institutions. Demonstrating that a problem existed was easy. Many graduates of Southern Baptist schools were now pastors of churches and knew the problems very well, since they recently had been students in those institutions. The second point was to show that a methodology existed to correct the problem. Few Southern Baptists knew how the system worked and how trustees were elected. They were ready to be educated. Thirdly, we needed to motivate people to attend the annual meeting of the SBC.

At no time was I more impressed with how much we needed to communicate the means of correcting the problem than when I met with Dr. W. A. Criswell, the respected, longtime pastor of First Baptist Church of Dallas, Texas. Dr. Criswell was attending a meeting of the International Conference on Biblical Inerrancy in Chicago October 26 to 28, 1978, when he learned firsthand about plans to start the conservative movement.

Paige and I were among the forty to fifty Southern Baptists attending that conference. Paige called a meeting to discuss the problems in the SBC. Among those present was Maxey Jarman of Nashville, a great Baptist lay leader who expressed approval of our desire to correct the direction of the convention. Dr. Criswell got up after Paige and I made a presentation and said this movement was definitely something that needed to be done, and affirmed his support. He further encouraged the group by saying that Paige and I were "fine young men" who could lead.

Later, Jerry Vines spoke in Dallas at Criswell College, and I went to the meetings. One night about 11 o'clock, Jerry, Paige, and I went to Dr. Criswell's home, where we talked for a long time about the problems and the methodology to correct them. We explained very carefully how the SBC president appoints the Committee on Committees, which nominates the Committee on Boards (now Nominations), which nominates all the trustees of the SBC—boards, agencies, and commissions. We talked about how a real impact could be made on our institutions through a continuation of conservative appointments.

After discussing this thoroughly, Dr. Criswell put his hands on the desk, pushed back, and looked at the three of us. His exact words still ring in my ears: "If I had only known what you have explained to me tonight when I was president of the convention, things could have been different."

He continued by illustrating: "Do you know what happened? How I made the appointments to the Committee on Committees? I received a call from Porter Routh (who was then executive secretary of the convention), and he said to me that I had to make the appointments in the near future. I said, 'Porter, I don't know who to appoint. How about your drawing up the list for me and letting me sign it?' And that's exactly what happened. Porter Routh drew up the list, and I signed what he gave me. I didn't know most of the men whom I appointed."

Then Dr. Criswell advised: "If you want to be successful, you must do two things. You must have presidents elected who not only are theologically conservative, but who will use their power as president to appoint other like-minded persons who desire to see changes made. Secondly, you must get to know people throughout the United States so that a president will have a reservoir of people from whom to make appointments in each state." These were wise words from Dr. Criswell, and his counsel proved a very valuable stimulus to Jerry, Paige, and me. The practical steps for proceeding were falling into place.

I needed to start visiting people, primarily pastors, and explain to them what could be done. When we had a week off in court or when I did not have oral arguments, I traveled. I would go from town to town for prearranged meetings with one to ten people in a community and explain to them what we were doing. I would illustrate the problem and then explain the methodology of dealing with it. Then I sought to motivate people to attend the SBC annual meeting and to be a voice there. Many people with whom I met had been looking for ways to express their concerns and to accomplish the needed changes.

When a reporter once asked me the greatest number of talks I made in a week regarding the convention situation, I told him that one week I made about forty or fifty. As that was reported, that figure immediately became inflated, and I was accused of making forty to fifty talks *every* week and neglecting my court duties. Such was not the case. Although I had numerous meetings, I had worked them carefully around the court schedule so that I neglected nothing.

About March or April of 1979, I called to make an appointment with Dr. W. M. Shamburger, pastor of First Baptist Church of Tyler, Texas. I briefly explained the purpose of my visit, but he said he was too busy to meet. Shortly after that an unwarranted attack against us appeared in the Texas *Baptist Standard* and then in other media. I have always wondered who gave them their information.

Although I am not a person who remembers dreams, I did have one which recurred during a three- to four-month period in the winter of 1978 and spring of 1979. Each time I dreamed it, I related it to Nancy. In the dream I saw a long line of people marching down Main Street in Houston and headed to the Summit, where the Southern Baptist Convention annual meeting would be held in June 1979. I remembered seeing two bright lines in the middle of the street (as if it were a no-passing zone) and no cars, only people. We were marching in a long line which was strung out, and as we marched, we sang the hymn, "We're Marching to Zion." I had no idea what the dream meant, nor did I try to understand it. To me at that time, it was just a strange experience and showed my preoccupation with convention events. But before long, I would understand clearly why the dream would be critical to what occurred in the days ahead.

CHAPTER 16

ℋOUSTON, 1979

As I traveled throughout the spring of 1979, I compiled a list of people who were interested in our concerns. Most of them lived in Texas, and since the 1979 annual meeting of the SBC was to be in Houston, more Texans would attend than persons from other states. That made our work in Texas crucial. I did travel out-of-state some but not extensively.

The election of a new president was not supposed to have been held at the Houston meeting. Dr. James L. Sullivan, longtime president of the Sunday School Board, was elected at the 1976 SBC meeting in Norfolk. His two one-year terms would have expired in 1978, meaning that a new president would have been elected that year and not in 1979. However, Dr. Sullivan refused to run for reelection in 1977 because of the pressure of the job and his health. Jimmy Allen of San Antonio was thus elected president in 1977 and reelected for a final term in 1978.

Jimmy Allen had campaigned extensively for the job. He had flown to airports where local pastors supporting his candidacy had assembled others so he could speak and gain their support. I understand that Jimmy Allen was the first ever to launch such a full-scale campaign for the presidency. Those attending his meetings reported his campaign pitch to be that if he were not elected, Adrian Rogers or somebody conservative like him would be, and they must head off the election of Adrian Rogers. Several Baptist newspapers had carried attacks on Adrian.

Adrian did not run for president in Kansas City in 1977. Jerry Vines and Richard Jackson, both conservatives, were candidates as well as Jimmy Allen. Conservatives supported both Jackson and Vines. Jackson was eliminated on the first ballot, and a runoff occurred between Allen and Vines. Before the runoff, false rumors had swept the meeting hall that Jerry Vines did not use Southern Baptist literature in his church. Although the combined votes for Richard Jackson and Jerry Vines reflected a heavy conservative majority, Jimmy Allen was elected. The rumor mill had worked. Jimmy was reelected the next year in Atlanta without opposition and was ineligible to be a candidate in Houston. I do not think that the leaders of the convention were particularly pleased that the

97

1979 election would not have an incumbent running, since Houston was considered conservative territory.

As we planned for the 1979 meeting, we knew that many people would take an interest in this particular SBC meeting for the first time in years. Numerous people had told me, "I will attend once, but I don't think there is any chance of success. We will come to Houston and give our support this one time, but don't count on us again if we fail."

Accusations surfaced that the conservatives bused in people. However, I know of only one bus. It transported about forty people from Austin whom conservatives organized to attend the Houston meeting. I did nothing to arrange it. Other than that, I know of no busing by the conservatives at any time during the fifteen-year struggle. I presume people did arrive at the meetings by bus, but the arrangements were their own doing. Perhaps one reason people accused us of busing stemmed from a memo I sent some of my friends. The memo explained the logistics of the SBC meeting. To furnish complete instructions on how to deal with parking, I referenced instructions that meeting planners at the SBC Executive Committee office gave me. The instructions included those for bus parking. The information originated from Tim Hedquist, vice president for SBC financial affairs and manager of the annual SBC meeting arrangements, and I just passed it on to be helpful.

Members of the news media played up my memo out of all proportions. Those who wanted to destroy the conservative movement tried to make it look like an organized machine rather than the grassroots movement it actually was.

The 1979 meeting was held at the Summit in Houston, where only a few restaurants were close to the convention hall. It was obvious that meals for participants would become a real problem during the meeting. Some of us who had been working in the conservative movement wanted to have lunch together to fellowship and to assess developments during the meeting. It was impossible to get a nearby hotel or restaurant room for twenty or thirty people.

A close friend of my father-in-law was chairman of the board of the M. W. Kellogg Company. Its offices were very near the Summit. This man and Nancy's father had attended school together on the South Side of Chicago. I called and asked him if he had a board, conference, or lunch room where about twenty or thirty of us could bring sandwiches and get together for lunch on Tuesday during the Houston meeting. He said that he certainly could provide that, but that he had something else in mind and would call me back. He called the next day and suggested that instead of their offices, we could have lunch in their company's skybox at the Summit. I asked him, "What are the skyboxes?" I had been in the Summit only a few times and had never noticed the skyboxes above the main hall. He invited me to come by, pick up a key, go to the Summit, and look at the skybox. If I wanted to use the skybox, I was to let him know. This occurred less than a week before the convention began meeting.

At the convention hall I ran into Tim Hedquist, the convention manager. Tim could not have been more helpful or more congenial. He showed me the way to the skyboxes. I told him what we were thinking of doing, and he did not object. The skybox was the perfect place for us to get together. While I was there on that side of the Summit, I noticed the names of the other companies which had skyboxes. Almost all of them were local Houston corporations, and I knew the presidents of many of them. I decided I would call and see whether some other skyboxes could be made available, since I knew they would not be used that week. As a result, most of the skyboxes on one side of the Summit were made available to us. None was rented. Their use was just a courtesy to me by friends.

The convention manager knew that we were using the skyboxes. No criticism or opposition was voiced as to their use until the SBC meeting was well under way. In fact, Tim and I worked out the way to get behind a registration area to the elevator that went to the skyboxes. I never dreamed that the use of the skyboxes would become controversial. Overlooked in the controversy was the fact that other skyboxes could have been available for any other group for the asking had others wanted them and the owners given permission.

In the course of our discussions about the skyboxes, Tim told me that he had read the letter I sent out to a few people about the convention arrangements. He said that I was accurate in every way except one, and he explained how I should have stated one matter differently. The fact that Tim had seen the letter amazed me, since it had not gone to many people. I didn't object to his reading it, since the letter contained nothing that was unsuitable for common knowledge. But it affirmed for me the fact that the only thing that worked perfectly in the Southern Baptist Convention was the grapevine. If I put something in writing, I could be assured that it would get to everybody else in the convention who wanted it.

It also showed me that some people played double agents. They appeared to be friendly to our cause but then passed on information to the establishment. I had hoped in Christian circles that believers would be straightforward and honest. How naive I was! To watch Christians acting this way through the years has been disappointing and has hurt me deeply.

The role I played in planning for the Houston SBC meeting also has been greatly exaggerated. The main thing I did was to alert people about how it was possible to make some changes in the convention direction. I didn't help people get to the meeting. I did make an effort to locate two or three motels and some reasonable housing facilities at the University of Houston that would be available if someone had difficulty locating a room. Probably no more than twenty-five people were helped in this way, and they all paid for their own rooms.

The Baptist state papers highly exaggerated and criticized our actions. We did not consider it the sinister plot, as implied, but merely a genuine effort to help people who were new at attending the annual SBC meeting. It also interested me that several years later no one criticized agencies and individuals who chartered airplanes and rented hotels for their friends and alumni to attend the meeting to vote for the moderate cause.

Also, in preparation for the SBC meeting, Nancy and I invited some leading pastors from several states to our home for dinner on the Sunday afternoon just before the Pastors' Conference. About thirty people attended for a time of fellowship and discussion.

For Monday evening June 1 after the Pastors' Conference afternoon session, I had engaged the cafeteria in the basement of One Shell Plaza. It was just a few blocks from the conference, which was held downtown in the Sam Houston Coliseum about seven miles from the Summit. The purpose of the dinner was for us to have prayer and fellowship, to give cohesion to the conservative movement, and to seek a consensus about who should be nominated the next day. Neither Paige, I, nor any of the other conservatives had any desire to impose our will on other people as to whom that candidate should be. It was all very open, very frank, and very unstructured.

No candidate had arisen prior to the meeting, although three names were prominently mentioned. They were Adrian Rogers, pastor of Bellevue Baptist Church in Memphis, Tennessee; Jerry Vines, then pastor of Dauphin Way Baptist Church in Mobile, Alabama; and Bailey Smith, then pastor of First Southern Baptist Church of Del City, Oklahoma. At this meeting, those who wished could make a contribution to pay for the dinner. Fortunately, we came out almost even. Some friends of mine and I paid the small deficit. Several people attended the meeting, ate, and were not part of the group, although they were allowed to stay. James Robison, an evangelist who was preaching at the Pastors' Conference, attended the meeting and led the discussion. We talked but mostly prayed on our knees.

Finally, participants were asked to write down their top three choices in order for whom they thought should be the next SBC president. These choices were tabulated, and the results were announced to the group. The clear choice of the approximately 350 people who attended the dinner was Adrian Rogers.

Later that evening, when he was informed of the vote, Adrian told me that he was sorry but that God had not told him to run, and he was not going to be nominated. He said he hoped that some other conservative would. I was discouraged because I did not know what would happen. The liberals had a well-organized group. We weren't even organized enough to have a candidate. We just urged people to attend, confident that God would give us a candidate. I was staying at home and returned there Monday night after the Pastors' Conference. I had no contact with anyone that night after leaving downtown and knew of no further developments as to whether we would have a candidate. I came to the convention hall on Tuesday morning, with the election to be held that afternoon, not knowing for whom I would vote at the SBC in 1979. I did not know what had transpired the night before.

A bit prior to the convention, Miss Bertha Smith, retired missionary to China and a great woman of God, spoke to Adrian and said, "Adrian, God has told me that you should be nominated for president of the Southern Baptist Convention." This shook Adrian very deeply because he knew what a great prayer warrior Bertha Smith was. When Miss Bertha reported what she believed God had told her, those who knew her knew she had heard from Him. Until her death in her late 90s, she was a great woman of prayer and a great supporter of Adrian Rogers. She walked with God and always sought His solution for every situation.

The person most opposed to Adrian's being nominated for president was his wife, Joyce. Later that evening, Joyce told Adrian that God was speaking to her heart and that she believed that perhaps he should be nominated. This disturbed him very much. Now the person to whom he was closest in the world—Joyce—and another person whom he highly respected—Miss Bertha—had both changed their minds. Besides this, Dr. Charlie Culpepper had also sent word to Adrian that he should run. Was this God speaking to him?

Adrian and Joyce were in their hotel room when Joyce told him about her changed perspective. Adrian and Joyce went to dinner, and as they went down the elevator and exited on the first floor, from one direction came Paige Patterson and from another direction came Jerry Vines. Adrian told both men what had occurred. The three decided they should pray together, and they returned to Adrian's hotel room, where they prayed with Joyce for a long period of time. Finally, Adrian knew that he had God's direction that he should run for president of the convention.

With so much activity surrounding the SBC meeting, I had delayed seeking to be named a messenger. A few weeks before the meeting started, I visited my pastor, John Bisagno of First Baptist Church of Houston, and asked about being a messenger. He said that unfortunately all the messenger positions had been filled. He then asked, "Aren't you serving as interim pastor of First Baptist Church of Bellaire?" I answered that I had done so for about a year and that the church had just called a new pastor. I had taught my Sunday School class at First Baptist of Houston and then dashed to First Baptist of Bellaire, a suburb of Houston, to preach on Sunday mornings as well as on Sunday evenings. In appreciation for my preaching for about a year without any pay or other compensation, the church had made me an honorary member for life, had given me a book on genealogy, and had made other non-monetary expressions of appreciation.

When I told John about this, he replied that he thought this connection might be the answer. He said when a person is serving as interim pastor, he assumed he has the right to be a messenger from that church. Not knowing the system and not having been that involved before, I did not check into the matter further. I was elected and received my credentials from First Baptist of Bellaire, and I registered as a messenger.

On the first day of the SBC meeting, when I arrived at the Summit, I heard that my credentials were being questioned. I went immediately to Registration Secretary Lee Porter—before any voting took place—and offered to turn in my ballots. He replied that I was already registered and that he could not unregister me. Although I told him I wanted to do what was right, he said that what was done was done. I did not realize that I would come under attack later for this. I still thought I had a right to be a messenger, but I did not want to do anything that would cast a shadow of doubt over the conservatives' actions at the SBC.

Later I was called an "illegal messenger." Baptist Press never reported the facts behind my registration and my attempt to turn in my credentials, although I reported these matters to the Baptist news organization. A few weeks later I discovered that at least two Southwestern Seminary professors had done exactly the same thing I had. They were messengers from churches where they served as interim pastors, although Baptist Press never mentioned them. Some of the attacks on me did seem to quiet down a little after this information about the professors was disseminated through the Southern Baptist grapevine, but the news media never reported it.

We decided to have some food available in the skyboxes to make sandwiches for lunch for messengers on the first day of the meeting. A friend of mine, Keith Actkinson, a member of First Baptist Church of Houston, and I were taking two large, cooked turkeys up to the skyboxes when we ran into Russell and Betty Dilday.

I had known Russell when he was pastor of Tallowood Baptist Church in Houston, and we had been friendly, although we had not been close friends. He was then a pastor in Atlanta, Georgia, and later he became president of Southwestern Seminary. I stopped to speak to him. Russell was talking to someone else, but he signaled that he wanted me to wait while he finished his other conversation. We felt awkward standing there holding the turkeys.

Russell told me that I had done a horrible thing in stirring up people. Betty asked Keith if he were a Southern Baptist. He told her he was a member of First Baptist Church of Houston. She asked how long he had been a member. Keith responded that he trusted the Lord five years before through student work at the University of Houston and after that joined First Baptist Church. She then asked if he had ever been to a Baptist school. Keith responded that he had not. She then asked if he had ever taken any seminary courses in a Baptist seminary. Again, Keith replied, "No."

Then she asked what right he had to participate in a Southern Baptist Convention if he didn't know Baptist work any better than he did. Keith said that he was just helping me carry the turkeys in and that he wasn't a messenger to the meeting. However, in what appeared to us to be a very smug and derogatory manner, Betty continued to berate my friend. I was very disquieted and embarrassed with the remarks of both Betty and Russell. They demonstrated no desire to communicate or be friendly, only to lecture us. It was as though we were outsiders who were treading on the private domain of someone who was fully in charge, and they deeply resented any intrusion. Often in years ahead I would experience this same attitude and demeanor from many in the group which had previously controlled the convention.

Many people had heard about the skyboxes and came to visit them. I did not know many of the visitors, but all were welcomed and none excluded. Several who came to the skyboxes would later be active in support of liberalism in our convention. One of these was Phil Lineberger, then pastor in Wichita, Kansas. The skyboxes were not maintained in an air of secrecy. Everything was open, and everybody was in on everything that was going on. I was often distracted since my son was quite ill at the time. Nancy was with him as he suffered excruciating headaches while he lay on a couch in one of the skyboxes.

When time arrived for the voting to occur, someone volunteered to collect all the ballots of the people in the skyboxes and deliver them to the floor. I protested strongly and said that each messenger must take his or her own ballot to the floor. I reasoned that if someone went into the meeting with a group of ballots, we could be accused of stuffing the ballot box. Therefore, each registered messenger who was in the skyboxes went down and handed his or her own ballot to an usher.

The time between the voting and the announcement of the results was filled with tension. Jimmy Allen, as president, went to the microphone and said that Lee Porter was there to announce the presidential election results. He stepped aside to let Lee approach the microphone, but Lee was not there. Confusion reigned on the platform. Finally, Jimmy called on the song leader to lead some music while they found Lee Porter. The song leader came to the microphone and announced that the messengers would stand and sing the hymn, "We're Marching to Zion." Immediately I remembered my recurring dream. Now I knew what it meant. I knew that Adrian Rogers had been elected president of the convention without a runoff. I believed that through the means of this dream, God had been telling me that He was in charge. I collapsed crying into my seat and told Paige (who was seated next to me) what I suspected had happened.

During the ensuing years of heartache when I personally—and conservatives in general—fell victim to the liberals' assaults, I was comforted by this sign that God had given me prior to the 1979 SBC meeting. Not being one who had believed in or expected signs, this was a precious thing to me. Remembering His comfort and His revelation to me in this way has gotten me through many difficult days. I believe that God teaches through His Word and never reveals anything contrary to His Word. However, from time to time, God does reassure and comfort through such events as this.

Adrian did win without a runoff. He received 6,129 votes, or 51.36 percent. Robert Naylor (also a conservative but not one pledged to correct the problems), who was president of Southwestern Seminary then, ran second with 2,791 votes, or 23.39 percent. Bill Self, who said the establishment leaders called him and told him that it was his time to run and who had positioned himself at the Atlanta SBC meeting the year before to run, ran third with 1,673 votes, or 14.02 percent.

The other candidates were as follows: Abner McCall, 643 votes, or 5.39 percent; Douglas Watterson, 474 votes, or 3.97 percent; Ed Price, 223 votes, or 1.87 percent. With this election, the conservative movement was under way and had started on what would prove to be a long path to climb that hill, the capture of which would bring our convention back to the principles on which it was founded.

Someone who was sitting close to Duke McCall, then-president of Southern Seminary, said that Dr. McCall and others of the leadership who had run the convention for so long reacted visually on hearing the news that Adrian Rogers had been elected SBC president. A few believed that this was the beginning of a very difficult period for them, but most were unaware that this was the beginning of the end of their control of the SBC. They reasoned that the election was due only to the personal popularity of Adrian Rogers. It is true that Adrian Rogers was elected because of his own popularity and not because of what Paige, others, and I had done. However, Paige has said on a number of occasions—and I think quite accurately so—that although Adrian would have been elected without our support, he would not have allowed himself to be nominated unless he had seen that his election could accomplish something.

The conservatives who had been elected president in previous years had accomplished little in changing the convention direction because they did not have a support team behind them. They accomplished little because they did not know how they could change the convention and what persons would be good appointees from various states. They were ineffective because they were forced to rely on the SBC bureaucracy. Because of the system, doing anything effective without the bureaucracy's guidance and control was extremely difficult. The powerful Committee on Nominations was heavily influenced by the executive secretary of the Executive Committee. The important Committee on Resolutions was dominated by the Baptist Joint Committee on Public Affairs and the Christian Life Commission. In every way the bureaucracy was involved in the actions that were taken. Members of the moderate group that controlled the convention at that time believed they could weather the storm. They had built a system in which the bureaucracy was dominant, and they did not believe it could be overcome.

An example of the way the liberal establishment sought to control everything emerged later in the 1979 meeting. Dr. Larry Lewis, then pastor of Tower Grove Baptist Church in St. Louis and later president of the Home Mission Board (now merged into the North American Mission Board), had proposed an inerrancy motion. It was known as motion #23 and was similar to one which had been passed in the Missouri state convention. It urged our schools to employ only teachers who believe:

> in the inerrancy of the original manuscripts, the existence of a personal devil and a literal Hell, the actual existence of a primeval couple named Adam and Eve, the literal occurrence of the miracles as recorded in the Bible, the virgin birth and bodily resurrection, and the personal return of the Lord Jesus Christ.

This resolution affirmed that the Bible was absolutely reliable and totally true.

Wayne Dehoney, former convention president, then went to the podium. A discussion, as the following transcription of the proceedings shows, occurred:

Dr. Wayne Dehoney: Dr. Allen, I call to attention this motion of #23 in your order of procedure and I will not read this statement. But I do have something to say of great significance and importance if you can bear with me long enough to get it all together here, that I think will make us all excited and happy. This statement represents, first of all, our Baptist Faith and Message statement of 1925 revised then in 1963 with a year of study spent, made up of a committee from the state presidents of the state conventions and others added to that committee. It came to our convention a unanimous recommendation in 1963 after a year of study and preparation. It was overwhelmingly adopted without changing one comma in the recommendation of 1963. It has served us well. It is an articulate, clear, and great statement of our historic position.

I have just come from the news conference with our new President, Dr. Adrian Rogers. And he has given me permission, he made this in the news conference, made this statement of his interpretation and understanding of this, and he has given me permission to say that he takes the same position that I do in that we should not change this historic statement and we should reaffirm it.

Dr. Rogers and I both take the same position and I want to read to you what his position and my position is on the interpretation of this—this phrase, this particular phrase, "The Word of God, it has God for its author, salvation for its end and truth without any mixture of error for its matter." *My interpretation and his interpretation of what that means, "without error," is that we understand this to mean that in the original autographs, God's revelation was perfect and without error, doctrinally, historically, scientifically, and philosophically.* If we can all say, "let's get together on this and go with it, we believe the Bible and we believe God's revelation was perfect to us, and if there are glosses or a passage here—a problem, a textual problem of a word or two, it is human error in the translation that has come, but the original autographs were God's revelation and we have His revelation for us today for the preaching of the gospel and salvation." I bring that and ask you to support it and let's move on with business here (emphasis added).

Dr. Larry Lewis: Thank you, Dr. Allen. I want to speak in support of Dr. Dehoney's resolution, affirming our historic Baptist belief in the Bible as the perfect treasure of divine instruction and truth without any mixture of error of any kind. As these men have interpreted it so, I accept it as so and thank God that Baptists have been and will continue to be a people of the Book who believe the Bible to be the infallible Word of God. I urge your support of this resolution.

Dr. Allen: We have one more who has asked to speak. I think I would let him speak whether he was for it or against it because he is Herschel Hobbs. Dr. Hobbs, you come.

Dr. Herschel Hobbs: Thank you, Brother President, and all of you out there and way up yonder. I just simply want to say this. Naturally, since I had the privilege of being the chairman of the committee that presented the revised form of the statement of faith and message of 1925, currently known as the one of 1963, I wanted to make this statement. I naturally support the motion of Dr. Dehoney, the position of our president-elect Adrian Rogers. I simply wanted to make this statement, not arguing for, but for clarification. I have received many letters through the years wanting to know if the committee meant that the Bible is "truth without any mixture of error," if that includes the entire Bible or does it just include the part that is truth. Well, obviously, we had reference to the original manuscripts, though no one has ever seen one— none of us has. But we accept by faith, not by sight. At the same time, I want to say this: The question raised to me by mail—did we mean that the whole Bible or just parts of it—never came up for a squeak of discussion in the committee. The committee understood and so recommended to this convention, and if the convention adopted it, the one in Kansas City, the committee understood that to include the whole Bible. Thank you.

Because of these definitions, a floor fight was avoided. The resolution passed. The discussion, however, was not reported in Baptist Press. Members of the group in control evidently did not want a record of it. It was also not appropriately reported in the SBC meeting record because Martin Bradley, registration secretary of the Southern Baptist Convention, for some reason merely reported as follows:

126. The Chair opened the floor for consideration of motions previously scheduled for this time. Wayne Dehoney (Ky.) spoke to his motion concerning reaffirmation of the section on the Scriptures in the 1963 Baptist Faith and Message Statement. (See Item 23.) Those discussing the motion were: Larry Lewis (Mo.), for; Bill Brock (Fla.), against; Herschel H. Hobbs (Okla.), for. The motion was passed.

When I asked these individuals why it had not been reported fully, they replied that they felt it was not something of interest to Southern Baptists. They should have known that this was one of the most vital issues to the conservatives at the meeting. Efforts by conservatives to have it clearly printed that Herschel Hobbs and Wayne Dehoney said unequivocally that the writers of the 1963 Baptist Faith and Message statement intended inerrancy in their reference to Scripture were ignored. Conservatives were offended and dismayed. We began to realize how strongly the bureaucracy was intent on keeping control of what was passed on to grassroots Southern Baptists.

The failure of Martin Bradley to record this discussion fully was a major reason for his defeat in 1990 for reelection as recording secretary. He was unopposed until then, but dissatisfaction had festered against him because of this. Had he recorded this, he probably would not have been opposed then. It also was a major factor in the change that was ultimately made in the Baptist Press leadership. Bad reporting in Baptist Press was a matter that conservatives realized had to be dealt with, but it was not the main issue. The main issue was the nature of Scripture. That very definition, as clarified in the 1979 SBC, had been kept from our Southern Baptist membership by Martin Bradley and the Baptist Press writers.

The conflict could have been resolved if, after Adrian Rogers was elected president of the SBC in 1979, those in authority had realized that a group of people believed they had been shut out of the processes of the convention and if those in authority had started to do two things. The first was to add to their faculties professors who personally held a traditional, conservative position and would have taught the traditional Southern Baptist belief that the Bible is completely true. The other was to halt the ridicule and attacks on students who defended the belief that the Bible was completely true. However, neither was done.

CHAPTER 17

$\mathcal{I}$N THE THICK OF BATTLE

I was not prepared for what happened after the 1979 Southern Baptist Convention meeting in Houston. Baptist Press and some secular papers began blasting conservatives unmercifully. It seemed we were called everything except children of God. Personal insinuations were made about Paige Patterson and me both individually and collectively. We were painted as terrible people in every way. Elsewhere in this book I have detailed some of these attacks.

We were concerned that our institutions teach the Bible based on a belief that the Bible is completely true. Some conservatives had tried in prior years to communicate with those in charge in the convention to get them to recognize the need for adding conservative scholars to the faculties of our institutions. Only when this method failed did we resort to other means. We believed that now, with the election of a conservative president, we should get the attention of those in power and accomplish change. We knew no other way to seek the modifications which we believed were necessary. We merely tried to get rank-and-file Southern Baptists to participate in convention events because we believed that they also wanted this. Elective power, therefore, was to be a means and not an end.

Strangely, the people who had held the power were the ones who began protesting most loudly that our desire and motivation merely was to gain power and control. Sometimes a person unconsciously ascribes his or her own motivation to other people. I believe this was what motivated some of our critics. I believe that either they were deliberately misrepresenting our position or else they genuinely misunderstood it. They were unwilling to dialogue or communicate with us, and I cannot help but suspect that they may have been projecting onto us their own motivations.

I thought that once we had made our point and elected a conservative as president, some of the leaders of our institutions would recognize that conservatives formed at least a major constituency in the convention and would begin to be responsive. Yet, while many attacked, some seemed to cooperate. Dr. Roy Honeycutt, president of Southern Baptist Theological Seminary in Louisville, Kentucky, arranged for evangelist James Robison to hold a Bible conference on campus during October 1979. Some conservatives took this as a gesture indicating that our convictions would be included. However, once the Bible conference ended and the conservatives left the campus, the conservative leadership continued to be roasted in many of the classes, and no conservative scholars were added to the faculty.

I deeply appreciated Dr. Honeycutt's gesture at that time, although I sometimes have had difficulty understanding him since then. At times he has been extremely gracious and cooperative, and at other times his comments have been unkind and derisive. I believe he occasionally took stands which he would not have taken if left to himself. His true nature seemed to be that of a gracious Christian gentleman who at the same time was surrounded by some individuals at Southern Seminary who maneuvered him into antagonism toward the conservative cause.

One person who was very helpful in seeking to facilitate communication between sides in the ensuing controversy was Huffman Baines, an insurance agent in Austin, Texas, and a cousin of President Lyndon Baines Johnson. Our families have been friends for many years, and we talked on several occasions. He was a trustee at Baylor University and was one of the people who sought to reach a consensus and to help people work together. He reached out and listened to what I had to say. Wanting to get me together with the people at Baylor, he arranged a luncheon with Baylor President Abner McCall.

I drove to Waco (through Austin to pick up Huff), and we dined with Abner at a country club on the lake. The three of us spent four or five hours talking about issues, including reading passages from the book *People of the Covenant*, coauthored by Jack Flanders, then chairman of the Baylor religion department. I later learned that Dr. Flanders had been pastor of First Baptist Church in Waco when Abner's first wife died and that he had ministered effectively to Abner and the family at that time. A close personal relationship between them existed that I had not known. I have found it interesting how personal relationships can color people's thinking and keep them from seeing the theological issues clearly. I read to the two men the following passage from page 497 of *People of the Covenant*:

> Daniel presents many historical problems. In fact, the number of historical inaccuracies has led Walter Harrelson to suspect the author to have misrepresented deliberately the historical events and notices in order to provide his readers with a subtle indication that he was actually writing in a much later period with quite a different historical enemy of God's people in mind. *Whether or not the errors are intentional, they illustrate* that the author writes

later than the events and redacts materials in light of his own purpose to inspire men of faith to endure temptation and hardship (emphasis added).

Four or five times I asked Abner how a person could say that the Book of Daniel contained errors and still believe the Bible was completely true. He always responded that Jack was a nice person and a fine Christian. As a lawyer, I persisted in asking my questions.

Finally, Abner admitted that the passage was contradictory to a belief that the Bible is completely true. He then said he guessed that Jack didn't have anything to do with the writing of that passage. I then asked why Dr. Flanders didn't publicly repudiate the statement and state his belief in the Bible as completely true. Abner said he would see what could be done. Nothing ever developed, and Abner and I never had any more discussion of the issues. After that event I felt that he hardened his position toward conservatives in general and toward me in particular.

Huff also informed me that he and Baylor executive vice president Herb Reynolds had agreed that Dr. Flanders and I should get together and get to know each other. On February 28, 1981, Nancy and I had planned to be in Waco for the wedding of a fine young man, Keet Lewis, who had trusted the Lord through one of our Bible studies, and Margaret Brown, who was from a prominent and outstanding Waco family. They had chosen to be married on the same day as our wedding anniversary. Huff arranged for me to call Dr. Flanders when I was in Waco on the Saturday morning of the wedding. After Nancy, the children, and I arrived in Waco, I called Dr. Flanders, who was expecting my call, at the arranged time and introduced myself.

Dr. Flanders immediately began shouting at me, saying that I had ruined his life and health. He launched into a bitter, personal attack on me, then slammed down the phone. I believe failure to communicate is evidence not of strength, but of weakness. Those who do not have anything to hide are not afraid of communication. I was extremely disappointed with this uncalled-for attack by Dr. Flanders and his unwillingness to go through with the meeting which his executive vice president said had been arranged. I told Huff what had happened in the conversation with Dr. Flanders. He said that he would look into it, but I never heard anything further.

Baylor has been a deep disappointment to me. I believe the Baylor religion department has spiritually harmed many students. I have observed some whose zeal for the Lord and testimony for Christ was destroyed or diminished by their Baylor experience. Why should Texas Baptists spend money which is used to harm our young people spiritually? I feel this personally since my great-great-great grandfather, Rev. Hosea Garrett, had been chairman of the Baylor board of trustees for thirty-eight of its first forty years of existence and my grandfather,

Judge E. E. Townes, served as a board member for many years. They served and gave because they wanted to see a Bible-based institution which built young people up in their faith. What a tragedy!

I was invited to a meeting in Lynchburg, Virginia, on September 12–13, 1980, hosted by Art Ballard, pastor of the Old Forest Road Baptist Church. Tom Miller of the *Religious Herald,* the state Baptist paper for Virginia, also attended and evidently recorded the meeting. I do not have a transcript of the meeting, and the context of my statements did not appear in news reports. However, I recall that during the question-and-answer period, I tried to explain the way the system worked. I said the conservatives had been winning the battles over the years, but we were losing the war. We won the Broadman Bible Commentary issue at an SBC annual meeting, but the Sunday School Board's trustees did not correct all the problems.

The Ralph Elliott issue was won on the convention floor, but he was dismissed as a professor at Midwestern Seminary, not because of his liberalism but because he refused to cease publishing his book. Evidently, he could have stayed at Midwestern Seminary teaching the same things that he espoused in *The Message of Genesis* so long as he did not have the book republished. Leaders at Midwestern Seminary acted as if they believed that his sin was publishing the book, which would let Southern Baptists know what he believed and was teaching, not the ideas themselves.

In my answer to a question, I emphasized that we needed to deal not only with the effects of liberalism, but we needed to deal with the root of the problem. The trustees were the lifeblood of the Southern Baptist Convention, and they alone could bring about change in their institutions. I said that we needed to be concerned about trustees. We needed to elect conservative trustees since trustees are the lifeblood of the convention. I used the sentence, "We need to go for the jugular," meaning that we need to get at the root of the problem. I was trying to explain how the convention operated.

The use of this metaphor was very unwise, as I would later learn. In retrospect, I will avoid using metaphors in the future. The Baptist newswriters seized on this to make me look like an angry monster. Presnall Wood of the *Baptist Standard* of Texas, on October 1, 1980, editorialized as follows: "'We are going for the jugular,' Pressler said of their attempt to gain control of Southern Baptist institutions. Such a harsh statement reflects a world of secular politics. No Baptist needs to be going for the jugular vein of any Baptist or anyone else."

This, of course, took my quote out of context and made it appear that I was seeking to destroy individuals—not just change the system. Ever since then, for about twenty years, almost every time my name was mentioned in some publications, it stated, "Paul Pressler, who said he was going for the jugular in order to try to control Southern Baptist institutions, said . . ." The liberals had the epitaph which they could attach to my name in an effort to smear me. I cannot help but suspect that this was a response born out of the inability of the liberals to discuss the issues before the Baptist public.

In this Lynchburg meeting, somebody also asked about giving to the Cooperative Program. I said that I supported the Cooperative Program fully and that it should be supported. The person then stated that the Cooperative Program funded many things he did not like. I told him to keep giving, because the prospects of changing the things he didn't like were good, and the Cooperative Program has so many more good things than bad things in it. I said we shouldn't throw the baby out with the bath water.

My questioner kept pressing me, citing problems in institutions supported by Cooperative Program dollars. I then encouraged conservative churches to give at least enough to the Cooperative Program so they could send a full contingent of messengers to the annual Southern Baptist Convention meeting. Giving for this purpose was as a last resort for urging Cooperative Program support. I had stated other reasons for its support. In his story Tom Miller summarized my remarks as follows:

> Pressler did, however, take a firm stand supporting the Cooperative Program. In answer to a question from his host pastor, Pressler advised not cutting the Cooperative Program from the budget. "Work within the framework of the Cooperative Program," Pressler said. "Give at least enough to have the maximum number of messengers."

In the same October 1, 1980, issue, Presnall Wood in his editorial took this and changed the meaning of what I said. He wrote as follows:

> Pressler's concept of the Cooperative Program as revealed in his statements in Virginia is unacceptable. In response to a question concerning a church cutting the Cooperative Program from the budget Pressler said, "Work within the framework of the Cooperative Program and give at least enough to have the maximum number of messengers."
>
> Is a vote in a convention the proper motive for a church giving to the Cooperative Program? For more than 50 years Southern Baptists have given to the Cooperative Program not in order to play politics but to propagate the gospel of Jesus Christ beyond the local church in missions, evangelism, benevolence and Christian education. Working a denominational political campaign is a foreign motive for church participation in the Cooperative Program.

Churches should share in the mission outreach of the Cooperative Program to win the world to Christ rather than win votes at some Baptist convention.

This was not what I intended, nor was it what I said. This was an inaccurate and unfair evaluation which I believe was deliberately calculated as an attack on me and thus on the movement. Baptist Press never reported fully my clarification and correction of these matters. In a number of speeches covered by various Baptist and secular reporters, I gave a full account of what I said. In various letters I also explained the full context. Still the context was not given, which has grieved me. However, the cause is too great to allow personal hurt to stand in the way of accomplishing the things that needed to be done. By attacking us, the press also caused people to wonder what the leaders of the conservative movement were like and why we were doing what we were trying to do. Therefore, people came to listen, to learn, and we told them.

If we had been ignored rather than attacked, perhaps we never would have gained an audience to present what concerned us. These events were in God's hands, and we realized that He would fight the battle His way and not ours.

$\mathcal{R}$OUND TWO: ANOTHER BIG WIN

A significant event happened while the James Robison Bible Conference was occurring at Southern Seminary in October 1979. One night after the meeting ended, I was with ten or fifteen conservative leaders in James Robison's room, and someone sent out for food. Many of the participants had their shoes off and their feet propped up on tables, and we were all relaxing and discussing various matters. In the middle of this relaxed atmosphere, Adrian Rogers suddenly announced: "You guys better look for someone who will be the next candidate for president of the convention, because I am not going to be nominated again next year."

All of us were surprised. I immediately protested strongly. Adrian then called our attention to an important consideration. He said if he were reelected for another one-year term in St. Louis in 1980, a new candidate would have to be advanced in the 1981 election in Los Angeles. Los Angeles would not be a good place for conservatives because grassroots pastors would have difficulty getting there. Individuals from wealthy, moderate churches and those with denominational expense accounts would be the main ones making the trip.

Adrian said this was not his reason for refusing to be nominated, but this might be a reason the Lord was clearly leading him not to run. All of us in the room urged Adrian to be renominated. He said he would wait and make his final decision in the spring. This was the first time Adrian had indicated that he would not be renominated.

The preparation of the conservatives for the 1980 SBC meeting in St. Louis was minimal. Paige, others, and I traveled with our three-point message: showing the problem, giving the solution, and motivating participation. Paige engaged in some debates, notably one with Cecil Sherman, then pastor of First Baptist Church of Asheville, North Carolina. Cecil made the attention-getting declaration that he would not exclude a person from teaching in our seminaries if he felt that "the Holy Spirit" led him "not to believe in the virgin birth." I considered this statement to be a real oxymoron.

Finally, in about March or April, Adrian gave the official word: he was not going to be renominated. He simply did not feel the liberty from the Lord to do so. Bailey Smith, pastor of First Southern Baptist Church in Del City, Oklahoma, felt led of the Lord to be nominated. He was one of six nominated for the post, the same number as in the Houston meeting. Another prominent candidate was Richard Jackson, pastor of North Phoenix Baptist Church in Phoenix, Arizona, who was hoping to combine both liberal and conservative support. The rumor swept the convention that he had made a deal with the liberals and was trying to hang on to his conservative support at the same time.

Jimmy Draper, George Harris, Richard Jackson, and Bailey Smith were all with John Bisagno in his room the night before the SBC meeting. George Harris had agreed to nominate Richard for president. George told Richard that he had doubts about nominating him since Bailey was so well-received at the Pastors' Conference earlier that day. Richard replied that he was so strong that a porter could "nominate me and I'd still be elected."

The next day Nancy, Paul, and I were sitting in the bleachers above Richard Jackson when the vote totals were announced. He ran fourth in the field of six, receiving less than 10 percent of the vote. The actual vote was: Jimmy Stroud, 167 votes, or 1.5 percent; Stan Boone, 213 votes, or 1.92 percent; Richard Jackson, 1,089 votes, or 9.81 percent; James Pleitz, 1,516 votes, or 13.65 percent; Frank Pollard, 2,382 votes, or 23.45 percent; and Bailey Smith, 5,739 votes, or 51.67 percent. When the results were announced, Richard looked as if he had been crushed. He and his wife soon left the convention hall. I said to Nancy, "Praise God, the Southern Baptist Convention is being saved." Unbeknownst to me, Cecil Sherman and his wife Dot were sitting in front of us and heard me say that. Cecil later had some rather caustic remarks to make about my statement that day.

Bailey's election in St. Louis was an amazing thing. He didn't have the prominence in the eastern part of the United States that Adrian Rogers had. The liberals had not considered him a force to be feared. His election really shook the establishment. They realized that conservative support was far deeper and far stronger than they had ever envisioned.

After speaking at the Pastors' Conference, John Bisagno had left on a vacation but told me that he knew Richard would be elected and that he would call me to find out the results. At first he thought I was joking when he called and I told him Bailey had won on the first ballot.

Adrian Rogers appointed the Resolutions Committee that was named in St. Louis. Just before the Resolutions Committee report on Thursday afternoon of the SBC meeting, Nancy, Paul, and I ate lunch in a hotel restaurant. I left before they finished dining to go to the convention hall to see some friends. Nancy came running over in a little while and found me. She said she had overheard a conversation from a group seated next to her in the restaurant. She had assumed they were people from the Christian Life Commission or Baptist Joint Committee on Public Affairs who had been talking about the proposed resolution entitled "On Women." These people had discussed how, if a resolution on women passed in the form in which the Resolutions Committee had approved it, they would claim that the Southern Baptist Convention had gone on record as endorsing the Equal Rights Amendment to the U.S. Constitution. Obviously, this was not what the committee had intended. The Christian Life Commission or the Baptist Joint Committee advisor to the Resolutions Committee had evidently suggested the wording, the ramifications of which were not understood by the Resolutions Committee. The last phrase of this resolution as then written was as follows:

> Be it further *Resolved,* That for women who need or want to work outside the home we urge employers to seek fairness for women in compensation, advancement, and opportunities for improvement.

When Nancy found me and informed me of this, we decided we needed to move quickly. We found our friend Ed Drake, a member of First Baptist Church of Dallas, a lawyer, and a member of the Resolutions Committee. Nancy told him what she had overheard. When the Resolutions Committee made its report to the convention, it had added the following statement:

> Be it finally *Resolved,* That this convention, reaffirming the biblical role which stresses the equal worth but not always the sameness of function of women, does not endorse the Equal Rights Amendment.

Very little discussion occurred on the resolution, a motion to delete the above statement was defeated, and the motion with the new statement passed easily. The purpose of the statement was to make the resolution completely neutral on the Equal Rights Amendment. Reporters misconstrued this, and it was widely reported that the Southern Baptist Convention had gone on record as opposing the Equal Rights Amendment. If Nancy had not overheard the conversation in the coffee shop, the SBC stand on the Equal Rights Amendment would have been reported differently. Perhaps this SBC stand played a role in the Equal Rights Amendment to the U.S. Constitution not being ratified.

The Committee on Boards (now called the Committee on Nominations) in 1980 was a result of Jimmy Allen's appointments. Conservatives believed in working within the system, and we did not oppose the report, although it possibly contained the most liberal group of nominees for convention trusteeships that had ever been nominated. The convention approved without discussion the nominations for the Committee on Boards for the following year which had been made by Adrian Rogers's Committee on Committees. Conservatives sat back to work within the system, not wanting to rush things.

Some of the nominations that Adrian made to the Committee on Committees were not reliable conservatives who wanted to change the direction of our institutions. This was because some people were perceived to be conservative when they actually were not. Also, Adrian was trying to be broad in his appointments and not appoint only from the group that had been working to reverse the direction of our Southern Baptist institutions. At the time, we did not know where many people stood.

Evangelist James Robison and Ed McAteer from Memphis conducted a Public Affairs Briefing in Dallas on August 21 and 22, 1980. At the urging of some friends, I decided to go. I did not expect much, but when I arrived, I found a packed arena, full of enthusiastic individuals hearing great speakers. I went to the phone after the first few hours, called Nancy, and said, "Get a baby-sitter for the children. You must come up here and hear what is going on." She flew to Dallas, and we had the opportunity to attend together. This was the first time either of us had met Ronald Reagan. Mary Crowley invited us to a reception for him at the Hyatt. Jimmy Carter had been invited to speak but did not attend.

This also was the occasion at which Bailey Smith, the convention president, made the widely reported statement that "God does not hear the prayers of the Jews." In the context of the statement, he was criticizing political meetings in which people from all different religions are paraded to the platform to use prayer for political purposes. He was talking generally about that improper use of prayer. As an aside, he talked about God hearing only the prayers of believers. If he had said that God does not hear the prayers of people who do not believe that Jesus Christ is the Messiah instead of singling out Jews, his remarks probably would not have had such a negative response. But the response was immediate, and he was denounced vehemently in the press. The liberals in the convention seized on this to try to defeat Bailey Smith for reelection in 1981.

As a result of this, Bailey met with Jewish leadership and observed Seder with some Jewish friends. He went further in establishing rapport and communication between Southern Baptists and Jewish leaders than any other SBC president has ever done. The net effect was that contact between Jews and Christians was strengthened.

I have personally participated on the Committee of Christians and Jews for Israel in Houston, spoken at meetings of the Anti-Defamation League of B'nai B'rith, and even addressed the international board of directors of B'nai B'rith. At the latter meeting, I was asked about Jewish evangelism. I told the directors that it was a matter of freedom of speech. I told them that if I had something that I knew was true that was very meaningful to me and did not share it with them, I was not being their friend. If they believed it was improper for me to tell them something that was meaningful to me, they were seeking to limit my freedom of speech. I told them I would limit no one's freedom of speech. We all had a right to say what we wanted to say. We live in a free country where no preference should be given to any religious group. My answer seemed to be well-received.

$\mathcal{T}$HE OPPOSITION MOBILIZES

After their unexpected defeat in St. Louis in 1980 by a person whom they considered to be a weak candidate, the liberals and those in control of the SBC evidently began to worry. They abandoned what appeared to be complacency and realized that the conservative movement would not soon pass. They recognized that we were serious and that we would not be content until conservative Southern Baptists were given a real place in the convention. The liberals evidently felt that they must reverse our momentum.

The Los Angeles SBC meeting in 1981 seemed to them a good place to start their return to power. Many people from the bureaucracy would be attending on denominational expense accounts. Many trustees of Southern Baptist agencies usually were present. A total of approximately one thousand trustees served. Most of them, along with their spouses, could be counted on to support the liberals. The opposition thought it had a real chance at this meeting, since it was held outside the area in which most Southern Baptists lived and where many grassroots Southern Baptists could not afford to go. The attendance would be smaller, and the bureaucracy and trustees would be overrepresented proportionately. A concerted effort was also made to get seminary students who were sympathetic to the liberals to attend.

The first major liberal organizational meeting which was reported was held in Gatlinburg, Tennessee, on September 25 and 26, 1980. It was stated that fifteen or twenty persons attended. Although no list of the attendees were released, the following were known to have attended: Kenneth Chafin, pastor of South Main Baptist Church in Houston and later a professor at Southern Seminary (the one whom I would later debate on the televised "Donahue" show); Cecil Sherman, pastor of First Baptist Church in Asheville, North Carolina, and later the first moderator of the Cooperative Baptist Fellowship; Carl Bates, pastor of First Baptist of Charlotte, North Carolina, and former convention president; Weldon Gaddy, pastor of Broadway Baptist Church in Fort Worth and later hired by Mercer University in Macon, Georgia; Bill Sherman, pastor of Woodmont Baptist Church in Nashville, Tennessee, and brother of Cecil Sherman; Vernon Davis, pastor of First Baptist Church of Alexandria, Virginia, and later dean at Midwestern Seminary; and Lavonn Brown, pastor of First Baptist Church, Norman, Oklahoma.

Of these seven known participants, two went on to leadership positions in Southern Baptist seminaries and another to a leadership position at a state Baptist college. This group made unflattering statements about conservatives and tried to organize to resist the conservative movement. Many conservatives irreverently referred to them as the "Gatlinburg Gang." The group continued for a while and later was replaced by other groups.

The first national liberal newspaper was authorized in November 1982. Some conservatives wondered why they thought forming a newspaper was necessary when they had such apparent support from so many of the state Baptist papers and from Baptist Press. From time to time conservatives had several newspapers. Each was an independent effort, and they all failed before too long. The liberals seemed much better organized than we were, and they used their organizational ability to fight us in every way they could.

The liberals decided to oppose Bailey Smith for reelection at the 1981 SBC meeting. I did not think their opposing an incumbent president was a good strategy. An incumbent had not been opposed since 1969 in New Orleans, when a small group of dedicated extremists opposed Dr. W. A. Criswell for reelection. They mustered only 450 votes against Dr. Criswell to his 7,482. The ones who opposed him lost credibility by running someone against him. Southern Baptists do not like ugliness and seek to resist anything that seems unkind or unfair. By opposing Bailey Smith for reelection in Los Angeles in a climate where for years the incumbent president had been allowed to run unopposed, the opposition made themselves look unnecessarily confrontational at this stage of the controversy.

The liberals agreed that Abner McCall would be their candidate for president of the SBC in 1981 in Los Angeles. Bailey Smith agreed to allow his name to be presented for reelection. On the day of the election, Abner and I walked into the convention hall together. I told him that I appreciated him and that I hoped he would not allow his name to be presented because it was obvious he would be defeated and would be embarrassed. Although I tried to express genuine affection for him, I felt he was very uncommunicative. At that time I still felt very fondly toward him. He received 4,524 votes, or 39.30 percent, while Bailey received 6,934 votes, or 60.24 percent.

Many uninvolved Southern Baptists were dismayed at the politicizing of a convention which should have been harmonious. On the other hand, the other side showed real strength in that they defeated five conservative nominees for trusteeships that the Committee on Boards presented. This was the first report nominating trustees that came from a committee elected as a result of the conservative resurgence, and it was attacked vehemently. Although five conservatives were defeated, more than one hundred new conservative trustees were elected. The conservative movement had borne its first fruit.

After the SBC meeting in Los Angeles, a number of conservative leaders and their families attended a School of the Prophets Bible Conference in Hawaii, hosted by Paige and Dorothy Patterson. Among the group attending were Dr. Criswell, Adrian Rogers, Bailey Smith, and other conservative leaders. Those of us who attended praised God for His tremendous blessings and for beginning to restore our denomination to its inerrancy roots. It was a wonderful Bible conference. However, my attention was directed to my son, who was having up to fourteen seizures a day and was not doing well.

Paul and I were sitting by the swimming pool when some of the young people, my daughters included, decided that throwing the president of the Southern Baptist Convention, fully clothed, into the swimming pool would be good sport. I appreciated Bailey's good-natured response. He is a person with a contagious personality, gracious manner, and openness to all people. Through the years I have grown to love and appreciate him more and more as I have seen the spirit of the Lord Jesus Christ in his life and in his actions with other people. I wondered how many previous presidents of the convention would have allowed themselves to be engaged in such undignified horseplay with teenagers.

At the 1982 SBC meeting in New Orleans, Bailey was ineligible for reelection. The liberals began organizing extensively. Conservatives had developed a network of communication, but we were not as organized as the other side. After much prayer and discussion, we concluded that if we created an organization with membership, we would expose our friends to retribution if the effort failed. Also, if people were members of an organization, they could be held responsible for the actions of that organization. If no membership existed, each one of us would be responsible for himself or herself and not for anybody else. This gave protection to everybody. We were a group of individuals who were bound together by our devotion to the Bible as God's inerrant Word. We were not bound together by an organization.

The contrast would become evident later when the liberals organized both the Cooperative Baptist Fellowship and the Baptist Alliance. They appeared to need the organizational patterns from which we shied away. We had a contact system in which information given to people in one area of the country could be conveyed to others throughout the convention. No elected or appointed leadership existed. Our group was just a network of people who were motivated by the same principles and by the same desires for the convention. Our lack of organization frustrated the liberals because they could never put a handle on what was going on. When I sent out letters to some friends, the liberals intercepted almost anything I wrote others. Therefore, after a while, I wrote everything as though everyone would eventually read it.

I continued my regular work on the appellate court while I increasingly spoke around the country. At the SBC meetings through New Orleans in 1982, when either Paige or I walked through a crowded room, it was like the parting of the Red Sea. We had received so much criticism that few people were willing to be seen with us. Many of the people who avoided us, however, did vote with us. They knew we were right and supported the cause. Some of them had grave reservations about us as individuals because the unflattering coverage in the media was having its effect. Although our reputations had been greatly harmed in their minds, they still believed in the cause. The cloud which the news coverage created hung over us as individuals but had not discouraged these people from voting their convictions. The attacks of the liberal establishment had failed to accomplish its real purpose of destroying the movement.

Four candidates for president emerged for the New Orleans SBC meeting in 1982. Duke McCall had agreed to carry the liberal banner. Dr. McCall possessed all the qualities that had previously elected convention presidents. He had served as executive secretary of the SBC, president of New Orleans Seminary, and, for many years, had been president of Southern Seminary in Louisville. He was then retired and had the time to serve. He was a well-known and well-respected gentleman who had many years of working with Baptists throughout the convention. It was believed that he would be a strong candidate.

Dr. Jimmy Draper, pastor of First Baptist Church of Euless, Texas, and a former associate pastor under Dr. Criswell, quickly emerged as the conservative choice. John Sullivan and Perry Sanders, both of Louisiana, the home state for the convention, were the other candidates. Both of them took a middle-of-the-road approach. They were theologically conservative, but they either did not recognize the problems in our institutions or did not approve of our method of doing something about them. This annual meeting obviously was going to be quite different.

Jimmy Draper was not as well-known as Adrian Rogers and had not preached as many revivals as Bailey Smith. However, Jimmy did have the right credentials. His father had been a faithful Southern Baptist pastor for many years, and both of his brothers were in the ministry. He had led many people to a saving knowledge of Jesus Christ and had built great churches wherever he pastored. He was greatly beloved because of his faithfulness to the Lord and His Word, his gracious manner, and his excellent preaching.

Attendance was up in New Orleans. The first presidential vote was taken Tuesday afternoon of the convention. It gave Jimmy Draper 8,081 votes, or 46.03 percent; Duke McCall 6,124 votes, or 34.88 percent; Perry Sanders 1,725 votes, or 9.83 percent; and John Sullivan 1,625 votes, or 9.26 percent.

Criswell College had engaged a ballroom for Tuesday evening to hold a fellowship dinner before the evening session. The runoff vote was taken before dinner, but the results had not been announced. At the fellowship, I was very discouraged. I thought that most of the votes that had gone to Perry Sanders and John Sullivan would now go to Duke McCall in the runoff. However, I was wrong, and the vote swung so that Jimmy Draper was elected decisively with 8,331 votes, or 56.97 percent. Dr. McCall had 6,282 votes, or 43.03 percent. Jimmy had gained 10 percent, and Dr. McCall had gained less than 9 percent.

The conservatives had withstood the liberal counterattack, and the conservative movement was becoming solidly established. This result stunned the old guard of the convention. Paige called Dr. Criswell to tell him the results. Dr. Criswell replied, "Do you mean to tell me that Jimmy Who? from Where? Texas has defeated the strongest politician in the Southern Baptist Convention? I can't believe it."

The conservative movement did sustain a reversal, however, when three of the nominees of the Committee on Boards (now Nominations) were replaced on motions by two individuals: Dr. Kenneth Chafin, then pastor of South Main Baptist Church in Houston and later professor at Southern Seminary, and Dr. Vernon Davis, then pastor of First Baptist Church in Alexandria, Virginia, and later dean of Midwestern Seminary. Both of these were members of the "Gatlinburg Gang." The chairman of the committee defending the report was Dr. Daniel Vestal, then pastor of First Baptist Church of Midland, Texas. He would later become the coordinator of the Cooperative Baptist Fellowship, formed years later by the liberals as a vehicle to oppose the programs of a conservatively led SBC. What a reversal of roles! Although we lost a few trustees, as in Los Angeles, a large number of new conservative trustees was elected. We now had some real representation on all boards.

Another event at this New Orleans meeting was the emergence of Morris Chapman, pastor of First Baptist Church of Wichita Falls, Texas, in conservative leadership. (He would later be elected SBC president and then president of the SBC Executive Committee.) Over the strong objections of the Christian Life Commission and the Baptist Joint Committee on Public Affairs leadership, he argued eloquently for a resolution on school prayer. We won the issue, which was a strong repudiation of the political leadership which had said for years that it represented Southern Baptist thinking. It was a portent of things to come in this area.

Except for 1983 in Pittsburgh, the liberals opposed every incumbent conservative president until 1991. Their practice was to run their strongest candidate against an incumbent and then often run him a second time the following year when the incumbent was ineligible. Thus, the second time their candidate ran, he was damaged from his prior defeat and had alienated those whom he offended by running against an incumbent. The liberals evidently never realized this. Some of them said they were helping their cause by having their defeated candidate run again, because he had gained prominence and publicity through his first race. I think this was a very flawed strategy which cost the liberals dearly.

The 1983 SBC meeting was the eye of the hurricane. It was conducted in Pittsburgh, out of traditional Southern Baptist territory. Jimmy Draper was unopposed for reelection. This was a real compliment to his open, friendly nature. It also showed that the liberals still thought that the conservative movement would collapse and was not a permanent threat to their control of the SBC. The liberals were very quiet in Pittsburgh and reversed their prior strategy.

At this SBC meeting, the liberals held a reception which later evolved into an alternative to the Pastors' Conference, probably because after several attempts they realized it was hopeless to elect someone sympathetic to their cause as president of the regular Pastors' Conference which was held for two days prior to the convention. At the earlier SBC meetings, the first contest had been the election of the president of the Pastors' Conference. By 1983, it was anticlimactic because the conservatives were firmly in control. Conservatives had their rallying point and a place to highlight our leaders in the Pastors' Conference. This was evidently quite frustrating to the liberals.

Another important development of the Pittsburgh SBC meeting was the beginning of Dr. Charles Stanley's participation in convention activities. As pastor of First Baptist Church in Atlanta, he had built a great soul-winning church which effectively touched his entire metropolitan area. Opposition to him from the liberal element in his area had been intense, even to the extent that someone physically assaulted him while he was in the pulpit. Liberals fought his call as pastor of First Baptist and heaped abuse on him, since he did not belong to their group. This had caused him to be less active in associational, state, and Southern Baptist activities than he otherwise might have been, and he was considered an outsider. Besides supporting the Cooperative Program, his church supported many missionaries affiliated with Campus Crusade for Christ and other parachurch organizations.

A friend of mine, Rick Summers, a young lawyer in Atlanta and a member of First Baptist Church there, was appointed to the Committee on Committees. I think I suggested to President Jimmy Draper that Rick be appointed, although I did not often make such recommendations. After he was appointed, Rick called and asked for suggestions as to whom he should nominate for the Committee on Boards (now Nominations). We thought about asking Charles Stanley to serve, as a means of getting him involved. Later, Rick and I decided to have Rick nominate Charles for chairman of the committee. He desired to be active in the convention and, until that time, had been excluded. I had been blessed by his ministry and considered him, as I do now, one of God's great leaders. I looked forward with pleasure to meeting him in Pittsburgh for the first time. After we met, Charles and I had lunch in his room, where I was privileged to describe the SBC system to him.

Charles Stanley's election as chairman of the Committee on Boards (now Nominations) seemed to be a lightning rod for the liberals. The fact that someone whom they had attempted to isolate was chairing the most important committee of the convention evidently frightened them. Since that committee nominates the trustees of all our institutions, this can make a major difference in the convention activities.

Terms on seminary boards are five years, most other boards and commissions are four years, and most committees are three years. A person can serve on a board for two terms. Therefore, on a regular basis, one-tenth or one-eighth of a board will be replaced. Additional vacancies exist as positions open up by persons who have moved, resigned, or died. We were aware of the fact that within a ten-year period, all members of every board should have changed. Our knowledge of this has caused us to be charged with having a ten-year plan for "controlling" the boards of the SBC.

Actually, the time required to change the majority is much less than that. The time for the complete changing of a board was an observation, not a program. The fact that it took some time for the ideological composition of a board to change showed two things: (1) liberals had done an outstanding job of excluding those not sympathetic with their control, and (2) conservatives did not appoint only those who were dedicated to their cause. If they had, the shift would have been quicker and more dramatic.

Pittsburgh was the first SBC meeting I really enjoyed. The undercurrent of antagonism existed, but it was not nearly so overt as before. Pittsburgh was truly the calm before the storm.

In 1980 and 1982, the conservative candidate had been obvious. For 1984, many outstanding possibilities existed, but no one individual had made the commitment to allow himself to be nominated. When the liberals began their intensive organization and messenger-recruitment program, we responded. However, we responded with promoting the cause, not a candidate. Actually that had always been the case, because we were much more intent on the message than we were the messengers who would lead. Many people assumed that Charles Stanley would be the conservative candidate, because the liberals were training their guns on him. Surely he was an imposing figure, and his joinder with the conservative movement evidently was most disconcerting to the liberals.

I personally traveled extensively in the fall of 1983 and the winter and spring of 1984. My nomination to the Executive Committee of the SBC in the March meeting of the Committee on Boards (now Nominations) caused me to be even more in the eye of the media. It amused and distressed me to see the vehemence with which I was opposed. To me, the issue was not me personally but whether the system was such that it would remain closed to conservative leadership. Would membership on our boards be open to all so that discussions of polity could take place as individuals from different perspectives and with different concerns sat down together and worked out their differences? I realized how closed the liberal, "good ol' boy" system had been.

However, I recognize now that my solution of having the boards be the forum for working out problems was naive at best. The attacks concerning my appointment to the Executive Committee changed my thinking. In a later chapter on the Executive Committee, I seek to demonstrate that under the liberals, the boards themselves were tightly controlled and were not places of free exchange. The tight control of the system showed me that the liberals had a basic fear of the democratic process of Southern Baptists. I came to see each board as a unified force to direct policy and not, as I had hoped, a forum for the presentation and compromise of diverse viewpoints. The nature of the liberal control showed me that they were unwilling to be open. One cannot work openly with someone who is using your openness as a means to manipulate you.

From that time on, many of us urged the Committee on Boards (now Nominations) to be as pure as possible and to nominate only true conservatives in its report. No longer was there any reason to elect those unsympathetic to the conservative cause so dialogue could occur on boards. That was not the desire of the liberals, and thus it became no longer ours. How different things could have been if they had looked on us as brothers in Christ with sincere concerns and not as enemies who should be defeated at all cost.

When June 1984 arrived, I was worn out. I was tired of the press distortions, the liberal attacks, the strain of traveling while keeping up my work at the court, and particularly the strain of attending our son, whose condition was worsening.

As I mentioned, prior to the SBC meeting that year, I hoped to rest in Illinois, where Nancy's parents were celebrating their golden wedding anniversary. Having to dash our son back for hospitalization, when he suddenly lost his eyesight, and my doing twenty-four-hour-a-day duty with him at the hospital left me completely exhausted.

When I left for Kansas City, it was difficult for me to put one foot in front of the other because of fatigue. Even worse than that, when I said goodbye to Paul, his situation was so grave that I didn't know if I would ever see him alive again. Paul, at eighteen, had such a deep walk with Christ that he told me I had to go because that was what God had led me to be involved in. Therefore, I went. My older daughter, Jean, went with me to Kansas City, while my younger daughter, Anne, stayed in Houston to help Nancy with Paul. It was a long drive to the airport and a difficult flight for Jean and me. We received a bad report on Paul the Monday morning after we arrived, as previously mentioned.

A small, lovely hotel just across the square from the convention center in Kansas City had not contracted with the meeting planners, and Russell Kaemmerling of the *Southern Baptist Advocate* had secured a block of rooms there. We were, thus, out of the main traffic flow of the SBC meeting and enjoyed some relative peace and quiet. This was where we and the Pattersons stayed, along with many other conservatives. Monday night after the Pastors' Conference, about fifteen of us gathered in Paige's room. Fred Powell, Ed Young, Charles Stanley, Adrian Rogers, Jim DeLoach, Bailey Smith, and others were there, as well as Paige and I.

We all had assumed that Charles would be nominated the next day. After a while, Charles interrupted the general flow of conversation and said, "You better find another person to be nominated tomorrow, because I will not be nominated." This took all of us by surprise, but Charles remained determined. He said that God had not told him to be nominated, and he couldn't do it without God's direction. In a little while, it finally dawned on us that Charles was absolutely serious. Dismay fell on the room.

Alternatives were discussed. Much time was spent in prayer, but no direction from the Lord seemed evident. When a waiter delivered soft drinks to the room, Bailey turned to the waiter and said, "We are looking for someone who is willing to be elected president of the Southern Baptist Convention tomorrow. Would you be willing to do it?" Bailey's humor relaxed the room somewhat. Finally someone turned to Ed Young and asked him if he would consider being nominated. Ed said that he had not considered it but would be glad to pray about it. He gave no assurance that he was available, but when we soon broke up for a few hours of sleep, I think most of the individuals felt as I did—that God was going to impress on Ed that he should be the candidate.

Ed prayed about it throughout the night and awakened Paige about 4 o'clock the next morning to say that he could not be nominated. God had not given him the release to do so. Word quickly spread among the group, and most reassembled about 7:30 in Paige's room. Ed was not there, since he was exhausted from his night of prayer. I have never been in a meeting where I saw such brokenness. Everyone was sobbing. All prayed silently, and from time to time, someone prayed out loud. I was kneeling with my face buried in a pillow on the couch. Thoughts kept going over and over in my mind. I prayed, "Lord, if you are in charge of the movement, and if we have been obedient to you in seeking a redirection of the convention, how can we not have a candidate? So many people have sacrificed to come here. If we have no candidate, does it mean that we misunderstood you and that we were acting on our own and not under your direction?" I have never sobbed more deeply.

About 9:30 Charles Stanley joined us in Paige's room. He had been in the prayer meeting for some time before he said anything. Finally, when he spoke, Charles Stanley said, "Men, I have been running from God. I don't want to be nominated today. If I am, I will probably be humiliated, but God told me before I left my room this morning that I have to be nominated. I don't want to be, but I must. Since He has told me, I must do it. Let Him humiliate me if He wants to. I will be nominated."

The reaction was electric. Shouts of "Amen," "Hallelujah," and "Praise the Lord" rocked the small room. Tears were wiped away, and hugs were universal. Any observer would have thought he or she were observing a group of Pentecostals. When the shouting died down a little, someone started singing the Doxology, and all joined in. Never has it been sung with greater enthusiasm or deeper appreciation:

> Praise God, from whom all blessings flow;
> Praise Him, all creatures here below;
> Praise Him above, ye heavenly host;
> Praise Father, Son, and Holy Ghost.

Only four hours later, the nominating speeches were to be made. We now had a conservative candidate, but we had no nominator, and no nominating speech had been prepared. Someone suggested that Jerry Vines would be an excellent nominator and that he had reason to believe that Jerry would be willing to do so. We dispersed as a group, with some trying to find Jerry to see if he would make the nomination.

As soon as the prayer meeting was over, Dorothy Patterson and my daughter Jean came to tell me that Nancy had called with news that Paul's condition had worsened. I called Nancy immediately, and we discussed what to do. She again insisted that Jean and I stay in Kansas City. When I put down the phone after our conversation, the roller coaster of emotions was almost too much to bear. I praise God that He is sufficient for every circumstance.

What happened then is in the history books. Jerry did nominate Charles, and he was elected. The vote was Charles Stanley, 7,692, or 52.18 percent; Grady Cothen, the candidate of the liberals, 3,874, or 26.28 percent; and John Sullivan, who also had run in 1982 and was attempting to be in the middle, 3,174, or 21.53 percent.

Winfred Moore, pastor of First Baptist Church in Amarillo, opposed my nomination to the Executive Committee by nominating Bruce McIver against me. Bailey Smith wonderfully supported and defended me. The vote was Paul Pressler, 5,462, or 53.93 percent, and Bruce McIver, 4,666, or 46.07 percent.

The low point of the meeting was the convention sermon by Russell Dilday. This address, which was intended to be for inspiration, was a clear attack upon the conservative movement.

A motion opposing the ordination of women passed 58.03 percent to 41.97 percent. This outraged the feminist element and their liberal supporters. Perhaps the resolution was a real warning to liberals that conservatives were intent on promoting their beliefs. This motion helped the liberals rally their own for the 1985 SBC meeting in Dallas.

Jean and I flew home on Wednesday afternoon as soon as my first meeting of the Executive Committee was over. I was never happier to be with our family, where together we could see Paul emerge from his crisis.

CHAPTER 20

$\mathcal{D}$ALLAS AND BEYOND

The liberals left the 1984 SBC meeting in real anger. They had been defeated in everything they tried. Charles Stanley had been elected president of the SBC, and I had been elected to the Executive Committee. Two individuals whom they deeply resented had won. They immediately began to prepare for 1985 in Dallas. Russell Dilday addressed students at rallies conducted on the property of Southwestern Seminary. Other organizational and mobilization efforts began. Conservatives stepped back for a couple of months to catch their breath and rest before the gathering storm.

I had seen Winfred Moore, pastor of First Baptist Church of Amarillo, on the street in Kansas City and went over to him to introduce myself. We had never met. I told him that I hoped he would be willing to get together after the SBC meeting so that knowing each other, we could perhaps work together. He said that if I came to Amarillo, he would see me. Our family had planned to stay in Colorado for a month during the summer of 1984. Paul was not well enough to ride in the car for a long distance, so he and Nancy flew. A friend of mine, Rod Mitchell, who had assisted me in some Bible studies, helped me drive to Colorado Springs. By arrangement, we stopped in Amarillo on the way to Colorado and met with Winfred at First Baptist Church.

We were admitted to his office on time. Exactly one hour later his secretary came in and told Winfred Moore he needed to do something else. During the hour we spent together, I neither felt that he understood what I was saying nor that he was interested in understanding. As with other attempts to dialogue and find common ground with those on the other side, I believed I had wasted my time. I realized that those with whom I sought to dialogue had already determined what to think about me, so no way existed to develop rapport.

After the state convention meetings were over in November, conservatives began to encourage attendance at the 1985 SBC annual meeting to be held in Dallas. I traveled and spoke as much as my court schedule would allow. By now press coverage had made the conservative movement well-known. Many people could see through the attacks on us and realized that we were supporting what they themselves believed.

Charles Stanley was well-known for his deeply spiritual In Touch Ministries. Since people had seen Charles on TV, unfiltered by the editorial opinions of others, the attacks on him discredited the attackers. Charles had a tremendous personal following. Those among his following who were Southern Baptists were energized by the attacks on him and were motivated to travel to Dallas to support him. My friends Marlin Maddoux and Pat Robertson gave me time on their nationwide broadcasts and let me tell the conservative side. This helped to rally and inform those who believed as we did and encourage them to attend the Dallas meeting.

Attend they did. The Dallas SBC meeting in 1985 was the largest Southern Baptist Convention meeting in history. Total number of messengers eligible to vote was 45,519. Probably this was the largest deliberative meeting of Christians in the history of the world. In fact, I do not know if any larger deliberative body has existed anywhere in the history of the world unless it would have been in one of the Greek city-states before the time of Christ. The logistics were overwhelming. Several halls were required to seat the crowd. Only messengers and credentialed press were allowed in these halls because of the space limitations. Charles Stanley presided with grace and ease. This seemed to antagonize the liberals, who were intent on restoring their power through making personal attacks on conservative leaders.

The Sunday before the meeting, we attended First Baptist Church of Dallas. After the service, I went up to express my appreciation to Dr. Criswell. He had always been very reserved with me, calling me "Judge," "My dear Judge," or some other formal title. This time, when I approached him, he grabbed both of my hands, held them in his, and excitedly said, "Paul, Tuesday we are going to have the greatest victory in the history of Christendom here in Dallas." Never before or since have I seen him so informally enthusiastic.

When Tuesday morning dawned, from our hotel room we could see thousands of messengers already lined up to enter the still-closed doors of the convention center. Many had driven all night, and all appeared eager to be in the main hall for the opening morning session and the crucial afternoon votes. The air was electric when we later arrived at the convention hall.

Winfred Moore was the liberals' candidate. He met the profile they wanted—a person who was considered a theological conservative but who was solidly on their side and dedicated to their cause. He had been elected president of the Baptist General Convention of Texas and thus was well-known and had a following in the area in which the SBC meeting was being held. Even with his candidacy, along with the diligent work of Keith Parks of the Foreign Mission Board (now the International Mission Board), Lloyd Elder of the Sunday School

Board (now LifeWay Christian Resources), seminary presidents Russell Dilday, Roy Honeycutt, and Randall Lolley, and the efforts of countless individuals involved in the liberal movement, the liberals lost. The vote was Charles Stanley, 24,452, or 55.3 percent, and Winfred Moore, 19,795, or 44.7 percent. The liberals put everything into their effort and failed.

The excitement did not end with the presidential election. As soon as Winfred was defeated, someone identified with the liberals proposed that Winfred be elected first vice president as a unifying gesture. This caught everyone by surprise. I personally suspect that this had been planned well before, but it looked spontaneous and was well-received. Winfred was elected to the position, which was entirely symbolic as long as the president remained well and healthy. However, this victory did salve the deep wound which Charles's reelection had inflicted on the liberals. It also emboldened the liberals to make further attacks.

During the meeting, the liberals made constant objections and points of order. It appeared that they were attempting to turn into chaos what they could not control. Charles conducted himself graciously but firmly. When motions were made to amend the Committee on Boards' (now Nominations) report for trustees, conflicting parliamentary maneuvers brought near bedlam. The convention adjourned, and time was given to study thoroughly the rulings of the chair and the points which had been raised. Wayne Allen of Memphis was ably serving as chief parliamentarian. I am sure that some people believed that I was behind the crucial ruling which was decided upon during the break. It ruled out of order certain attempts to change the Committee on Boards (now Nominations) report.

Nancy, Paul, and our attorney friend, Marshall Albritton of Nashville, took me to our room and put me to bed. I was experiencing either a heart problem, hyperventilation, or some other kind of disorder, which profoundly worried all four of us. Fortunately, the problem passed in an hour or so and has never recurred. The tension and exhaustion of the convention temporarily took their toll and kept me from effective leadership during the meeting. I was, therefore, no part of the afternoon deliberations in Charles's suite.

An important action of the Dallas meeting was the creation of the Peace Committee. This was the idea of former convention president Franklin Paschall, a man whom I have always deeply respected and appreciated. He felt that a broad-based committee could examine the issues thoroughly. I liked the principle but was afraid of what might occur. Having seen how committees were manipulated in Southern Baptist life, I was not sure whether the committee would function appropriately. Paige had no such reservations, and I basically kept mine to myself. Although the Peace Committee was very diverse, its study showed the existence of liberalism in our seminaries as we had been claiming and the falsity of all the attacks against us. The Peace Committee turned out to be most helpful to the conservative resurgence. Paige was right, and I was wrong.

The press attention to the Dallas meeting was unprecedented. All the major media were there. For many years, I had been a trustee of KHCB-FM, our oldest Christian radio station in Houston. Because of the media interest, KHCB asked me to represent the station and give direct broadcasts from the SBC meeting to listeners in the Houston area. When I entered the SBC pressroom, which seemed to be the inner sanctum of liberal control, I felt that many received me rudely. It was as though I had invaded a liberal enclave, the territory of those who were attending the meeting as press.

Ted Koppel called me from Nightline, and we discussed what was occurring. I felt he was very open and truly wanted to understand. He interviewed me briefly on that program. I believe that he did a fair and competent job of reporting. I debated Russell Dilday on the "MacNeil-Lehrer Report." It was live and gave each of us the opportunity to present his case. The major program on the convention was the "Donahue" show, for which Nancy and I traveled to New York several days after the meeting ended. In chapter 25 in this book, I describe that experience.

The 1985 meeting in Dallas was, in many ways, the culmination of the convention controversy. The conservatives won decisively against all the liberals could muster. The liberals would continue to oppose the new direction of the convention, but after Dallas, many of them began to realize the futility of their cause. The people in the pews did not support their position, and now, with the new trustees elected in Dallas, the ability of the agency heads to lead the liberal cause was being curtailed. It was the pivotal event in the history of the SBC and a defeat from which the liberals would and could never recover.

Vacation time in the summer of 1985 allowed me to catch up on some items which I had let slide while preparing for the Dallas meeting. One was a challenge from Dr. E. Harmon Moore, former executive secretary of the Indiana Baptist convention, for me to name names and give quotes of liberalism so they could be printed in the *Indiana Baptist*. David Simpson, a solid conservative, was editor. He agreed to print the results of my research as Dr. Moore had requested. On September 3, 1985, I wrote him with forty-seven pages of examples. Appendix B of this book is this letter with its examples.

After David and Dr. Moore received my letter, Dr. Moore completely reversed his position and asked David not to print the information I had sent. David called to tell me about this. I assume that Dr. Moore realized that most Southern Baptists would not approve of these statements. However, my friends and I widely circulated this letter along with the examples. When I spoke, I always had copies available. From time to time, some of the leaders of the liberals would make some type of critical reference to these examples. They tried to shift the discussion by saying that some of the individuals cited were then teachers in Southern Baptist seminaries and that some quoted were from colleges that were state institutions.

However, it was difficult for them to deny or to defend these remarks. I had set these forth as only a few examples of what was being taught in schools supported by Southern Baptist money.

Preparation for the 1986 SBC meeting in Atlanta was not as hectic as for the previous year. Winfred Moore again was to be the candidate for the liberals. They followed a strategy for the next several years which still remains puzzling to me. Winfred, Daniel Vestal, and Richard Jackson all three ran against an incumbent president and then ran in an open election the year after having been defeated by an incumbent. I'll always marvel at the ways in which the liberals could have short-circuited us if they had not made tactical blunders.

Not only did Winfred enter the election in Atlanta as the one who had lost the year before; he also ran in an area of the country beyond his base. He was not well-known east of the Mississippi. Adrian Rogers, who had declined to be nominated for the customary second term in 1980, agreed to allow his nomination in Atlanta. The liberals tried, but Winfred was defeated. Adrian Rogers received 21,201 votes, or 54.22 percent. Winfred Moore received 17,898 votes, or 45.78 percent. More conservative trustees were added to the boards, and real changes were beginning there. The conservative cause was making headway.

The liberals supported Richard Jackson for president in St. Louis in 1987, although Adrian Rogers was nominated for reelection. Richard was defeated in his third quest for the presidency. Adrian Rogers received 13,980 votes, or 59.97 percent. Richard Jackson received 9,331 votes, or 40.03 percent—far better than he did seven years before in St. Louis, when he ran fourth in a field of six.

For conservatives, three critical votes always occurred at each SBC meeting. They were (1) the presidential election; (2) the approval of the Committee on Nominations for the following year, and (3) the approval of that year's Committee on Nominations report nominating the new trustees. All of these were important because they determined who would become trustees. Conservatives had won all votes on matters 1 and 2 beginning in 1979. The last time item 3 was amended was 1982 in New Orleans. Therefore, conservatives were feeling confident that their dominance in these areas would continue, and it did. Also, the Pastors' Conference was now so firmly under conservative leadership that the liberals no longer contested it after 1982.

The Peace Committee worked diligently. Its members visited seminary campuses, dialogued with various Southern Baptists, and studied the data presented to its members. I had the opportunity to appear before the committee. Answering committee members' questions was easy. The transcript of the Peace Committee was sealed for ten years. I hope that all Southern Baptists will read it now that it has been released. The fact that the committee was not diverted from its task, even though no solid conservative majority was on the committee, is remarkable to me. The presentation of the committee's report was the highlight of the St. Louis SBC meeting in 1987.

The Peace Committee met late into the night before finalizing its report for presentation the next day. Although the report contained several compromises, none did any damage to the conservative movement. From my point of view, the most significant portions in the findings were as follows:

> The Peace Committee has completed a preliminary investigation of the theological situation in our SBC seminaries. We have found significant theological diversity within our seminaries, reflective of the diversity within our wider constituency. These divergences are found among those who claim to hold a high view of Scripture and to teach in accordance with, and not contrary to, the Baptist Faith and Message Statement of 1963.
>
> Examples of this diversity include the following, which are intended to be illustrative but not exhaustive:
>
> (1) Some accept and affirm the direct creation and historicity of Adam and Eve, while others view them instead as representative of the human race in its creation and fall.
>
> (2) Some understand the historicity of every event in Scripture as reported by the original source while others hold that the historicity can be clarified and revised by the findings of modern historical scholarship.
>
> (3) Some hold to the stated authorship of every book in the Bible while others hold that in some cases such attribution may not refer to the final author or may be pseudonymous.
>
> (4) Some hold that every miracle in the Bible is intended to be taken as a historical event while others hold that some miracles are intended to be taken as parabolic.

They also found as follows:

> It is the conclusion of the majority of the Peace Committee that the cause of peace within the Southern Baptist Convention will be greatly enhanced by the affirmation of the whole Bible as being not errant in any area of reality.

Therefore we exhort the trustees and administrators of our seminaries and other agencies affiliated with or supported by the Southern Baptist Convention to faithfully discharge their responsibility to carefully preserve the doctrinal integrity of our institutions receiving our support, and only employ professional staff who believe in the divine inspiration of the whole Bible and that the Bible is truth without any mixture of error.

They then found as follows:

We, as a Peace Committee, have found that most Southern Baptists see truth without any mixture of error for its matter, as meaning, for example, that

(1) They believe in direct creation of mankind and therefore they believe Adam and Eve were real persons.

(2) They believe the named authors did indeed write the biblical books attributed to them by those books.

(3) They believe the miracles described in Scripture did indeed occur as supernatural events in history.

(4) They believe that the historical narratives given by biblical authors are indeed accurate and reliable as given by those authors.

They then issued this charge:

We call upon Southern Baptist institutions to recognize the number of Southern Baptists who believe this interpretation of our confessional statement and, in the future, to build their professional staffs and faculties from those who clearly reflect such dominant convictions and beliefs held by Southern Baptists at large.

As to the charges that we violated the electoral process, the Peace Committee found, "There was no evidence of widespread or organized misuse of the ballot by any political group and no evidence of massive voter irregularities related to annual meetings."

A vote of more than 95 percent of the messengers approved the Peace Committee report. Conservatives believed that the report verified the fact that theological problems existed. This was the concern which had motivated the conservative movement. It also showed that all charges against us which they studied were untrue. The Peace Committee report failed to give the liberals any arguments to use against us. It did nothing which would detrimentally affect the solid progress conservatives had made.

Soon after the St. Louis meeting, I received a letter dated July 11, 1987, from my friend, Dr. W. O. Vaught, a spiritual giant who was pastor of Immanuel

Baptist Church in Little Rock for many years and who had served as vice president of the convention. It read in part as follows:

> I saw Herschel Hobbs at the airport in St. Louis and I asked him to give me his estimate of the St. Louis meeting. This is what he said, "W. O., we entered a deep, dark woods about ten years ago and things got black. The storm really broke on us in Dallas and Atlanta and it appeared that we might lose the battle. But in St. Louis we moved on through the deep, dark woods and came out into a clearing again and the sun is shining again and we can see the blue sky even more. The battle is not over, but it is being won." I thought this was quite a statement for Hobbs to make and I pass it on to you for whatever it is worth.

Dr. Hobbs was obviously talking about the convention itself when he used the term "we." However, I think this letter shows that he and the other true centrists such as he recognized where the convention was headed and were content.

The liberals made two other major efforts. One occurred the next year in San Antonio. They again ran Richard Jackson. Since this was his fourth attempt to be elected president, he could not be considered a new face. This removed some of the luster from his effort. Jerry Vines was the consensus candidate supported by conservatives. Richard had roots in Texas, and Jerry was from the East Coast. This was somewhat of a problem for conservatives.

The biggest problem, however, was that San Antonio did not have enough hotel rooms to deal with the crowd. Conservatives did what we had not done before. We hired a person half time to help our friends get hotel rooms. A church hired him, he worked on programs for the church, and I raised funds to pay half of his salary. We disseminated his name and phone number among our friends. He helped many people obtain rooms so conservatives could attend the meeting.

The only other paid employees that I know of who worked for the conservative movement, except the ones who edited newspapers supportive of conservatives, were a series of young people who, one at a time, worked for me part time in the former garage at my house. Having them there kept Baptist telephone calls away from my office. They planned my trips, provided information to those who called, and filed data concerning the controversy. I assume some people on the staffs of pastors and other conservative leaders had assistants who helped them with the cause, but I know of none hired specifically for that purpose.

The bureaucrats and liberals of the convention were not timid in using Cooperative Program money to fight us. At Southwestern Seminary Russell

Dilday rallied his students against us. At Southern Seminary Roy Honeycutt declared "holy war" against us. Keith Parks used the bully pulpit of the Foreign (now International) Mission Board to rally furloughing missionaries and other Southern Baptists to oppose the conservative resurgence. At a meeting in his home church, First Baptist of Washington, D.C., James Dunn confessed that he as an agency head had done all he could do to resist conservatives.

The most blatant example, however, was Foy Valentine, who, as executive director of the Christian Life Commission, bragged about how many messengers he recruited to attend the Kansas City SBC meeting in 1984. All of these individuals were salaried by Southern Baptists and directed agencies funded by Southern Baptists (except for James Dunn, whose organization was only partially funded by the SBC). Large amounts of Southern Baptists' money were used to fight Southern Baptists in the conservative movement. We used a little of our own money to resist. They used a lot of our money to fight us.

The vote in San Antonio was the closest of all the contested annual meetings. However, God again gave the victory. Jerry Vines received 15,804 votes, or 50.53 percent. Richard Jackson received 15,112 votes, or 48.32 percent. This defeat was a bitter pill for the liberals. They had really expected to win.

In what I considered a sophomoric, melodramatic gesture, Randall Lolley led a few messengers to walk several blocks from the convention hall to the Alamo, where they burned their ballots. They said that freedom was being extinguished in the Southern Baptist Convention. This seemed an odd position to take, since Southern Baptists had already freely voted ten times in all parts of the convention territory to elect a conservative president. Southern Baptists had said that we had the freedom to determine what was being taught in the institutions we owned and supported and that our employees did not have the freedom to take our money and contradict what we believed. That message was loud and clear, but some just didn't get it.

In 1989, Daniel Vestal emerged as the candidate whom the liberals supported. I wonder what would have happened in San Antonio if he had run in 1988. It was his home area. A former conservative supporter, Daniel was new to the liberal movement and was not tarnished by prior efforts. However, in accordance with the liberal strategy, he ran in 1989 against an incumbent outside of his home base. Thus, he was damaged by a defeat when he ran the second time in 1990 in a nonincumbent year.

The 1989 meeting in Las Vegas was a unique one for Southern Baptists. Las Vegas has never been accused of being a buckle on the Bible Belt or even a part of it. The gaudy neon lights and the round-the-clock gambling casinos were somewhat of a change for most, if not all, of the messengers. I have never understood either why we wanted to meet there or why they wanted us. The yarn is often told about Baptists who go to an annual SBC meeting with the Ten Commandments in one pocket and a ten-dollar bill in another and never break either one. This joke has an element of truth in it. If any messenger had been tempted to gamble, the presence of other messengers would have been an inhibiting influence. The Las Vegas Convention Bureau should have known that.

Perhaps Las Vegas was using our meeting as an effort to change its image. I do not know, but I really don't see how it could have been very profitable to them to have us. Las Vegas has low hotel rates, low meal costs, and low air fares in order to attract gamblers. Southern Baptists profited financially from being there, as the meeting was less expensive for messengers.

Jerry Vines was easily reelected over Daniel Vestal. Jerry received 10,754 votes, or 56.58 percent, to 8,248, or 43.39 percent for Daniel. I had worried about the Las Vegas SBC meeting since I knew that many conservatives had a real aversion to going to that city. However, my fears were unjustified, and a sufficient number attended.

While in Las Vegas, I participated in a debate before the Religion Newswriters Association. I have never done a worse job in communicating. What could have been an opportunity to give the press a glimpse of what I considered to be the real me was lost. I was completely exhausted going into the debate. The tension of the contested convention, the fatigue of the years of conflict, and the emotional upset of being before those whom I considered to be dedicated to destroying me and promoting the other side took its toll. I resolved never to debate again just before an annual meeting.

Daniel Vestal campaigned diligently for the presidency before the 1990 SBC meeting in New Orleans. Afterwards, he said that he thought he could win, but he campaigned as a prior loser. The liberals put everything into their effort. The number voting for president increased from about 19,000 at the Las Vegas meeting to more than 36,000 in New Orleans. Only 31,000 had voted in San Antonio in 1988. Morris Chapman, pastor of First Baptist Church of Wichita Falls, Texas, was the conservative candidate. Seven years before, when the convention met in New Orleans in 1983, he had emerged as a forceful spokesman for conservatives on moral issues. The next time we met in New Orleans, he became our president. Morris received 21,471 votes, or 57.65 percent, and Daniel received 15,753 votes, or 42.32 percent. In spite of all the liberals' work, Daniel received a smaller percentage than he received in Las Vegas.

This was the final blow which ended the liberals' attempts to elect a convention president. Conservatives had won from Atlanta to Los Angeles and Las

Vegas and from St. Louis and Kansas City to Dallas, Houston, New Orleans, and San Antonio. Many liberals left New Orleans vowing to "do their own thing" and not to return to a Southern Baptist Convention meeting. At that time, they still controlled numerous state conventions. Their state victories lifted their spirits, and they resolved to hold on to these enclaves of strength.

Much has been said by liberal leaders and repeated in the Baptist state papers about how the conservative candidates emerged, but a remarkable lack of attention is paid to the selection of the liberals' candidates. It has been alleged that the conservatives had a "college of cardinals" who chose their candidate and directed their activities. No such allegations were made concerning the liberal selection process. I am not privy to how it worked for them, but I would guess that some of the state editors not only knew but also might have participated in selecting the liberal candidates.

The selection of the conservative candidate in Houston in 1979 and in Kansas City in 1984 has already been described. At other times, the selection was most informal. Conservative leaders listened. They did not direct. Sometimes such an obvious consensus candidate arose that little discussion occurred about whom the candidate should be. The discussion among conservatives in those years was how to encourage the messengers to attend the annual meeting in order to win. In 1980 in St. Louis, Bailey Smith was clearly the consensus choice. He, Adrian Rogers, and Jerry Vines had been the consensus candidates at the Houston meeting. Jerry was not ready to be nominated in St. Louis, so everyone expected Bailey to be nominated. He agreed to do so. Jimmy Draper had emerged as a consensus choice well before New Orleans in 1982. His leadership and preaching ability caused him to stand out. No one in particular selected him—conservatives in general implored him to run.

In 1986, again the nominee was obvious. Adrian Rogers had stepped aside in 1980 after serving only one year. Once he was ready to take up the mantle of leadership again, all conservatives joined in support. In 1988, Jerry Vines and Homer Lindsay Jr. were firmly established in their joint pastorate of First Baptist Church in Jacksonville, Florida. Since Jerry was the only one of the three leading prospects considered in Houston in 1979 who had not been elected, conservatives were awaiting his availability. Once he agreed, all conservatives flocked to his support. Perhaps no leader has ever had greater rapport with pastors of small churches than Jerry Vines. He was always available to everyone, and conservatives had been awaiting the time that he felt God's leadership to be nominated. Thus, from 1979 through 1989, the nominees were the three suggested in 1979, plus Charles Stanley and Jimmy Draper, both of whom were

obvious consensus leaders. No "College of Cardinals" or any selection committee existed.

During the 1980s, several conservative leaders had arisen who were great
men of God and had a compassion for souls and an ability to articulate the
gospel clearly. While a dearth of charismatic leaders existed among the liberals,
an abundance existed among the conservatives. In 1990 and thereafter, some
meetings were held among conservative leaders. Basically these were to find out
what was being said at the grass roots. The meetings were broad-based in order
that all sections of the convention could be heard. A consensus at the grass roots
was that Morris Chapman, Ed Young, and Fred Wolfe should be elected president. The whole process was informal and from the people.

The 1991 SBC meeting in Atlanta was basically uneventful. Morris
Chapman was reelected without opposition. I felt pleasantly relieved to be able
to relax at an SBC meeting and to sit back and enjoy everything.

In 1992 support for two different persons developed among conservatives.
Some wanted Edwin Young, pastor of Second Baptist Church in Houston, and
some wanted Nelson Price, pastor of Roswell Street in Marietta, Georgia. I could
have enthusiastically supported either one and have tremendous respect and
admiration for both. Both are close friends of mine. Each would have made an
excellent president. I supported Edwin since he was the pastor of my son and
was a neighbor. I was glad that both were nominated.

A third candidate, Jess Moody of First Baptist Church of Van Nuys,
California, emerged. He was not as much a part of the conservative movement
as were Edwin and Nelson. He was supported by the dwindling number of those
who still thought a compromise over theology could occur. The SBC meeting
was held in Indianapolis. Ed Young received 9,981 votes, or 62.05 percent. Jess
Moody received 3,485 votes, or 21.66 percent, and Nelson Price received 2,619
votes, or 16.28 percent. Solid conservatives received almost 80 percent of the
presidential vote in Indianapolis. The future looked bright.

The unhappy part of the Indianapolis convention meeting for me was the
opposition to my serving as a trustee on the Foreign (now International) Mission
Board. Although I knew that no real opposition to me existed at the grassroots
level and believed I would win, the anticipated contest and the unkindness of
some purported friends kept me on edge. I was most gratified when I received
more than 80 percent of the vote. This was just about the combined percentage
for Ed and Nelson in the presidential race.

In 1993 at the SBC meeting in Houston, Ed was reelected without opposition. It was good to be able to enjoy the convention fellowship again without
stress or concern.

The 1994 meeting in Orlando became a contest. This time it was not between a conservative and liberal but rather between two conservatives. One of them, Fred Wolfe, pastor of Cottage Hills Baptist Church in Mobile, had been with the movement all the time; the other, Jim Henry, pastor of First Baptist Church of Orlando, Florida, was conservative in his personal theology but did not see the same theological danger to the convention as some of the rest of us. Jim was a good man, but I could not vote for him. I believed that he was too trusting of some individuals who were not dedicated to making sure that sound doctrine was taught in our seminaries. I was also concerned that some of his supporters made unkind and derogatory remarks about some of us who had been active in the conservative movement. I was very worried about how these two factors would affect Jim Henry's appointments if he were elected president. Fred Wolfe had also emerged as a conservative candidate. Reports from all over the convention indicated that he was the choice of grassroots conservative leadership.

Several factors caused Jim Henry to win. The SBC meeting was held in his hometown of Orlando. He was known as a theological conservative and had successfully built a great church. He also was an effective pastor. In the speech in which he was nominated, he was hailed as one who would nominate only those who believed in the inerrancy of Scripture.

I had always urged conservatives not to engage in controversial matters after January 1 if at all possible. The state papers could keep a controversy going for only so long. This recommendation was not followed in 1994. Controversy erupted when the trustees at Southwestern Seminary correctly found it necessary to fire its president, Russell Dilday, in the spring of 1994. The need for doing so was greater than the risk of doing it only a couple of months before the SBC meeting. The trustees believed that if Russell had been allowed to remain, with the faculty retirements which would soon occur, he could appoint many to the faculty who were not sympathetic to the conservative theology. This would have guaranteed a seminary that would be out of sympathy with the leadership of the Southern Baptist Convention for years to come.

The controversy over the firing had been fanned by the state papers and the other regular opponents of the conservative movement. It created a backlash against the conservative movement. Russell had friends and former students who viewed him differently from the way many of us in the conservative movement viewed him. These factors combined to elect Jim Henry. He received 9,876 votes, or 55.18 percent, and Fred Wolfe received 8,023 votes, or 44.82 percent.

Some people tried to make it appear that the conservative movement was hopelessly divided as a result of Jim's election. Such was not the case. Jim was a theological conservative. Although in some states his appointments were not as strong as those which had been made in recent years, these did not have a detrimental effect on the conservative resurgence. The unsympathetic trustees resulting from his appointments were relatively few. Also, when some of these individuals started serving on the then-conservative boards, they saw the gracious, loving, and non-threatening demeanor of the conservatives and became valuable, contributing board members. Jim made a few remarks which some regarded as vague attacks on the conservative leadership, but all these remarks tended to do was to isolate him from some who had voted for him and left many of us wondering exactly whom he was attacking.

The next year in Atlanta, Jim was reelected without opposition. The 1995 SBC meeting was basically uneventful. More conservatives were added to the convention boards, and the liberals continued to absent themselves. It was increasingly clear that the contest for control of the Southern Baptist Convention was over. The contests had shifted to the states.

The question as to who would be nominated for president in 1996 started even before the 1995 convention meeting. Many conservatives considered Jim Henry's presidency a plateau on the climb to theological fidelity and were looking forward to moving on. Several names were discussed. Some people believed that the time had arrived to elect Paige Patterson. Others believed that electing Tom Elliff, a former missionary and then pastor of First Southern Baptist Church of Del City, Oklahoma, would be wise. No real consensus existed. The individuals who had backed Jim Henry were divided among themselves. Since no clear consensus existed, Adrian Rogers invited almost one hundred conservatives to meet in Atlanta. These were laymen, evangelists, and pastors. Some of the pastors had large churches, and some were pastors of small congregations. All were good listeners and knew what Southern Baptists in their part of the country were thinking.

We met for prayer and a time of sharing what God had been doing among his people spiritually. After lunch, the talk turned into a discussion of who should be elected president in 1996. Several names were suggested. Each person was then asked to take a slip of paper and write the name of his preference. When these were counted, although five or six persons were mentioned, more than 90 percent of the attendees had written the name of either Tom Elliff or Paige Patterson. The number mentioning each of them was about the same. Paige then asked Tom to step outside so the two of them could talk. In a few minutes they returned. Paige had asked Tom to be nominated and had retracted his willingness to serve. The group was elated, believing that God's will had become clear to the group.

Tom was nominated at the 1996 SBC meeting in New Orleans and elected without opposition. The 1996 meeting was a noncontroversial time for worship and praise. The only controversy had occurred behind the scenes without any publicity. My close friend, Lillian Butler of Kentucky, had suggested to the Committee on Order of Business that I be one of six persons to present a theme interpretation at the New Orleans meeting. Jim Henry, who served on the committee because he was SBC president, immediately opposed it. For almost half an hour, he spoke about how disruptive and bad it would be for me to do so. The committee listened patiently. When Jim was finished, someone acted as though Jim had never spoken and moved that I be approved. No further discussion occurred, and all six regular members of the committee voted against the expressed wishes of the president.

I enjoyed speaking at the SBC meeting. It was the first time I had addressed this body except for a couple of times when I spoke on controversial matters. I finally believed that for me, the controversy was over. I could now be the positive, supportive person I have always wanted to be.

The 1997 annual meeting in Dallas was a time of fellowship, feasting on the Word, and enjoying being Southern Baptists on mission with God. I hope and pray that it will be one of many such meetings to come.

Discussion of the 1998 SBC meeting in Salt Lake City began soon after the one in Dallas ended. Since Paige Patterson had been the other top choice of those in

Judge Paul Pressler preaching a theme interpretation at the New Orleans Southern Baptist Convention, June, 1996

Atlanta two years earlier, attention immediately centered on him. Paige did not want to be nominated unless both the conservative leadership and the conservative rank-and-file members supported him. Soon it appeared that overwhelming, enthusiastic support existed for his candidacy. Therefore, he agreed to allow his nomination in June 1998.

In his *Baptist Standard* editorial on January 14, 1998, Toby Druin attempted to derail Paige's election but conceded that "if Patterson is nominated, he will be the new president." Toby went on to say:

> There will be a nominee; apparently it will be Patterson, and we will have him for two years since a second term in 1999 would be customary. And after that there is Pressler. His term on the International Mission Board expires in the year 2000, and he will be available.

I thank Toby for his "nomination," but once again, he just doesn't understand. What I desire most is to see the students in our institutions built up and supported in their faith and not have their faith undermined by individuals we pay to teach in our schools. I have no desire to be SBC president. I want to rejoice in the fruits of the victory: an increase in missions and evangelism, not to be president. My cup is full as I see the wonderful results which are now being achieved in our seminaries.

Paige's unopposed election as president in 1998 shows how complete the change in the convention has been. (Appendix C shows the vote totals from all SBC presidential elections from 1979 to 1998.)

CHAPTER 21

$\mathcal{T}$HE HEART OF THE ISSUE

On August 26, 1976, three professors at Southern Seminary—G. Willis Bennett, E. Glenn Hinson, and Henlee Barnette—approved a thesis entitled "A Sociological Analysis of the Degrees of 'Christian Orthodoxy' Among Selected Students in The Southern Baptist Theological Seminary," by student Noel Wesley Hollyfield, Jr. All of those approving the thesis would later become leaders in the attacks on the conservative movement. Because of his stands on a number of liberal issues, Glenn Hinson later would become one of the major examples of conservative concern. The fact that these three accepted the validity of the thesis did tremendous harm to liberal control of the convention. The thesis traced the orthodoxy of the beliefs of students at Southern Seminary.

A chart compiled from the thesis appears below. The chart shows that the longer a student was at Southern Seminary, the less that student believed in fundamental Christian doctrines such as the virgin birth and the miracles reported in the Bible.

Changing Views of Southern Seminary Students

	Diploma Students	First Year	Final Year	Ph.D.–Th.M. Students
I know God really exists: I have no doubts about it.	100%	74%	65%	63%
Jesus is the Divine Son of God: I have no doubts about it.	100%	87%	63%	63%
I believe the miracles happened as the Bible said they did.	96%	61%	40%	37%
Jesus was born of a virgin: completely true.	96%	66%	33%	32%
Belief in Jesus Christ as Savior: absolutely necessary	100%	85%	60%	59%
	(p. 52–54)	(p. 60–61)	(p. 63–64)	(p. 70–71)

The statistics accumulated by Hollyfield and approved by these Southern Seminary professors illustrated in a serious and dramatic way that Southern Baptists were paying to have professors destroy the faith of those who attended our seminaries. Therefore, a basic issue in the convention controversy was whether Southern Baptists had any recourse against such an institution and whether we could insist that the schools which we owned, supported, and prayed for could be required to be faithful to their Southern Baptist constituency.

The debate in the Southern Baptist Convention concerns how completely we can rely on the authority of the Bible. To many the word *authority* is an ugly word. Many of us can remember with frustration the complete control which was exercised over us when we were in the military. Some people cringe when reminded of the authority parents exercised over them when they were young. Rules and regulations of governmental authorities are resented by all and defied by many. All people want to be free—free to express themselves, free to do as they wish, free so that nobody controls them. The desire of the natural person is to be free.

Christians know that we have freedom in Jesus. We are free from the bondage of the old sin nature which causes us to do things which are contrary to the will of God. However, with the freedom we have in Christ, we need to surrender our wills to His. He should become our Lord as well as our Savior. When we call someone "Lord," we are saying that this person has authority over us.

If we are under some authority, we need to know what the person or thing who has authority requires. In the military both written and direct oral commands exist. Few parents have written rules. These rules are sometimes arbitrary, sometimes changing, but they are frequently strongly enforced. Governmental authority is asserted through voluminous pages of laws, regulations, legal opinions, and other directions so copious that they are almost impossible to follow, particularly when seemingly mindless bureaucrats administer them. All of us resent some aspects of the authorities above us.

Christians have several ways to learn what our Lord desires of us. The Holy Spirit indwells a believer and guides those who are sensitive to His leadership. The Lord speaks through other believers, pastors, and lay persons of the past and present, as they minister to us. The Lord speaks to gatherings in churches and conventions. All of these, however, are situations in which individuals can misinterpret what our Lord is saying because a subjective response is required of each individual believer.

The only objective record which our Lord has given to us is the Bible. It tells us about our sin, our need for redemption, and the love of our Savior who was incarnated, led a sinless life, and died our perfect substitute to pay the price of our sins. It also shows us what the Lord requires of us in Christian living after we have received Him as Savior and Lord.

Conservatives believe the Bible is completely accurate and true because it came from God. A perfect God is able to communicate perfectly. He does not stutter, misunderstand, or miscommunicate. He is not limited by the fallible human beings through whom He gave His Truth. Therefore, the Bible is "Truth without any mixture of error," as is stated by the Baptist Faith and Message statement the Southern Baptist Convention approved in 1963.

For the liberals, the Bible contains a human element which keeps it from being absolutely perfect in all that it says. Since the views of liberals have a great variance as to how much of the Bible is to be accepted and how much is not, I define a liberal as one who believes the Bible does or could contain errors or make mistakes. (Appendix B contains examples of writings which most Southern Baptists would find unacceptable.) If someone believes that the Bible does contain error, a means must exist for that person to determine what portion of the Scripture is error and what portion is not. Some have quipped that the liberals have a Dalmatian theory about the inspiration of Scripture. According to the quip, liberals believe Scripture is inspired in spots and that they are inspired to spot the spots. I think it is dangerous to attempt to edit God. What objective standard exists for doing the editing if a person believes that only portions of the Bible are inspired?

The question then arises as to what is the basis for belief that certain portions of Scripture are inaccurate. At one time the accuracy of some of the historical sections of Scripture were debated more than they are today. Archaeology has assisted in resolving some of these debates in favor of the accuracy of Scripture. Nowhere has the Bible been proven to be in historical error. Some people would attack Scripture as not being scientifically accurate, but supposed conflicts usually occur when someone claims too much for science or too much for Scripture. Sometimes people have overclaimed for the Bible, contending that it says things that it really does not say. On the other hand, the Bible contains many scientific truths which only in recent years science has come to understand. Splendid books have been written demonstrating the reliability of the Bible. The fulfillment of its prophecy and its tremendous accuracy shows that it is the work of God and not merely of human beings. This book is not written to argue the point.

Where is the source of liberalism? In many cases, I think, it occurs because individuals have never been exposed to a sufficient proclamation of biblical truth. I have never been impressed with the intellectual validity of the attacks on Scripture, although I have been confronted by such at Exeter, Princeton, Union Theological Seminary, and various other places. In my experience, conservative schools generally do a much better job of teaching what is liberal theology than liberal schools do in teaching what is conservative *or* liberal theology.

Telling the simple gospel story glorifies the Savior and not the one telling the story. In the academic world, a need exists to publish something that is new and exciting. A professor usually wants to be known as the "learned doctor." One professor might deviate from biblical truth in order to be respected in academic circles. The next professor must go farther in order to attract further attention. This is another source of liberalism.

In some instances a student has gone to an institution and has been befriended by professors whom the student respected. The professors tell the student how bright he or she is and how the professors are willing to help the student escape the limited background from which he has sprung. In this way some professors create a circle of students who follow them. They will train the students in what the professors believe. Such groups can be used to glorify the professor rather than the Savior and can become another source of liberalism.

One Sunday afternoon when I was in college, I was leaving to preach in a nearby Baptist church for its evening service when Mr. Fullerton, the teacher of our Bible study on campus, stopped me. He looked me in the eye and said, "Paul, when you stand in the pulpit tonight, you can do one of two things. Either you can show those in the congregation that Jesus Christ is wonderful, or you can try to convince them that Paul Pressler is a reasonably intelligent young man. You can't do both." These were wise words which everyone who teaches or preaches should contemplate.

One cannot believe the Bible is true and continue in a lifestyle which is contrary to its teachings. Either the person has to change his or her lifestyle or find some justification for his or her behavior. Frequently such justification comes from changing one's theology and rejecting the truthfulness of God's revelation. In these cases, not believing Scripture is a heart problem and not a head problem.

The more I study the Bible, the greater confidence I have in its complete accuracy and truth. I cannot believe in a perfect God who sees imperfect human beings in need of assistance, intervenes in the events of humanity by sending His Son to be our Savior, and then either does not care enough or does not have enough power to give us an accurate record of His dealings with people. To me the fact that a perfect God exists means that a perfect revelation must exist also.

The conservative movement was not motivated by a desire for power or the promotion of the conservative leaders' personalities. Many people in the liberal movement tried to make that the issue. They did everything they could to divert the issue from that of theology to trying to make conservatives look as bad as possible. Some liberals charged that we were in the conservative movement for personal greed and personal power. In fact, as quoted in the October 4, 1980, issue of the *Dallas Morning News,* one of their leaders, Ken Chafin, then a Houston pastor, said of conservatives, "They are people with different sets of sick egos with different ego needs—one old one that should retire, one with a secular vocation wanting to be in a religious vocation, and one with a second-rate institution wanting to be in a first-rate institution." The fact that the liberals accused us of this caused me to worry about them. I again remember that people often project their own motivations on other people.

I have hoped to belie their attacks against me by getting out of convention activity as quickly as possible. Someone once asked me, "What do you hope to get out of the conservative movement?" I replied, "What I hope to get out of it is to get out of it as quickly as possible." That was a sincere response. However, the attacks by the liberals have not allowed me the luxury of withdrawal. You cannot quit when under attack. The issue was never the personalities of the people involved in the conservative movement. The issue was never power. Power came through the utilization of the democratic processes of the Southern Baptist Convention to allow the position of the majority of Southern Baptists to be expressed and for rank-and-file Southern Baptists to be able to control the institutions which we collectively own as Southern Baptists.

The issue in the convention also was not the autonomy of the local congregation. Baptists are congregational in their belief and practice concerning church government. Each congregation is completely independent and can give its mission money as it wishes. It can belong to any association of churches it wants, so long as that association will admit the church to membership. I believe that in practice, conservatives have been even more congregational, or democratic, than the liberals.

As a Christian, a Baptist, and a believer in the complete authority of the Word of God, I believe that the New Testament teaches that the divinely constituted institution is the local New Testament church. Everything that is constructed above the local New Testament church is extrabiblical (not unbiblical but extrabiblical) and is a device that people use to help carry out the Great Commission. Conventions and denominations are people's institutions, certainly with divine blessing but founded by people. They are extrabiblical organizations which do those things which a local church cannot do as well in isolation. Therefore, these institutions are creations of the local congregations and belong to the local churches.

When the institutions try to dictate to the churches, biblical principle is violated. Those institutions should be under the control of the churches. The churches are not under their control. If the institutions are created by the local churches and are under the control of the local churches, the local churches have a right to decide how these institutions should be run and what should be taught in them. I do not believe in the autonomy of these extrabiblical institutions. These extrabiblical institutions are the servants of the churches which created them. When local churches, through the democratic processes of the convention, exercise control over their institutions, it does not violate the autonomy of the local church or violate Baptist polity. To exercise such control is what Baptist polity expects.

In many ways those supporting the liberals have violated this principle during and before the years of the controversy. One example is through the role of the director of missions (DOM). A director of missions is the leader of a Southern Baptist association, roughly the equivalent of a county organization of Southern Baptist churches. One DOM who is a very strong supporter of the liberal movement told a friend of mine that he could not be the pastor of a church which was a member of his association if he promoted having elders in the church. Through pressure he kept a man from serving as pastor even though the local church had voted to call the man. The DOM is supposed to minister to all the churches in his association. Instead, in this instance, the DOM intervened in a decision that a local church made and tried to limit whom it could call as pastor. This does not promote the autonomy of the local church.

At other times directors of missions have interfered with pulpit committees and attempted to direct who should be called as pastors. I know of some directors of missions who have actually tried to stir up opposition to pastors within those pastors' churches because these pastors were identified with the conservative cause in the convention. To me, that smacks of a hierarchical form of church government. It makes the DOM a petty bishop. This is not the Baptist way. Liberals might mouth platitudes about the autonomy of the local church, but conservatives practice it.

It was a sad day for Southern Baptists when some leading associations started calling their paid leaders "directors of missions" rather than calling them "associational missionaries." The person in this position shouldn't direct—he should serve! Creating "directors" must be the way the first-century local, independent, New Testament churches developed into a hierarchical system later known as the Roman Catholic Church. We must not let history repeat itself here. Directors of missions are to serve the churches, not control them or dictate to them.

Despite what the liberals tried to say, the issue in the convention was not the priesthood of the believer. No individuals could believe more strongly in the priesthood of the believers than do those in the conservative movement. To the conservative, the "priesthood of the believer" means that when a person comes to know the Lord Jesus Christ as personal Savior, the Holy Spirit resides in that person. That believer thus has the right to go to the Word of God and let the Holy Spirit, who wrote it, interpret it to that person. The priesthood of the believer means that a believer can have direct contact with God and does not need to go through any priest, pope, ecclesiastical organization, or anything or anyone else.

Conservative Southern Baptists have always believed and do believe in the absolute priesthood of the believer. However, primary to the priesthood of the believer is the fact that a person must be a believer. That person's priesthood is the privilege and ability to decide issues based on what the Word of God says under the leadership of the Holy Spirit, who wrote it. Priesthood of the believer applies to all born-again believers. A false rendition of the priesthood of the believer is proclaiming that it is the right of anybody to believe anything he or she wants and then teach in a Baptist institution using money that Southern Baptists have provided. People have the right to believe what they want, but they do not have the right to teach it in institutions we as Southern Baptists have created and support.

Sometimes, to the liberals, the doctrine of the priesthood of the believer seems to mean the priesthood of the elite. When some students wanted me to speak at Southeastern Baptist Theological Seminary in Wake Forest, North Carolina, Dr. Randall Lolley, then president, wrote a memo on January 27, 1983. It said in part as follows:

> Southeastern Seminary is an accredited graduate theological school. If Mr. Pressler is invited to speak it should be in the area of his expertise—i.e., the law and courts system. Otherwise, you will be placing him in a position of being an authority quite outside his field and his opinions will be judged accordingly. In short, he is not a theologian or an expert in Biblical studies. Naturally, he has opinions on these matters, but they are scarcely informed by a lifetime and/or career in these disciplines.

Randall's note is not consistent with my understanding of the priesthood of the believer. He seems to be espousing a limited priesthood. I personally believe that any unschooled believer with a vital relationship with the Lord Jesus Christ and a love of His Word is a better priest and promoter of the gospel than is a professor or anyone else who is so educated beyond his intelligence that he rejects the plain statements of God's Word.

A similar instance occurred in the northeast corner of Louisiana on February 26, 1985, in the Green Acres Baptist Church outside Bastrop, where Jim Richards was pastor. Jim asked me to speak to an area meeting, which some three to four hundred persons, many of whom were bivocational pastors, attended. After my presentation, we had a question-and-answer session. Dr. G. Earl Gwinn, former president of Louisiana College (a state Baptist institution), rose and spoke. A verbatim account of what he said follows:

> Those of us who have come through the seminaries in the last fifty years or so have been trained in the historical method of biblical interpretation. Now, it seems to me that what you, as a layman, are advocating, without any background whatsoever in theological education. Why here in Louisiana, if a man starts practicing law without having studied law, he can be called into court. Yet there is no such prohibition against practicing theology.

Dr. Gwinn continued at great length. When he stopped, I replied as follows to the implication of his remarks:

> I think it is very interesting that you think that I do not have the right to speak on theological issues because I haven't been to seminary. Now when I trusted Jesus Christ as my personal Savior, the Holy Spirit of God came into my heart and into my life. I believe in the priesthood of the believer. I believe that a born-again child of God has the right to go to the Word of God, to study the Word of God. I think it is tragic when we have a royal priesthood which allows only seminary graduates to interpret the Word of God. Our most effective soul-winners frequently have been people that the only degree they have is a Born-Again Degree. I am grateful for them. I am grateful that in the Southern Baptist Convention, many of our churches are pastored by people who, although they haven't had the money and privilege of going to seminary, have been able to stand up and proclaim the unsearchable riches of Christ with love and power and with the power of the Holy Spirit so that people are saved under their ministry. I don't believe that a seminary education is a criterion for leading someone to a saving knowledge of Jesus Christ.

To a chorus of "amens" Dr. Gwinn sank into his seat. So much for the liberals' claim that they are the ones who uphold the priesthood of the believer!

Along with the doctrine of the priesthood of the believer is the doctrine of the responsibility of the believer. Believers must be responsible in their conduct. They must be responsible in their doctrine. They are responsible for being loyal to Christ. They are responsible for being faithful in their testimony. A believer should never exercise his priesthood without responsibility. For a local church democratically to decide that it wishes to do a certain thing and then do it is one matter. For an individual teaching in an institution created by the local churches to be unresponsive to these local churches is another.

Teaching irresponsibly is not a valid exercise of the priesthood of the believer. Directing the institutions created by the local churches and owned by the convention is a sacred trust. That trust must be exercised with responsibility. It is not a violation of anyone's priesthood to say that when a person takes Southern Baptists' money, he or she should be responsible to advocate in our institutions that which Southern Baptists believe. It is only logical and reasonable to think that anyone who takes a position of responsibility in one of our institutions must be responsive and faithful to the constituency which he is selected to serve. The real issue in the convention was not the *priesthood* of the believer but the *responsibility* of the believer.

Another issue has been, should Southern Baptists have to fund that which they do not believe? Some people in the convention would say that academic freedom means that a professor has a right to take money from Southern Baptists to teach contrary to what Southern Baptists believe. I do not believe that it is proper for a person to take Southern Baptist money to teach in a Southern Baptist institution and attempt to undermine what Southern Baptists believe. Some liberals, on the basis of academic freedom, would support an absolute right of an employee to do anything and to teach anything regardless of how contradictory it is to the beliefs of those who pay the bills. We oppose this. People who take a position of trust from Southern Baptists must be responsible to their constituency. Such people don't have to take the job, but if they do, they must hold it with responsibility!

The promotion of a conservative political agenda was also not an issue in the convention. Charges have been made that conservatives were in league with the Republican Party. At the time these accusations were being made, I was actually an elected Democrat. I was elected to political office six times as a Democrat and for twenty-five years held office to which I was elected as a Democrat. Subsequent to that, I became a Republican out of conviction. I certainly was not conspiring with or working for the Republican Party, nor was anyone else that I know of in the conservative movement. I am sure I would have known of it, if this had occurred. (Chapter 28, "Southern Baptists and Government," discusses why I believe conservative Christians tend to be conservative politically and economically and why theological liberals tend to be liberal on these issues.)

The issue in the convention was neither an interpretation of Scripture nor an effort to create unity of thinking on theological issues. My friend, Dr. Wallace Henley, pastor of the Encourager Church in Houston and a former president of the Alabama convention, is a man of deep convictions about the things of God. He has a strong desire to win people to a saving knowledge of Jesus Christ. He and I met several times during the early days of the conservative resurgence. The liberals had said that after the conservatives finished with those who held different views of the nature of the Bible, they would begin attacking the charismatics (neo-Pentecostals). They also alleged that conservatives would later attack various other groups until they "purified" every aspect of convention life. They said conservatives wanted to make everybody think just as they do.

Such a charge was ludicrous, but it did worry some people such as my friend, Wally Henley, who had charismatic leanings. I assured him the issue was not the charismatic movement. Although I am not a charismatic, I have referred people with charismatic convictions to his church, which leans charismatic. I assured him that Paige, our friends, and I would not turn on charismatics after the battle over biblical authority was won. He trusted us, and he and others have now seen that this issue will not be a test of fellowship. Charismatic worship and understanding of spiritual gifts is an interpretation of Scripture. That was not our concern. Our concern was the nature of Scripture.

The liberals have tried to make much of the fact that some Calvinists exist within the conservative movement. Calvinism also is an interpretation of Scripture. Although I am not a five-point Calvinist, I am perfectly content with persons who seek to convince others to have Calvinist convictions from the teaching of the Word of God. That is a side issue and not the main issue. Liberals misunderstand conservatives. They think we will divide on this issue. We will not. An interpretation of Scripture is a derivative issue and not a primary one. Interpretation is not a hill on which to die. In fact, the presence of such persuasions as Calvinist and charismatic in the conservative ranks merely shows that conservatives never sought to have all Southern Baptists think exactly alike. All we wanted was for people to base what they believe on an intelligent study of what the Bible says.

Another issue which the liberals have used to sidetrack attention from the real issue is the ordination of women. People have asked me what I believe about the ordination of women, and I have always responded, "I believe that the issue should be decided by what Scripture says and not by anybody's sociological opinions." That answer always made the liberals angry, because even they knew that a careful analysis of Scripture would lead most people to a conclusion that was adverse to their position. I was perfectly honest and forthright in answering the question. My concern was not so much about the result that was to be reached but rather about the way in which the result was reached. People should reach conclusions because they truly believe that the Word of God teaches that something is true.

What was the issue? The issue was Scripture, not an interpretation of Scripture but rather the *nature* of Scripture. Is all Scripture given by inspiration of God, or is Scripture the work of humanity reaching up to conceive the idea of God? If Scripture represents the very words of God, then we are bound by all that Scripture says. If Scripture is the opinion of people who lived many years ago, we should weigh it as other opinions of people are weighed. The nature of Scripture was, is, and forever will be the concern of the conservative movement. The conservative movement will not fracture because we are united on that point.

Conservatives will always stand on the truthfulness of the Word of God because it is absolutely essential to all sound doctrine. The conservative movement will prosper if we are obedient to the Lord, because preaching the Truth of God based on the authority of His Word is biblical, Holy Spirit-blessed, and Christ-directed.

The issue was not an interpretation of Scripture, but the nature of Scripture—the complete, absolute reliability of Scripture: the complete truthfulness of Scripture and—may I dare say—the complete infallibility and inerrancy of Scripture. *Inerrancy* is a word that the liberals do not like because they have not yet been able to redefine it to give it a less than exact meaning. It once was sufficient to say that Scripture was inspired, which meant that it was God-breathed. Some liberals will say the Scripture is inspired like Beethoven was inspired when he wrote his Fifth Symphony, or like Dante was inspired when he wrote his *Divine Comedy*. That never was the meaning of the word *inspired*. Inspired means "God-breathed." As the liberals find new definitions for old terms, we must constantly be finding new terms, the meaning of which is absolutely understood.

Russell Dilday, former president of Southwestern Seminary, has tried to use *inerrancy* in a different way. He has talked about "inerrancy of purpose" rather than "inerrancy of the text." This use of the phrase "inerrancy of purpose" implies that the purpose for which Scripture was written was true, but it does not necessarily mean that the entirety of the text is true. We must watch for redefinitions. The issue was and is the complete, absolute, total accuracy and integrity of the revelation that God has given us in His Book—the Bible. This is the hill on which to die!

CHAPTER 22

*H*OW THE LIBERALS FOUGHT THE BATTLE

When the controversy began, those of us in the conservative movement hoped for a course correction for the Southern Baptist Convention. We expected intelligent dialogue through which the individuals in charge of our institutions would recognize that they had not been fair to conservatives in the way people were hired for faculty and other positions of leadership. We were not prepared for the attacks which were leveled against us. However, the way the liberals attacked us strengthened our conviction that something was dreadfully wrong. People who have nothing to hide do not react in the way in which the convention's liberals reacted. Their attacks did not weaken our resolve. Their methods strengthened it.

An adage for lawyers says, "When the law is on your side, argue the law. When the facts are on your side, argue the facts. When you have neither the law nor the facts, attack the opposing side with all the vehemence you can and blacken their character in such a way that you can win." Many liberal Southern Baptists must have been trained in this legal tactic. Here are some examples.

Using a letter that I wrote, some liberals, whom I believe were associated with Baylor University, attempted to destroy me. They falsely charged that I had used stationery belonging to my court for a letter about convention matters. The letter they cited, however, was written on my own personal stationery, which I had the receipts to prove that I had purchased with personal funds. Court stationery lists all the judges on the court. My stationery had only my name on it. These liberals seized on this letter to attempt to hurt me through the Judicial Qualifications Commission, which supervises the conduct of sitting judges. A group of lawyers wrote letters to the commission. Judge Ed Coulson, who was then a member of this commission and also a justice of the Fourteenth Court of Appeals, showed me the letters that were written. Each one was from somebody who was connected in some way with Baylor. Their letters all contained the same theme. They claimed that I had used court stationery to promote the conservative movement in the convention.

161

The commission's rules require that a private investigation be made of all complaints and that no publicity be given until the commission has finished and issued a report. However, someone violated this rule and reported the complaint to the media. The Houston papers did not cover the story. However, in the *Dallas Morning News*, a newspaper more than two hundred miles away from where I lived, it became a front-page lead story on September 30, 1980. Rarely do newspapers concern themselves with such matters in a faraway judicial district. The headline proclaimed, "Judge's Use of Stationery Called Illegal." An unflattering picture of me also was printed. It is obvious that someone sought a newspaper that would carry the story about the matter during the time these Baylor supporters were complaining about me to the commission.

Maurice Dotson, who was then head of the Judicial Qualifications Commission, investigated the matter. He traveled to Houston to meet with me. I showed him the letterhead that was court stationery and then showed him my private stationery. My private stationery did have my return address at the court. I also showed him the receipt proving that I paid for the stationery personally. We went through everything. I promised him that I had not and would not use court stationery to do anything concerning the Southern Baptist Convention. I have kept that promise. The commission dismissed the matter and took no action. The *Dallas Morning News* never printed the fact that the commission completely exonerated me.

Several years later, a lawyer identified with the liberal side of the SBC went to the Harris County treasurer's office to try to get the records of any telephone calls that I had made and charged to the state. The county treasurer's office turned the person down, since these were private records. Then this individual went to the county attorney's office, which turned the person down for the same reason. The person then went to the state attorney general's office, which likewise refused. All of this probably took a year or so.

The first I knew that someone was seeking these records was when the person later came to the chief justice of my court in a final attempt to obtain them. The chief justice asked me what to do. I told him that I had nothing to hide and gave permission to open my records and let anybody who wanted have access to them. The records showed that in the prior two years, the only period for which records were available, I had charged less than five dollars to the state. This was for four calls to the governor's office and one to another state agency. That was all. On each occasion, the chief justice had asked me to make these calls. The matter turned out to be a dead end for the person inquiring. I'll always wonder who was behind these inquiries.

Later, someone filed another grievance against me with the Judicial Qualifications Commission. The person who was behind it again was someone related to the liberal side of the SBC. The grievance accused me of using court supplies and the court photocopier for conservative convention-related activities. The commission dismissed the charge as groundless. The person then went to the district attorney's office with the charge. I was not even contacted about it because there was no evidence of misuse. I learned of it later from reporters, who obviously had been tipped off about the investigation.

When they came and asked me about the charge, I showed them checks for approximately one hundred dollars a month which I had paid for years into the court's petty cash fund to cover any incidental usage of court supplies that I might have made. The chief justice of our court also made this type of contribution to the petty cash fund for similar reasons. I know of no other judges in the state of Texas who contributed in this manner.

The most hurtful attack of all occurred when I was being considered for a federal appointment in 1989. Chase Untermeyer, whom I had known for some time, was head of the Office of White House Personnel. He called and told me that Frank Nebeker, who had been director of the Office of Government Ethics, was resigning to take another governmental position. Chase asked me if I would consider the appointment. In a couple of days, I called him back and told him I would consider it but could make no commitment.

In evaluating this, I studied the pros and cons. One pro was that this job would provide a way of stepping out of the convention controversy. If I took this position, I could no longer be active in convention activities. I had become a point of attack by the liberals. My withdrawal could diffuse the hostility that had been built up against me. The conservative leadership was in good hands, as others had capably assumed leadership roles, and I felt I could step aside. The position in Washington was also a nonideological one. It was the type of work that I had been doing as a judge. I believed that I could do a good job enforcing ethics without ideological controversy. This would have removed me both from the controversy in the convention and from controversial decisions. I was ready for—and needed—such a rest.

Over the years my family and I have been friends of George Bush, who was then President of the United States. I felt loyalty to him and a desire to serve in his administration. Probably the most significant benefit in my taking the job would have been closer contact with both our daughters, who were then living in the Washington, D.C. area. Both of them were married and were beginning to have children. We knew the move would allow us to spend more time with the grandchildren.

On the other hand, I had great reservations because at the time both of my parents were in their late eighties. They felt that I had not participated sufficiently in family matters because of my work in the Southern Baptist conservative resurgence. My parents were extremely reluctant for me to leave town and not be available to them. A move to Washington would be expensive and dissettling. Also, I looked forward to retirement, and this appointment would involve taking on another very difficult job. Life had been hectic for me, and I wanted to catch my breath, get some rest, and get my own personal matters in order. I also needed to serve in the state judiciary for less than an additional year in order to draw my retirement pay before I was sixty-five. Taking this job in Washington would delay my ability to retire.

These and various other things were weighing on my mind as I considered whether to accept the nomination. Most importantly, I needed to pray it through and really know what God wanted me to do.

I worked on the required government forms and prayed about the matter but did not give a definitive answer. On September 1, 1989, I was in San Francisco, California, with my wife, son, daughter Anne, and her husband, Les Csorba, attending a meeting of the Council for National Policy, a conservative think tank. When we returned from dinner, a call from a reporter awaited me. The reporter said my nomination was in jeopardy because of various personal attacks which were being made against me. He asked me to comment. Knowing nothing, I did not comment. This was the first that I had heard of any opposition. I thought that the liberals in the convention would be glad for me to step aside from convention activity. The attack was completely unanticipated. I checked with Chase the next day, and he said that the appointment was still on and that I had nothing to worry about. I told him I was reluctant to get into a fight on the matter.

Ed Meese, attorney general and chief of staff under President Reagan, was one of the leaders of the Council for National Policy. He and I have both served as president of the group. The next day our family of five and Ed had lunch at the Mark Hopkins Hotel to discuss the pros and cons of continuing to consider the nomination. He told about his experience and the experience of many of his friends in dealing with the Washington press in particular and liberals in general. We discussed the pattern of personal vendetta in which liberals engage to destroy innocent people. Ed said he believed that once the liberals decide that they need to destroy a person, they will continue unmercifully, with no way for the person to recover. At that luncheon, I decided that it just wasn't worth it to accept the nomination, particularly when so many other reasons existed for me not to do so.

Shortly thereafter, I received a call from John Sununu, who was chief of staff at the White House. I had known John when he was governor of New Hampshire. At my invitation, he and I both spoke on the program when a Southern Baptist church was being constituted at Exeter, New Hampshire, where I had attended school.

John's call was to ask me to come to Washington on October 12, 1989, and meet with the chief of staff and the President. This I did. I met John in his office, and we went down the hall to the Oval Office. President Bush and Vice President Dan Quayle had just finished lunch, and the President introduced me to the vice president. The four of us could not have had a more gracious time. The President told the vice president and John about how my father had befriended him when he came to Houston in 1959 and about our family connections.

Then the President turned to me, asked about the position in the Office of Government Ethics, and offered it to me. I told him that I had really considered taking it, but I could not; it was not worth the fight. The President told me that they would do anything I wanted to do about it, but if I didn't take this position, he wanted me to do something else in his administration. I told him I would be glad to serve elsewhere if it wouldn't entail a fight and wouldn't require my moving to Washington. He told me to see Chase Untermeyer about a place I would like to serve.

The President could not have been more generous and helpful. The visit lasted twenty minutes. As we walked from the Oval Office back to the office of the chief of staff, John Sununu remarked that it was extremely rare for someone to spend so much time with the President in what was to have been a formal meeting. I shall ever be grateful for the concern and support that this great man, President Bush, showed me. He was ready and willing to stand by me, but I did not want the conflict, particularly considering the other drawbacks to taking the job. After I refused the appointment, the President issued the following statement:

THE WHITE HOUSE
WASHINGTON
October 12, 1989

Judge Paul Pressler is a man whom I have known and admired for many years. His integrity, outstanding qualifications and exhibition of the highest ethical standards prompted me to again urge him today to accept the nomination as Director of the Office of Governmental Ethics.

Judge Paul Pressler in the Oval Office with (left to right) Chief of Staff John Sununu, President George Bush, and Vice President Dan Quayle on October 12, 1989, when Judge Pressler was asked to become the Director of the Office of Government Ethics

Unfortunately, Judge Pressler informs me that due to professional, religious and family obligations, he is unable to accept a full-time government position at this time. He, therefore, withdrew his candidacy for Director of the Office of Government Ethics. I am disappointed by that decision. However, Judge Pressler assured me that he would be willing to accept another position that would not conflict with his personal obligations.

I am grateful to Judge Pressler for his enthusiastic support and agreement to serve our country.

The following letter from Chase Untermeyer later summarized the situation:

THE WHITE HOUSE
WASHINGTON
17 June 1990
Mr. Edward Dufner
National Editor
Dallas Morning News
Dallas, Texas 75265

Dear Mr. Dufner,

A copy of your letter of 22 May to Mrs. Stuart Blackshear regarding Judge Paul Pressler has been forwarded to me.

At the time Judge Pressler was under consideration for nomination as director of the Office of Government Ethics (OGE), there was a great deal of unkind comment against him entered into his file. While I hesitate to venture into that perilous landscape, it seemed clear to me that all this arose directly from Judge Pressler's involvement in the internal politics of the Southern Baptist Convention. This caused some lower-echelon White House staffers to speculate, unwisely and, as things developed, tragically for Judge Pressler's reputation, to the press that his nomination was in trouble. As things happen in Washington, this speculation fed on itself and soon became "truth."

The facts remain: President Bush on 12 October 1989 offered the directorship of OGE to Judge Paul Pressler, who declined it for professional, religious and family reasons. The President then offered Judge Pressler appointment to his Drug Advisory Committee, a part-time position which he felt he could accept. Given the high ethical standards of the Bush administration and the sensitivity of the drug issue, the President would not have done this if he believed there was any truth to the scurrilous comments against Judge Pressler.

I hope this serves to clarify the record, and I thank you for the opportunity to do so.

Sincerely,
Chase Untermeyer
Assistant to the President and Director of Presidential Personnel

The press referred to it as a "face-saving" meeting. They knew the way they wanted to spin the story and refused to allow the facts to divert them from their purpose. In this instance, as in many others, I will always believe that the press was the willing accomplice of the liberal movement within the SBC.

Lloyd Bentsen, our Democratic senator from Texas at the time, had written and pledged his support if I were nominated. I believe that I would have been confirmed, but it just wasn't worth it. Personally, it was best for me not to take the job except that it provided a way for me to get out of the SBC controversy. I took this development as God saying that I had to finish the job in the convention which He had given me to do. The President appointed me to his Drug Commission. I enjoyed serving there and hope that I made a contribution to that important effort.

I have always been a highly private person who has not wanted attention in the media. My parents have always shunned controversy and publicity. This whole episode was most distasteful to all of us, but this is the way the liberals fought the battle.

Various approaches were made to stop Paige's involvement, too. In 1980 or 1981, Paige received a call from Dr. James Landes, executive director of the Baptist General Convention of Texas, requesting that he meet with Dr. Landes for lunch at the Fairmont Hotel in Dallas. In order that no misunderstanding develop about what occurred, Paige asked Richard Land, then vice president of Criswell College, to accompany him. Dr. Landes brought someone from the Baptist Building.

Pleasant dialogue began the meeting. Dr. Landes then moved to the purpose of his invitation. He indicated that Paige's concerns had been heard but that any further protests would be detrimental to the convention. He suggested that Paige agree to remain silent, in return for which Landes and others would see to it that "something very significant and permanent in the denomination" would come Paige's way. This position, of course, was contingent on Paige's removing himself from participation in the conservative movement.

Without hesitation Paige politely but firmly rejected the offer. When Dr. Landes asked why, Paige simply replied, "Because I fear God more than I fear the denomination." A look of puzzlement crossed the face of Dr. Landes, and the meeting concluded with its failure to divert Paige.

In 1980 Dr. Bill Pinson, president of Golden Gate Seminary, called Dr. Criswell. He said that the six seminary presidents wanted to meet with him privately, without any publicity. They requested a late-night meeting in Dr. Criswell's office, and Dr. Criswell agreed. At the appointed hour, they arrived at the church in two taxis, thinking they were unobserved. However, Richard Land and Lamar Cooper, both faculty members of Criswell College, watched their approach from a strategic vantage point nearby. In the meeting, which lasted about two hours, the seminary presidents, with tears and great emotion, delivered their message: Paige had to be stopped, and Dr. Criswell was the one who could end his participation or fire him. This they demanded that Dr. Criswell do.

In a slow and measured response, Dr. Criswell told the assembled presidents that God told Paige what to do and that he (Dr. Criswell) could not. He then said that if he fired him, Paige would become a martyr, and such a firing would create sympathy and momentum for the conservative cause. He would not give in to their demand. Then, to their great surprise, Dr. Criswell said, "And besides that, I agree with Paige." A defeated and deflated group of seminary presidents returned to their hotel. They knew that great trouble loomed ahead for them.

These cited examples, along with many others, such as death threats made against me and Paige and his children, have left me overwhelmingly disgusted with people whom I originally thought were reasonable, nice individuals with whom I merely differed theologically. Much of the joy of life has departed because I see many people differently. That great "theologian" Abigail Van Buren once said, "You cannot wrestle with a skunk and come out smelling like a rose." The cost of conflict has been great and has left many scars.

A person must be convinced that his or her involvement is a hill on which to die when fierce conflict is waged. Many people do "die."

Many other people suffered far more than I. Some have lost their churches because of the intervention of denominational leaders. Others have had their reputations blackened because they had the temerity to stand against those who had been running the convention. All I can say is, "Praise God. The convention has been returned to its biblical base and those who perpetuated such things have been repudiated." The liberals have now started building their own organizations, and I think they will get out of the Southern Baptist Convention if and when they can obtain the support to do so. Originally I wanted to hold everything together and be conciliatory. Now I believe we should bid them farewell, if that is what they want to do. I have lost my desire to work with those who fought the battle in the manner in which some of them did.

CHAPTER 23

*W*ITHIN THE INNER SANCTUM

Although conservatives had been dominant on the Committee on Nominations (then the Committee on Boards) for several years, I had never seriously considered serving on any of the SBC's boards, agencies, or commissions. However, in 1984, the Texas members of the committee approached me and asked me to pray about whether I should serve. I was reluctant to be nominated because I knew that nominees had been rejected in Los Angeles in 1981 and in New Orleans in 1982. In 1983 no challenges had occurred, so none of the nominees was rejected. Strong objections to my nomination would surface, but the question basically was whether I could be more effective working within the system or outside of it.

After much prayer and consultation with friends, I felt that I could do more within the system. I let the committee members know that I desired to build and support our denomination and not merely to appear to criticize from outside the system. From my viewpoint, my election to the Executive Committee would be a strengthening and unifying force showing how we could work together. Based on this belief, I decided to allow my name to be placed in nomination at the Kansas City SBC meeting in June 1984. Weldon Gaddy, a member of the "Gatlinburg Gang," had resigned as pastor of Broadway Baptist Church in Fort Worth to join Mercer University in Georgia. He had served one year of his second term on the Executive Committee. I would be nominated for the three remaining years of his term.

At the March meeting of the Committee on Boards in Nashville, the two Texas members—Paul Martin, a Houston attorney, and Gordon Graham, then the pastor of First Baptist Church in New Braunfels, Texas—nominated me. The whole committee approved the nomination, but after that, a great reaction occurred. Although nominations were supposed to be kept secret and the results of the committee's meeting was to be confidential for a month or so, the fact that I had been nominated was immediately the talk of the SBC Building in Nashville and, within a few hours, seemed to be known across the convention. I had hoped it would be taken as a conciliatory move of my desire to work within the system, but it was not seen that way. Rather, I was viewed as an outsider seeking to break into the system.

This concerned me and raised several questions. Why did the system seek to exclude those who had questions about the way things were going? Did this mean that the system was so tightly controlled that no room existed for anyone who was not part of the controlling group? Did this mean that, within the system, things were going on that must be kept from other Southern Baptists? Did it mean that the people in control believed that the Southern Baptist Convention was their exclusive province? Did it mean that the bureaucracy was unwilling to be open to conservatives and to unify the convention by allowing broader participation on our boards and in our agencies? These questions bothered me and at the same time strengthened my resolve to serve. They settled any doubts that I might have had about whether my nomination was the proper course to take.

Several weeks before the 1984 meeting, Dr. Winfred Moore, pastor of the First Baptist Church of Amarillo, Texas, announced that he would nominate Dr. Bruce McIver, pastor of Wilshire Baptist Church in Dallas, as a candidate for the Executive Committee, in opposition to my nomination by the Committee on Boards. At that point I had not met Dr. Moore and was surprised that neither he nor any of the others who opposed me made any effort to get to know me and know how or why I would be willing to serve on the Executive Committee. The only person on the liberal side who did call me to express reservations about my nomination was Dr. Russell Dilday, president of Southwestern Seminary. (This was five years after the incident I described earlier in which he and his wife made remarks to me and a friend as we were carrying turkeys to the skyboxes.) As I mentioned, Russell and I had been casual friends for some years while he was pastor of Tallowood Baptist Church in Houston. I lived in the area of town close to that church.

When Russell called, he said that he had heard rumors that I was going to be nominated for the Executive Committee and wanted to know if it was true. I told him that it was. He said that this upset him because the Executive Committee was the group that set his seminary budget and that serving on it placed a person in a very powerful position. Since I was an outsider, he did not think that it was appropriate for me to serve there. He said that friends of his were very angry about my proposed nomination. I told him that I hoped that these friends would talk to me, get to know me, know my intent in serving and could, through personal communication, see that my desire was not to disrupt but rather to try to work together. He said that he would talk to them. I never heard from any of these persons to whom he alluded. I still wonder whose sentiments he was voicing—his or someone else's.

The choice of Bruce McIver was questionable in several ways. At that time, he was serving on the Committee on Order of Business. He was rotating off in 1984. A question arose about whether a person should be allowed to rotate off one board and the same day be elected to another committee or agency of the Southern Baptist Convention. Also, Bruce's wife was then serving on the Home Mission Board (now merged into the North American Mission Board). Under liberal domination of the SBC, it was not unusual for liberal husbands and wives to serve simultaneously on different boards.

Milton Cunningham, pastor of Westbury Baptist Church in Houston, an active moderate, was then serving on the Southeastern Seminary trustee board, and his wife was serving as a trustee on the Foreign (now International) Mission Board. In 1981, moderate Bill Self of Wieuca Road Baptist Church in Atlanta was serving as a trustee on the Foreign Mission Board and his wife was serving as a trustee on the Golden Gate Seminary board.

Most Southern Baptists would think that this amounted to an undue concentration of power in certain families who had been absolutely loyal to the liberal system and the "good ol' boy" network. During the press discussion of the contested nomination, Baptist Press never reported the board memberships of Bruce McIver and his wife, although conservatives mentioned this fact to Baptist Press on numerous occasions. I often wonder how these matters would have been treated had the "double dippers" been conservatives.

The 1984 SBC meeting in Kansas City was one of the most difficult times of my life. The details of my son's illness at that particular time appear in chapter 13. Under this very difficult cloud, events began to unfold when the report of the Committee on Boards was presented. Winfred Moore did, in fact, nominate Bruce McIver. Bailey Smith, former SBC president, eloquently defended me. He quoted my pastor, Dr. John Bisagno, as to the fact that I was a soul winner, Sunday School teacher, deacon, and active participant in First Baptist Church of Houston. During a floor debate, Fred Wiesen, pastor of North Oaks Baptist Church in Houston, asked whether the Bruce McIver who was nominated for this position was the same one who was then serving on the Committee on Order of Business and whose wife was then serving on the Home Mission Board. The question was answered in the affirmative. In this way the information bypassed Baptist Press and was presented to the convention messengers without personal attacks being made on Bruce. Bailey Smith's speech and Fred Wiesen's question greatly helped my nomination.

Convention president Jimmy Draper asked for a show of hands on the question. It looked as if my nomination had been affirmed. However, in order that no one might ever question his impartiality and doubt the validity of the vote, the president properly asked for a ballot vote. While the ballots were being counted, Louis Moore, then religion editor of the *Houston Chronicle,* approached me and asked certain questions, assuming that I would be serving on the Executive Committee. I told him that I really didn't want to answer the questions because the vote had not been tabulated. He said that based on the show of hands during the voting, he and others in the press room believed that I had been elected.

A little while later, the tellers committee reported that the vote tabulation showed that I had received 5,462 votes and Bruce McIver had received 4,666 votes. I won by a margin of 53.93 percent to 46.07 percent. This showed how far the conservative movement had progressed. Less controversial nominations had been rejected in prior SBC meetings.

The first meeting of the new Executive Committee occurred on the Wednesday afternoon of the convention. Of course, I attended. Most members received me in an extremely chilly manner, not with the friendship for which I had hoped. Rather, most greeted me as an outsider who was forcing himself into the inner sanctum of those who knew what was best for all and who would run the Executive Committee accordingly. I felt it was obvious that my purpose for serving on the Executive Committee would not be fulfilled in the near future. As soon as the Executive Committee meeting was over, I immediately went to the airport and flew to Houston to join my family at the bedside of my son in Texas Children's Hospital. Eventually my son began to improve. Long hours at his bedside brought time for reflection and introspection considering "the ways of God to man," as Milton wrote in *Paradise Lost.*

My second Executive Committee meeting occurred in the fall of 1984 in Nashville. The Executive Committee conducts four full meetings each year. Two are at the time of the SBC annual meeting. The Monday meeting is comprised of the old Executive Committee, and the Wednesday meeting includes the newly elected members. In September and February the meetings are conducted in Nashville. Additionally, a meeting of the budget subcommittee is held in January in order to provide time for the extensive hearings required to prepare the budget.

In September, Nancy and I went to Nashville for the Fall meeting. I hoped that the cool reception which greeted my arrival at the first meeting would have somewhat dissipated. I resolved to sit quietly and to say very little until I experienced a growing atmosphere of acceptance. However, events surrounding that meeting did not allow me to fulfill my intent. The matter which caused my first controversy on the Executive Committee is reported in this book's Chapter 26 on Baptist Press.

The Executive Committee met at the SBC annual meeting in Dallas in 1985. Dewey Presley, a Dallas layman who was a firm supporter of the liberal cause, had finished his two terms as committee chairman. At that meeting, David Maddox, a layman from California, was elected as his replacement.

David had a very different style from Dewey's. He sought to reach out to everyone and brought an entirely different atmosphere to the Executive Committee. David is as thoroughly kind a Christian gentleman as I have ever known. If he had been chairman of the Executive Committee when I was first elected, things might have been quite different. The resentments engendered from the previous leadership probably would not have developed. Although David's friends were basically those on the liberal side of the controversy, he had an attitude of including everyone. This brought some peace to the Executive Committee during the year of 1985.

However, a basic problem still existed. All of the matters to be dealt with were carefully worked out before we arrived. I learned that the six officers were meeting with staff to review the recommendations only on the Sunday night before the Executive Committee began on Monday. The staff had prepared all of the material, and the officers met only for a couple of hours over dinner to review it. Since everything was already printed, this meant that no meaningful input could occur from the officers before the material went to the full committee. Everything was presented as a recommendation of the officers. It appeared to me that it was merely a recommendation from the staff and then, to give credibility, said to be a recommendation from the officers.

It appeared to me that the Executive Committee was tightly controlled by a small group who worked out what action should be taken on all matters presented to it. Only in rare instances did the membership speak up sufficiently to cause a different result. This situation was not unique to the Executive Committee. It was similar on other SBC boards as well. The system rewarded those people who did not make waves. Individuals who were safe team players were put in crucial positions where they would not fight against those in the bureaucracy. Thus, even membership on a board was not of great consequence in determining the direction of policy for most of the one thousand people who served on the boards of an SBC agency or commission. The bureaucracy was in charge, along with a few very supportive members.

Realizing this helped me to understand how the system really worked. A convention of fifteen million people had been managed and controlled, not by its membership or even by one thousand trustees, but by a very small handful of paid employees combined with a few elected officers of the various boards and commissions.

Some people have wondered why conservatives took such a long time to make changes in the Southern Baptist Convention. A number of reasons exist: (1) Conservatives wanted to move slowly so they would not disrupt the system. (2) The source of real power in the convention was distributed among so few people that penetrating the inner sanctum of those in control was most difficult. (3) Not only did conservatives have to obtain a voting majority on a board, but they also had to elect officers of that board who would make crucial appointments and promote people who would not be under the control of the bureaucracy. (4) Real change occurred only when the heads of agencies left and people sympathetic to the conservative movement replaced them. (5) The policies of the new agency head could not be implemented fully until the new head had had the opportunity to hire key staff who would work for him and not against him.

David Maddox did several things that made conservatives feel more comfortable. He appointed a couple of conservatives, myself included, to the committee studying the Baptist Joint Committee on Public Affairs. I discuss this committee in more detail in chapter 28. He also talked to conservatives about our feelings and generally tried to create an atmosphere on the Executive Committee that was conducive to peace and understanding.

However, one event did occur during Maddox's chairmanship that caused much disharmony and set the stage for conservative dominance after he was no longer chairman. W. C. Fields announced his retirement as head of Baptist Press. This occurred either because the power structure believed that conservatives were soon to become a majority on the Executive Committee and wanted W. C. to retire early so they could replace him with someone sympathetic and helpful to their cause, or it could have been merely W. C.'s personal desire to retire a year or so early with no ulterior motive. A parallel situation occurred later when Christian Life Commission director Foy Valentine sought early retirement, citing heart problems. This too caused suspicion because it occurred while a slim majority of liberals still existed on the Christian Life Commission trustee board. Whatever the reason, W. C. Fields resigned just before conservatives would have been so dominant on the Executive Committee that they could have picked their own choice as his successor.

Earlier, a person had been hired for a more minor staff position on the Executive Committee. The general membership of the Executive Committee received no information on this candidate before the meeting at which we were to approve the selection. Many of us were very concerned about this, since we were asked to approve someone without our having sufficient information. At that time, several of us told Executive Committee President/Treasurer Harold Bennett that this was unacceptable and that we wanted to be involved earlier in all such decisions. He told us that in the future, he would work with us and provide us with full information about any sensitive appointments.

Later, a vacancy occurred in the position of feature editor for Baptist Press. The general membership of the Executive Committee had no input whatsoever in that appointment until it was announced. The Executive Committee bylaws then in effect stated that the president/treasurer would make nominations and that the Executive Committee could act only on the nominations made by him. For this vacancy, Marv Knox had been selected, reviewed by a small committee, and the Executive Committee as a whole was allowed to ask very few questions. It was obvious from reading his writings as associate editor of the Louisiana state paper that grave questions existed which needed to be investigated. Many of the articles which he had written were coauthored with Lynn Clayton, the paper's editor, who at that point was clearly in the liberals' corner. A need existed to find out how Marv would actually perform and whether he could be fair to both sides in the convention controversy.

Complicating the situation was our previous statement to Harold that we would not again rubber-stamp one of his appointments without first having the chance to screen the candidate. We were told it would be very embarrassing if we did not approve Marv since he had already been proposed. It would be personally damaging to him and other candidates who might have already quit their previous jobs, anticipating approval of the Executive Committee. Nevertheless, I was allowed to meet with Marv Knox in Harold Bennett's office, but only after the proposed appointment had been made public. We were to meet for about an hour.

The first forty-five minutes were taken up with the others present giving many plaudits to Marv and making statements about his qualifications. It appeared to me that he was being completely protected from my questioning. Finally, I said, "Well, I guess this is the first of two meetings, because I asked for a meeting so that I could ask him some questions. I suppose we're going to reconvene at a later time so I can ask the questions that this meeting was set up to have answered." Harold then quickly allowed me to start asking questions.

I based my questions on some of the things that Marv had written. I was not satisfied with the answers or with his position as reflected in his work with the Louisiana *Baptist Message*, but I felt that nothing could be done at this stage. I was confronted with a completed action. I could only plead with Marv to be fair. However, his subsequent writings did not show any understanding of the true motivations of the conservative movement. (He is now editor of the *Baptist Standard* in Texas. In my opinion, his track record for the past decade has been clearly that of a moderate in step with the Cooperative Baptist Fellowship.)

With the retirement of W. C. Fields, various conservative members of the Executive Committee tried to give input. Almost half of the committee wrote Harold requesting that David Simpson, editor of the *Indiana Baptist,* be nominated. Harold and his staff never allowed conservatives to have any meaningful participation in the selection process. Any time we asked how the selection process was going, we were told, "We're working on it," and nothing was revealed to us. Any suggestions that we made were taken under advisement, and no comment was made one way or the other.

About a week before the recommended successor to W. C. was to be announced, word surfaced that Harold planned to nominate Al Shackleford, editor of *The Baptist and Reflector,* the Baptist state newspaper in Tennessee. I called Harold and expressed my extreme displeasure. Harold said that this was what he had decided. He said he thought the Lord had led him in that direction, and he was going to the Executive Committee with that recommendation. It was a done deal as far as Harold was concerned. Numerous protests came from other members of the Executive Committee. Harold paid no attention to the emerging conservative majority on his board of trustees. This lack of attentiveness and failure of openness divided the Executive Committee further. It became a wedge that was permanently driven by Harold between himself and many members of the Executive Committee. It would affect the remainder of his tenure.

Harold Bennett is a person who loves the Lord Jesus Christ, and I respect him as my brother in Christ. His intentions were good, but he was well-schooled in the methods of bureaucratic control which had been so dominant in the SBC. It seemed to me that Harold had been trained to dominate and control his board. He operated as one of the old order which now, thankfully, has passed away. Nothing herein is to be taken as a criticism of Harold personally. He merely acted as he was taught a Southern Baptist executive or bureaucrat should act.

With real anguish conservatives arrived in Nashville for the February 1987 Executive Committee meeting. We felt that we had been excluded from the selection process of the Baptist Press director and that our desires and concerns were not considered at all. We felt that although we were almost a majority on the Executive Committee, we had no chance for meaningful participation in the selection of the person for this highly important position.

For the first time to my knowledge, conservatives met as a group before an Executive Committee meeting. We met in the hotel room of one of the members. We did not anticipate the fact that more than twenty would attend. The vehement opposition to the nomination of Shackleford by so many members who previously had not expressed themselves was a real surprise to many of us. The Executive Committee was being polarized. Conservatives, who had been willing to go along because of David Maddox's leadership, decided that they had to get involved. We were not willing for Harold to dictate to us who W. C.'s successor would be.

We suspected that Harold had worked very closely in this selection with state paper editors and with Frank Ingraham, a lawyer from Nashville and Executive Committee member from Tennessee. Harold seemed more responsive to these editors than to his own board. In the meeting in the hotel room, we decided that we would definitely vote against the nomination. We knew of some who would agree to table the nomination and postpone it but would not directly vote against the nominee. Some would vote with us on a secret ballot, not wanting to vote against the nominee in a show of hands and thus risk the wrath of the members who controlled the Executive Committee. Therefore, a strategy was developed at the meeting. The fact that we had met was vehemently attacked as an improper conservative caucus. When Harold or liberal groups held secret meetings, it was considered a function of the Executive Committee. When we met, it was characterized as a sinister event.

Frank Ingraham was called on to lead the devotional for the Executive Committee. It turned out to be a campaign speech for Al Shackleford. Many members of the Executive Committee did not receive this well, and, from my viewpoint, this caused Frank later not to be elected chairman and to lose his influence with many members.

When the nomination was presented the next day, a motion was made to table it. The parliamentary maneuvering at the Executive Committee had long been handled for the liberals by John Sullivan, a member from Louisiana and then pastor of Broadmoor Baptist Church in Shreveport. Later John became executive director of the Florida Baptist Convention. Conservatives thought we had the votes to table the nomination and would probably win 30 to 29. However, Darrell Robinson, a member from Alabama, was called back to Mobile for a matter in his church and did not return in time to vote on the Shackleford appointment. The establishment pulled out all the stops. Al, his wife, and family members were introduced to the Executive Committee. Various members talked about what a wonderful family person he was. The vote on the motion to table was by secret ballot. Martha Gaddis, Harold's secretary, and Tim Hedquist, one of Harold's vice presidents, counted the votes. They counted and recounted. The vote was a tie, 29 to 29.

Many of us thought that because of the tie vote, Harold would not proceed with the nomination. David Maddox, as chairman, had voted in the initial balloting. Presumably he voted not to table the nomination, since he participated in the recommendation. If the chair had abstained from voting, as was customary, the motion to table would have carried. Surprisingly Harold immediately got up and moved for the acceptance of Al Shackleford's nomination. I had with me copies of many editorials and articles that Al, as editor of the *Baptist and Reflector,* had written. Many other conservatives and I deemed these writings absolutely unacceptable. I pulled these from my briefcase and prayed about whether or not to introduce them, which would be tantamount to a frontal attack on Al. Although I was prepared to make the speech, I felt that the Lord was telling me not to do it. It was clear now that Al would be elected. I did not make my speech. The final vote was 32 in favor of hiring him and 26 against. Three members who had voted to table voted to approve the nomination.

Al was asked whether he would accept. He asked for time to pray about the matter overnight. Immediately Julian Pentecost and other notable liberals who were state editors surrounded Al. They stated regret that he had been opposed and asked him to accept. Their immediate outpouring of support indicated to many of us their involvement in the process of selecting him. We felt that Frank Ingraham, with nonmembers of the Executive Committee, had engineered his election. Next morning, as anticipated, Al Shackleford delivered a well-prepared speech, accepting the position and asking for a year's grace to prove himself. The liberals had been successful in putting in place a new head of Baptist Press on whom they thought they could depend. As later events showed, their victory occurred at an extremely high price.

The battle over Al Shackleford furthered the developing cohesion of the conservatives on the board. It also developed a militancy on the part of many who had earlier been less involved. We strengthened the coordination of our activities, and many of us began talking among ourselves as to whom we would like to have elected as the new chairman of the Executive Committee. A profile was developed of the person who would be desirable so we could support certain leadership characteristics and not just an individual with personal charisma. It was first decided that we should elect someone who had been actively engaged in the effort to defeat Al Shackleford. This was because we knew that such a person could be counted on to take a stand and to include conservatives in the group which was actually running the Executive Committee.

A consensus developed for Charles W. Sullivan, pastor of First Baptist Church of Lenoir City, Tennessee (now executive director of the Indiana Baptist convention). Charles had made a speech against Al Shackleford, although he was a member of the Executive Committee from Al's state of Tennessee. He had shown real courage. While on the Executive Committee, he had always conducted himself as a gracious gentleman. The conservatives, therefore, decided that he would make an excellent chairman.

The liberals were very active in their efforts to elect the chairman. Frank Lady, a conservative member of the Executive Committee, had gone to school with Frank Ingraham. Frank Lady approached me about supporting Frank Ingraham as chairman. It was obvious that Frank Ingraham was the one whom the liberals had been grooming to take over from David Maddox. Frank is basically a conservative person and joined the Executive Committee as a conservative. However, his father had been with the Sunday School Board (now LifeWay Christian Resources), and he had strong ties to the bureaucracy. This alone had created some reservations in the minds of many of us. When he led the fight for Al Shackleford, that ended any support which he might have received from conservatives and cost him the chairmanship.

The election of the new chairman of the Executive Committee occurs on the Wednesday of the SBC annual meeting, right after the new members of the Executive Committee have been elected. When the report of the Committee on Boards revealed the new Executive Committee nominees, it was evident that conservative strength would be enhanced and that we would have a much better chance of electing the chairman than we did of defeating Al Shackleford. When Frank Lady suggested to me that Frank Ingraham would be a good chairman, I responded very strongly, outlining what Frank Ingraham had done in the Shackleford matter. Evidently, others reacted as I had when Frank Lady questioned them about this proposed candidacy. Frank Ingraham was never nominated.

After the trial balloon for Frank Ingraham had been punctured, the liberals decided to support Darrell Robinson. They thought he was electable since they anticipated he would get some conservative support. Darrell, pastor of Dauphin Way Baptist Church in Mobile, Alabama, was a Bible-believing, conservative preacher who was well-liked by everyone. However, he had left the Executive Committee meeting before the vote on Al Shackleford and did not return. Regardless of the validity of his reason, most conservatives believed that we needed someone who had been involved in the fight and whose election would signal that we would no longer put up with appointments being rammed through the Executive Committee without consulting all the members.

In June 1987 the liberals appeared very confident of electing Darrell, but I knew the oncoming members of the Executive Committee better than they. I knew of enough conservative votes to elect Charles W. Sullivan. However, it would be a close election. I was worried when Doyle Collins, an outstanding conservative pastor and former president of the Northwest Baptist Convention, was unable to attend the meeting. I still believed we had a margin of two votes. Immediately before the vote on Wednesday afternoon in Atlanta, I looked around and saw that Adrian Rogers was not present. Being president of the convention, he was a voting member of the Executive Committee. My wife agreed to try to locate him. She came back with word that he was autographing books in the bookstore and said he would come to the meeting as soon as possible. Much to my dismay, he did not arrive until after the vote had been taken. Charles W. Sullivan was elected by a vote of 30 to 29 over Darrell Robinson. We had lost two votes we had counted on but still won.

When the results were announced, I watched Harold Bennett's face become ashen. This was a defeat the liberals had not expected. It was one caused by the tactics they had used in the election of Al Shackleford. Darrell Robinson was not the liberals' first choice. He was an outstanding person who would ordinarily have been acceptable to everyone and would have worked with all. Charles Sullivan was clearly the one whom the liberals opposed. In the other two contests for Executive Committee officers, conservatives also won. Charles Sullivan did such a good job as chairman that conservative leadership was assured for the future. A shift in power from the close-knit control group to the new conservative majority had taken place.

During the next several years, numerous examples of what conservatives considered to be poor reporting and discrimination against them in Baptist Press were brought to the attention of Al Shackleford and his assistant, Dan Martin. These problems were not rectified.

The chairmanship of Charles Sullivan was characterized by excellent, gracious leadership, goodwill, and cooperation with few divisive issues. We had both a conservative chairman and a conservative majority. Therefore, real harmony was developing on the Executive Committee. Our intent was basically to accept the status quo and make no major structural changes for several years, since they would have generated suspicion by those on the other side.

When Charles Sullivan's second year as chairman ended in June 1989, Sam Pace was elevated from vice chairman to chairman. James Jones of Kentucky was nominated against him. Sam, the director of missions of the Comanche Cotton Association, which included Lawton, Oklahoma, was a man short in stature but tall in ability and in his walk with God. Sam had been president of the Oklahoma Baptist convention. He also was a most intelligent and gracious chairman and was determined that the Executive Committee would represent all Southern Baptists. He and Charles W. Sullivan both sought to include those who had been voting on the other side in key appointments. Both of their chairmanships created a spirit of working together for the entire Executive Committee.

When Sam was elected chairman, I was elected vice chairman. James Jones was nominated against me. It was obvious to me that Kenny Mahanes of Ohio and Frank Lady of Arkansas, both doctrinal conservatives, were leading the opposition to the new majority on the Executive Committee. Many people believe that the reason that James was asked to run against Sam for chairman was in order to create a sympathy vote for James after he had been defeated for chairman and hence to help him defeat me for vice chairman. James, a former president of the Kentucky Baptist Convention, is also a conservative and a gracious man. By a vote of 43 to 26, I was elected. Some people believed that the remaining liberals on the Executive Committee were using James, Frank, and Kenny, rather than their being in sympathy with the liberal agenda.

I agreed to be nominated for vice chairman because, as an officer, I would be in the inner group. From the inside I could help open up the procedures with which the Executive Committee operated. I insisted that we conduct the officers' meeting at least three weeks in advance of the Executive Committee meetings so that we could go over the entire agenda at great length and in detail. We would then meet again the Sunday night before the Executive Committee started on Monday to review everything and make sure all recommendations were exactly as we had decided.

This would also allow us to see what the issues were going to be, to talk to other members of the Executive Committee by telephone, and to develop a consensus among the Executive Committee membership rather than having members merely presented with a decision that had been made by the staff, said to be recommended by the officers, and intended to be rubber-stamped by the members of the Executive Committee. This would allow us to move from a staff-run to a member-run Executive Committee. It effectively opened up the Executive Committee process.

This did not always work. When we arrived in September 1990 for the officers' meeting three weeks in advance of the Executive Committee meeting, Harold told us that the recommendations had already gone to press and were being printed at the Sunday School Board. We immediately recessed the meeting so he could call and stop the printing. We did not want to have the extra expense of having to reprint matters that were not approved, and we wanted to tell Harold that nothing should be finally printed until the officers approved the matter. On several of the matters on which decisions had already gone to press, the officers differed with solutions that Harold had already had typed and was having printed in bulk.

One of the lengthy items Harold was having printed was a recommendation to have a new program assignment for the Christian Life Commission. It spelled out in great detail a religious liberty assignment. The Christian Life Commission had not sought this. Since we had just debated that matter at the June 1990 SBC meeting, it was something that we did not wish to open up again. However, Harold personally wanted it. The officers turned him down. Later the Christian Life Commission received a new program assignment, but only after careful, deliberate thought by the officers and Executive Committee members, along with the trustees of the Christian Life Commission. Today, the name of the Christian Life Commission is the Ethics and Religious Liberty Commission.

The officers developed a bylaw amendment to allow the Executive Committee officers, working as a committee, to hire a new staff member on an interim basis only after the full membership of the Executive Committee had, by a two-thirds vote, declared an emergency and authorized the officers to do so. The officers worked out a carefully worded bylaw which they instructed Harold to include in the recommendations going to the Executive Committee. When we met on the Sunday night before the Executive Committee meeting in September and reviewed the prepared recommendations, we discovered that Harold had omitted one of the crucial portions of the bylaw that all six officers had decided on. Unilaterally he had changed one of the key provisions. The stricken provision provided that during this interim period, recommendations could be taken not only from the present president/treasurer (which he was), but also from any member of the Executive Committee or any other Southern Baptist.

The officers expressed their extreme displeasure with Harold's unilateral editing out of this provision without advising us what he had done. We had decided on the form in which it was to be presented, and he had changed it without notice. Harold's excuse was that it appeared to be in conflict with another portion of the bylaws of the Executive Committee. That was not correct. It was not an amendment to the regular process of selecting staff but was merely a procedure which spelled out provisions for handling a matter during an emergency. He had not even called a single officer before he made that change. It was discovered only when I proofread what had already been printed. This event did a great deal to harm the trust level between Harold and the officers.

At the same Sunday night officers' meeting, Harold proposed several people to be interviewed for staff positions. One of them, Richard P. (Bucky) Rosenbaum, appeared to be imminently qualified both spiritually and professionally for the position of vice president for financial affairs. He seemed to be agreeable to all of the officers. However, we wished to check him out and to bring other members of the Executive Committee into the process. We also were unwilling to allow this recommendation to be approved without moving ahead on filling the positions of vice president of Baptist Press and vice president for public relations. (Al Shackleford had now been fired. More about this situation appears in the next chapter. W. C. Fields's previous position had been split into the two vice presidential positions.) If we approved a vice president for finance, we would have lost some of our leverage. Other staff members were very pressed to do that work. They would no longer feel the urgency of hiring new staff for other positions if they had been relieved of the work which would be assigned to Bucky.

The position of vice president for public relations was most essential. While we flew to Nashville, my wife asked me who I thought would be the best candidate for that position. I told Nancy that I thought that Dr. Mark T. Coppenger, the executive director of the Indiana Baptist convention, would be by far the best candidate. Nancy was the only one to whom I expressed myself.

At lunch during a break from the Executive Committee meetings, I was eating with Charles Sullivan, Sam Pace, and Guy Sanders, a member from Florida. We were discussing new personnel, and Sam Pace volunteered that he thought that Mark Coppenger would make a great vice president for public relations. Charles Sullivan said, "Well, you know, I'm so glad you said that, because he's exactly the one on my mind." I listened to them talk for a little while and then expressed my great pleasure at what they had said. Mark could bring to this position brilliance and spiritual discernment. He had an earned doctorate from Vanderbilt University and was clearly qualified in every way to lead in this important aspect of convention life.

When we later met in Dallas to interview additional applicants, it was clear that Mark was the one. Although he was extremely reluctant even to consider the position, we were elated that he was selected. After a weekend of prayer, he agreed to accept. We believed that having a vice president for public relations who could communicate by newsletter or computer directly with churches to provide them with accurate information on what was happening in the convention would be highly beneficial. By separating the positions of public relations and Baptist Press, we would have on one hand a person who would promote the SBC and on the other, someone who would disseminate news factually and impartially. Mark served in an outstanding manner and is now president of Midwestern Baptist Seminary, where he is leading the school to greatness. The true story of Southern Baptists needed to be communicated not only to our own constituency but also to the public at large. Mark did this.

Another example of how the bureaucracy in the Executive Committee dealt with matters concerned the Religion in American Life (RIAL) appropriation in the committee's budget. For several years, this had been a line item for at least $10,000. Each time someone on the committee asked about it, we received vague answers. In September of 1988, Executive Committee member Kenneth Barnett began asking perceptive questions about this appropriation. Harold Bennett indicated that he did not know much about the group but said it was "a group of Christians who put up notices in hotels and promoted church attendance." The group's exact form and structure seemed very nebulous.

Kenneth, a pastor from Colorado, is an intelligent and tenacious person and a good friend. I admire his dedication to detail and to researching information. Not being satisfied with the vague answers he received, he went to the office of Ernest Mosley, Harold's executive vice president, and asked him questions. At first, Ernest seemed very reluctant to give answers. Kenneth then announced that he would sit in Ernest's office day and night until he received the answers. Ernest, knowing the threat was real, then turned over to Kenneth the file on RIAL. The file revealed that Harold was a member of the executive committee of RIAL and was its treasurer. He was very much involved in its activities. Not only were Christian groups in RIAL, but Unitarians, Moslem, and Jewish groups were also involved. In the file was a discussion about how to pray not using the name of Christ so that the persons praying would not offend Moslems and Jews. Once Kenneth had the information, the appropriation for RIAL was doomed. No more discussion occurred.

I now understand how a bureaucracy perpetuates itself and guards itself from the trustees who are elected to see that its administration conforms to what the constituency wishes. Turning the convention around was not merely a matter of electing a majority of trustees on a board. It also involved electing trustees who would not only stand firmly but would also have the tenacity to dig into the records to find pertinent information and not compromise even when doing so makes one extremely unpopular.

One of the things I worked on most diligently while I was on the Executive Committee was a revision of the bylaws. This revision was adopted at my last full board meeting in February 1991. The rewritten bylaws provided for the officers' committee and its meeting being held sufficiently in advance of the Executive Committee session so that the recommendations made to the full committee could be the recommendations of the officers and not just a rubber stamp of the staff recommendations. The practice which we had developed was now incorporated into the bylaws.

The new bylaws also established a legal committee which would check the amount of legal fees paid to all lawyers. None of us on the Executive Committee ever knew how much was being paid to our legal counsel, and nobody was ever given these bills for review. The legal committee also could check out opinions the legal counsel issued and could provide a tremendous amount of legal assistance free of charge. An incident brought this need into focus. Harold wanted the Executive Committee to review a particular matter. I was on the subcommittee to which it was referred. The committee's legal counsel issued a report on the matter, and it was strongly slanted toward the position Harold wanted.

After the counsel's presentation, I spoke. I told him that in my experience basically two types of legal briefs were submitted to me. One was an advocacy brief, which gave all the reasons why I as judge should take a certain position. The other was an analytical brief, which gave all sides of a matter and allowed me to make my own decision after receiving all the information. I then asked the attorney if he had presented to us an advocacy brief or an analytical brief. He knew that it was necessary for him to have presented an analytical brief and answered that he had done such. I then asked him why, if it were an analytical brief, he had not included certain additional factors. After I had mentioned several omitted items, he sank red-faced into his seat.

It seemed that in the workings of Southern Baptists under the old system, lawyers were expected to give the reasons which would permit the executive to do what he wanted to do. Lawyers sometimes would become the spokespersons for the bureaucracy. Members of a board would give credence to the lawyer's words, thinking the attorney was rendering a legal opinion that was balanced and had to be followed. By setting up a legal committee, lawyers' remarks could be examined first by their peers so these peers could determine whether the lawyers' reports really set forth the legal requirements or were merely arguments for the executive's position couched in legal terms.

The old bylaws did not allow members to call a special meeting of the Executive Committee. If the chairman did not call a meeting, no alternate way existed for having one. The new bylaws rectified this. The bylaws also originally stated that no one could be nominated for a staff position except by the president/treasurer, who was then Harold Bennett. The new bylaws provided procedures to bypass this in emergency situations. These bylaw changes, on which I worked very diligently, opened up the system. I am proud of this accomplishment.

In June 1991 I had served my allotted time and rotated off the Executive Committee. I was very relieved to end my term. From the beginning, it had been a contentious and difficult experience. I left the Executive Committee believing that every single battle that conservatives had fought there was now won. In Baptist Press we had a new director whom I hoped would be fair. We had an outstanding public relations director who agreed with the direction the convention was headed and an excellent finance officer. We had new bylaws which would allow the members of the Executive Committee to exercise control. The Baptist Joint Committee had been defunded and eliminated from the Constitution and Bylaws of the Southern Baptist Convention (more on this in chapter 28). The committee had excellent officers and a solid conservative majority. Many had worked diligently to accomplish this.

At the same time I rotated off the Executive Committee, Harold Bennett decided to retire as president/treasurer. This opened the way for someone who was sympathetic with the conservative movement to be elected. The new leadership could take over and lead without the scars of these battles and without the resultant hard feelings and heartaches that naturally come from such events. I am so glad that Dr. Morris Chapman is now president/treasurer of the Executive Committee. He is outstanding.

The Executive Committee of the SBC is extremely important. It sets the budget and gives other major recommendations. It has a great deal of influence. The Executive Committee is now on a solid course, leading and directing the convention along the paths of soul winning and evangelism which Southern Baptists wished to travel, based on the fact that the blood of the Lord Jesus Christ is the only answer to the sin problem, the Bible is completely true, and this should be proclaimed through the power of the Holy Spirit.

CHAPTER 24

$\mathcal{T}$HE MEDIA

From the early days of the conservative resurgence, the news media, both secular and denominational, has played an important, and from my perspective, mostly negative role. Perhaps it was understandable that we would get bad press from the Baptist media because the people running it had been part of the bureaucracy for years. Many had close friendships with leaders of the moderate cause and had decidedly moderate personal theological convictions themselves.

In about 1970, when Dr. Joe Odle retired as editor of the Mississippi *Baptist Record*, great rejoicing occurred at Southern Seminary and throughout the liberal establishment because the last of the conservative editors was departing the scene. The liberals believed that the new group of editors being selected ensured that the denominational press would be securely in their hands. The reaction of the secular media, however, was a great surprise. Many in it misunderstood, misrepresented, and caricatured the conservative movement through the years of the battle.

One reason suggested for this is that the secular press saw the controversy through the eyes of the Baptist Press. On February 16, 1982, W. C. Fields, who was then its editor, wrote a letter to all of the secular news media that were planning to cover the SBC meeting that year. In this letter he stated that "a take-over attempt by a dissident group of fundamentalists has been in progress for about three years." This statement showed where W. C. Fields himself stood and how he characterized the conservative resurgence. Evidently, many of the secular press bought his line. He called us "fundamentalists." He called us "dissidents." He called it "a take-over attempt." These accusations have since recurred frequently in the characterizations of the conservative movement by the secular press. W. C. Fields's position is further reflected in an article in the *Richmond Times-Dispatch* in June 1984 where it reported as follows:

> Meanwhile, at River Road Baptist Church, Dr. Wilmer C. Fields, assistant to the executive secretary and director of public affairs for the Southern Baptist Convention, urged the members not to be discouraged or to despair at some of the actions of the convention.

189

He said, "Keep in mind there is no binding force at work here. They represent only the opinion of those present at the convention."

He added, "Don't give up. Hang on . . . There are brighter days ahead of us."

During a Sunday School class earlier, Dr. Fields said the current fundamentalist controlling group "may tell us they represent the majority of Southern Baptists, but they (the controlling faction) are a tiny group among the 14.1 million Southern Baptists in the nation."

I corresponded with Harold Bennett to express my concern about these statements by Fields.

After he retired from the SBC Executive Committee, Fields's feelings toward the conservative movement became even more open and obvious. In a column April 25, 1987, in the *Houston Post,* religion editor Richard Vara, then a *Post* reporter who now works for the *Houston Chronicle,* expressed his disappointment with Fields. The headline of the article said, "W. C. Fields let anger get best of him." Vara cited an instance in which Fields stated that the denomination's agencies are "being kept in turmoil and disarray by an unrelenting, shameless takeover by a narrowly partisan political group thinly disguised now and then by pious phraseology." He noted that Fields went on to say, "May God in his wisdom have mercy on all who have a part in perpetrating this tragedy and on all whose misguided zeal causes it to continue."

Vara wrote, "Fields is angry and he let that anger get to him." He went on to say, "There are few Baptists who love the SBC more than Fields does. And no one wants to see something he loves entangled in a brutal, angry dispute. But, if he sincerely felt this way, why didn't he say this earlier? Why wait until he was safely retired?"

Another reason suggested for the mistreatment we received from the press is that reporters frequently are much more politically liberal than is the populace at large. Numerous studies have shown this. At first I did not understand why the secular press should be interested in what was a theological controversy within a denomination and not a political movement. Evidently they saw political and sociological ramifications in the success of the movement which those of us who were involved did not see at the outset.

It has been appropriately argued that the secular liberal agenda has been to change the whole complexion of our American society and move us to a post-Christian era. If Southern Baptists had gone along with this trend, no moral bulwark would have existed among Protestants which would have been sufficiently large and powerful to resist the liberal agenda for our nation. The national liberal movement evidently felt that it needed to destroy the conservative movement in the Southern Baptist Convention. A liberal press was its ally in so doing.

Some reporters, like many people in general, are basically lazy. They borrow their research and materials from each other. Therefore, at times, when one writer who had a liberal bent wrote something, whether he heard it from Baptist Press or in some other way, other writers picked it up and repeated it until fiction became reality in the press.

Another suggested reason was the SBC liberals' effective courting of the media. Some Baptist institutions controlled by liberals have given awards and recognition to some members of the media without regard for the person's fidelity to Christ, to his or her marriage vows, or to the principles upon which the institution was founded. These favors have purchased the loyalty of certain people in the media.

The prejudice of the press can be documented. During the 1979 Houston SBC meeting, Louis Moore, then religion editor of the *Houston Chronicle,* had a visit from Robert O'Brien, who worked under Fields at Baptist Press. Before the SBC meeting, Louis had written a story about me in which he referred to me as a "conservative." The article was extremely fair and well written. Robert told him that Baptist Press had decided that the new conservative group should be called "ultraconservatives" and berated Louis for not referring to me as such. "Ultra," of course, means "too much" or "extreme." Thus, by definition, the press was seeking to brand us as a far-out, unacceptable group.

Several days later, the *Chronicle's* news editor, a Methodist, changed Louis's use of the word from "conservative" to "fundamentalist" in the paper's front page lead article about the election of Adrian Rogers as president. Though the news editor said at the time it was his personal preference, Louis is still not sure what or who prompted the decision to make the change. Because the meeting was in Houston and the *Chronicle* was the largest newspaper in Texas at that time, other newspapers followed suit and the term *fundamentalists* quickly replaced *ultraconservatives* in the press nationwide.

Perhaps the reason for this is that the term *fundamentalist* has been used for many years as a derogatory term. Its original meaning—when it was first used shortly after the beginning of the twentieth century—meant a person who believed in the fundamentals of the Christian faith such as the deity of Christ, His virgin birth, and His bodily resurrection. The term was derived from a group of position papers, called *The Fundamentals,* issued by conservative theologians, some of whom were Southern Baptists. These papers reasserted the fundamental doctrines of the Christian faith against the early inroads of theological liberalism. "Fundamentalists" were originally merely those who believed in the fundamentals of the Christian faith. It later became a derisive term during the 1920s as a result of the propaganda surrounding the Scopes trial when the national press propaganda mill was deifying Clarence Darrow and crucifying William Jennings Bryan. Cartoons showed a person labeled a "fundamentalist" in black clothes with a long, bony finger pointing at someone saying, "Thou shalt not. . ."

Another negative connotation of the term was derived from the fact that Dr. J. Frank Norris, a Texas Baptist who led a conservative movement in the 1920s and 1930s, was called a fundamentalist. The methodology reported to have been used by Dr. Norris and the attacks on him and his movement in the press had alienated many Southern Baptists from him and his type of fundamentalism. In the minds of many, to brand anybody a "Norrisite" or a "fundamentalist" or a "Norrisite fundamentalist" was to say one of the worst things that could possibly be said about a Southern Baptist. Our opponents knew that identification with fundamentalism could destroy a movement within the Southern Baptist Convention because of its negative connotation.

Not only did the term *fundamentalist* have connotations in Christian circles; the press also wrote about Moslem fundamentalists such as the Ayatollah Khomeini and others opposing the United States in the Middle East. The term *fundamentalist* had no good—only bad—connotations. Almost everybody, regardless of whether they were religiously oriented or not, would understand it as a derogatory term. The fundamentalist label stuck. Its use was promoted by the Baptist Press, W. C. Fields, the secular media, and in conversations in the press room.

Another term the press used to misrepresent conservatives was that we were *literalists* and that we were those who "demanded a literal interpretation of Scripture." This was incorrect reporting. We were not talking about an interpretation of Scripture. Rather, we were talking about the *nature* of Scripture. We believe the Scripture should be approached in a context of faith, with a belief that it is true. That is not an interpretation of Scripture. Interpretation is an analysis of what Scripture says, not an examination of the nature of Scripture.

Every time the press reported that the battle was over "interpretation" of Scripture, they deliberately and willfully misidentified the entire nature of the controversy. The correct terminology was constantly pointed out to individuals in the press, but they persisted in saying that the controversy was a matter of interpretation of Scripture. The following is one of the many illustrations I used to try to point this difference out to them:

> I believe that the first two chapters of Genesis, like all other portions of
> Scripture, are absolutely accurate, true, and correct. However, I am not sure

about certain details of what occurred in the initial act of creation by the Lord. A debate occurs as to what Scripture means when it says the earth was created in six periods, each of which is called a *yom*. Can the Hebrew word *yom,* which is used in Genesis and is translated "day" in the King James translation, also mean a period of time? To say the Scripture is completely true is one thing— that affirmation speaks to its nature. To say the word *yom* must mean a twenty-four-hour day or must not mean a twenty-four-hour day is another. It is an interpretation. To decide the interpretation, one must study what the Hebrew language meant and compare this passage with other passages of Scripture to see what was intended.

When the phrase "literal interpretation" is used, the press has compounded its error. As stated before, we were not focusing on an interpretation but rather on the nature of Scripture. When they say we demand "a literal interpretation," that again is not accurate. We recognize, with all other Bible believers, that literary expressions, including poetry and parables, occur in Scripture. When our Lord stated that something was a parable, He was clearly saying that it was not necessarily an historical event. To say that we require that all passages be taken literally is incorrect. This, again, has been explained to many members of the news media, but they have refused to acknowledge it. They have refused to report our position accurately.

Another phrase the press has used incorrectly to compound its misrepresentation is that we require "a strict literal interpretation." "Strict" means narrow. Southern Baptist conservatives simply believe that the Bible is completely true. We believe that varying interpretations exist but that when a person comes to Scripture, he or she should come with a conviction that it is true. This does not require a certain "interpretation." It does not require a "literal interpretation." It does not require a "strict literal interpretation." It just seeks an agreement that the Word of God is correct and that believers should try to understand it based on the words it uses. Members of the news media know or should know this, but they haven't reported it.

The word *political* is another term that the press has often wrongfully used to describe the convention controversy. The movement is political in one sense. Any system in which elected officers exist and people can vote is a system that has a political process. Until soon before the conservative movement began, no individual ever announced that he or she would "run" for convention office. A candidate pretended to be nonpolitical by saying that he "had been asked to allow his name to be presented" to the convention. No matter how the election was defined, it was a political election and the system was political. The methodology for correcting the problems in the convention involved working within this system and voting to elect officers and make changes. Therefore, it was political in this sense of the term.

However, the way in which the term was applied was not only to refer to the methodology of correcting the problem but also to create an implication that our motivation and the reason for our actions were for secular political ends rather than for the spiritual ends which we actually sought. Therefore, a double meaning of the term created confusion. This was misleading and unfair.

The news media accused us of having a "new right agenda" in a political sense. This is wrong. It sought to make us look as though we were concerned primarily with secular politics rather than theology. The media never defined a "new right agenda." If a "new right agenda" means opposing the killing of the unborn, the use of tax dollars to fund obscene art, or other matters such as these, most Southern Baptists are dedicated to a "new right agenda." The repeated use of a term which is undefined and does not have any clear meaning is wrong.

Transgressions by the secular media are so numerous that only a few will be cited to illustrate the problems. Current *Houston Chronicle* religion editor Cecile Holmes-White said in an "analysis" on May 28, 1988, the convention's conservatives "believe that they are unfairly linked to conservative organizations as diverse as the Republican Party and the Council for National Policy, a right-wing forum and think tank that serves as an umbrella group for organizations including the John Birch Society and Phyllis Schlafly's Eagle Forum." Even though this linkage was stated as something that conservatives object to, the mere mention of any such alleged connections without any basis in fact was outlandish. I was president of the Council for National Policy. It has individuals as members—not groups. I know of no persons in it who had any relationship with the John Birch Society. This was an inexcusable attempt to create guilt by association. I so told Cecile. She neither apologized nor presented any basis for this attack.

I decided to give Cecile another chance. I gave her the data from a former student at Baylor, Jerry Nanson, which he had prepared and used for a paper in a marketing course, MKT 137, in the spring of 1984. I gave her Jerry's name and telephone number. He had used a random selection process to obtain a cross section of Baylor students. He then contacted them and obtained the answers to various questions that he had prepared. Some of the questions and the percentage of the students who gave each answer are as follows:

> **Question:** Do you feel that the Baylor religion faculty's teaching on God and the Bible reflects that of the average Southern Baptist?

> **Answer:** YES (22.9 percent); NO (77.1 percent).

Question: Do you feel that the (Baylor) religion professors present the Bible as:

Answer: (a) the inspired, inerrant word of God? (20.0 percent);
(b) the inspired word of God but with some human error? (61 percent);
(c) a historical account of biblical times with little application to the people of today? (16 percent).

Question: Do you feel that the religion professors at Baylor are concerned about your spiritual well-being?

Answer: YES (57 percent); NO (42 percent).

I considered these responses to be very damaging to Baylor's credibility. Cecile told me she would consider using the data I had given her. A few days later she called and said she had talked to her supervisor about a possible story. She said the *Chronicle* would report the data only if it were done within the context of my making an accusation against Baylor. I replied that an accusation against Baylor was not the issue; the issue was the student's data collected for the class and the fact that the paper he prepared was accepted and approved in his course. I feared that if I were involved, the story would twist the facts and the focus would be shifted onto me and away from the damaging responses of Baylor students in the data collected. Therefore, I refused to make the charges. I was not any more involved in the collection of the data than was Cecile, and no reason existed for me to make a charge. The story should have stood on its own. However, it never appeared.

Richard Vara, then a *Houston Post* reporter, wrote a story that included me on a list of supporters of Pat Robertson in his presidential bid in 1988. After being unable to reach Richard Vara, I called the *Houston Post* editor and complained that I was fond of Pat Robertson and his wife Dede, but as a judge, I had to maintain strict neutrality in political matters. I also had other connections. Jack Kemp and my wife's brother are married to sisters. George and Barbara Bush have been friends for thirty years and are now neighbors. But as a judge, I could take no public stands. For the paper to say that I was supporting Pat was wrong and extremely embarrassing. Richard admitted to his editor that he had made a mistake, and the *Houston Post* wrote a very excellent correction, which I deeply appreciated. If all the press had been so responsible, this chapter would not have been written. I still find it curious as to why and how such grievous errors ever get into print in the first place.

Marjorie Hyer wrote in the *Washington Post* under a byline from Atlanta on June 9, 1986, referring to the 1979 SBC annual meeting as follows: "Moderates were outraged that year when the fundamentalists' chief strategist, Texas state appeals court Judge Paul Pressler, used a skybox high above the convention floor in Houston to deploy aides armed with walkie-talkies to capture the presidency for Rogers."

Of course, this was an absolute fabrication. We had no floor workers. We had no walkie-talkies. On July 1, 1986, I wrote the writer to try to find out where she had received that information and to deny what she had reported. She never even acknowledged my letter. Later I found an earlier story in the *Christian Century* written by Stan Hastey, then head of the Washington Bureau of Baptist Press and later the paid director of the Southern Baptist Alliance, the extreme left wing of the liberal movement. His false report stated, among other inaccuracies, that there were walkie-talkies and floor lieutenants at the 1979 SBC meeting. I always wondered if Marjorie Hyer picked up this error from the article by Stan Hastey.

Neither Marjorie Hyer nor Stan Hastey nor any of the others who later used it ever acknowledged the error or attempted to correct it. In the same article Marjorie Hyer also wrote as follows: "Some fundamentalist leaders have offered cash awards—dubbed 'snitch prizes' by critics—to seminary students who will report 'unbiblical' comments made by their professors." This was a complete and total fabrication with no basis in truth. Again a retraction never occurred.

A further insult occurred in a story written by Marv Knox, then editor of the Kentucky Baptist Convention's *Western Recorder* and now editor of the *Baptist Standard* in Texas, shortly after the New Orleans convention in 1990. On the night Paige Patterson and I first met in the 1960s, we went with our wives to the Cafe du Monde in the French Quarter. Some of our lawyer friends— Cactus Cagle, Paul Martin, and Walt Carpenter (all from Houston)—knew of our going there that night. On Wednesday night after the SBC session, they wanted to have some fun commemorating our first meeting. They formed what they called the Zenas Fellowship (Zenas was a lawyer mentioned in Titus 3:13). They gave a party under that name.

At the time the get-together was planned, no one knew how the convention would turn out. This meeting was not to be a victory celebration but simply a gathering of friends. Engraved invitations were prepared a month in advance and handed out to friends when we arrived in New Orleans. After the session on Wednesday night, many of us showed up at the Cafe du Monde. The event was unorganized, except for free tickets for coffee, hot chocolate, and beignets, which were passed out to friends and paid for by the Zenas Fellowship. The group had not reserved the Cafe du Monde, and other people were in the restaurant.

A group of students from Southern Seminary were on the other side of the restaurant from where we were gathered. When they saw some of the conservative leadership, they began yelling, "Shame! shame!" In order to drown them out and to keep them from disrupting our gathering, someone said, "Let's sing something" and then "What shall we sing?" Someone else replied that a good Baptist song was "Victory in Jesus." Someone else asked, "Who will lead it?" Someone replied that Barry McCarty had a good voice and got him to stand on a chair and lead us in singing "Victory in Jesus." Barry, the convention parliamentarian, was there because he was responsible for accompanying the SBC president, Jerry Vines, who was attending. It was all spontaneous, and no program had been planned. Our singing was in response to the rudeness of the Southern Seminary students.

In a story in the *Western Recorder,* Marv Knox gave an erroneous account that included the following assumptions: (1) The gathering at the Cafe du Monde was an organized meeting; (2) it was a victory celebration; and (3) Barry McCarty, as the SBC parliamentarian, was the leader of the meeting. If Marv had checked with anyone related to our fellowship, he would have learned the facts. State Baptist papers picked up the story of the "victory rally" presided over by the "parliamentarian." This simply was not true.

Another glaring example of media prejudice was an article on April 25, 1990, by Gus Niebuhr, then the religion editor of the *Wall Street Journal.* Gus is from the same family as Richard and Reinhold Niebuhr, leaders of the neo-orthodox school of theology, and people whom many liberals in the SBC revere. Gus emphasized one or two negative statistics, including a slight slowdown in the denomination's baptism rate the previous year, out of many more positive statistics available and concluded that the Southern Baptist Convention had ceased to grow because of the controversy. In my opinion, he also misrepresented some of the positions the convention had taken. This was a very disappointing article and one I felt was grossly unfair. I told him so.

Bob Allen, then editor of the *True Union,* the Baptist paper in Maryland-Delaware, used his news space to rebut statements that I made. This is acceptable in an editorial but is most unusual in a news column that a supposedly unbiased reporter writes. The incident occurred in 1988 when I was in Maryland speaking across the state. Bob, who is now appropriately assistant editor of the Associated Baptist Press, the news organization of the liberal movement, attended two of the meetings. In one story that he covered for the *True Union,* he used phrases such as "Pressler did not mention . . ." and "he did not mention . . . ," and gave data to which I had not referred.

Actually, I believe that the information he inserted (which he noted I did not say) was inaccurate. He was trying to rebut or counter what I said. This was not appropriate for a news column in which facts are to be reported. In the next speech I made in Maryland after that article appeared, I referred to it and complained. Afterward, Bob told me that he had thought I would not like the article. Obviously he knew what he was doing at the time he wrote the article. To his credit the second news story, on September 22, 1988, reported my objection as follows:

> Pressler called a story in the May 5, 1988, *True Union* reporting an April 25 address by Pressler at a CBF (Conservative Baptist Fellowship)-sponsored Bible conference in Edgewood "not poor journalism, but bad journalism." At that meeting Pressler read excerpts from writing and manuscripts which he presented as evidence of theological "problems" at SBC seminaries. The *True Union* report summarized the content of some of the excerpts, quoted remarks by Pressler and in two instances observed that Pressler "did not mention" that actions possibly contributing to resolution of the discussed concerns had taken place.
>
> "The rebutting of remarks had no place in a news account," Pressler complained. "When the writer of a story doesn't like what the speaker says and does research to insert rebuttals . . . it is bad journalism and unfair." Pressler also charged the writer omitted important parts of the content of his address and chose descriptive verbs which distorted his intent. In one instance the story alluded to a group of students whom Pressler at one time "taught" in a youth group. Pressler said a more precise description of his relationship is that he led a Bible study in which many of the young people were won to the Lord. The story also reported Pressler "assailed" a person who at the time of the speech was a seminary professor. Pressler denied he "assailed" the individual, but merely read part of a transcript of remarks the professor had made.
>
> "One of the reasons we are having problems in the denomination is because in many places this is the type of reporting we have," Pressler said. He added later: "(One reason) I speak to groups like this as often as I get invitations (is) I am unfiltered by Baptist Press."

Of course, in quoting my criticism of his reporting, Bob toned down the examples which I gave in the second speech.

In 1989, after the Southern Baptist Convention, Nancy, Paul, and I went to Europe for a rest. I always felt refreshed when I got away to a place where I was not harassed by the media and could not see what the media was reporting. During that time Dan Martin of Baptist Press wrote, without my response, a story about me which I considered very unfair. When I returned to the United States, I asked him why he had not called me. He said he had obtained my itinerary from my daughter, which I had told her to give to anybody who wanted it, and he tried to call me in Seville, Spain. He said that nobody at the hotel could speak English, and therefore, he couldn't leave a message.

In Seville we were attending a meeting at the Alfonso XIII, which is one of the premier hotels of Europe. All of our meetings and meals were in the hotel, so we could have been reached at almost any hour. Everyone who worked the switchboard whom I encountered spoke fluent English. I don't see how they could have had a non-English-speaking person working the phones at such a prominent international hotel. I have always been very puzzled about Dan's statement and wondered just how diligently he tried to reach me.

Subtle prejudice against conservatives continues, sometimes in unanticipated sources. After the 1998 meeting of the SBC, an article appeared in what once was considered a leading evangelical magazine, *Christianity Today.* My letter to *Christianity Today,* which was as follows, showed some of the problems with the article.

July 27, 1998
Christianity Today, Inc.
465 Gundersen Drive
Carol Stream, Illinois 60188
Dear Sirs:

I am commenting on your article on the SBC in the July 13, 1998, edition. You state in it: "Bitterly fought battles throughout the 1980s spurred disenfranchised Southern Baptists . . ." I wonder what you mean by the word "disenfranchised." Disenfranchised means that a person no longer has the franchise or the right to vote. Who has been disenfranchised in the Southern Baptist Convention? Liberals are no longer elected to positions of leadership, but that is because they lose the vote and not because they did not have the right to vote. Yours is an extremely misleading statement.

Later it is said that Paige Patterson was elected president "without even a show of hands." This gives the implication that those who want to dissent were not allowed to do so. That is contrary to the fact. The rules say that when there is not another nominee, a unanimous ballot is cast. The rules were followed. There could not have been a show of hands. Why, therefore, would you comment that it was without even a show of hands?

The article further states that "The Texas Baptist convention is expected to give final passage to a bylaw that will make it more autonomous and will allow official links with the CBF and the Baptist World Alliance." First of all, the Baptist General Convention of Texas and every state convention is completely autonomous, and there is no interlocking. Therefore, the one who wrote the article does not understand Baptist church organization. Something that is completely autonomous cannot be more autonomous. Can a pregnant person be more pregnant than pregnant? The Texas Baptist convention already has ties to the CBF by channeling funds to them, and so that could not be a result of the bylaw change.

I have just returned from the Baptist World Alliance meeting where I served as a voting member of the General Council. The Baptist World Alliance will not admit the Texas convention or the CBF at the present time. The passage of the bylaw is to "disenfranchise" (your word) some who would like to participate in the Texas convention by creating a monetary requirement (or poll tax) for a church. Now there is no monetary requirement. The liberals are trying to amend the bylaw in order to disenfranchise (i.e., keep from being able to vote) some conservatives who are now voting. This is where your word "disenfranchise" should be used, not where you used it.

Yours very truly,
Paul Pressler

The only response I received from *Christianity Today* was a form printed postcard.

The feeding frenzy of the liberals on the addition to the Baptist Faith and Message Statement during the 1998 SBC was unbelievable. Perhaps the errors in reporting were best summarized in an article by Paul Greenberg of the *Arkansas Democrat-Gazette*. His article was headlined, "'Submission' by Baptists not as was oft reported: Even *The New York Times* buried full text until near the bottom of the story." The first two paragraphs read:

> More revealing than the Southern Baptists' new statement of belief about the family is how widely misunderstood it has been. It's not exactly news that we live in a biblically illiterate society, but one suspects there's something going on here besides ignorance. Maybe it's willful ignorance.
>
> How else to explain the incomplete, and therefore distorted, news coverage of what was in fact a carefully qualified theological position? Time and again, its key phrases were glossed over or omitted entirely in the coverage of the Statement of Belief adopted by the Baptists last week in Salt Lake City.

Can anyone wonder why I have a bumper sticker in my office which says, "I Don't Believe the Liberal Media"?

CHAPTER 25

$\mathcal{D}$ONAHUE

Television also devoted time to the controversy. Two programs, both in June 1985, presented both sides and did a commendable job. "The MacNeil-Lehrer Report" featured Russell Dilday and me. It was broadcast live, so no prejudicial editing could have occurred. The second one was "Nightline." It was compiled after the show talked to and taped many people. Ted Koppel of "Nightline"called me personally, and we talked for several minutes. He asked good questions and seemed to understand what was happening. The program allowed conservatives to state their case. Although it gave a great deal more time to the liberals, the program presented an overall, fair picture.

Perhaps the most-watched show on television concerning the Southern Baptist Convention was the "Donahue" show in June 1985. Ken Chafin represented the liberals, and I represented the conservatives. I don't think I had ever seen the show before I appeared on it, so I didn't really know what to anticipate. The show was produced live, so no editing occurred. Nancy went with me to New York. I had asked in advance that she be admitted to the studio to watch the show. Also, two of my closest friends from Exeter and Princeton (who were not Baptists) were living in New York, and I requested tickets for them. They were refused outright, and the show's representatives told us that Nancy would be considered later.

Ken Chafin, Nancy, and I were transported from the hotel together. All went well until we arrived at the building from which the broadcast would be aired. When we entered the building, someone approached Ken and told him that a group was present, presumably supporting him, and everything was under control. I then became worried that I was being set up and raised the issue with the staff of the show. They denied any kind of set-up. They finally agreed to allow Nancy into the studio on the condition that she sit in a remote area on the side and promise not to say anything.

In the latter part of the program, the group that appeared to be there supporting Ken began asking questions. These questions were not difficult, but the fact that they had one particular slant was disturbing. Several friends had strongly advised me not to appear on the program. They told me that I would

201

be set up, but I felt the Lord indicated that I should do it. I am glad that I did, because probably ten million people saw the program. Many people have told me that through viewing it, they understood the issues for the first time. When Ken revealed what he believed, it shocked many Southern Baptists.

The show itself was fair, although Phil clearly did not agree with the conservative position. He seemed genuinely interested in how conservatives could believe what we do and why those beliefs do not generate strife and conflict with others who do not share our beliefs. He didn't seem to realize that the essence of the gospel is that you respect all people regardless of whether you agree with them, since each person is created in God's image and has the possibility of fellowship with God through our Lord Jesus Christ. At the same time Phil seemed to be concerned with what appeared to be Ken's sometimes lack of forthrightness in revealing what he believed.

Three things on the program particularly revealed the difference in our beliefs. One was when a woman stated the following:

> I am not a Christian, but I live by all the ethical rules. I don't harm anybody. I do all the wonderful things that we should do as citizens of this world. Am I doomed? Do you think I will go to heaven?

I said, "The Scripture says very clearly that all have sinned and come short of the glory of God. I'm a sinner; everyone in this room is a sinner. The question is, have we taken God's solution to the sin problem . . . ?" Ken interrupted me by saying, "Jesus said to love God and love your neighbor as yourself and that sums it all up." I believe I was presenting the grace-alone scriptural answer to her question, while Ken, in his own words, revealed a works-based theology.

The second revealing moment occurred when Ken said he believed he would see his rabbi friend, Dr. Hyman Judah Shachtel, who to my knowledge had not accepted Jesus Christ as his personal Savior, in heaven some day.

> **Dr. Chafin:** "You can ask down in Houston—you can ask Hy Shachtel, retired rabbi, and Hy and I work together, we're close together. And I say, does Hy know God? I think he knows God."
>
> **Phil Donahue:** "And Hy is going to enjoy his reward with you in the everlasting world prepared for us?"
>
> **Dr. Chafin:** "Yes, I think that it is probably because of what God has done through Jesus Christ."

Again, I believe Ken sidestepped the issue. The Bible says that no one can come to God except through Jesus Christ. What God did through Jesus Christ was to provide a means for our salvation, when Christ took the punishment for our sins. I still am not sure how Ken thought he was answering Phil Donahue's question by stating that last answer as it applied to the eternal salvation of the rabbi.

A third illustration that surprised many occurred when Ken gave his thoughts about evolution. He said:

> I think the evolutionary process is the best scientific position that we have.
>
> When I look at the first eleven chapters of Genesis and the creation story, I don't see that there is a scientific description of how the world came to be. I see a religious description—who made it and why.
>
> (The Creation story) is a fantastic statement that basically affirms that the world didn't just happen. It was created without opposition and without assistance for the purpose of God, so that the creation science that they are trying to push into our school systems—I don't believe is good science and a good understanding of the Word of God.

Again, Ken revealed his personal theology in such a way that he surprised many Southern Baptists who believe the first eleven chapters of Genesis are true and without any mixture of error. I didn't have to say Ken's theology was liberal; much to my surprise and the surprise of millions of other faithful believers, Ken described it for himself.

During the "Donahue" program several telephone calls were received and put on the air. All were extremely negative toward Christians, Baptists, and conservative Southern Baptists in particular. It appeared to me that they all had the same theme. Not until several years later, while viewing a tape of the program, did I realize that no telephone number was displayed for people to call to have their questions aired on the program. How did these people know the number to call? Why were all questions directed the same way? Why did not calls occur that were sympathetic to the conservative Christian cause? I guess I shall never know the answers to these questions. I wonder if possibly the program set up these calls to hurt our cause. I am very glad the program was broadcast live and therefore could not be edited.

A month of so after the program aired, I received a call from one of the women on the staff of the "Donahue" program. She said she had heard the program was being watched and listened to on tape all over the country and that it was a violation to show it without authorization. I told her that many people had recorded the program as it was aired on television, and that as far as I knew, they were merely showing it to their families and friends. She said she believed that Dr. Chafin was a very nice man and that the "Donahue" staff did not want him destroyed by the program. I wondered if Ken or one of his supporters had called and complained about people watching tapes of the show. We did not show the

"Donahue" program at meetings, but many individuals had copies and showed them to various people on their own. I had no control over the situation. The program awakened many Southern Baptists to the fact that the problems we had were real and substantive.

I also studied carefully the great interest that TV personality Bill Moyers took in the Southern Baptist Convention. Bill attended East Texas Baptist University and Southwestern Seminary, both institutions heavily subsidized by Texas Baptists or Southern Baptists. As an adult, Bill left the SBC for the United Church of Christ, a very liberal denomination. Bruce Buursma of the *Chicago Tribune* quoted Bill in the Monday, April 19, 1982, edition of the *Fort Wayne News-Sentinel* as saying that he left his Southern Baptist roots for "another way of seeing and believing."

Bill had many friends who were still in the Southern Baptist Convention, but he told me he was a member of a United Church of Christ congregation on Long Island, where he lived. Later I heard he joined a Baptist church on Manhattan many miles from his home. Many people wondered why he was coming back into a Southern Baptist church after many years of absence. Was it a doctrinal conversion experience, or was it a desire just to become more effective in supporting his views among Southern Baptists?

I was also concerned about what I considered a highly prejudiced program that Bill Moyers produced that aired on the Public Broadcasting System and focused on the convention. By a 42 to 14 vote, the Executive Committee of the Southern Baptist Convention on February 22, 1989, passed a resolution decrying its bias. The resolution was as follows:

> That the Executive Committee of the SBC expresses its concern about the biased content of the Bill Moyers special series "God and Politics" and directs its officers and encourages its individuals to express their personal concern about it to its sponsors and to the Public Broadcasting System concerning the timing of the showing of "Battle for the Bible" and the use of federal tax dollars to support one faction in the SBC controversy through the use of the Public Broadcasting System.

On Bill's program were soft questions to the supporters of the liberals, such as James Dunn of the Baptist Joint Committee on Public Affairs and Nancy Sehested, the pastor of Prescott Memorial Baptist Church in Memphis. Some of the questions asked of them seemed to pave the way for them to air their viewpoints. Some of us on the conservative side were asked difficult questions which seemed to me to seek to destroy our credibility. I believe several things about the interview were most unfair. After I left Bill's interview with me, new questions were recorded and then inserted before some of my answers. This was obvious because Bill brought only one camera to the interview. It was focused full-faced on me during the entirety of the interview while I was there. Some of the questions on the program showed him full face. Therefore, this part had to be recorded at a later time. He had remained in my office for some time after I left, so the questions could have been recorded then. (Nancy was out of town, and I had to get to Paul IV, who was having a seizure problem.)

When I asked him about this seeming discrepancy after the program aired, he attempted to justify the appearance of the new questions by saying that they were essentially the same. Quite a difference exists between a question being exactly the same and essentially the same. If a question is essentially the same, some nuance of wording might cause the person questioned to answer in a slightly different way. As I watched the program, I believed that I would have changed my answers to certain questions to be more responsive to the specific questions asked me if I had been responding to the actual questions which were on camera.

Bill did several other objectionable things. He tried to ask me questions concerning the Council for National Policy, a conservative think tank to which I belong. The Council for National Policy takes no stands on any issues. It merely has conservative speakers who allow members to gain insight into the workings of government and the issues facing the nation. It is an organization that does not allow reporters, so the speakers can be very candid and open. Bill Moyers tried to imply that the Council for National Policy was a sinister operation. Fortunately, he didn't know that I was on its executive committee and would soon serve as president.

Another thing he did was try to align me with Coors beer business. Joseph Coors was a member of the Council for National Policy, and Bill tried to imply that I was aligned with the beer industry because we were members of the same organization. Of course, this was absurd. Anybody who knows me well knows that I have never drunk any alcoholic beverage in my life. I do not serve liquor and never have. Just because I am a member of an organization with several hundred people and one person happens to be in a certain business does not align me with the business of that person. That is a gross form of guilt by association. Knowing that most Southern Baptists oppose the liquor traffic, Bill tried to ally me with it. If someone is in Rotary, Kiwanis, or Lions Club with somebody who is later proved to be dishonest, does that mean other club members are guilty of dishonesty by association? Certainly not! This was an uncalled-for and an improper attack.

Bill also tried to imply that because I had political interests in addition to my religious interest, that made my activity in the Southern Baptist Convention a political activity. His rationale and accusations were completely unfair.

Bill also claimed on his program that I became angry and stormed out of the interview. That is totally false. When he finished asking me about the convention and started asking me about the Council for National Policy, I politely got up and said in effect that he had asked to interview me about the convention, which I had agreed for him to do. Now he was delving into matters completely irrelevant to the convention, and I saw no reason to proceed. At that point, I stood up. I did not move from my place. I did not remove the microphone with which I was wired. After he assured me that he would deal only with convention matters, I continued the interview. In comments afterwards, Bill completely and totally misrepresented this incident, not only on his first program but also on the rerun. In the rerun he inserted concluding remarks attacking me further. Several times thereafter the PBS station where a national convention was to be held reran the program just before the convention. This I considered to be a propagandizing effort to help the liberals win.

I objected to the fact that Bill Moyers's program ran on public television. This seems to be a violation of separation of church and state. I do not believe that public facilities or monies should be used to promote a certain brand of religion. A charitable foundation and a major oil company financed Bill Moyers's program on public television. I understand that about 17 percent of the money for public television is derived from tax dollars. This program showed what I believe to be a very narrow and negative viewpoint of the Southern Baptist Convention and advanced a particular theological position. If biblical Christianity were promoted on public television, I imagine that many people would allege that the program failed the test of separation of church and state. Where were the Baptist Joint Committee's and James Dunn's objections to PBS's running the Moyers program?

CHAPTER 26

$\mathcal{B}$APTIST PRESS

Baptist Press, the official news service of the Southern Baptist Convention, was far more biased in its coverage of the conservative resurgence than was the secular press. This began early in the controversy. Baptist Press reported that possible vote fraud occurred in Adrian Rogers's election in 1979. The accusations were couched in terms that seemed to imply that only conservatives were guilty and that the activity was organized. The Peace Committee later found in its investigation that a few isolated, improper things might have been done by a few individuals on both sides but that no evidence existed of any organized attempt to do anything incorrectly. This was, of course, true.

One of the most distasteful events concerning Baptist Press developed in 1984 and 1985 and involved a Southern Seminary student. The following is the factual background of the matter, as I reported it to the Executive Committee in February 1985:

I was invited to speak in Louisville on February 12, 1984, at Dr. Laverne Butler's fiftieth anniversary celebration at Ninth and O Baptist Church. This invitation came approximately three weeks before the event. Upon accepting the invitation, I contacted a member of the Executive Committee, Alan Sears. I told Mr. Sears that I had never to my knowledge met Dr. Honeycutt (Southern Seminary president) and felt that it would promote understanding and harmony for the two of us to get together. My request was relayed to Dr. Honeycutt. Mr. Sears called to tell me that he felt that things would be worked out for Dr. Honeycutt and me to get together. Therefore, I made my plane reservation so as to stay in Louisville until later on Monday in the hope that we would meet. Mr. Sears informed me that he was told I was to receive a letter from Dr. Honeycutt, but he did not know its contents. I left most of my plans in Louisville open until right before my departure from Texas.

By Friday, February 10, before I was to leave for Louisville on Sunday, I had not received his letter. I checked to see what other individuals I knew in the Louisville area so that I could utilize my time Monday if Dr. Honeycutt did not respond favorably to my suggestion that we get together. In my file on

Kentucky were the names of some individuals whom I had known in the past. One of those was Staff Durham who, in 1978 or 1979 with his wife, had visited a couple in Houston who were in the Sunday School class I taught. They attended a retreat with us. In October of 1979, I went to the Heart of America Bible Conference held on the Southern Seminary campus at which Drs. Paige Patterson, James Robison, Bailey Smith, Adrian Rogers, and others were preaching. Because the couple in my Sunday School class did not know how Staff was getting along spiritually, they asked me to contact him and his wife and ask them to come and join us for the conference. This I did. He joined us, but she did not. This had been my last contact with him.

The letter which he wrote me after the Bible conference referred graciously to his heroes being such men as Paige Patterson, James Robison, Bailey Smith, and Adrian Rogers. That letter follows:

November 7, 1979
Dear Paul,

I hope your flight back to Houston was comfortable, but I sure was sorry to see you go so soon. I only wish we had had a longer time to share before our separation, but I can honestly say that our experience in Louisville was one of real spiritual uplifting that I continue to praise the Lord for every day.

Paul, I can't express my gratitude for all you've done for me. I want you to know that you made it possible for an old mountain boy to have the thrill of his life and a time that he will never forget. My heroes are not any movie stars or even sports figures, but the men I was in the room with Monday night. And through you, the Lord gave me that chance to meet them. Without you taking me under your arm and being my friend, I would have never had the opportunity to meet those men under the circumstances that we did. Thank you from the bottom of my heart.

I relayed the request to Paige that you asked me to, and he was grateful for the compliment. I respect those men and what they are doing so much, only eternity will reveal my feelings. James' message on Wednesday morning touched me to the core of my being. I really feel he is called of God.

Paul, thank you so much, and Terye and I are looking forward to visiting and sharing with you and Nancy soon. I will remember you in my prayers.

Yours through Christ Jesus our Lord,
Staff Durham

My report went on as follows:

On Friday, February 10, 1984, I left for our ranch near Austin to hold a Bible conference for the Sunday School class from First Baptist of Houston which I teach. When I talked to my wife on Saturday afternoon, the letter from Dr. Honeycutt had still not come. I asked my wife to call the couple who had been in my Sunday School class to find out whether Staff was in Louisville and to get his telephone number from them if he was. When I talked to my wife from the ranch on Saturday night, she had talked to Staff's friends and found out that he was indeed at the Seminary and obtained his telephone number from them which she then gave me. That was all the information that I had about him. On Sunday morning during the singing before a Bible study, I slipped out of the main room of our ranch house to call Staff from the phone in the hall. The phone call was approximately five minutes, and my recollection of it is as follows: I told him I was going to be in Louisville and asked if he would like to get together. He said he lived out from town and did not come in on Mondays. I said I was sorry not to get a chance to see him and said if he was going to be at the convention in June, I would enjoy getting together then. He said he was going. I asked if his wife was going. He said he did not think she was. I said my wife and I would be there, gave him the name of the hotel where we would be staying and said I would like to get together. I asked him how things were going at school. I might have commented something such as "this is going to be an interesting convention" and "do you know whom the liberals are going to run for president." There was some general conversation along these lines. This is all the conversation I remember from this very brief call.

It should be noted that if I were trying to obtain information from anybody, I would not have called on a Sunday morning. I would not have called when I was just slipping out of a meeting. I would not have called when the person was obviously getting ready to assume his responsibilities at church. I would have called at a relaxed time and have laid some predicate for my conversation. There were no further calls. If I had been seeking information, I certainly would have pursued the matter.

My friendly, personal call to Staff was an after-thought to fill the time left open by Roy Honeycutt's failure for almost three weeks to respond to my gesture of friendship. It was evidently reported by Staff to Roy Honeycutt. Either Staff misunderstood the call or someone else seized upon it as an opportunity of making it into an episode which could be used as an attempt to embarrass me.

Dr. Honeycutt's letter did finally arrive. Although it was dated Feb. 3, 1984, it was not postmarked until February 6 and not received by me until my return from Louisville (see letters attached). In the fall of 1984 Roy Honeycutt in his well known speech declaring "Holy War" upon other Southern Baptists, said that somebody had "invaded the privacy of the president's office to say nothing of my personal life." I had no idea what he was talking about when first asked about it (his reference to someone trying to get information from the student who was his personal driver). When later I found out that Dr. Honeycutt's office was accusing me of being involved, I went through my files to see what possibly could have happened. It was then that I ran across Staff's name. This was the first suggestion that I had that there might be some link between me and that accusation. Staff was the only student at Southern Seminary whom I ever remember talking to on the phone about anything. Therefore, on Saturday morning September 1, I called Staff to find out whether he drove for Roy Honeycutt. I was very surprised to learn that he did. I took the precaution of taping the conversation for several reasons: (1) Certain individuals on the liberal side in the convention have completely and totally misrepresented conversations I had with them. (See Dilday comments attached.) (2) I felt that if Staff had been involved, he had obviously either mis-represented my February telephone call or had taken information from my pri-vate telephone call with him to other persons who had deliberately and will-fully misconstrued my conversation. If they had done it once, they might try to do it again. For self-protection it was, therefore, necessary to have a record of the telephone conversation. I did not plan to use the contents of the tele-phone conversation unless misrepresentations were made and it became neces-sary to correct these misrepresentations. In this telephone conversation, Staff stated: (1) that I did not tell him I knew he drove for Honeycutt; (2) that he did not tell me he drove for Honeycutt; (3) that he had merely made that assumption that I knew; and (4) that the whole thing had been blown out of proportion. I thought that this would end the matter.

Several days later a reporter from the *Houston Chronicle* called me and asked me to comment on statements that Staff had made which were totally inconsistent with the remarks that he had made to me over the telephone the previous Saturday. After hearing the remarks and feeling that they were in direct contradiction, I allowed the reporter to listen to the tape and therefore, he was able to see the inconsistencies in Staff's statements. The *Chronicle* story was written from the benefit of having Staff's two conflicting statements. I felt that I was justified in correcting the erroneous statements and showing the inconsistencies in what this young man had said.

I then learned a complaint was being filed by Staff with the FCC. This complaint was filed under an inapplicable or nonexistent portion of the FCC code. He accused me of "illegal" activities when there was no law, federal or state that would cause this to be illegal. I have wondered many times who directed him to the FCC? Who paid for his telephone calls to the FCC? And who orchestrated this new attack?

The Baptist Press stories were written later. In the same article to the Executive Committee I gave the factual background of the writing of the stories as follows:

My wife and I left Houston on Thursday, September 13, 1984, driving our daughter's car to Nashville (where she attended Vanderbilt University) to attend a meeting of the Southern Baptist Executive Committee. When we arrived in Nashville, there was a call waiting from Russ Kaemmerling of the *Southern Baptist Advocate*. When I returned the call, he informed me that Dan Martin (of Baptist Press) had been trying to reach me because of another attack from Roy Honeycutt and his agents at Southern Seminary in their "holy war." He said that he had given Dan the name of the hotel in which I was staying and the arrival time. He further advised that Dan said he would be calling me. I said that was fine. We spent Friday evening with our daughter and no call was awaiting us Friday night when we returned to our hotel. Saturday I spent the day with Dr. James Sullivan, former president of the Southern Baptist Convention, and went to his home outside of Nashville. When I returned, there was a call from Dan Martin. I immediately returned his call. He came from his office to the hotel. He told me about the attacks being made and said that he would like to interview me about it on Monday. I told him I was available to be interviewed right then. He said he did not have time. He said he had to get his clothes out of the cleaners before they closed and, therefore did not have time. I told him I would see him on Monday morning. Knowing the schedule with which I was confronted Monday morning, I prepared a statement so that I could give it to him. (See attached.) I went to the orientation meeting for new members of the Executive Committee which began either at 8:30 or 9:00 A.M. After that I stopped by Dan Martin's office and gave him my statement. He wanted to engage in a lengthy conversation about the story, but I was overdue at Dr. Harold Bennett's office. In fact, shortly after I arrived in Dan Martin's office, Dr. Bennett's secretary called to locate me to tell me that they were waiting for me in Dr. Bennett's office. I could have discussed the matter at length on Saturday, but was under pressure because of Executive Committee responsibilities on Monday. My meeting with Dan Martin in his office was approximately at 9:30 in the morning.

I understand that the story containing only the attack and with no rebuttal was released after 10:00 on that morning. Dan Martin had my rebuttal at the time of the release of the story. The next day, on a break from the administrative committee, I picked up a copy of the *Baptist and Reflector* in the hall and saw in it the full attack on me without any rebuttal whatsoever. I went to W. C. Fields's office and protested the story. He informed me that it was his decision to release the first story without any rebuttal and then to release the rebuttal information later. I went straight from his office into the administrative committee and during miscellaneous business expressed my extreme displeasure with the manner in which Baptist Press handled this matter. This led to the investigation meeting that was held by the public affairs committee which led to the approval of the investigation of Baptist Press by the full Executive Committee and the meetings which are now being held.

The statement I gave to Dan Martin at Baptist Press was as follows:

> Roy Honeycutt in conducting his "holy war" against other Southern Baptists has attempted to turn nonissues into issues in order to divert attention from legitimate concerns which many have for the spiritual quality of education in our institutions. Dr. Honeycutt made charges which have since been clearly refuted. Since Honeycutt's representations can no longer be asserted successfully, a student which was involved now complains because his comments can be accurately quoted.
>
> If individuals are to be effectively reached for Christ, we, as believers, must conduct ourselves with utmost honesty and integrity. The Scriptures enjoin us to let our aye be aye and our nay be nay. We are responsible for what we say. No honest person should object to a record being kept of what he says in order that he might not be misrepresented.
>
> Recent experiences have caused me to be most careful in communication with certain people to make sure that the content of conversations will not be misrepresented.

The whole focus of this story became, not the invalidity of the charges that had been made against me, which were proven by the tape recording, but the fact that I had recorded the conversation. Under Texas law, wiretapping exists when a person who is not a party to a conversation tapes that conversation. Since I was a party to the call, I did nothing illegal, and no wiretapping occurred. For illustration, if a person has a tape recorder in his briefcase, has it running, and is taping a meeting that he is in, that is perfectly proper. However, if he leaves the room for a couple of minutes for any purpose, it is illegal for his recorder to be taping the meeting while he is out of the room. Since I had been a party to the telephone conversation the entire time, it was not improper for me to record it, particularly when I needed to safeguard myself against misrepresentations which had been made previously.

I found it interesting that when (Arkansas pastor) David Montoya later recorded a conversation with conservative leaders in Arkansas in 1989, no Baptist or secular press people accused him of improperly recording the conversation. The difference between his recording and mine was that he was acting as an undercover agent for the liberals and I was a conservative. He recorded for the purpose of revealing the meeting. I recorded only to protect myself in case my conversation was falsely reported.

My report to the Executive Committee then proceeded to deal with the reaction to the story as follows:

> During the initial hearing of the Public Relations Sub-committee, an attack was launched against Paul Pressler by Gene Puckett, editor of the *Biblical Recorder*. As reported in the Baptists United News of North Carolina on November 7, 1984, "It was Gene Puckett, editor of the *Biblical Recorder*, who asked to speak before the Committee and made nasty and abusive remarks about Paul Pressler. His remarks drew a rebuke from Chairman, Jimmy Jackson, who said, "What you said was unethical and the way you said it was unchristian and no more remarks like that will be tolerated as long as I am Chairman of this Committee." A North Carolina member of the Executive Committee commented that Puckett's conduct was "an embarrassment to North Carolina Baptists." Bob Terry and Al Shackleford both jumped up to defend the Baptist Press before the Committee. When the matter went to the full Administrative Committee, Dr. John Lewis from First Baptist, Raleigh, North Carolina, proposed that no investigation be had until after all "the court hearings" were over. He referred to the trial that would result from the taping. It was brought to his attention that his remarks were the prime reason why the Baptist Press story was unfair. He, a leading pastor and a very intelligent person, after reading the Baptist Press story, was led to believe that there would be legal action taken against Paul Pressler because of the taping incident. This is of course absolutely false and shows the harm of the story. Julian Pentecost, in *The Religious Herald*, and Bob Terry, in the *Word and Way*, immediately jumped to defense of the Baptist Press in editorials to their papers.
>
> The *Houston Chronicle* commented on the article and the remarks that were made about the *Chronicle* in correspondence with Dr. Harold Bennett. (See attached.) These letters should be closely examined. Vulgarity by Dan Martin is referred to in the third paragraph from the last on the first page of the letter of September 20, 1984. The description of what is fairness in report-

ing is spelled out in the letter of October 5. The application of these principles is not only to the reporting about the *Chronicle,* but also to the reporting about Paul Pressler.

The letters referred to are as follows:

Thursday, September 20, 1984
Dr. Harold Bennett
Executive Secretary of the Executive Committee
of the Southern Baptist Convention

Dear Dr. Bennett:

I am writing to you in regard to a story that appeared in Baptist Press on Monday, Sept. 17, 1984.

The part of the story that concerns me is the third paragraph where Baptist Press reports that the tape of the conversation between Judge Paul Pressler and Southern Seminary student Stafford Durham was revealed in a "carelessly written" story in the *Houston Chronicle.*

Nowhere is there an explanation of what "carelessly written" means. Then, in the tenth paragraph Baptist Press quotes Mr. Durham as saying the story in the *Houston Chronicle* "was not accurately written." Again, Baptist Press does not explain this statement.

I am the religion editor of the *Houston Chronicle.* The story in question was written by my able associate, Steve Maynard, the *Chronicle's* religion writer. Mr. Maynard's story was not only carefully written but also accurate. We have all the tape recordings to prove this.

The Baptist Press story does not contain a response from me or from Mr. Maynard.

The use of the words "carelessly written" is a slander directed against Mr. Maynard. Complicating the situation is the fact that Baptist Press writer Dan Martin has expressed to me personally and directly an unnecessary and unprofessional dislike for Mr. Maynard, calling him a seven-letter profane name.

The fact that Mr. Maynard's name does not appear in the Baptist Press story widens the slander to include me. It is widely known by people who receive Baptist Press stories that I am the religion editor and Mr. Maynard is the religion writer of the *Houston Chronicle.*

Through this story and the lack of a printed rebuttal, Baptist Press has acted in a vicious manner to cast doubts and undermine confidence in mine and Mr. Maynard's work. The story is written in such a way as to defame and damage our professional reputations and characters.

The *Chronicle* has a sterling reputation for covering all religions including Southern Baptists. A recent article in the *Los Angeles Times* reviewing religion coverage throughout the United States said that I have a wide reputation for being "fair." I am the current president of the Religion Newswriters Association, the only professional association for religion reporters on secular newspapers in the U.S. and Canada. As an active member and tither of a Southern Baptist church which contributes heavily to the Cooperative Program, I am asking you to look into this matter.

At the very least, I expect a retraction and letters of apology from the director of Baptist Press and the writer of the story.

Sincerely,
Louis Moore
Religion Editor, the Houston Chronicle

September 28, 1984
Mr. Louis Moore, Religion Editor
Houston Chronicle

Dear Mr. Moore:

This letter acknowledges your letter of September 20, 1984, related to the Baptist Press article, "Student Files Complaint Against Texan Pressler" by Dan Martin and released September 17, 1984. I was out of the city when the letter came but read it on Monday. I appreciate the fact that you were willing to write me. I am happy to respond.

Wilmer C. Fields, Dan Martin, and I have discussed in detail your letter and the news article.

We regret you and Steve Maynard were offended by references to the *Houston Chronicle* in the Baptist Press story.

The two references to the newspaper reporting are clearly attributed to the student, J. Stafford Durham. Baptist Press made no judgment about the quality of the *Houston Chronicle* reporting. The opinions expressed are those of Mr. Durham, not of Baptist Press.

It is our feeling that no fair-minded person will find "vicious" motives in the Baptist Press story. On the contrary, the personnel of Baptist Press have frequently and over many years sighted (c.q.) the *Houston Chronicle* as a leader in the nation in religion coverage. We congratulate you.

Again, we reaffirm our pledge in the attempt to practice the highest journalism standards in Baptist Press, even as you follow a similar procedure.

Sincerely,
Harold C. Bennett

Friday, October 5, 1984
Dr. Harold C. Bennett
Executive Secretary-Treasurer
Executive Committee
Southern Baptist Convention

Dear Dr. Bennett:

I am responding to your letter of September 28, 1984, which was in reply to my earlier letter. I appreciate your prompt response. Tony Pederson, the *Chronicle's* managing editor, and I have studied your letter in detail. We believe you have not heard what I said in my first letter, and we do not find your response acceptable.

We realize you are trained in theology and not in journalism. If you were familiar with the basics of journalism, you would immediately realize the problems associated with the Sept. 17, 1984, Baptist Press article, "Student Files Complaint Against Texan Pressler."

The basic texts of journalism all point out that controversial statements must be treated with fairness and balance. Statements that are slanderous or damage someone's reputation should be printed only if the news source has substantial reason to believe those statements are true. In addition, every effort should be made to see that an offended party has the opportunity to respond in defense.

Baptist Press printed untrue statements about Steve Maynard's story which were injurious to his reputation as a journalist and to the *Houston Chronicle* as a public medium. No effort was made by Baptist Press to obtain the truth or to clarify the remarks attributed to J. Stafford Durham and no reply was obtained from us as it should have been.

It is not sufficient defense for you to say, "The two references to the newspaper reporting are clearly attributed to the student, J. Stafford Durham."

Again, I repeat, we believe Steve Maynard's story was accurate and not, as Baptist Press quoted J. Stafford Durham as saying, "carelessly written" and "not accurately written." We have tapes to back up the accuracy of our story.

It is not sufficient for you to say you "regret" that Steve Maynard and I are "offended by references to the *Houston Chronicle* in the Baptist Press story." You regret our feelings but not Baptist Press' unprofessional actions.

As an indication of your willingness to be fair, I expect an apology on behalf of Baptist Press, and not a deceptively worded "regret."

However, I have spoken my final word on this matter and this will be my last time to correspond with you on this matter.

I would appreciate your concluding this exchange with integrity.

Sincerely,
Louis Moore
Religion Editor

No response was ever received from either Harold Bennett or any representative of Baptist Press.

This event polarized the Executive Committee immediately and from the outset cast me in an adversarial position with certain members of its paid staff. If this had not occurred, it is quite possible that some of the polarization and division on the Executive Committee would not have occurred.

Dewey Presley, an influential layman from Texas, was chairman at that time. He ran a very tight ship, dealing with matters through the officers and the committee chairmen. Many of us believed that we were not allowed to have input before his group made decisions and passed them on to the Executive Committee as a whole for routine approval.

The move by some members of the Executive Committee to investigate Baptist Press came up on the floor suddenly, and Dewey was unable to deal with it through his normal procedural channels. Enough members of the Executive Committee felt that the matter merited consideration, so the vote was in favor of conducting a study.

I found it interesting to see how Baptist Press responded. The following is from the report I made to the Executive Committee in February 1985:

> Not one time since the meeting in September has anyone tried to contact me to discuss the article, to discuss reaching an understanding, or otherwise try to work out our difficulties. I understand that there has been no contact with the *Houston Chronicle* subsequent to their letter of October 5th. The only contact that I have had with anybody from the Executive Committee concerning this matter has been with Dr. Harold Bennett and later with Dr. Jimmy Jackson to express concern over the shortness of time allocated to the hearing on this matter when the situation needed to be thoroughly explored.
>
> I received a call from Bob Terry of the *Word and Way* in December in which he requested that I write down all the objections to the story. I told him that Dr. Everett Sneed of the *Arkansas Baptist* had proposed to me in the spring of 1984 that I come to the February meeting of the Baptist State Editors and speak before lunch and answer questions after lunch. Then when I had not heard back from Dr. Sneed, I called him in the fall only to find out that there was going to be no invitation to dialogue with members of the Baptist Press.

When Mr. Terry called in December, I told him I was still willing to dialogue and would be glad to discuss at length with them my objections to the story and the related matters with Baptist Press as well as to let them ask any questions that they wanted to ask of me. I have not heard again from Mr. Terry after his December call.

I also received a letter from a Dr. John DeMott of the Department of Journalism of Memphis State University dated January 23, 1985, a copy of which is attached. I immediately wrote Dr. DeMott asking him for information prior to answering his letter. It seemed to me that somebody was paying for a study to be made by someone upon whom he could count to support him on the story. The questions that I asked in my response to Dr. DeMott are ones I think this committee should ask if a study from DeMott is submitted. I received no further communication from Dr. DeMott.

His letter was as follows:

January 23, 1985
Dear Judge Pressler:

With some professional associates, I am researching the controversy over the Southern Baptist Convention Press Service's reporting of a news event involving the taping by you of a telephone conversation with Stafford Durham, a student at Southern Baptist Seminary, at Louisville, Kentucky.

At the heart of the controversy, it appears to us, are the news service's reports of September 17th and 18th.

Are there any inaccuracies in either or both of those stories in your opinion? If so, what, specifically, are those inaccuracies? If there are no specific inaccuracies, factually, what criticism do you have, if any, of either or both stories?

Whatever responses you can give me to the preceding questions—plus whatever perspective on related matters you may have time to provide—will be appreciated deeply.

Thanks, so much, for your cooperation.

My return note at the bottom of his letter was as follows:

I don't understand your letter. Please let me know the following:
1. Who are you?
2. Of what Southern Baptist church in Memphis are you a member?
3. Who are your "professional associates"?
4. How did you decide to make this study?
5. Who asked you to get involved?

6. Who is paying you and how much?

7. What will you do with your "research"?

I concluded my report to the Executive Committee as follows:

> It is also well known that members of Baptist Press have been calling and writing around the country to solicit letters of support from various religious news writers. If a few of such are presented before this Committee, it would be extremely pertinent to ask who was solicited that did not write letters and the extent to which arm twisting was utilized in order to obtain the letters presented. If none are presented, it is probably an evidence that a respectable showing could not be made even with pressure applied.

When the Executive Committee met in February 1985 I found out that Dr. DeMott was a member of a committee of three journalism professors evidently appointed and financed by some Baptist state editors to investigate the events surrounding the February Baptist Press story and to make a report to the Executive Committee. I thought it rather strange that the only communication that I ever received from this group was the letter quoted above written January 23, 1985, just a few days before the group's final report was completed. The group had gathered information from other people concerning the event but did not interview the one who made the complaint and was also the subject of the questioned reporting until immediately before the report was finalized. The group never met with me or obtained any input from me, and Dr. DeMott never answered the questions I wrote when I returned his letter. This appeared to me to be a very careful plan by some state Baptist editors to protect their friends in Baptist Press. Once the investigation was authorized, it seemed that a very strong effort at damage control was undertaken. I felt that Baptist Press and its supporters wanted this report to make it look as if they had tried to get information from me and to finalize the investigation without further study by the Executive Committee. There was no way I could have responded adequately with the short time that they gave me.

The investigation of Baptist Press was a major issue at the February Executive Committee board meeting. Here again, I was unwillingly thrust into the limelight. However, I believed that my side had to be presented. The committee charged with the responsibility of hearing the matter was the administrative sub-committee chaired by Nashville lawyer Frank Ingraham. I had prepared an approximately fifty-page document setting forth specific instances which I considered to be improper and prejudiced reporting by Baptist Press. Some of that narrative is quoted above.

When I came into the committee room with a suitcase full of these reports so that one could be distributed to every committee member and asked for time to make a presentation, I heard howls of anguish. Finally a motion was made to allow me to make my presentation. The vote was 15 to 6 to allow me to speak. I found it amazing that anyone should oppose having the other side told, but this taught me a great deal about how the Executive Committee was a tightly run ship under the leadership of Dewey Presley and Harold Bennett. Those things that were discordant or did not suit the direction in which they were trying to lead were handled quietly and firmly.

I was allowed forty-five minutes to make my presentation and was firmly interrupted when the forty-five minutes were over. Without my knowledge, included in my time were ten minutes required to hand out the report and to reach decisions with the committee about the method of presentation. I watched the clock very closely and thought I had ten minutes left, but I was informed that my time had expired.

The final vote of the Executive Committee cleared Baptist Press, but control of the discussion had not been as tight as those in charge might have desired. Information concerning the manner in which the Baptist Press operated had been disseminated. In the minds of most, the report of the three professors had been discredited. I never heard the report referred to again. The stage had been set for a more careful look at Baptist Press, its method of operation, and whether it was being fair to all. The report which I had prepared, although not released through the committee, was widely distributed by me and my friends. In some ways this resembled the course my report took years before when I wrote to the deacons at Second Baptist Church about the Elliott matter.

Baptist Press made a serious mistake. Instead of admitting the stories were mismanaged, apologizing, and promising to do better in the future, Baptist Press circled the wagons and wrapped itself in robes of self-righteousness. This caused me to conclude that fairness from Baptist Press was impossible. I was particularly offended by the manner in which it tried to justify that which was not justifiable.

I hoped that when W. C. Fields retired, an attempt would be made to find a Baptist Press director who would be fair to all Baptists. Several others and I communicated this desire to Harold Bennett. As described in chapter 23, meaningful participation in this matter was denied to us.

After his election, Al Shackleford asked for one year to prove his fairness. In the three years that he was granted, he was constantly admonished and often shown specifically what we felt was unfairness to conservatives. These communications were both written and oral. At no time did he seem to respond positively. To many of us on the Executive Committee, it appeared that Al Shackleford felt that Bob Terry and the other state editors were his bosses and the persons to whom he needed to relate. It seemed to us that he felt no responsibility to the members of the Executive Committee to be fair to conservatives. State editors Julian Pentecost of Virginia, Bob Allen of Maryland (and later Associated Baptist Press), Gene Puckett of North Carolina, and Don McGregor of Mississippi seemed to me to be the most vitriolic against conservatives. Bob Terry seemed to me to exercise a great deal of control behind the scenes.

Finally, Al Shackleford and Dan Martin were fired in the summer of 1990. At the time of this incident, I was in Europe with my family on a trip that we had planned for a long time. The Executive Committee did what I believe had to be done. If this had not occurred, we would still be faced with the same unfair treatment that we received for so many years from the Baptist Press, and peace could not have returned to the convention. We hoped by having someone fair and impartial at the Baptist Press helm, we would see an end to liberal propagandizing through Baptist Press. We needed to redirect BP's approach in such a way that conservatives would receive fair treatment. Only the future will reveal whether this has occurred.

Herb Hollinger, state editor in California, was selected new Baptist Press director in 1991. I hope that my vote both as a member of the Officers Committee, which served as a search committee, and as an Executive Committee member for Herb is one that I will not regret in future years. The question is whether he can withstand the pressure that, even as I write this, the liberal editors are applying to steer Herb toward their camp or cause him to resign in frustration. I was extremely disappointed in his reporting about my election to the International Mission Board trustee board in 1992. Time will tell about his performance.

The loss of circulation by state Baptist papers has interested me greatly. Had I edited a paper which lost 40 or 50 percent of its circulation, I would have been more than passively interested in knowing why. A survey of lost readers or some sort of study would have seemed only reasonable. However, if the paper's leadership feared what might be found by such a study, it might have hesitated to investigate why cancellations occurred. I know of no study which has been made.

Some people have alleged that the drop in circulation is due to increased subscription prices because of the mailing costs or because of a change in reader habits. These explanations do not really answer the question. The cost of everything has increased. People read what interests them. The circulation and readership of such secular newspapers as the *Houston Chronicle* and the *Dallas Morning News* have increased dramatically during the same time that the circulation of such state papers as the (Texas) *Baptist Standard* and the (North Carolina) *Biblical Recorder* have declined drastically. Most secular papers would close their doors and go out of business if faced with the decline of some of the Baptist state newspapers.

Baptist Press and state paper editors were very quick to back a study when they felt they needed to protect their credibility in 1984 and 1985. Why do they hesitate to back a study which would be vital to their continued effectiveness? Do they fear what it might show? State papers should realistically determine what the support which some of them gave to the liberal establishment cost them in credibility and readership. This would help if they desire to heal and appeal to all Southern Baptists.

The following circulation totals for 1998, 1996, 1987, 1983 and 1980 are taken from the Southern Baptist Annuals. The 1980 total is taken from the state convention reports. The figures for the other years are from the Denominational Press Report to the convention. The year given is that of the Annual in which they appeared. These are not my figures but are figures the state papers themselves supplied to the Executive Committee of the SBC. The circulation of the major papers is as follows:

	1998	1996	1987	1983	1980	% decline
Alabama	110,000	113,318	139,000	165,000	156,000	29%
Arkansas	35,000	37,000	56,000	61,300	72,200	52%
Florida	45,000	44,343	92,000	94,100	87,500	48%
Georgia	61,734	59,000	98,000	110,000	125,000	52%
Kentucky	45,000	48,000	60,000	60,000	60,000	25%
Louisiana	43,500	44,750	64,000	69,000	69,000	37%
Mississippi	102,500	102,000	121,262	126,000	128,339	20%
Missouri	45,000	50,000	60,000	60,000	67,235	32%
N. Carolina	50,000	55,000	95,400	100,379	118,156	58%
Oklahoma	93,620	100,167	120,000	113,891	96,800	3%
S. Carolina	99,165	103,000	125,000	124,000	127,000	22%
Tennessee	56,000	60,000	75,000	77,000	82,000	32%
Texas	188,858	204,008	337,755	376,544	392,196	52%
Virginia	23,500	30,000	40,000	40,000	50,000	54%
Total Circ.	1,206,561	1,265,399	1,719,767	1,816,842	1,865,174	35%
of all State	(p. 271 of	(p. 327 of	(p. 230 of	(p. 217 of	(p. 385-396	
Papers	Annual)	Annual)	Annual)	Annual)	of Annual)	
(including						
those above)						

The net decrease in circulation of all the state papers between 1979 and 1998 was approximately 35 percent. The decrease of circulation in certain states was far greater. In North Carolina, Georgia, Virginia, Arkansas, and Texas, the loss was 52 percent or more during this period. Florida lost almost 48 percent. On the other hand, the relatively conservative state paper in Oklahoma lost only 3 percent in circulation during the same period. Additional Texas figures are interesting. In the October 22, 1997, issue of the *Baptist Standard* the U.S. Postal Service Statement of Ownership, Management, and Circulation was published as required. In very small print which a person could read only with great magnification, it said the following:

Average Number of Copies Each Issue During Preceding 12 Months
Press Run: 199,998
Total Paid and/or Requested Mail Subscription: 184,555
Average Number of Copies of Single Issue Published
Nearest to Filing Run Press Run: 199,573
Total Paid and/or Requested Mail Subscription: 181,601

Any way you look at it, since 1979 the Texas *Baptist Standard* has decreased in circulation dramatically. The decline to a total paid figure of 181,601 is eye-popping. While the number of Texas Baptists increased, the once-mighty state paper lost more than 200,000 subscribers, according to the SBC Annuals and more than 210,000, if you use the most recent figures published by the *Standard*. But what happened in Texas was merely the benchmark for the declines elsewhere. Subscribers have been voting with their subscriptions, and they have cast their ballots against these liberal-biased relics of the past.

In a column in the September 16, 1997, issue of *Baptists Today*, an independent paper supporting liberal causes, its then-editor Jack Harwell stated as follows:

Along with Mike Clinginpeel in Virginia and Mark Wingfield in Kentucky, Gene (Puckett) and Toby (Druin) are currently doing some of the best editorial writing found among Baptist editors. I recently saw a needlepoint plaque which read, "In the cookies of life, friends are the chocolate chips." Toby Druin and Gene Puckett have been chocolate chips for me. Thanks, fellows for your friendship!

It is interesting to note that the ones with whom this leading supporter of the liberal cause identified are editors of papers which show such marked decline in circulation. Three of these papers are among the five which have lost more than half of their circulation—far more than the average loss of 35 percent. A fourth paper which lost more than half of its circulation was in Georgia, where Jack Harwell himself was the former editor. This should tell us something.

In an editorial on October 1, 1997, entitled "*Baptist Standard:* The People's Paper," editor Toby Druin stated, "This editor wants the *Standard* to be the *Standard* of all Texas Baptists. I believe this column reflects it." He continues as follows:

> Some people, particularly some pastors, do not want their members reading about other Baptist groups or about things controversial and have led their churches to stop sending the *Standard* to their families in spite of the fact that every issue contains stories that offer good examples of what Baptists are doing to fulfill their responsibilities as Christians.

On page 2 of the same issue a story is entitled "Wade cites reasons why Texas stays 'free.'" The story quotes Charles Wade, at that time president of the Baptist General Convention of Texas (BGCT) as well as pastor of First Baptist Church of Arlington, Texas. Wade is a moderate. Part of the *Standard* article reads as follows:

> Wade addressed one of 17 rallies being sponsored by Texas Baptists Committed, a group supportive of BGCT leadership, prior to the state convention's annual meeting in Austin, Nov. 10–11. People frequently ask why the BGCT has not fallen to the conservative movement that captured control of the SBC and turned it sharply to the right, said Wade, pastor of First Church in Arlington. "First, we know each other well enough that they can't lie about us without having to face up to their lies," Wade said. He cited two examples . . .

The *Standard* article implied that what Charles Wade called "lies" were actually circulated by conservatives. Conservatives had no opportunity to refute what Wade accused us of doing. This is the type of treatment which we now expect from the *Standard* and many other state papers because it happens so often. Toby could have read elsewhere in that issue of his paper to understand why "some people, particularly pastors, do not want their members reading . . ." Studying his own magazine's articles could have shown him why his paper had lost at least 52 percent of the ones who were once his audience—he and many other state editors have simply not been fair or even reasonable with Southern Baptist conservatives.

CHAPTER 27

$\mathcal{A}$ HEART FOR MISSIONS

My service as a trustee with the Foreign Mission Board (FMB) of the Southern Baptist Convention, now International Mission Board (IMB), followed a lifelong interest in missions and numerous opportunities to spread the gospel overseas. As a child in Sunday School and Training Union, the wonderful accounts of missionaries started my interest. This interest became stronger when, as a college student, I had the opportunity to give my testimony in a church in Mexico. To see people in less-developed countries who have neither spiritual nor physical bread was a real heartache for me.

I read the stories of Lottie Moon, David Brainerd, Hudson Taylor, William Carey, and many other Christians who gave their lives on the mission field. I have always believed that bringing people into a saving knowledge of the Lord Jesus Christ is the most important thing that a believer can do. The command of the Great Commission is worldwide. We cannot sit back in comfort while people throughout the world are headed for a Christless eternity.

In 1954, on my first trip abroad, I had the opportunity in Greece and Israel to share my testimony. This gave me an even stronger desire to speak at other times and in other places abroad.

Our first trip to Eastern Europe was in 1971. Before we left, Nancy and I talked to a friend who was on the board of a group that smuggled Bibles behind the Iron Curtain. He asked us to take some Bibles into Russia. We agreed to do so, and he supplied us with eight Russian-language Bibles. Because these Bibles were few in number, we filled a suitcase with additional Christian literature, including "Four Spiritual Laws" tracts, Good News English translations of the New Testament, and children's material.

When Nancy and I arrived in the Moscow airport, we were placed in a line to go through customs. The officials were checking every piece of paper in everyone's suitcases. We grew apprehensive, since we had one full suitcase of Christian literature, not just in English but also the eight Bibles in Russian. As we moved forward in the line for about forty-five minutes, we both prayed fervently. When we were about fifteen minutes away from being checked, we noticed a group of people, dressed as Westerners, who had been given VIP treatment in a back

225

room. (Later, we heard that these people were attending an international tuber-culosis conference in Moscow.) After they had been checked and cleared, the customs officials moved our line and the line next to us aside to clear a space for these people to walk between our two lines. Nancy and I looked at each other and did not say a word. We picked up our suitcases and got in the middle of this group that had already been checked. We walked through the customs area without having a bag opened. This truly was a miracle of God.

When we got to the other side of customs, we found the person who would be our guide and under whose surveillance we would be for the days we were in Moscow. After we exchanged pleasantries, the first question he asked me was, "Where is your money voucher?" I handed him the voucher which we had filled out declaring all currency and securities which we were bringing into Russia. He looked at it and said, "But it is not stamped." (The money voucher was to be stamped after clearance by customs.) I replied, "Yes, he did not stamp it." (I decided that it was best *not* to tell him why the customs official did not stamp it.) Our guide then said, "But nobody ever gets into Russia without having his money voucher stamped!" I replied, "We're in Russia, and we don't have our money voucher stamped. What are you going to do about it?" The guide said some things in Russian which I'm very glad that I did not understand and then took our money voucher, went over to a friend's desk, stamped it with the official stamp, initialed it, and brought it back to us. Thus, the problem of getting the literature into Russia was solved.

Later, we met a Catholic priest who been forced to hand over one of two English-language Daily Missals he had with him and to see it destroyed. The customs officials told him he could not personally use two Missals while he was in Russia.

The remaining problem, however, was that we had a suitcase full of material that the Russian government classified as "contraband and subversive literature," and we had to deliver it. We arrived at a plan. For a couple of days as we went on our tour bus, we took our carry-on baggage with sweaters, cameras, and various other items. We spread them around so everybody would know what we had in our carry-on bags.

On the third day, we had a later invitation for dinner at the American embassy with some friends in the U.S. State Department. The morning before that evening invitation, we put all the Russian Bibles and most of the Christian literature in the carry-on luggage with a few other things on top. We told the guide about our invitation. At the appropriate time she called a taxi to take us back to the hotel so we could freshen up before going to the embassy. When we were out of sight of the guide, I handed the taxi driver a little slip of paper which had instructions in Russian. I could not read it. It was supposed to request a ride to the address of the contact point for delivering the Bibles. The guide pointed to the paper and then pointed to Nancy and me. I nodded, and he started off across the city. It was not possible for us to read the Russian street signs because their alphabet is different. We were completely isolated. We felt the danger of the Cold War, but we knew we were in God's hands.

Finally the taxi driver pulled up in front of a door. I got out and knocked on the door while Nancy, keeping one of the bags, remained in the cab. The person who answered spoke only Russian. I opened the carry-on bag, and he could see a Bible. He seemed very pleased, and I knew we obviously were at the right place. I quickly went and got Nancy and the rest of the literature. By that time someone who spoke English had come to the door. I can now say that our contact was the Central Baptist Church of Moscow, where years later I would preach. With tears welling up in their eyes, the people told us they were amazed that we were able to bring this Christian literature. They said it was almost impossible to get a Bible through customs at that time. When we delivered the eight Russian-language Bibles and the other Christian literature, they could not believe what had happened and said that it was truly a miracle from God. We knew that it was!

Our new Russian friends told us about two women who, in order to get a Bible, had walked six hundred kilometers to Moscow from their village. The women were part of a congregation of about one thousand, but not even the pastor had a full Bible. The day before we arrived, the persons at the delivery point had told the women that they knew of no way they could get a Bible to them. The next day, the women were to return to their homes, unsuccessful in their twelve-hundred-kilometer trek. By closing the eyes of the customs officials, the Lord provided them with a Bible. This heightened our concern for Eastern Europe and our desire to reach other people there for Jesus Christ.

A highlight of our visit in Moscow was attending services in Central Baptist Church. We saw more than twenty people follow the Lord in baptism. Three questions were posed to them: (1) "Do you know that you are a sinner and that Jesus Christ died to pay the price for your sins?" (2) "Have you personally accepted Jesus Christ as your Savior?" (3) "Are you willing to live for the Lord Jesus Christ regardless of what it costs?" The third question affected us particularly, because at that time those who identified themselves as believers and followed the Lord in baptism were losing their opportunity to hold meaningful jobs or to have a good education for their children. We thought about the easy Christianity in America contrasted with the deep sacrifice of these people as they risked their whole material future in this world by following the Lord Jesus Christ.

In 1973, Nancy and I took our three children, then ages ten, eight, and seven, along with twenty teenagers—ten boys and ten girls—on an evangelistic tour in Europe. The trip was planned in cooperation with Dr. D. H. "Dub" Jackson and his World Evangelism Foundation. I admire Dub tremendously. He developed a concept of partnership evangelism where teams of Southern Baptists go into other countries and conduct evangelistic campaigns in various cooperating churches. I think we were his first youth evangelism team. It was an experience having twenty-three teenagers and preteenagers in our care for six weeks. God gave grace to all the young people, and Nancy and I, as the only adults, had a minimum of problems.

We flew to England, and our first meetings were in the South Oxford Baptist Church. The pastor was our friend Richard Land, who had been a teacher in our summer Bible studies and now is president of the Ethics and Religious Liberty Commission of the Southern Baptist Convention. Richard was working on his Ph.D. at Oxford. Individuals in our youth group had adopted him and raised money to help defray his expenses. We were at the church for a high tea and an evening service. That night a young man who was a Ph.D. physics student at Oxford came to know Jesus Christ as personal Savior.

Several years before, in one of the Bible studies I had led in the sand hills of Pennsylvania while I was in the Navy, a young man who was mentally retarded had prayed with me to accept Christ. I thought how wonderful it is that a God of grace and mercy can save both that young man and a Ph.D. graduate student at Oxford with the same simple message of salvation through the blood of Jesus Christ.

After our time in England, we went to Germany and joined other Americans in the ballroom of the Dusseldorf Hilton. As we entered, a soloist was singing "The King is Coming." What a thrill! Hundreds dispersed from Dusseldorf to churches all over Germany. We went to Nordheim, a city in the Hanover area. God mightily blessed that week. Richard Land was the primary preacher, and the young people and Nancy and I led Bible studies and the worship

We were in a very interesting church. The pastor had resigned soon after he agreed for us to hold the meeting, so not much preparation for our visit had occurred. The lay leadership was outstanding, and what could have been a disaster was remedied by the laity. Our emphasis was to be with young people. The youth director was an intelligent and fine young man, but he had a completely different view from ours about the gospel of Christ. For the first two or three days of the meeting, everything was very formal. Finally, the youth director confronted me and said that we did not preach the way he believed. He said we talked about nothing but the Bible and that we thought that the Bible had all the answers. He said that the church wanted to discuss other issues and asked us to be more open to other ideas.

I asked him if he believed all that the Old Testament prophets have said. He said he did not because the Old Testament was the work of men. I took him to the passage in Luke 24:25, 27 where Christ said to his disciples, "O fools, and slow of heart to believe all that the prophets have spoken . . . And beginning at Moses and all the prophets, he expounded unto them in all the scriptures the things concerning himself." We used a parallel-column German/English Bible. After he read the passage in German, I asked him what Christ had called His disciples in His day if they refused to believe all that the prophets had spoken. In his strongly accented English, he replied, "He called them fools." I then asked what He would call a person today who did not believe all that the prophets had spoken. He said, "He would call me a fool." This is a type of confrontation in which I usually did not engage, but I felt it was called for at that time.

From then on the whole spirit of the meeting changed. The youth director changed his attitude, the resistance ended, and the schools were opened for our young people to present the gospel. Attendance at the meeting increased tremendously, and by the end of the week, we saw a number of young people come to know Jesus Christ as personal Savior. Despite the cold reception we received when we arrived, we left with tearful embraces. A drizzling rain fell as we left Nordheim. One of our hosts told us that they had a saying in Germany that when a painful separation occurs, even the heavens weep.

The next place to interact with Christians on our tour was Yugoslavia. We were to contact a woman called "Sister Fanny" and see what we could do to assist in the area of Opatia (now in Croatia). With real difficulty we located Sister Fanny. In 1973 the Cold War was intense, and we had to ask directions many times. Finally we found her on an upper story in a communist-style apartment building. She greeted us very warmly and insisted that I preach the next day. The church, which was in the adjoining city of Rijeka, was across the street from the communist army barracks. As I preached the gospel of the saving grace of our Lord Jesus Christ, the communist troops were practicing their drills outside the open window. The contrast was overwhelming.

While staying at our hotel on the beach at Opatia, our young people met two students from the Yugoslavian merchant marine academy. Although they were preparing for their final exams, they spent a good bit of time with our young people. One night, we were sitting on the shore of the Adriatic Sea teaching these students Christian hymns in this atheistic communist country. One of the choruses that we sang talked about the second coming of the Lord, when "the man that says there is no God will know that he's a fool." We still keep in contact with one of these men.

In the late 1960s, I joined the board of directors of International Students Incorporated (ISI), an organization involved in friendship evangelism with internationals in the United States. Hal Guffey was then president. He and his wife, Betsy, are two of our close friends. In 1975, with the Guffeys and other board members, Nancy and I traveled to Central and South America. In Costa Rica and Ecuador were a number of persons who had trusted Jesus Christ as personal Savior while in the United States through ISI and other groups. They needed follow-up now that they had returned home. Also many evangelistic opportunities had developed. In Costa Rica some of the leading citizens of the country had been reached through ISI. Zulay Carmona, a staff member, had organized meetings for us. One at which I spoke was a breakfast with more than sixty leaders of the country, including several justices of the supreme court of Costa Rica.

In Ecuador a woman named Isabella Cuevas began ISI's work there. She went to the United States as a nanny for some Americans in the diplomatic service. While in Washington D.C., she had trusted the Lord through an international Bible study sponsored by ISI. She developed a burden for her people and gave ISI a tract of land and ten thousand dollars to start a mission in her hometown. This gift represented almost all of her life savings. We stayed at the mission station near the slopes of Mt. Cotopoxy, south of Quito. We were impressed with seeing more than four hundred Indians walk miles and miles into the mission station for the church services on Sunday morning. Other services were being held in even more remote areas. More than one thousand Indians had been saved because of the gift and sacrifice of one woman. The conditions were primitive. No water pump existed. We watched as the Indians worked all night to bring water in pails from the well to fill the baptistry so a baptismal service could be held the next morning. On this mission trip we learned much from the Lord. After our return, the mission received a pump from friends in Houston.

Another important mission trip was with ISI in 1976. We had been very concerned about strengthening our ties with returnees to the Orient who had trusted the Lord through ISI while in the United States. Nancy and I agreed to take a group of twenty to the Orient, where I preached twenty-nine times in nine countries in thirty-five days. We went to encourage the returnees and to develop ways of having young people who would be coming to the United States referred to ISI before they arrived. On this trip were four adults and eleven young people from our youth group plus Nancy and me and our three children, who were then thirteen, eleven, and ten. We had meetings in Japan, Korea, Taiwan, Hong Kong, Thailand, East and West Malaysia, Singapore, and the Philippines. Also, we rested for a few days on the island of Bali in Indonesia, where we were excited to find a Christian orphanage. Seeing precious people throughout Southeast Asia who were paying a price for their witness for the Lord Jesus Christ inspired us and opened our eyes even more to evangelistic opportunities.

We had other mission trips and other opportunities, but these were the most important in formulating and reinforcing our desire to support and be involved in missions. We have also been involved in friendship evangelism with internationals in the United States through ISI and our local church's program. In 1998, the president of the University of Houston presented us with a plaque designating us as "Host Family of the Year."

In 1984, to celebrate their fiftieth anniversary, Nancy's parents took their children and grandchildren to Switzerland, where they had engaged a chalet for Christmas. Nancy, Paul, and I flew over early. Because of Paul's illness, he needed time to rest after the long flight before getting involved in the activities with the rest of the family. Since we were flying straight to Zurich, I called Bill O'Brien, then an officer with the Foreign (now International) Mission Board. I had known Bill in Texas. He came to a Bible conference held at our ranch. I told him we were going to Zurich and that I had heard that the Baptist Theological Seminary at Ruschlikon was near there. I told him I would be interested in seeing it and wondered if I could take a cab or train out to the seminary. Bill said that he would arrange everything.

When we arrived at our hotel from the airport, the seminary president, Altus Newell, was waiting at the registration desk. We quickly put our bags in the room and went with him to the village of Ruschlikon, where the seminary was located. We were extremely surprised to find very few people on

Judge and Mrs. Paul Pressler and son Paul IV on visit to Ruschlikon Baptist Seminary in Switzerland. December 1984

campus. Our tour was quite restricted. In the cafeteria were students who sat at the far end. I asked whether I could meet them and was quickly told that it could not be allowed on our schedule. We had tea with one of the staff members and the president and received an excellent tour of the physical facilities. We were completely isolated from contact with anyone except the president and this particular staff member.

I heard later that the students who had not already left for Christmas were told to leave campus for the day and that everyone was instructed not to have any contact with us. My desire to see the seminary evidently was taken as a threat and as an investigatory tour. I concluded that they did not want me to find out certain things about the seminary. This was humorous to me, because my interest had been merely to see and understand the seminary so I could be supportive. This type of paranoia bothered me greatly.

In 1991, the year before I was elected a mission board trustee, I had an opportunity to preach in the former Soviet Union. Rev. Tolly Jaloshin, who was then head of an independent mission work with Slavic people, arranged for and took me on this trip. I first went to Romania and met with Baptist leaders. Then I took the train from Budapest to Kiev, where I met Tolly. He had arranged meetings with Baptist and governmental leaders as well as preaching opportunities in Baptist churches. I was extremely impressed with Dr. Jakob Dukhonchenko, now deceased, who was head of the Baptist work in the Ukraine. We spent a full day with him and were grateful for his gracious manner and his desire to reach his people for Christ. Not only did I speak in one of the largest churches in Kiev, I also saw the construction of new Baptist churches.

From Kiev we went to Moscow, where I had the opportunity to preach on Sunday morning in Central Baptist Church, the congregation to which we delivered Bibles and where we worshiped in 1971. The difference in atmosphere between 1971 and 1991 was remarkable. I enjoyed conferring with Dr. Ivan Korablev, who was pastor of the church. Russian Baptists have good leaders who believe the Word and preach the blood of Christ as payment for the price of our sins.

I also met on religious liberty issues with the assistant to the attorney general for the Russian Republic and her assistants. They could not comprehend the concept of complete freedom of religion without governmental registration and regulation of churches.

We met with the officers of the Book Society, the Society of Learning, and the Deaf Society in order to expedite the presentation of the gospel among members of these groups. One of these meetings was with the communist, Russian member of Parliament who sponsored the Deaf Society. This society was said to have more than ten million members. The president and secretary of the society attended the meeting with the Parliament member. It was held in a dark, dingy Russian restaurant, far away from the places where tourists usually go. As the member of Parliament gave his blessing to the opening of evangelistic work among the members of the society at their regular meetings, he consumed large quantities of vodka. Before the meeting ended, he confided that he knew that Christianity was true and that, therefore, he would become a Christian some day, but for the present, he was unwilling to give up his drinking and his women. At least he understood that trusting the Lord would lead to a change in his pattern of life.

Some of these contacts were very valuable when I returned in March 1993 to teach at the Baptist Bible Academy in Obninsk. My friend Brad Ray of Dallas and several others involved in ministry to the deaf went on that second trip. A thriving ministry among the deaf in Russia now exists as a result of these contacts.

From Moscow we went to St. Petersburg, where I preached on Thursday night and Sunday morning in their largest Baptist church. I have never seen such brokenness as we saw on Thursday night. God blessed in a remarkable way, and many decisions, mostly by young people, occurred. I also had the privilege of speaking in a new Baptist church which was being renovated by a team from the United States. God blessed on that mission trip, and it, coupled with other preaching opportunities in Romania, the Ukraine, and East Germany, gave me

Judge Paul Pressler preaching at a Baptist Church in Romania, summer of 1991

a burden for Eastern Europe and a commitment to see that the gospel is preached forcefully, effectively, and clearly there.

My time on the Executive Committee ended in 1991. This service had been difficult because so many changes needed to be made. By 1992, the conflict in the Southern Baptist Convention appeared to be over. The attacks against me still hurt deeply. I was eager to do something to let people know who I really was. I longed to return to a noncontroversial Christian testimony as I had experienced before the SBC controversy began. After being approached about serving on the FMB (now IMB) trustee board to replace my close friend Paul Martin, a lawyer from Houston, and praying about the matter, I told the Texas members of the Committee on Nominations that I would accept nomination to the trustee board if it were forthcoming. I considered that this would be a positive step which would channel my activities constructively. The Ruschlikon seminary by then had been defunded (an explanation of this follows), and it appeared that the needed changes were already occurring at the mission board.

I was tremendously surprised at what occurred. Soon after I was nominated, and while the nomination was still supposed to be confidential, I received telephone calls and letters from a few people urging me not to be nominated to the FMB trustee board. They professed appreciation for me but said that I should not serve for several reasons: (1) I was too controversial; (2) I had already served on a board and needed to step aside and let some other people serve; (3) it would be very disharmonious for me to serve on this trustee board because of my involvement with the conservative movement; and (4) such a groundswell of antagonism existed against me personally that I probably would be defeated on the floor if the nomination were presented to the convention.

When the first few calls came in, Nancy and I prayed about the matter again. We felt no leading from the Lord whatsoever to withdraw my name from nomination. A few conservative leaders then put a great deal of pressure on me. They seemed to react to a few others who had never been my friends. They were more intent on responding to these than on supporting me. This lack of support from friends hurt me more than anything else that happened in the Southern Baptist Convention controversy. The period of time from my nomination by the committee in March until my election to the board in June was the most difficult time I had in the entire controversy.

I received more than one hundred letters concerning my nomination. The large majority urged me not to withdraw. Those who did urge me to withdraw made basically one or more of the four points above. One letter from a pastor in Texas was particularly troublesome. He said he knew pastors in his hometown who had supported the conservative movement because they saw it as an opportunity for them to serve on boards and commissions where previously they would have been excluded. He said that if I was going to be elected to a board or commission after having served before, that would keep one of them from serving and his friends would probably stop supporting the conservative movement.

I wrote him back and told him that if anyone was supporting the conservative movement because that person hoped to have any personal gain from it, like serving on a board or commission, his or her motivation was entirely wrong. Such a person should be excluded from service because of that attitude. I believe this very strongly. Many of those who urged me not to withdraw said that if I did, it would tell those who had paid the price for working in the conservative movement that they, too, would be disqualified from service. This would be the wrong message to send.

I never wavered in my conviction that God was calling me to serve as an FMB trustee. I could not understand why some people who had asked me to pray about the matter could not accept the fact that, after much prayer, God had given me the answer that they did not want. Did they believe that I wasn't open to God's leadership or that they had a more superior path to God than a layman had?

I did throw out one fleece. A person who was in a position to place me in an alternative place of service had put pressure on me to withdraw. I told him that if he would appoint me to a position which would give me a reason to withdraw my nomination, I would. Without even praying over the matter, he immediately refused to do this. If I had withdrawn as a nominee, the liberal press would have said that something obviously was in my background that kept me from being qualified to serve and that I had refused the appointment to avoid embarrassment from revelations surfacing about me. The fact that this would occur was something that some of those persons seeking my withdrawal never recognized, although I explained it to them numerous times. It seemed that they never considered the ramifications of my withdrawal. What the liberals could not do in years of attack, a few conservatives did in one month. They broke my spirit.

When it became obvious that I would not withdraw, some of those who requested my withdrawal actually started supporting my nomination. Some did begrudgingly and some enthusiastically. One of those who had opposed my serving was Bill Hancock of Kentucky. He was then rotating off the FMB trustee board and was just ending two years of service as board chairman. Bill and I had worked together closely in the past, and I did not understand his vehement opposition to my serving. I have always wondered if Keith Parks, president of the mission board, put pressure on Bill to oppose me.

My close friend, Dr. Laverne Butler, arranged a conference call with himself, Bill, and me. We discussed the matter at length. When I refused Bill's request to withdraw my nomination, Bill finally said that he "guessed" he would not oppose me. Two individuals had told others that they would nominate someone against me. One of these who made this threat was also a trustee of the FMB. I found his desire to be friends after I was elected very interesting. He never knew whether I knew of his threats. I was pleasant and never indicated I had heard. I hold nothing against these people. I was extremely hurt, however, that they did not consider the full ramifications of their opposition.

Right up until the time of the Indianapolis SBC meeting at which the vote occurred, rumors concerning opposition to my nomination still surfaced. When the time came, someone was nominated against me, but neither he nor the nominator was well-known. I received an estimated 80 to 85 percent of the vote, which was by show of hands. I took this as a tremendous affirmation by Southern Baptists.

Then another distressing event occurred. The press release about my election merely said that I was elected and then quoted one of my detractors talking about my winning by a small margin. This really bothered me. The article did not mention the 80- to 85-percent margin which I received. Those with Baptist Press and the author of the article admitted to me that the article was not well-written. They revised the article to make it satisfactory, but most of the state papers ran the earlier version. Somehow, from my objecting strenuously to the article, someone started the fallacious story that I was trying to get the new editor of Baptist Press fired because of this poor story. This was simply not true.

Right after the SBC meeting, as I usually did, I left for Europe with my family to try to recover from the pressures and heartaches of the convention controversy. Although I could have been reached any evening of the trip, no one tried to contact me about the unfounded and false rumor that I was trying to get Herb Hollinger fired. I contacted Herb several times and told him how upset I was about this rumor. The only possible basis for the rumor I could think of is that I had remarked to Herb that we had gone through the turmoil of firing the previous Baptist Press editor and I wondered if we had come out with anything better. I never threatened his job, nor did I want to do so. No effort was made to find out the truth and what I actually said.

I did not attend my first board meeting because I had planned the European trip before my nomination. The last thing I wanted to do was attend another meeting where I was not sure I was wanted. I had entertained a number of thoughts. One was that of resigning immediately, as soon as I was elected, so that someone else could be elected. I also considered serving a year and then resigning, or serving my first term and then not be a candidate for reelection. By the time I was elected, the whole matter had become so thoroughly distasteful that I had personally lost my desire to serve as a mission board trustee. I realized that if I resigned from the board, the liberal press would probably make up a story claiming I had made a deal with certain people not to oppose me in exchange for my promise to resign. Therefore, I did not have the liberty of resigning. I believed that anything I would do that would be out of the ordinary would be misconstrued, misrepresented, and lied about by the liberals and their allies in the press.

I decided that I would serve my full time on the trustee board so nobody could say that I made a deal. Now, as the hurt has eased and time has passed, my original enthusiasm about serving on this trustee board has returned. My desire for God to use me in international missions could not be stronger.

I went on the FMB (now IMB) trustee board in the waning days of Keith Parks's presidency. I am glad I did not have to vote on the Ruschlikon seminary matter or on the matters that Keith Parks used to try to make an issue for his departure from the FMB. Those things were history before I went on the board. I cannot justly be accused of being responsible. However, for historical purposes, the events which occurred before my service should be detailed. No better analysis of what happened exists than the letter sent to the trustee board by Ron Wilson, a California pastor, who served with distinction on the board and provided astute, dedicated leadership. Ron's letter details events as follows:

> Let me explain the purpose of this letter. It deals with our vote when we gave away Ruschlikon seminary to the EBF (European Baptist Federation).
>
> You will recall this vote finally happened after much chess playing by the staff and the Europeans with our board. Remember that originally we were examining the possibility of selling Ruschlikon Seminary, changing its emphasis and relocating the property we could buy and renovate in Brussels, Belgium. Dr. Cal Guy and others were convinced the Brussels property would accommodate 500 students and could serve as a retreat center and a training ground with Eastern Europe Christian leadership as the primary focus. The cost at the time for the purchase and renovation would have been in the neighborhood of four to five million dollars. The value of the Ruschlikon property at that time was nearly twenty-seven million dollars.
>
> A committee was formed to go over and examine this possibility, but liberal European leadership was ready for them. Trustees were presented with a

scenario of doom and destruction if Ruschlikon were to be sold and a different kind of ministry developed.

In Richmond the script was prepared to bring fear to the board if we moved in the direction of Brussels. Then a campaign by the "butters" ensued (definition time again: butters—a theological conservative, even an inerrantist, who comes up with an excuse to defend a vote that would contradict the purpose of his election and biblical stand; not to be confused with a meteorologist which is one who sticks his finger in the air to ascertain which way the wind is blowing).

One knows he is in trouble when he hears a conservative say, "I am a conservative, but . . ."

Pressure was brought upon the board through various means. I have in my possession an anonymous letter sent to me by some employee at the FMB that in essence states that former leadership helped stir up the Europeans so that pressure could be brought on the board to not sell Ruschlikon. The "butters" began to work the halls of the Holiday Inn and the FMB and the meteorologists were watchful. It didn't make any difference that we had supported this liberal institution for 40 years and accomplished little. All of a sudden, we were moving too fast and we shouldn't listen to the extremists.

Then the committee came back from Europe and brought what was a unique solution to the problem—just give the property to the Europeans.

Debate time. Isam (Ballenger), Keith Parks, and others made it clear that to sell the property and move the location of the school would kill the school, that its uniqueness and success (whatever that was) was based on the location. In fact, (I) remember a tearful, pleading Isam Ballenger indicating that to move this institution to Brussels would destroy it and destroy all the mission work that we had done previously in Europe. Indeed, if we did not give this 27 million dollar property to the Europeans, they would have their feelings hurt and become angry with us. Well, we certainly did not want to hurt or make the Europeans angry so, the "butters" had a reason to vote for the continuation of liberal theology at Ruschlikon.

During the debates, Dr. Paige Patterson, among others, made a clear argument for not giving Ruschlikon away and in fact gave reasons for selling and moving it. Although I do not remember all of his argument that day (for he made statements in the Europe Committee and in other venues), his argument included:

1. The opportunity would be lost with the Brussels property.

2. If we gave the property to the Europeans, they would not support the institution to the degree that it would be able to stay in Ruschlikon.

3. Declaring that its success was tied to its location was an empty argument because he predicted that they would be forced to sell that property and be forced to move elsewhere in Europe.

4. At that point, when the institution would be moved, there would be an endowment created that would help perpetuate theological liberalism in Europe for decades.

So the argument ultimately rested upon the assurances of Ballenger and Parks that the institution would change and turn in a conservative direction and stay there in Switzerland against Patterson's and some of the radicals' argument that we needed a new direction in a new place with greater effectiveness of ministry. With the assurance that we were headed in a conservative direction and with the support of the chairman of the Board, Dr. Mark Corts, the motion to give the institution away to the Europeans was passed. It was a happy day in Europe . . . in some circles. They got a 27 million dollar gift. Twenty-seven million dollars! The trustees were certainly in a philanthropic mood that day. How did we explain giving away 27 million dollars? How did we plead for Lottie Moon support that year with a straight face?

Enough years have passed for a somewhat accurate evaluation of those exciting days to be made. Time does not permit me to go over what could be called in history, Ruschlikon II. I simply say the Europeans did not carry through on their part of the agreement of Ruschlikon I and the FMB disassociated itself totally from the institution. This brought resignations in protest of our actions and helped start what is now known as the Cooperative Baptist Fellowship. "Ruschlikon" became their battle cry. At least Ruschlikon II will save Southern Baptists over a million dollars a year and will save us that much for years to come. That million a year can be put to wonderful use in Eastern Europe. That action was easy to explain to the convention.

"But now," as the man on the radio says, "for the rest of the story." I noted in the state paper not long ago that the trustees of Ruschlikon Seminary were negotiating the sale of the school. We had been told that you couldn't sell it because it was an historical site, but what's a technical error or lie here or there! The sale price was twenty million dollars! Twenty million dollars for a piece of property in Switzerland. The same article indicated they were going to move the seminary to another location, some place in eastern Europe. Why would they do that? Isam Ballenger told us that to move the institution would be to kill the institution. Why do the current trustees of Ruschlikon desire to kill the school? Are they crazy or were the trustees of the FMB misled and given false information when we gave away a twenty-seven million dollar piece of property? Friends, we are not talking about thousands or hundreds of thousands. We are talking millions. Those zeroes begin to mean big bucks.

I read from another news source this action was necessitated because there was inadequate income for the school. This must puzzle us all. We were assured the Europeans would support this institution. "Just give it to us and see what we can do." We did. They didn't. "Ah," but they say, "you reneged on the agreement," but in return we say, "You never kept the agreement." The CBF, under the leadership of Mr. Integrity himself, took up the slack "so that the Europeans would never have to doubt true Southern Baptists."

A quick diversion: Although this letter is a walk down memory lane, there is the question of, if not the legality, the morality of giving assets away and then becoming a beneficiary directly or indirectly. My guess—and it is exactly that—is the CBF got tired of giving most of their money to an institution doing so very little for missions, and the trustees of Ruschlikon, sensing their concern, knew it was time to move on. Certainly they do so with big smiles and thankful hearts, and an obviously large bank account.

Which brings us to Paige Patterson's warnings or predictions or even, if you will, prophetical statements:

1. Did we lose the opportunity in Brussels? Yes.
2. Did the Europeans rally sufficient support to the school? No.
3. Are they selling the property and moving? Yes.
4. What kind of theology is going to be taught at the new location of Ruschlikon Seminary? Does anyone really think that it is going to be a conservative theology? No.

Our actions do make a difference. We gave away millions, but more importantly, what could have been accomplished with those finances is lost forever. Trusteeship is and was difficult. I hope that we will all pray that never again will any Board of Trustees of any of our institutions make such a colossal error as the FMB made on that fateful day.

By the way, if by chance anyone has a prick of conscience (20 million) and feels guilty (20 million) and wants to confess (lost opportunity) "I'm sorry," or "I was wrong," Dr. Paige Patterson now resides at Southeastern Baptist Theological Seminary. You know, that's the seminary that was supposed to die when he became president because he was an "extremist inerrantist." They now have grown from 300 to almost 1,000 students and are having to turn students away for lack of housing. A great spiritual renewal and revival permeates the campus.

Cordially,
Ron Wilson

P.S. If anyone wants to take this letter and place it on the bulletin board at Ruschlikon or Southern Seminary, you certainly have my permission. Last time you forgot to get it.

For those of you at Southern, be sure and say hello to Al Mohler for me. He is the new president of that institution and is known to be an extreme fundamentalist inerrantist. I understand revival is also breaking out there. It's a shame the same cannot be said for Ruschlikon.

The first year as a trustee, I was assigned to the Cooperative Services International (CSI) committee, which worked in closed areas with difficult-to-reach people groups. It was a very interesting and vital ministry. However, my heart was in reaching Europe for Christ. We have cousins who still live in the town where my family moved before 1680 and which later was in the former East Germany. We kept in touch with these cousins and visited them before the Berlin Wall came down. We also have traveled throughout all of Europe visiting every country except Albania, Molvoda, and a couple of the new Islamic Russian republics. Knowing the people, having talked to them about the Lord, and knowing what is occurring sociologically and spiritually in Europe has created a strong desire on my part to be associated with Europe. I was very grateful when, for my second year on the board, I was appointed to the European committee and then later as chairman of the Western Europe committee.

Board service was noncontroversial except for a couple of matters. The chairman, John Jackson, whom I supported and considered to be excellent, was opposed for reelection in 1993. This was a polarizing action that many saw as generated by those who had voted to continue funding Ruschlikon. He was reelected, and most of those who opposed John for reelection rotated off the board shortly thereafter.

The other major event was the election of the new Foreign Mission Board president. When Keith Parks announced his retirement, Bill Hancock, as chairman, appointed a search committee. It was already in place before I joined the board. I favored no particular candidate but wanted somebody who was theologically knowledgeable and who would be alert in dealing with some of the theological challenges. Word began to circulate that Dr. Jerry Rankin, a longtime missionary in Asia and then area director in Southeast Asia, was to be nominated.

I did not know him and did not feel peace in my heart about his nomination. I did not know how firmly he would stand theologically or whether, because he had been a missionary for many years, he had friendships which would keep him from taking the firm leadership position which would be required. When he was nominated at the time of the SBC meeting in Houston in 1993, fourteen of us voted against him. This was short of the one-third required to defeat his nomination.

Immediately after the vote, I rose and stated that since Jerry Rankin had been elected president, it was clearly God's will. I wanted to support him. I moved that the election be unanimous, and it was so ordered. I felt strongly from my heart that we needed to have a unified trustee board and a president elected out of that unity. As time has passed and I have grown to know him and observe his leadership, I am very pleased with Jerry Rankin as president. He is a gracious man who loves the Lord Jesus Christ. He is doctrinally astute and has been greatly used of God in making necessary fundamental changes both in personnel and in procedures. The people whom he has brought on staff have been outstanding. He has built a wonderful team. I believe that the International Mission Board is moving in the right direction with God's man as president and God's people in staff leadership. The remaining problems can and will be dealt with, I feel sure.

I have had the privilege of serving under four pastors who served as chairmen of the IMB. They were John Jackson of California, Leon Hyatt of Louisiana, Bill Blanchard of Tennessee, and Bill Sutton of Texas. Leon had also served in a state convention office after being a pastor. All four are great Christian gentlemen, and they led with firm and gracious dedication to the cause of Christ. Each contributed greatly to the smooth and successful operation of the IMB.

Recent International Mission Board statistics confirm the blessings of God. The Lottie Moon Christmas offering for the year 1996 was ninety-three million dollars, the largest in history. It was 4.57 percent above the 1995 offering, which had set the previous record. The 1997 Lottie Moon offering topped one hundred million dollars for the first time in history. This was an increase of 7.49%. That, coupled with the increase in giving to the Cooperative Program, bodes extremely well for the future. As of December 31, 1998, we have an all-time record of 4,581 missionaries serving on international fields. In 1998 we appointed 885 new missionaries. This was twice the number appointed in any prior year and also produced the largest net gain in number of SBC missionaries in history. The applications for 1999 indicate even more growth. The total number of IMB missionaries should pass 5,000 during the year 2000. This is most remarkable. The caliber of the people who are being appointed is outstanding.

Baptisms on the international field have gone from about 85,000 in 1970 to about 302,000 a year in 1995. In 1998, the number exceeded 333,000, which is 10% more than in any previous year. The number of churches and preaching points on the field has increased dramatically as well.

At the end of 1998, we had 46,000 churches on the international mission field, a gain of 4,200 or almost 10% over the previous year. There are also additionally over 31,000 preaching points for our missionaries. This makes a total of 78,000 places the gospel is presented through our mission efforts.

It should also be noted that in 1985 only 1% of our missionaries worked with the 30% of the world's population which lived in areas where the gospel was not presented. Today 20% of Southern Baptist missionaries work with these difficult to reach people groups. The future for Southern Baptists' international missions is bright. The number to be reached for the Lord will be limited only by our failure to support financially those whom God has called, and their failure to respond to His call. We cannot fail—a lost and dying world calls us, and we cannot fail Him.

CHAPTER **28**

ɈOUTHERN BAPTISTS AND GOVERNMENT

One day in the early 1980s, while I dined with a prominent and respected Houston businessman, he made a comment that added a new dimension to my understanding of the conflict in the Southern Baptist Convention. He told me he believed that the conservative movement which was seeking to restore the SBC to its theological roots was the most important event occurring in the world at that time. Since I knew him to be a person not given to exaggeration, I protested. He explained that he considered Southern Baptists to be the last remaining religious group which had enough strength to keep our country from drifting into relativism and moral bankruptcy which would ultimately lead to internal collapse. He went on to say that the United States was the world leader for freedom, and if we failed as a nation, the world would fall under the control of one or more totalitarian systems—either communism, fascism, Islamic fundamentalism, or some other type of despotism. This was a sobering comment.

When we started, those of us in the conservative movement did not realize the sociological ramifications of what would occur. We were interested in winning souls for Christ. We were motivated to direct our own institutions so that we would not finance the destruction by our employees of those principles in which we believed. We looked inwardly at the Southern Baptist Convention. The conservative movement in the SBC was always a means to an end—the end being the evangelization of the world with the uncompromised gospel of Jesus Christ.

At first, we did not look outwardly at the effect that a return of the Southern Baptist Convention to our biblical base would have on society as a whole. The liberal media understood much better than we. It seems that those with a far-left agenda decided that Southern Baptist Convention conservatives had to be stopped.

A bit of background helps clarify this perspective. When I graduated from high school in 1948, our society was basically grounded on Christian morality, which held the fundamental values taught in Scripture, promoted the traditional

245

home and traditional marriage, and allowed a religious predicate for instruction in our public institutions (not religious instruction). We had a good foundation in Judeo-Christian ethics. Today, we are moving in quite the opposite direction.

Many people in academic communities attempt to undermine the teaching of Western culture and to substitute for it the promotion of various other cultures. Ironically, the same people who have promoted these changes under the pretense of being open-minded often seek to enforce "politically correct" speech in narrow-minded ways. Those who criticize these persons' agenda or otherwise do something "unacceptable" to liberals are often disciplined or ousted from educational employment, educational opportunities, or public service for so doing. Freedom of speech is denied to those who differ with them. Those promulgating a "politically correct" dogma and a new "post-Christian morality" from the pulpits of the media, educational establishments, liberal churches, and government agencies have tried to change the whole fabric of our society.

Some people have suggested that those who push for this new society saw the SBC conservative resurgence as a threat to their emerging consensus. Some other denominations have succumbed to liberal positions and no longer are a bulwark of resistance to them by continuing to uphold biblical morality. If we, as Southern Baptists, also were to abandon our biblical roots, no strong, organized spiritual resistance would remain to oppose them.

If the media, educational institutions, and churches in a country are controlled by a certain type of thinking, that way of thinking will certainly permeate all of society in a relatively short period of time. I believe that the media is strongly in the hands of the liberals as is the educational establishment, not only at the college level, but increasingly in the public schools of our nation through the National Education Association's influence. Most large Protestant denominations have succumbed to liberal theology. The Southern Baptist Convention, various Pentecostals, Missouri Synod Lutherans, independents, Bible churches, and some smaller groups, along with minority elements in mainline denominations, are the ones now resisting the trend. If Southern Baptists were lost to this group, the liberal establishment in Protestantism would be entrenched. Since Protestants account for over half of the total American population, the liberal domination of our country would be ensured. Perhaps this is a reason why the media and the liberal establishment in the country treated us so badly.

The conservative movement in the SBC was not motivated by secular politics, but as it turned out, it did have sociological and political ramifications. Because the Southern Baptist Convention is so large, and all Baptist groups together comprise almost 20 percent of the population of the United States, what happens in Baptist circles cannot fail to influence the rest of the nation. A person need only look at the demographics of the religious composition of America to see how profoundly influential Southern Baptists are in the region stretching from Virginia to Texas. In this area, Baptists comprise more than 50 percent of the population of most counties. Although this includes various types of Baptists, Southern Baptists are by far the largest and most influential group. The way Southern Baptists think is very important in influencing the thinking of others.

Before the conservative movement began, the political education of our people carried on by the Christian Life Commission (now the Ethics and Religious Liberty Commission) and the Baptist Joint Committee on Public Affairs was not directed toward taking conservative stands on moral issues such as abortion, the death penalty, true welfare reform, prayer in school, moral purity, and other conservative concerns.

The change of leadership in the convention did, in fact, effect a tremendous change in the thinking of Southern Baptist pastors. Dr. James L. Guth, a Furman University political science professor, conducted various surveys to gauge this thinking. In 1980-81, he found that 29 percent of Southern Baptist clergymen called themselves Republican, 41 percent called themselves Democrat, and 30 percent call themselves Independent. By a similar survey in 1984 he found 66 percent were Republican, 25 percent Democrat, and 9 percent Independent. Before the late 1970s Southern Baptists by and large considered themselves Southern Democrats. The following chart is from Dr. Guth's surveys:

	1980-81	1984	Change
Republican	29 percent	66 percent	+37 percent
Democrat	41 percent	25 percent	-16 percent
Independent	30 percent	9 percent	-21 percent

Guth stated that the margin of error was 3.5 to 4 percent. He commented about the switch as follows: "I believe this is occurring largely because the Republican Party is addressing sound issues that are relevant to the ministers and that the right inside the Southern Baptist Convention is for the first time forcing ministers to choose sides."

The emergence of conservative leadership among Southern Baptists has helped them understand issues and thus to vote politically more conservatively. The political revolution in 1994 which changed Congress and elected not only Republicans, but, more importantly, many more evangelical Christians, has made a profound effect on the nation. Many of the Republican gains occurred in areas of strong Baptist influence. This revolution continued in the 1996 congressional elections. The possibility of its continuing is far greater than some of the pundits would think. A change in the thinking of many people was the basis of this political upheaval.

Therefore, an unanticipated effect of the conservative movement in the Southern Baptist Convention could possibly be a long-term change in the political climate and the public policy thinking of some Americans. During the preceding thirty years, the religion of secular humanism had been promoted with great effectiveness by the media and many secular and religious elites. Now the establishment of the religion of secular humanism possibly can be destroyed and true freedom of religion can be restored to America.

I long for an America without enforced political correctness and without the governmentally promoted atheistic religion of secular humanism. I long for an America where each person will be able to espouse his or her religious beliefs without being called "narrow-minded" or "bigoted," where each person can advocate the principles in which he or she believes, and where the marketplace of ideas is open to all, even evangelical Christians.

Why do conservative Christians tend to be conservative politically and economically? Why do those who are liberal in theology also tend to be liberal in politics? A very basic reason exists for this. Those who believe the Bible to be completely true believe in the sinfulness of each person and yet the intrinsic worth of all individuals, since each person is created in the image of God. We believe that all have sinned and come short of the glory of God; that there is none who seeks after God; that there is none who seeks after righteousness. Only as the Holy Spirit of God enters a person's heart and a person's life is transformed does he or she have the capacity for doing those things which are truly pleasing in God's sight.

The consistent liberal, on the other hand, believes in the basic goodness of human beings. Therefore, many liberals do not believe in the need for personal regeneration. To some of them, "accepting Jesus Christ" merely means the redirection of the path a person should follow. To some of them salvation is not personal regeneration that is a life-transforming experience which is the result of a new birth.

The person who believes that people are basically good believes that a major function of government is to give people a different environment through supporting welfare programs and pouring money into changing peoples' conditions. Many liberals believe that when the physical condition, the environment, or the education of a person is changed, the person himself or herself will change. A person who believes that people are basically sinful has different secular political principles from one who believes that people are basically good. Conservatives believe that when people are changed from within, they will change their actions. It has been well stated that socialism will put a new suit on an old man, but Christianity will put a new man in the old suit.

The tragic situation of some young people illustrates the difference between the conservative and liberal approaches. Liberals say that higher teacher salaries, better buildings, and a curriculum that affirms the student, whether he or she learns or not, will correct the problems with education. Liberals would solve the problem of violence by banning guns. Although some of these tactics might help in some instances, conservatives believe that these address the effects of the problem, not the problem itself. Conservatives see the problem is in the moral and spiritual fiber of our young people. We see the problem as being the one who uses the gun, not the gun itself. Liberals teach young people that we are merely a higher form of animal and then express surprise when they act as animals.

Some liberal religionists, using the shibboleth of "separation of church and state," seek to remove prayer, the Ten Commandments, and all other recognition of basic moral and spiritual values from our schools. Then they express surprise that our school systems fail to turn out responsible individuals. Conservatives believe people are basically selfish and that they need to be redeemed and changed. Liberals attempt to bring in their brave, new world by changing the environment, not changing the person.

Our political system is based on the biblical understanding of the nature of people. The framers of our Constitution did not believe in unbridled democracy. The major pure governmental democracies that have existed in the history of the world were the Greek city-states, in which all the citizens gathered in the amphitheater and decided everything by vote. However, problems existed. Sometimes a very brilliant orator would sway the crowd and would cause a decision of a Greek city-state to be erroneous.

In the United States, we do not have a pure democracy, and I am so grateful. Everyone is subject to being swayed by a demagogue. All of us are susceptible to failing to think things through, and we can very quickly make irrational decisions. Our system doesn't trust an uneducated populace. We send people to Washington to make laws for us. We don't make laws by a democratic vote. Those laws are not made in one house of Congress but by both houses of Congress. If something does not pass both houses of Congress, it cannot become law.

Other restraints also exist. The chief executive can veto legislation which he believes is harmful. The courts can determine if legislation is constitutional. With legislative, executive, and judicial branches, each one of which is both independent and interdependent, a quick, unbridled majority is prevented from acting precipitously for selfish reasons. We have checks and balances because we are afraid of the tyranny of a temporary, transitory majority. Our system is based on the rule of law with built-in protections for the basic rights of people who find themselves in the minority on an issue.

We also have a written contract of government called our Constitution. It is very difficult to amend. In more than two hundred years of the American Republic, after the adoption of the Bill of Rights, we have amended it only seventeen times. An amendment must pass both houses of Congress by a two-thirds vote, and then three-fourths of the states must ratify it. This keeps bad amendments from being passed quickly without sufficient reflection. Our system recognizes that sinful people will use government for their own selfish benefit if they have the opportunity. If we do not have restraints, people will prey on other individuals and promote themselves.

Government protects the life, liberty, property, and pursuit of happiness of every individual within society. Such inalienable rights are granted by God since we are created in His image. The Declaration of Independence so recognizes. The only just government is a government that restrains the selfishness of people. It is true that the government which governs best is the government which governs least. It is one which stimulates people and does not stifle them.

We also have an economic system that stimulates productivity. Its basic proposition is that if you don't work, you don't eat. Most people choose to work instead of starving to death. Obviously, some individuals within society who have handicaps cannot be productive. The exception to the rule of work is, therefore, the obligation of society to take care of those who cannot compete. When we move from subsidizing those who cannot work to subsidizing those who will not work, we are destined for failure. When those who will not work find that they can get along by taking from those who are productive, the system collapses. When government overtaxes to take away from those who are productive, those who are productive become discouraged. Making people work in order to enjoy the benefits of our society creates an economic system which takes advantage of the fact that people are basically self-centered and basically selfish. Thus, we stimulate the productivity of our people.

Why does America have such a small percentage of the world's population and such a large percentage of the world's wealth? It is not merely because we are blessed with natural resources. Other parts of the world have equal or greater natural resources than the United States does. It is because our economic system has spurred the productivity of our people.

The communist system is based on a marvelous theory. It proclaims that if you destroy the bourgeois society with its corporations and the economic structures which control society, the state will ultimately wither away and everyone will live in harmony. However, communism was an absolute failure. Karl Marx did not understand what would happen. The state did not wither away. It became all-powerful because of the necessity of the state's forcing people to work in undesirable jobs. All people were paid, whether they drove a truck, sat in an executive office, cleaned latrines, or stayed at home. Very understandably, no one wanted to clean latrines. When communism supported all people, whether they worked or not, the state had to substitute something to replace the removal of the economic incentive for productivity. This was the state. Thus, communism was an economic and political disaster. The communists didn't understand the nature of man as Scripture sets forth—that people are basically self-centered and do not act out of pure altruism.

In 1979, when the conservative resurgence movement first supported a candidate who was elected president of the convention, Southern Baptists supported two entities which dealt with public affairs. The one owned by the convention was the Christian Life Commission (CLC). The other was the Baptist Joint Committee on Public Affairs (BJCPA), in which we cooperated with other Baptist conventions.

The Christian Life Commission was headquartered in Nashville. When the new Executive Committee building was built in the mid-1980s, the CLC officed there. The convention elected its trustees, just as it did the trustees of the other convention-owned entities. Its executive director was Dr. Foy Valentine.

I had met Foy in 1949 or 1950 when he preached several times at the new River Oaks Baptist Church in Houston. My grandfather led the church's organization and was the first moderator. I considered Foy to be a pleasant, undynamic person who preached pleasant sermons lacking depth. Some people wanted him as pastor of River Oaks. I was relieved that he was not interested, since I had decided at that time that I would have to oppose his selection.

Foy became very politically active. He was one of the founders of the National Abortion Rights Council, opposed the death penalty, and took other political positions which I considered very liberal. He also became very active in opposing the conservative movement in our convention. He put a good deal of effort into the annual meeting of the SBC in Kansas City in 1984 and boasted that he had eight thousand messengers attending the SBC meeting in order to support the liberal cause. This, of course, did not materialize, but many of us were concerned that the time and resources of a paid employee were utilized in an attempt to assist one faction of the convention.

Although the seminaries were the primary concern of conservatives, Foy's activities caused the board of the CLC to receive attention. The Committee on Nominations (then Boards) added some outstanding women to the CLC trustee board. Foy soon tired of the pressure of CLC board members Skeet Workman, Alma Ruth Morgan, Liz Minnick, Deborah Glanville, Marilyn Simmons, along with many of the men on the board. These individuals knew what they believed and would not allow Foy to push them around.

Judge Paul Pressler addressing Texas House of Representatives in 1986 as a former member

They worked to alter the direction of the CLC. In May 1986, Foy resigned before conservatives had a majority on the trustee board and while liberals would still control the search committee selecting his replacement. He said he had heart problems, but his schedule after retirement caused some people to believe the purpose of his retirement was actually to allow the election of a liberal successor.

In January 1987, the search committee nominated Nathan Larry Baker as CLC executive, and the trustees approved him by a 16 to 13 vote—hardly a mandate. It was reported that others had turned the search committee down because they knew they would not have the support of a majority of trustees for long. At the time of his election, Larry was pastor of First Baptist Church of Fayetteville, Arkansas, where he had succeeded Paige Patterson. Larry fit the mold that Foy and his supporters desired. However, with conservative trustees becoming more dominant with each SBC annual meeting, his term of office was short.

On September 15, 1987, a motion to dismiss Larry lost by a tie vote of 15-15. The resentment over what was conceived as Foy's contrived reasons for retirement, Larry's acceptance of the position after such a close vote, and the dedication of the conservative trustees to their principles made his resignation or firing inevitable. Larry resigned May 15, 1988, after only sixteen months in office. He went to First Baptist Church of Pineville, Louisiana, was active in the liberal movement in Louisiana, and is now retired.

The conservative search committee appointed to recommend Larry's successor quickly moved to recommend Dr. Richard Land, a solid conservative whom I had known well since his high school days in Houston. He was elected on September 12, 1988.

Richard had outstanding qualifications. He graduated magna cum laude from Princeton University and received the Th.M. degree from New Orleans Baptist Theological Seminary, where he received the Broadman Seminarian Award as the outstanding graduate student and also served as the elected student body president. He also received a doctor of philosophy degree in theology from Oxford University in England. Richard had been a pastor, taught, and at the time of his election was a top assistant to Governor Bill Clements of Texas. His government job was to deal with moral and religious liberty concerns. He hardly fit the stereotype of the conservatives which the liberals sought to create. The vote to elect Richard was 21 to 2. He has led well.

In 1997 the agency was renamed the Ethics and Religious Liberty Commission. Its responsibility was broadened and its budget markedly increased. Its program statement was widened to allow it to have a presence in Washington, D.C. The ELRC recently began a half-hour, nationwide radio call-in program, "For Faith and Family," featuring Richard Land. This program addresses moral issues which concern Southern Baptists. Now we have an agency responsive to Southern Baptists and influential in helping our nation move in a biblical direction in public affairs.

The Baptist Joint Committee on Public Affairs (BJCPA) was begun in about 1936. It became the joint effort of nine Baptist bodies. Southern Baptists were by far the largest, having more than half of the combined membership of its constituent bodies in 1986. That year Southern Baptists provided $427,000 for its operation. This was 90 percent of its denominational support. We had eighteen representatives on its forty-seven-member board, which was 38.3 percent of the board membership. Of the eighteen Southern Baptist members of its board, twelve were members by virtue of their positions as agency heads and only six were freely elected by the SBC.

This created a situation in which conservatives could exert very little influence until the time in which our agency heads were changed. Even then, when all Southern Baptist members were in sync with rank-and-file Southern Baptists, no vote could be won on the board without the help of other constituent bodies. The Baptist Joint Committee was Southern Baptists' sole representation in Washington before the Ethics and Religious Liberty Commission took on this program assignment. This was the situation with which conservatives had to deal.

Until his retirement in 1980, James Wood was head of the BJCPA. Dr. Wood had many views which were not in keeping with the thinking of many Southern Baptists, but his style was such that he did not engender great controversy. His replacement was James Dunn, who had been head of the Texas Christian Life Commission. Dunn was elected in October 1980. His style was more confrontational than was Dr. Wood's.

In 1980, Southern Baptist Jimmy Carter, a Democrat, was running for reelection against Ronald Reagan, a Republican. Dunn delayed leaving the Texas Christian Life Commission until after the election. Secular politics spilled over into the Southern Baptist Convention. James Dunn, as head of the CLC (BGCT), was a member of the Carter Reelection Committee. Although he was receiving his salary from Texas Baptists and later from the BJCPA, he spent much of his time on the Carter reelection effort. Jim Jones, reporter for the *Fort Worth Star-Telegram,* reported as follows: "At the same time he (Dunn) openly supports President Carter, serving on the President's State Steering Committee claiming that his denominational job doesn't mean that he has to be a political eunuch."

Dunn had written a book about Christians' involvement in politics, and he, while an employee of the BGCT and then the Southern Baptist Convention, was certainly following his own recommendations. Later, calling it a violation of separation of church and state, he objected to—and still objects to—conservatives doing much less than he did.

With his confrontational style, James took many positions which most Southern Baptists would consider liberal. In a bombastic way he opposed school prayer. In a May 6, 1982 press release, he blasted President Reagan's call for a constitutional amendment allowing school prayer. He stated: "It is despicable demagoguery for the President to play petty politics with prayer." Even some who agreed with James' position were concerned with his method of expressing himself.

When the Kansas-Nebraska convention voiced its concern, James defended his use of the phrase "ultraconservative crazies" to describe his opponents and held to his position opposing school prayer.

James also was a member of the executive committee of the twenty-eight-member board of People for the American Way (PAW). This organization was founded by television producer Norman Lear. Many considered Lear to be a prime promoter of television programs which undermined moral values. The largest contribution Hugh Hefner's Playboy Foundation made in 1983 was to PAW. It gave forty thousand dollars. The next-highest grants were twenty thousand dollars each. They went to the National Organization for Reform of Marijuana Laws, Committee Against Registration and the Draft, and the ACLU/National Development Grant. These grants indicate the types of organization which the Playboy Foundation was interested in financing. In a Baptist Press release that the *Baptist Standard* of Texas printed on January 25, 1984, Dunn is quoted as follows:

> "I declined renomination to the board of that organization (PAW). On that date I told the nominating committee that since I rotated off the board Dec. 31, 1983, I would not serve a second (three-year) term.
>
> "It is important to emphasize that I made this decision in part because of time and energy spent dealing with a very few Southern Baptists who had been engaged in a smear and harassment campaign. Leaving the leadership . . . (of PAW) does not reflect any retreat from working with groups with different degrees of disagreement."
>
> The head of the Washington-based BJCPA noted such attacks "may be instructive to all of our agencies if we recognize the challenge to the precious right of free association, if we identify the tactics of those with a personal and political agenda attempting to use Southern Baptists and if we determine to know the facts and not be misled by distortion and untruth."
>
> He noted the attacks on him and BJCPA—an organization of nine Baptist bodies in the U.S. and Canada—have "required a great deal of forbearance and forgiveness on our part."
>
> He commented he remains "one of the 104,000 members of People for the American Way," which he described as a "broad-based people's movement." He added he believed his membership in PAW, as well as his leadership role, was as "an individual . . . any place organization names were listed in it was understood to be for identification purposes only."

On March 28, 1988, Kerry Knott, administrative assistant to Congressman Dick Armey of Texas, wrote a letter to former Congressman Albert Lee Smith, who was then serving as a Southern Baptist member of the board of BJCPA. In it, as follows, he described the tactics of James Dunn:

Dear Albert Lee,

During the recent battle over the Civil Rights Restoration Act, many members were confused about where certain religious organizations stood on the issue. I had heard that the Baptist Joint Committee on Public Affairs was supporting the bill, and I was, frankly, surprised. In my effort to verify this, an interesting thing happened that I thought you should know about.

After calling the office of the Baptist Joint Committee and being told that they had not endorsed the bill, nor had they mailed any statement to any members unless they requested it, I asked if they would send me a copy of the "fact sheet" I had heard about from another hill staffer.

Dr. James Dunn personally brought me a copy of the fact sheet and spent a few minutes talking to me about the bill. He said this fact sheet was "not an endorsement of the bill, but rather an effort to get the real facts out about the bill." He further said that "there has been a great deal of misinformation about this bill, and we just wanted to set the record straight. There's been a bunch of crazies, and you know who they are—people like Gary Bauer, James Dobson, Jerry Falwell and the Moral Majority types—they're the ones spreading all this misinformation." He then went on to tell me that all the hype about how the bill would affect religious institutions, particularly on the question of hiring homosexuals, was completely off base.

I told them that my impression from looking at the "fact sheet" (which I've enclosed for you) is that the Baptist Joint Committee was supporting the bill. He again said that they had taken no position on it, but were just making sure they set the record straight regarding the provisions of the bill.

I was surprised to find Dr. Dunn, as the spokesman for the Baptist Joint Committee, refer to Gary Bauer, the President's domestic policy advisor, James Dobson, and Jerry Falwell as "crazies." As you know, I've worked with each of these people on legislative matters before. My opinion, and Congressman Armey's opinion, is that each has served our country well in the fight for religious freedom (and for conservative principles across the board), and should be given a bit more respect from Dr. Dunn. I hope his opinion is not the opinion of the organization at large.

In any event, I just wanted to make sure that you were aware of this interesting exchange. Please give me a call if I can ever be of assistance to you in any way.

"With best wishes,
"Sincerely,
"Kerry Knott, Administrative Assistant"

On September 29, 1983, Jim Castelli, in a special release he wrote for *USA Today*, quotes James Dunn as follows:

"Senate defeat of New Right abortion and school-prayer measures show 'most people have the inherent good sense not to be forever misled by religious or political demagoguery," says James Dunn, a prominent critic of the New Right.

Dunn, a Southern Baptist minister, is executive director of the Baptist Joint Committee for Public Affairs, representing 29 million members. He is also a board member of Norman Lear's People for the American Way . . . Dunn was pleased with the defeat of the Helms abortion measure, because of what he sees as its attack on the courts. And he was even more pleased with the defeat of the school-prayer measure.

Before this, Jim Jones, reporter for the *Fort Worth Star-Telegram,* had written:

Dr. James Dunn, head of the Texas Baptist Christian Life Commission, said the resolution is contrary to abortion statements in the commission's report made to the convention, and he said he was disappointed over the opposition to use of public funds for abortion.

Dunn and other Baptists said thousands of teen-agers are victims of rape and incest each year and could not afford private hospitals for abortion.

Christianity Today carried a report of the Southern Baptist Convention meeting in New Orleans on July 16, 1982. Resolutions which Dunn opposed were passed. The following excerpts from this article imply Dunn's contempt for rank-and-file Southern Baptists:

A reporter noted to Dunn that he had sat near the table reserved for SBC agency heads and observed they had voted by a ten-to-one margin with Dunn and against the majority of messengers on the church and state matters.

"Agency heads, without exception, are extremely well-educated," Dunn said. "They are not susceptible to sloganizing, bumper sticker answers, and emotionalism."

Inerrantist Paige Patterson, president of the Criswell Center of Biblical Studies in Dallas, overheard Dunn's remarks.

He said, "This voting by agency heads against the will of the majority is' exactly what all this protesting by conservatives has been about . . . The inadequacy, slowness, even reluctance, with which convention agencies have treated the expressions of the will and concern of the people are the occasions for this whole situation. Total peace can only come when the agencies become sensitive to the majority."

Two of James's top assistants at the BJCPA were Stan Hastey and Buzz Thomas. Stan was also the Baptist Press representative in the District of Columbia. When Stan left the BJCPA, he became head of the Alliance of Baptists, the left wing of the Southern Baptist liberal movement—more liberal than the Cooperative Baptist Fellowship. Stan recently announced that the Alliance would hold its meeting in the year 2000 at the University Baptist Church in Austin, Texas, described in the April 23, 1998, issue of *Baptists' Today* as "a congregation recently kicked out of the Baptist General Convention of Texas for accepting homosexuals."

The same article went on to state that in his annual state of the Alliance address, Hastey denounced Baptist agencies that take punitive action against pro-gay and pro-lesbian congregations.

Soon after he left the BJCPA, Buzz Thomas became a Washington representative of the National Council of Churches. Hastey and Thomas really help us understand the types of convictions James welcomed on his staff. Perhaps they also define James.

In his letter to the editor of the *Florida Baptist Witness* and published in the July 31, 1986, edition, Dunn voiced his position on another subject: "In reference to letters regarding my cautionary words about how churches celebrate the Fourth of July, I warned against the use of military honor guards in worship services simply because it seems strangely inappropriate to have weapons of war parading in the worship place of the Prince of Peace."

At the same time James was able to work with People for the American Way and make confrontational statements, it appears he was not doing his homework with the members of Congress. In making a study about the BJCPA, the SBC Executive Committee sent out a questionnaire. Congressman Tom DeLay, from a district near Houston, and now majority whip of the House of Representatives, replied as follows:

February 4, 1987

Dear Dr. Bennett:

   I am writing in regard to a questionnaire brought to my attention by Mr. Paul Weyrich about the activities of the Baptist Joint Committee on Public Affairs located in Washington, D.C.

   I was somewhat surprised by this questionnaire as I was unaware of the existence of this office until seeing your communication.

   That is not to say that I believe an office of this nature would not serve a very useful purpose. However, in order to make an impact on national affairs, it is important to be highly visible.

For example, I have been in Washington for over two years now and have never been contacted by this office; yet I am listed in every congressional directory as a Baptist, and have long been active in church affairs.

I would certainly welcome the opportunity to have the SBC's input on the issues before Congress. Towards that end, I hope that my comments will be taken as constructive criticism and help to set the Public Affairs Office on a more active course of congressional interaction.

Sincerely,
Tom DeLay, Member of Congress

One can easily see how different James was from the average Southern Baptist. Had someone less outspoken, more conciliatory, and less confrontational held his office, something could possibly have been worked out which would have preserved Southern Baptist participation in the Baptist Joint Committee. With James Dunn there, the result was inevitable.

The SBC made several unsuccessful efforts to defund the BJCPA. With an increased conservative presence on the Executive Committee and with Southern Baptists becoming more aware of James's style and positions, something obviously had to be done to deal with the issue. Therefore, at its September 1986 meeting, the Executive Committee authorized a subcommittee to study the matter. David Maddox, chairman of the Executive Committee, appointed the members of the subcommittee. My appointment to the subcommittee was an example of David's sincere desire to be inclusive. Although it appeared that a majority of the subcommittee members were dedicated to protecting James and the BJCPA, conservatives at least had a vote.

I did not approve of the wording of the questionnaire (mentioned previously) that the subcommittee sent out. I believed the wording of the questions was calculated to help the BJCPA, but it really didn't make much difference. Those who wanted to protect the BJCPA knew that some action needed to be taken which would give the impression that something was being done. I, on the other hand, knew that the subcommittee would not move very far, and I needed to settle for any movement I could get. Everyone was ready to compromise. They hoped the compromise would end the controversy. I hoped that the compromise would be the first step in ending our association with the BJCPA. I was willing to be incremental in my approach.

The committee decided to go to Washington to see the BJCPA operation and interview the staff. That was fine with me, but I wanted to do more while I was there. Knowing that we would be subject to a sales promotion, I wanted some balance and requested that I be allowed to have some persons from

Congress and some from the Reagan White House, whom I knew, testify. I asked that they be allowed to express their feelings about James Dunn and the BJCPA, their positions, their reputations, and their effectiveness. This was the last thing James wanted. My request was denied, but as a compromise, it was decided that nobody would summon any outside witnesses.

While we met, Senator Mark Hatfield of Oregon, one of James's best friends in Congress, walked in. He said that he had heard we were meeting and just wanted to stop by and see how we were doing. James immediately suggested that since Senator Hatfield was there, he should say a few words to the committee. I considered this to be a typical James Dunn trick and a direct violation of the agreement we had reached. However, nothing could be done, and I accepted the fact that I had been outmaneuvered. This certainly didn't increase my respect for James.

After Senator Hatfield made his statement and others dialogued with him, I asked to be allowed to interact with him. This was allowed. I began by saying, "Senator, I know you don't remember me, but we had a good visit before a breakfast at Fourth Presbyterian Church (in Bethesda, Maryland) about 10 years ago." (I had spoken at a conference there in 1976. The senator arrived early for a breakfast at which I was speaking, and we had talked then.) The senator replied that he remembered the visit but that he had also seen me on television.

That was a most interesting remark since, surprisingly, I knew the event to which he referred. It was the "Donahue" program where Ken Chafin and I had appeared a year and one-half before. A close friend who was a congressman had been discussing a legislative matter in the senator's office right after the "Donahue" program aired. James called the senator, and the congressman heard him tell James, in effect, to get another spokesman besides Ken because "the Judge had torn his spokesman up in the debate." I had appreciated the compliment.

Another thing which irritated me happened in Washington at our subcommittee meeting. During our time in Washington I suffered with the flu and with the fever, chills, and fatigue associated with it. I made it through a full day of meetings but went up to my room as soon as possible. In about an hour, Executive Committee chairman David Maddox, who served as an ex-officio member of the subcommittee, called me on the phone. He said that he and James Dunn were in the lobby and James wanted to come up and talk to me. I told him that I felt very ill. He talked to James but reported that James insisted on coming up. I reluctantly agreed and asked that they stay only a few minutes. They stayed an hour, with James talking almost the whole time. I really don't know what he thought his harangue could accomplish. The only thing it convinced me of was a lack of judgment and sensitivity on James's part.

The committee worked diligently. It reached a compromise which decreased the number of Southern Baptist members of the BJCPA board who were members because they were agency heads. It replaced them with members elected by the Southern Baptist Convention. Now a majority of the PAC would be grassroots Southern Baptists. Equally significant was the authorization given to the Southern Baptist members of the BJCPA (called the Public Affairs Committee but more commonly referred to as the PAC) to function separately. Although this did not separate us from the Baptist Joint Committee, it accomplished almost everything else I wanted. I was so pleased, I had to contain my joy.

The Executive Committee easily approved this approach and presented the plan to the 1987 SBC. When the committee asked me to present this compromise, I demurred. I believed that if I were to present it, it would be identified as my motion and thus immediately be suspect by some people on the other side. I knew that I could convince my friends to support it even though it was only a step in the right direction. I could convince them what a truly large step it was. I agreed to speak for the proposal while refusing to be the prime mover. The motion passed overwhelmingly, far surpassing the required two-thirds vote.

We now had what we needed to lay the groundwork for disassociating ourselves from the BJCPA. The Southern Baptist group had a majority within it to request an audit, to make public statements about the BJCPA, to supervise its operation, and also to operate on its own. The most notable action it took as an independent group occurred on August 25, 1987, when it endorsed the nomination of Judge Robert H. Bork for the U.S. Supreme Court. This brought howls of protest from liberals. They hated Judge Bork because of his brilliance and his articulate affirmation of conservative principles. Only then did the liberals realize the result of their compromise. Conservatives now had a voice in Washington, and it was part of their revered organization, the Baptist Joint Committee. They also knew that they could no longer muster a two-thirds vote at any Southern Baptist Convention to change anything unless the change was something to which conservatives agreed.

The great strides made in 1987 and the controversy over the Bork endorsement caused us to be more reserved in 1988. All we did was to reduce the budget appropriation for the Baptist Joint Committee from $410,000 to $391,000. That showed that we still were working on the matter but that we were willing to go slowly. Southern Baptists were just beginning to understand the positions of James Dunn and what he was supporting through the Baptist Joint Committee.

In 1989, the Executive Committee by a 42 to 27 vote proposed a separate Religious Liberty Commission for the SBC. I wasn't sure that a separate agency was the way to go, but I went along with it. I would have preferred to have had the Christian Life Commission take over that function and have just one agency dealing with public affairs. The proposal for the Religious Liberty Commission created quite a controversy. SBC President Jerry Vines requested that the proposal be withdrawn to avoid controversy, and the Executive Committee agreed.

At the 1989 SBC meeting, a motion came from the floor to completely defund the BJCPA. The motion lost narrowly. Southern Baptists are much more likely to support a committee recommendation than they are a motion from the floor. To have the defunding motion from the floor fail so narrowly greatly worried James and his supporters. They began to see the handwriting on the wall—the Baptist Joint Committee would be defunded before too long. Sentiment was building.

In 1990 the budget which the Executive Committee recommended cut BJCPA support from $391,000 to $50,000. It transferred the remainder of the funds to the Christian Life Commission under the leadership of Richard Land. In 1991, the BJCPA was completely defunded. In 1992, the slow death of Southern Baptist involvement in the Baptist Joint Committee ended. The convention passed a recommendation as follows:

> The Executive Committee of the Southern Baptist Convention recommends that the Southern Baptist Convention terminate the convention's participation in the Baptist Joint Committee on Public Affairs without restricting the right of The Christian Life Commission of the Southern Baptist Convention to relate to the Baptist Joint Committee on Public Affairs in any manner it may deem appropriate.

The battle had been difficult. The press would not adequately report our concerns with the positions of James Dunn and the Baptist Joint Committee, so we had to educate our people slowly.

Two outstanding laymen—Judge Sam Currin of North Carolina and Congressman Albert Lee Smith of Alabama—led the work on the PAC and through it the work on the Baptist Joint Committee. Two finer leaders never existed. Both were highly principled, brilliant, knowledgeable, and dedicated to conservative principles. They worked long and diligently. We conservatives owe them a great debt of gratitude for eliminating the liberal voice of the BJCPA and ultimately creating a responsive and responsible Southern Baptist voice in the Ethics and Religious Liberty Commission.

CHAPTER 29

𝓑ITS AND PIECES

Many events that occurred in the long battle for biblical authority did not make the headlines but provide important background for understanding the movement. Some of the items included in this chapter are designed to correct the record. Some are humorous, and others represent a pathetic commentary on the events as they unfolded.

I pray that reporting this potpourri of vignettes will go a long way toward filling in some information gaps that will benefit all who study these critical years.

* * * * *

I consider Dr. Francis Schaeffer to be one of the greatest intellects and greatest proponents of the Christian faith of our century. His books and his conference center at L'Abri, Switzerland, have profoundly influenced countless individuals and society in general. We have seen several friends and a cousin profit tremendously by studying at L'Abri upon our recommendation.

One of my friends, Jess Crain, who operated a Christian bookstore in Houston, told me about a conversation that he had with Dr. Schaeffer. Not long before Dr. Schaeffer's death, they were talking together at the Christian Booksellers Convention in Dallas. Dr. Schaeffer asked Jess about the conservative movement in the Southern Baptist Convention and whether he knew me since Jess was from Houston. He stated that he did know me. Dr. Schaeffer told him to tell me that he prayed for me and the others in the conservative movement every day because the future of evangelical Christianity in America depended on what happened in the Southern Baptist Convention. He said that it was the only group that had the numbers and resources to influence American society for good and to win a large segment of the American population to a saving knowledge of Jesus Christ. Learning about this comment gave me an awesome sense of responsibility.

* * * * *

On July 21, 1988, Nancy, Paul, and I were in New Mexico to see the Santa Fe Opera, as we do almost every other year. Nancy had an aunt and uncle who were almost ninety years old and had a home in Santa Fe. We had arranged to go out for dinner with them. When the hour approached for them to meet us at the hotel, Paul and I went outside and sat in front so they would not have to get out of their car. Two people whom I did not recognize but whom I thought I had seen before passed the place where Paul and I sat. They said, "Hello, Judge Pressler," and I responded casually. The incident occurred without my giving it a second thought.

A day or so later, Paige Patterson called me at the hotel. When I answered, he said, "You really are in Santa Fe!" I said, "Yes, where are you?" He replied that he was in Glorieta, just down the road from Santa Fe, for the trustee meeting of the Foreign (now International) Mission Board . I told him I didn't realize we were in the same area. Paige said Keith Parks, then-president of the FMB, had accused him and other conservatives at Glorieta of talking to me in Santa Fe and that I was directing the activities of the Foreign Mission Board from a command point at a hotel there. I told him we were there to see Nancy's aunt and uncle and to go to the opera. Paige and I had a good laugh about it.

However, as I reflect on it, I think it shows the paranoia under which certain leaders of the liberal cause were operating. To anything that Paige or I did, they ascribed sinister motives. They could not understand that we had lives other than our participation in the convention. I have surmised that the rumors were started by the two men who spoke to me by name in front of the hotel. They evidently must have had some connection with the Foreign Mission Board. They apparently added two and two and got 105!

* * * * *

After the SBC meeting in Kansas City in 1984, a rumor began that the conservative leadership wore uniforms at the annual meeting so individuals to whom we were "giving instructions" could recognize us. A reporter called Paige to ask whether we had worn uniforms and what they were. Paige replied, laughing, that we wore polka dot hats with roto blades on top to make sure we weren't missed! The reporter was so humorless that he didn't realize Paige was ridiculing the false story. I wondered how such a story could have begun.

Finally, I think I know. Someone I did not know called and wanted to meet me at the convention hall. I don't remember whether it was a reporter. Since he did not know what I looked like, he asked me where I would be sitting and what I would be wearing. I told him I would be wearing a blue suit and red tie and would sit in a certain area. Evidently, in trying to locate me, he inquired of others and told them I was wearing a blue suit and red tie. This somehow became exaggerated into a report that conservative leaders all wore blue suits and red ties. An additional rumor was that we did this so people who wanted to know how to vote could contact us.

This was absolutely ridiculous paranoia on the part of liberals because at no time did we have any contact people on the floor of any SBC meeting to tell anybody how to vote. We did have friends who sat near some microphones who were ready independently to speak to matters which were being discussed; so did the liberals. That was all the "organization" we had at the annual meetings.

* * * * *

In 1991, Nancy, Paul, and I went to Europe. My close friend, General Erle Cocke of Washington, D.C., who labored to make the Baptist World Alliance an effective organization, suggested that I get to know the then-BWA president, Dr. Knud Wumpelmann, when we were in Copenhagen. When we visited the

Judge Paul Pressler with map of Texas made by his great-grandfather, Charles W. Pressler, in background

city, we called the Wumpelmanns, who lived about an hour west of town. Knud and his wife Karen very graciously invited us to their home for the afternoon and dinner. We spent a delightful time there. They showed us through their home and around the adjacent Baptist school. We had several pleasant hours of conversation.

Toward the end of the evening, Knud brought the conversation around to the subject of the Baptist Theological Seminary at Ruschlikon. He said Ruschlikon was important to European Baptists and commented on how many leaders in European Baptist circles had graduated from Ruschlikon. He said Southern Baptists must continue to support Ruschlikon. I told him this could be guaranteed if the school would immediately add knowledgeable and outstanding conservatives to its faculty. He quickly changed the subject.

I think he possibly knew that I had outlined a course of action the school would not take. Very likely he already was aware that Dr. Glenn Hinson, a Southern Seminary professor whom many Southern Baptists considered very liberal, was about to start teaching at Ruschlikon. The visit was a failure in that regard, but we enjoyed getting to know the Wumpelmanns, who are a wonderful Christian couple.

* * * * *

In 1985, Dr. Fisher Humphries, a professor at New Orleans Seminary, called and requested to interview me for the seminary publication, the *Theological Educator.* We had been friends through the years, although he was considered to be on the other side of the controversy. He, Paige Patterson, and I were three of the four groomsmen in the wedding of Becky and Richard Land. He agreed to come to Houston for the interview; he would transcribe the interview verbatim without editing, and the interview would occur in our home. When he arrived, I told him I also wanted to record the interview so no question would exist about what was said. He, of course, agreed. I thought the interview went very well. Some excerpts from it are as follows:

> **Educator:** Let me come at this question a different way. I know that you yourself are committed to the inerrancy of the Bible. In your view, what action should the convention instruct institutional trustees to take toward faculty members or other employees who love Jesus Christ, believe the gospel, accept the Bible as the uniquely inspired Word of God and the ultimate authority on earth, but who reject the biblical inerrancy?
>
> **Judge Pressler:** Well, it depends on what you mean by rejecting biblical inerrancy. First of all, you explain to me how much of the Bible you can reject and still believe in the authority of the Scripture. You explain that to me and then I'll answer your question.
>
> **Educator:** All right. Let's suppose we have a professor in the seminary. This person says, "I love Jesus Christ. I trust him. I believe in the message of the Bible. I believe in one God, the creator, who is a personal God . . ."
>
> **Judge Pressler:** Again, you are putting it affirmatively and not telling me what you are negating.
>
> **Educator:** ". . . and this loving God became incarnate as Jesus of Nazareth, he died upon the cross (and I'm using these words just as they are used by ordinary Baptists) for our sins, he was raised bodily from the dead on the third day by the Father; he gave his Spirit to the church; the church is the people of God; salvation is through Jesus Christ by grace through faith in him who died and was raised again from the dead; and then there is the hope in the hearts of all these people for the coming of Christ and for heaven." But you have such a person who nevertheless says, "I will not describe the Bible as inerrant."
>
> **Judge Pressler:** Nobody wants him to describe it in any terms that anybody has. I want to know what he doesn't believe about Scripture and what you

would say that he can disbelieve that is contained in Scripture and still use Scripture as authoritative.

Educator: Let's say the person says, "I will not use the word inerrancy."

Judge Pressler: Nobody has ever asked anybody to use the word "inerrancy." What can you disbelieve in Scripture, and still feel that you ought to be paid with Southern Baptist money to teach in one of our institutions?

Educator: First of all, I am not sure the question that I would want to deal with is the question of what you disbelieve.

Judge Pressler: You asked me whether a person couldn't believe in inerrancy and teach in Seminary. I'm asking you to define your question and what he doesn't believe about Scripture. And I think we'll go a long way towards understanding if you all will define what you can deny about Scripture and still be in our Southern Baptist frame of communion.

Educator: All right. Let me ask you then, if a person believes in the full religious message but does not believe in the scientific accuracy of the Bible, would that amount to disbelief?

Judge Pressler: Who is going to define what is religious and what is scientific? Is the resurrection of Jesus Christ religious or scientific? Which is it?

Educator: Let's stipulate that the person who denied the resurrection shouldn't teach in our seminary.

Judge Pressler: You are setting up a doctrinal creed. What I am asking is, how much can you disbelieve? You are telling me that a person ought to believe in the bodily resurrection to teach in one of our schools. Are you?

Educator: Judge, I really intended for me to interview you, not for you . . .

Judge Pressler: But you're asking me questions you want me to answer.

Educator: What I want to know is, Do you think that a person must believe not only in the message of the Bible about God and Jesus and faith and the church and salvation, but also that any allusions in the Bible have to be scientifically accurate?

Judge Pressler: What is an allusion to science? The bodily resurrection is science, because it describes something that is not in accordance with regular scientific events, a supernatural event. Now that deals with science. I believe that where the Bible touches on science, it is scientifically accurate. Now what is it that you can disbelieve and say that the Bible is wrong about? And what you've done if you say that you believe that the Bible can make mistakes, then you define the areas where the Bible makes mistakes, and you define the term "scientific," and so you have made yourself the judge of Scripture rather than Scripture being your judge, when you set up categories where the Scripture can be wrong. And with the resurrection, I am trying to show you that it depends on your definition of "scientific" as to whether a person can be a Bible-believer and deny the bodily resurrection of Christ, in the terminology that you are seeking to make me use.

About three weeks later, Fisher called and in a sheepish voice said his recorder had not worked properly. He said some areas of the interview didn't come through. He asked if mine had worked. I told him that I had listened to every word of it, and it all came through very clearly. I sensed obvious disappointment in his voice when he asked me to send him a complete recording of it so he could transcribe the whole thing verbatim. I made a copy of the tape and sent it to him. If I had not recorded the interview, I wonder what portions would not have been available.

* * * * *

From my viewpoint, one of the most unfortunate incidents in the controversy occurred at the Southern Baptist Convention in New Orleans in 1982. Someone who was then a leader among conservatives had begun a rumor that Dr. Duke McCall, former president of Southern Seminary, had a drinking problem. The rumor seems to have been based on a story that Dr. McCall reportedly took a few sips of beer in China because beer was the only thing available to drink on a boat on which he was riding at a particular time. This was parlayed into saying that he had a drinking problem. This was wrong, untrue, unfair, and unfortunate. The story that circulated did not reflect the true event.

Although I do not drink at all and have never done so, I can understand the extreme circumstance in which Dr. McCall is alleged to have done this. Almost anyone would have done the same thing as he did. Dr. McCall is reliably reported to be strongly against liquor and does not use it. I was extremely upset about this event, because this was an obvious attempt to destroy a person on the other side. It was not the Christian thing to do. The person who circulated this story was soon out of leadership in the conservative movement, and fortunately no incident like this was repeated.

Dr. McCall is my brother in Christ. He has accomplished much in God's work and for Southern Baptists. Fortunately, his character is such that it could never be damaged by such an unkind attack. Paige Patterson took the microphone at the convention, denounced the attack, and supported Dr. McCall. No part of the controversy should ever have been fought that way.

* * * * *

One of the more ridiculous charges that has been brought against me is that I support reconstructionism and dominion theology. Anyone who accuses me of this is willfully ignorant. I have often attempted to set the record straight, but the Baptist media have not reported my statements, and people making the charges seem determined to keep themselves ignorant of the facts. I know very little about this type of theology, but from what I'm able to piece together, dominion theology expects to bring in the kingdom of God on earth through peoples' actions—political or otherwise. Theologians would classify this as a postmillennial position—that Christ will come again after mankind has brought in the millennium era on earth.

That is not my position. I believe the Scripture teaches that the world will get worse and worse and then Christ will physically return to earth and set up His kingdom. (This is a premillennial position.) The two positions are completely opposite. The postmillennial position says people will do it. The premillennial position says people will fail.

The only way I can possibly suggest that this foolishness began is that I allowed Dr. Gary North, a reconstructionist who holds to dominion theology, to interview me, and his interview was well-circulated. I have always allowed anyone to interview me if it is convenient. Being interviewed by someone does not mean that I agree with that person's position. If it did, I would never have consented to the interviews I gave Bill Moyers, Fisher Humphries, Dan Martin, Toby Druin, Greg Warner, Gus Niebuhr, Bob Allen, and others.

The bankruptcy of the liberal position is shown by the liberals making such a ridiculous charge. I am not, never have been, and never will be one who holds to reconstruction or dominion theology. It is entirely contrary to my understanding of what the Bible teaches about the nature of man and the future of the world.

* * * * *

At the Dallas meeting of the SBC in 1985, Donnie (Mrs. Harlan) Caton was talking on a pay phone. (Her husband was pastor of Spring Baptist Church near Houston before his untimely death.) Next to her, on another phone, was Ken Chafin. Donnie believes he was talking to someone with the "Donahue" program on which he and I were soon to appear. Donnie overheard Ken running down my character and making very unkind, false, and misleading attacks. Having heard this, she confronted him after he finished his call. It was interesting that on the "Donahue" show, Phil Donahue said to me,

> I believe you when you say that you have—your life as a citizen has been exemplary. Your life as a public citizen and on the bench is scandal free. You have every reason to brag to your grandchildren about your own service, not only to your church but to your country. So you are to be sure, one of the "good guys."

When I found out about Ken's telephone call that Donnie Caton overheard, I understood why Phil made these remarks. He apparently had investigated what Ken had been saying.

* * * * *

Soon after I joined the Executive Committee, I received a call from a leader of the group which controlled the SBC before 1979. He asked me to arrive a day early for an Executive Committee meeting and to spend some time with him. I, of course, did this, since I always looked forward to any opportunity for enhanced communication. We had a pleasant day except for several remarks he made. At one time he asked if the real reason Paige Patterson was involved in the conservative effort was because he had been a poor student and was trying to get revenge on his professors. Anyone who knows Paige knows how ridiculous such a statement is! Paige is a brilliant scholar who always performed well academically.

Later, the man with whom I met referred to a certain person who had become a Southern Baptist. He said he understood that this man once was a Methodist but that the United Methodists "kicked him out" and he became a Baptist. He said that he didn't know why the United Methodists "kicked out" this man but theorized that he was homosexual. The individual about whom he spoke was a very distinguished person of great moral and theological conviction who had left the Methodist denomination because of its bent toward liberalism. These and other remarks bothered me greatly. It appeared that the man with whom I spoke was trying to destroy by innuendo various leaders of the conservative movement and thus was trying to wean me away from it. This was not the only time I saw the liberals use such a tactic.

* * * * *

Although conservatives were accused of using walkie-talkies in Houston in 1979, that accusation has no basis in fact. However, the liberals did make limited use of walkie-talkies in New Orleans in 1982. Richard Land observed more than one person trailing Paige Patterson from time to time and told Paige. Paige told Richard he was too conspiratorial and made fun of the report, much to Richard's consternation. Then Richard spotted one of the persons with the walkie-talkies and pointed him out to Paige. Paige decided to test Richard's theory and see if the young man would follow him to the men's room. Paige entered and immediately stepped behind a door. In a few seconds the individual with the walkie-talkie stepped inside, only to meet Paige face to face. Paige asked him, "Are you looking for me?" The person broke out in a sweat and could only stammer. On being questioned, he told Paige he was a New Orleans

Seminary student and said, "They (plural) told us (plural) to follow you and report on what you were doing." "They" was not defined.

* * * * *

In New Orleans in 1982, Lee Porter, registration secretary, a bitter opponent of the conservative resurgence, had a pair of binoculars which he used to scan the seats of the messengers. When he located a group of us, he continued watching from his vantage point on the platform. When we realized what he was doing, Russell Kaemmerling, editor of the *Southern Baptist Advocate,* stuck out his tongue at Lee to annoy him. Later Lee confronted Russell in the hall and said that he was going to "punch him out" for his act. Of course, his reaction and challege verified the fact that he was spying on us. How silly can anyone be!

* * * * *

A newsletter written by an author using the pseudonym "Dr. U. Ben Took" provided humorous relief at the SBC annual meetings. The newsletter had limited distribution and offered commentary on various aspects of the convention. It was neither liberal nor conservative but poked fun at all. I had nothing to do with this publication. It was always delivered to me and others anonymously.

* * * * *

My friend Bill Dudley, a Missouri pastor, asked me to speak at an associational "M" night in the Ozark mountains of southwestern Missouri. It was agreed that we would say nothing about the conservative movement or about the controversy in the convention. Everything went well in the meeting until a man neither Bill nor I knew was called on to close in prayer. He prayed eloquently and at great length. Finally he prayed, "And Lord, we pray that you will save those liberals and forgive those moderates for covering up for them." Our efforts to be completely noncontroversial had been lost. I'm sure that some people thought the conservatives put him up to doing this, but that certainly was not the case.

* * * * *

On several occasions I met with Dr. Franklin Paschall, former president of the SBC and former pastor of First Baptist Church of Nashville. At all times Dr. Paschall was courteous and polite. He was never unkind or critical, although many people considered him to be part of the establishment. I believe that he was most gracious, sympathetic, and inclusive. After one of the sessions at the 1988 SBC meeting in San Antonio, I ran into Dr. Paschall at the elevators on the first floor of the Marriott Hotel. He was with Dr. Herschel Hobbs and Dr. Porter Routh. Conservatives had just won another victory. All three of these men were most gracious and stated that they thought some corrections had been needed and they were glad that these corrections were being made. It was a friendly and kind conversation. I shall always remember it with appreciation.

* * * * *

The Peace Committee was Dr. Paschall's idea. He called me, as he did several people on both sides of the controversy, to promote the committee. I was very concerned about the idea of a committee, particularly when I saw the names of those who were proposed to be on it. It did not have a conservative majority by any stretch of the imagination. It was a miracle of God that the Peace Committee came down so conservatively on each issue. Certainly the Peace Committee was not my idea. Paige supported its formation much more than I did. I thought it would be a disaster, but my faith was small. I think it contributed in a major way to resolving the controversy in a conservative direction. It honestly determined what was going on and confirmed the fact that theological problems existed. We shall always be indebted to those on this committee who served long hours so sacrificially and who were determined to discover the truth.

* * * * *

From time to time, conservative leadership met to pray, fellowship, assess what was transpiring, and strategize. We would discuss various ideas and pray about them. At one of the meetings a conservative leader suggested that we enter into a truce with the liberals, give them Southern Seminary, and have the other five seminaries as conservative. I rarely questioned the wisdom of my spiritual leaders, but I did so on that occasion. I told the group that only two things were wrong with the suggestion.

First, it would give the liberals a permanent base from which to operate. The convention battle, therefore, would never end, and we would always have the factions vying for leadership. Secondly, and even more important, if Southern were to be a liberal school, it would turn out liberal pastors who would go into the churches of Kentucky, the Midwest, and other states, and many souls who could have been reached for Christ would go to hell because they would never hear the message of redemption through the blood of the Lord Jesus Christ. As soon as I stopped talking, the individual who had made the proposal said that since we had decided that matter, we should discuss something else. It was never considered again.

* * * * *

In 1990, James Dunn was seeking to build support for the Baptist Joint Committee on Public Affairs. He invited the Baptist state paper editors to Washington for a briefing. When I learned that a White House meeting was on the schedule, I called and told a friend who was a leader in the Bush White House

Herman and Elsie Pressler with family. Christmas, 1994

about James Dunn's work on the Carter reelection campaign. I also gave him information about James's calling President Reagan "deliberately dishonest" and that it was "despicable demagoguery for the President to play petty politics with prayer."

The White House called me a few days later and said they had decided not to cancel the meeting but asked me to attend with a couple of other individuals so James would be denied the limelight. I felt that what James wanted was his picture with President Bush to be in all of the Baptist state papers just before the 1990 SBC meeting, where his funding would be an issue. The White House promised it would make sure that no such picture would be given out, and it wasn't.

When James and the editors arrived, they were shocked to see former Congressman Albert Lee Smith, Norris Sydnor (both members of the Southern Baptist PAC), and me in the reception room of the west wing of the White House. They were even more surprised when I was ushered back to the Oval Office before anyone was admitted to the Roosevelt Room for the meeting. Later, I entered the Roosevelt Room from the same door the President would use to enter and occupied a reserved seat on one side of the President, while Albert Lee was already seated in his assigned seat on the other side. When the President entered, he greeted Albert Lee, Norris, and me by name and then said "Hello" to the rest as a group. I enjoyed watching James's face.

*****

Dewey Presley, former chairman of the Executive Committee, strongly supported the establishment and defended the liberals in the convention. He asked for a meeting with Dr. Criswell, Paige, Russell Dilday, Keith Parks, me, and various others. We met in Dallas a couple of years after the controversy began. This became an effort to draw Dr. Criswell away from the conservative movement. A great deal of conversation occurred, while Dr. Criswell remained silent.

Finally, Dewey turned to Dr. Criswell and told him that what happened during the next few years in the convention would determine how history treated him. He told Dr. Criswell that everyone knew that he could rein in the conservative movement and stop it. He told Dr. Criswell that if he allowed Paige Patterson and Paul Pressler to continue, it would destroy Dr. Criswell's reputation, thus assigning him to a role in history as the one who divided the Southern Baptist Convention.

Everyone waited expectantly for Dr. Criswell to speak. Dr. Criswell took a deep breath and surveyed the audience. He looked at Paige and me and then told everyone that we were "his boys." He said that Paige was speaking the truth, that he supported him, and stood with him in every way. He said some kind words about me also. Dewey Presley's efforts to cut Dr. Criswell away from the conservative movement had failed, and the supporters of the establishment knew they had real problems.

CHAPTER 30

*M*Y HEROES OF THE RESURGENCE

Many Southern Baptists know the names of the individuals who were elected as convention president and who provided the top leadership for the conservative resurgence. However, numerous other persons contributed dramatically to restoring biblical integrity in our institutions. Literally thousands gave of themselves. To name a few is extremely difficult, because so many existed.

Of course, proper credit must be given to those who served at the helm. These provided articulate, able leadership for the conservative cause. Their service as SBC presidents took them away from their churches and families, and they were diverted from many tasks that they ordinarily would have performed. They did this cheerfully, willingly, and sacrificially. Two or three of those who served as president suffered particularly because of their service.

Bailey Smith became a target of the liberals. Some people fought against his conducting evangelistic meetings in their area and, in some cases, successfully had meetings canceled. It seems unthinkable that people would fight having the gospel presented and would cancel a meeting in their locality just because they opposed the particular evangelist's stand within the convention. However, some people were so antagonistic against Bailey that they did this for revenge.

I particularly regret these attacks on Bailey. He protected and supported me when few others would. He defended me when Winfred Moore and others fought against my election to the Executive Committee at the 1984 SBC meeting in Kansas City. He did this articulately, with conviction and with great passion. Some of his friends attacked him for supporting me. He has constantly gone out of his way to say kind things such as he did at the 1995 SBC meeting, when he referred to Paige Patterson and me when he was recognized as a former president. When I have felt low, Bailey Smith has called me more frequently than anyone to express personal support. I am eternally grateful to him. I will always deeply regret the suffering inflicted on him and the attacks on his ministry.

Charles Stanley labored long and diligently. To stand for the cause, he took time away from his In Touch Ministries as well as from his family and church. He was always clear, consistent, insightful, and dedicated. No one could have acted in a more godly manner than he did. I can never adequately express my admiration for this great man of God.

Jerry Vines also had a special way of calling and expressing encouragement just when I needed it most. He was always gracious and caring. Perhaps the fact that we both are parents of "special" children gave us an identity and understanding for each other. He always blesses me.

Everyone identified with the conservative cause owes a deep debt of gratitude to Adrian Rogers, Bailey Smith, Jimmy Draper, Charles Stanley, Jerry Vines, Morris Chapman, Ed Young, Tom Elliff, and Paige Patterson—those who were the conservative presidents during the resurgence years. Each is a great man of God—as genuine out of the pulpit as in it. These former presidents performed well in their leadership roles as servants of our Lord. They did not, however, have the time to do all that was necessary to make the resurgence succeed. The former presidents were, for the most part, not the ones who could answer the constant telephone calls, the requests for information, the searching inquiries, or could maintain the grassroots contacts required for the movement to succeed. This had to be done by Paige Patterson, myself, and a host of others.

The person who suffered most during the early days was Paige Patterson. He was constantly under attack by persons who sought to destroy his ministry, to undermine his leadership at Criswell College, and to have him blackballed from preaching engagements. Threats to one's children, which both he and I sustained, were frightening and disconcerting. One prominent conservative leader told Paige that he would fight the convention battle to the last drop of Paige's blood! Through all this, Paige stood firm and unwavering, and God blessed his efforts. He now leads Southeastern Baptist Theological Seminary in its period of greatest growth, its greatest productivity, and its greatest testimony for our Lord Jesus Christ.

If two outstanding heroes of the conservative resurgence exist, it would be Paige Patterson and his wife Dorothy, who stood through thick and thin. She ministered faithfully at his side with brilliance and integrity. I have been in Paige's office on many occasions and have seen the telephone calls of that day lined up. Some thirty, forty, or fifty calls a day would be waiting for him to return. Physically it has been almost impossible to meet the demands placed on him, but he has dealt with them well.

One of the reasons that Paige and I succeeded, humanly speaking, is because we were instantly and totally available to every single person who desired contact. Our telephone bills were enormous. People who had been blackballed, ostracized, attacked, belittled, and made fun of for many years by directors of missions, executive secretaries, state paper editors, professors, and the general liberal establishment finally found in us people who were interested in them and who would listen to them. People often called to obtain correct information. Particularly when state Baptist papers ran misleading reports, a rash of telephone calls would occur to seek the facts behind a story.

The Baptist state editors never realized the extent of the communication between conservatives. Therefore, they never understood how we could rebut those things they were doing to caricature, attack, and make fun of the conservative movement. Grassroots Baptists lost confidence in many state Baptist papers and in Baptist Press. When they had the answers, they disseminated the truth among their friends, and their friends further disseminated the truth. The Baptist state papers were the losers. Their precipitous drop in circulation is merely one indication of how they fell in public esteem.

Conservative individuals called to find out with whom in their area they could fellowship and in whom they could have confidence. We never set up an organization; we never had officers nor did an organizational structure exist, but we did have contact with friends in every part of the convention. I kept accurate lists of whom to contact where. The liberal organization, on the other hand, was carefully worked out. They created organization charts such as one which I have disseminated at a meeting at Johnny Baugh's ranch at which Richard Jackson was the speaker on September 1, 1987. This chart lists their organizational structure for the state of Texas. One of their state leaders was Charles Wade, now president of the BGCT. Dick Maples, now on the BGCT staff to work with churches, was zone leader for his area.

The conservative movement was a network, not an organization. This network was busy on the phone, and many people participated. Through this network, individuals surfaced who had leadership potential and were willing to sacrifice their time and energy to serve on committees, boards, and agencies of the convention. Their names were communicated unofficially as information to the SBC presidents and the members of the Committees on Committees and Nominations.

For conservatives, service on a board and agency was not just an honor; it was a responsibility. The "good ol' boy" system, which the liberals ran, rewarded its own by giving them positions of honor on boards and agencies where the agency heads would host them royally. Some people believed this was their payoff for faithful service, and consequently they would remain loyal to the people who got them there in the first place and would merely enjoy the perks of office. Conservatives, on the other hand, saw service not as a perk or benefit but as an awesome responsibility that diverted them from their real interest in church building, soul winning, and mission activity. Most conservatives would rather have been actively involved in personal evangelism and church building than in serving on a board.

Many of my heroes of the conservative resurgence were those individuals who were involved in transmitting information and thus circumventing the power of the press and the bureaucracy. Most of these names are unfamiliar to the majority of Southern Baptists. They are not perfect persons. They, like all the rest of us, make mistakes, but they, among many others, gave themselves for the cause. Most paid a high price. I list no one who is now pastor of a large church or who works for the national denomination. Among the ones whom I think deserve special attention, listed in alphabetical order, are the following:

Marty Angell. The youngest person on this list, he was a student at Baylor University during many of the hectic days of the conservative resurgence. He fearlessly stated his position in classes and as a result spent a great deal of time defending his position before deans and the president of the university. His graduation was at times in doubt. As a college student and thereafter, Marty made a tremendous contribution.

Rev. and Mrs. Kenneth Barnett. He was a pastor in Cache, Oklahoma, when he made the motion concerning the Broadman Bible Commentary at the Denver SBC meeting in 1963. His director of missions treated him rudely and ultimately caused him to lose his church. Kenneth is one of the most thorough, hard-working individuals I have ever known. His ministry was undermined on several occasions, but he has continued to stand tall. He even took a second job to allow him to continue in a bivocational ministry. No one has worked more tirlessly, more successfully, and more conscientiously than Kenneth Barnett, supported by his wife, Patsy. He now is a pastor and leader among Colorado Baptists.

The Brumbelow family. Joe Brumbelow was a pastor at First Baptist Church of Dawson, Texas, near Corsicana, when we first met. Now he is on the staff of First Baptist Church of Lake Jackson, Texas. He and his wife, Bonnie, are the parents of three sons, two of whom also have served as Southern Baptist pastors. Steve built a fine work in West Virginia, where building churches is difficult. We served together on the Executive Committee. Now he is an evangelist. The second son, David, now pastors effectively in Highlands, near Houston. Their other son, Mark, is in business and is a deacon and Sunday School teacher in a Southern Baptist church. They represent what a Christian family should be. They love the Lord, serve Him faithfully, and have unselfishly given of themselves. They and others like them are the heart and soul of the conservative movement.

Dr. and Mrs. LaVerne Butler. LaVerne and Lillian have long been leaders for the cause of Christ. At the time the controversy began, he was pastor of Ninth and O Baptist Church in Louisville, Kentucky, and conducted a soul-winning evangelistic ministry that was well-known and respected, not only in Kentucky, but also in Illinois, Indiana, and throughout the SBC. Dr. Butler left Ninth & O to become president of Mid-Continent Baptist Bible College in Maysville, Kentucky, and carried on a very outstanding ministry there. Lillian has conducted a ladies' ministry, frequently speaks at women's conferences, and leads for the cause of Christ.

Kent Cochran. As a businessman, he was active in helping Missouri Baptists fight against liberal dominance. He was attacked when he was nominated to the board of Midwestern Seminary. Inside information about Midwestern Seminary that he uncovered and presented caused the smooth transition to Dr. Mark Coppenger's presidency of the school. Had Kent not served on the board, I do not believe Midwestern would have made its change so quickly.

Dr. and Mrs. Robert Crowley. For thirty-nine years Bob was pastor of Montrose Baptist Church, which he made into one of the finest ministries in the state of Maryland. Libby led in the music ministry and in many other ways. Maryland has not been an easy area for Southern Baptists, but Bob Crowley ministered very effectively there. Although not an early participant in the conservative movement, he was elected to serve on the Southeastern Seminary board of trustees and became one who led, helping cause the resignation of Randall Lolley. He guided the transition at Southeastern. He served as chairman of the Southeastern board at a crucial time. Southern Baptists owe a great debt of gratitude to him. I particularly do, because he has conscientiously pastored my daughter and son-in-law, Jean and Joe Visy, and three of my grandchildren. Joe was baptized under his ministry. In retirement, Libby and Bob Crowley are now developing a Bible conference and retreat center called Middle Creek, in southern Pennsylvania. I believe their present work will greatly impact the Washington, D.C. and East Coast areas.

Dr. and Mrs. James DeLoach. Jim was a professor at Southeastern Seminary in its early days. One of his pupils was Ed Young. Later, when Ed became pastor of Second Baptist Church in Houston, Jim was his associate. Jim also was a member of the Southeastern Seminary board of trustees, served as its chairman, stood firmly, and helped turn that seminary in a conservative direction. While he was at Second Baptist, he and his wife Doris ministered tremendously to my son, Paul, and to my daughter and son-in-law, Anne and Les Csorba.

Rev. and Mrs. David Eppling. This book would not have been written without David and his wife, Lea. David volunteered to spend innumerable hours typing and correcting my dictation and revisions. I am forever indebted to him and his family. He serves as pastor of a small church in Virginia while he completes his education. He and many other students have assisted me with great dedication, encouragement, and consistency. They are the greatest.

Mr. and Mrs. Neil Griffin. Neil and Elizabeth are two of the most giving people I have ever known. Though highly successful in business, they always put the Lord first. Their home is always open to God's people. Although they do not serve as messengers, they drive to each SBC meeting so they can be available to help others. They chauffeur conservatives, save seats for others, and wonderfully give of themselves. As one of our daughters appropriately said, "They both have true servant hearts."

Rev. and Mrs. Jerry Johnson. In his mid-twenties, Jerry became Colorado's representative on the board of Southern Seminary while he served as pastor of Central Baptist Church in Aurora, Colorado. He researched thoroughly, asked good questions, and incurred the antagonism of the liberal establishment at Southern Seminary. Jerry stood firm despite tremendous criticism. Even before he was thirty and had graduated from seminary, he had affected the future course of Southern Seminary. Now married, he has left his pastorate in Colorado for further study at Southern Seminary, where he previously served as chairman of the board of trustees.

Mr. and Mrs. Paul Martin. Lay leaders in Houston, Betty Lou and Paul Martin have always been available and have been two of our closest friends. They lead in their church. Paul served as a Baylor University trustee before conservatives were excluded from service there. He also served with distinction as a trustee of the Foreign (now International) Mission Board. They showed the depth of their commitment to the cause when they contributed the money they had saved for a new car to help with the expenses of the conservative movement.

Dr. and Mrs. Reuel May. He is an oral surgeon who led in Mississippi and serves on the SBC Executive Committee. Reuel is well-known and well-respected throughout the state of Mississippi and has given of himself in conservative causes.

The McGuire family. Pete and Peggy McGuire faithfully attended SBC meetings throughout the years and longed for the restoration of biblical fidelity in our institutions. Pete has served both as a pastor and as an evangelist. In their son John they instilled their deep love for our Savior. John, a pastor, with his wife Susan have labored long and diligently for the cause of Christ. This family is one of the very best the SBC has to offer. They and others like them were the backbone of the conservative resurgence. They have ministered primarily in the east Texas area.

Dr. and Mrs. Eldridge Miller. Eldridge and Jene are the parents of nine children, most of whom are in the ministry. He recently retired as pastor of First Baptist Church of Salisaw, Oklahoma and went home to be with the Lord as this book was being finalized. He, together with Sam Pace, Anthony Jordan, and many others, led effectively in the Oklahoma convention. He also was a person of strength on the SBC Executive Committee. Jene was always at his side. His excellent articles analyzed problems in the convention.

Dr. M. O. Owens, Dr. Calvin Capps, and Dr. Gerald Primm. These leaders deserve special recognition for their service since the 1960s. They recognized what was happening to the convention before many others did. They were perceptive and knew that something must be done. They tried to encourage conservatives to correct the problems, even when the destruction of biblical faith had not reached such proportions that it was evident to many. Their foresight, wisdom, and self-sacrifice caused the conservative movement to begin. The early deterioration of biblical faith in North Carolina helped them recognize the problem and awaken other Southern Baptists to what was occurring and to the need for a conservative resurgence. They deserve much credit, and we must not forget the early concerns that they voiced.

Dr. and Mrs. William Robert Parker. Gloria and Bob were among the early leaders in Louisville, Kentucky, where he served as pastor. They have consistently led effectively. He now serves as pastor at First Baptist Church of Markham Woods in Florida. He also served well on the SBC Executive Committee.

Gen. and Mrs. T. C. Pinckney. T. C. had a distinguished career as a general in the U.S. Air Force. He has served as commanding officer of bases. In retirement he hiked hundreds of miles each summer, but he gave up this pastime in order to devote almost full time to the conservative effort in the infertile ground of Virginia. Progress has occurred. He distinguished himself as an outstanding leader on the Executive Committee and as a leader of conservatives among Virginia Baptists. A great tragedy was his defeat by one vote for chairman of the Executive Committee. Harsh and unkind criticism has been heaped on him, but God has given him a gracious spirit that has allowed him to survive all of these attacks. His wife, Shady, has been a full partner in his efforts.

Dr. and Mrs. Bill Powell. Bill and his wife, Betty, performed exhausting and sacrificial service for the conservative movement. As I mentioned earlier, it was he who told me how the Southern Baptist system worked and explained the power of the presidency. He served as executive director of the Chicago Baptist Association. At great financial sacrifice, he left a position with the Home

Pressler children with sons-in-law Les Csorba and Joe Visy in Budapest in 1989

Mission Board to become director of the Baptist Faith and Message Fellowship. He suffered greatly because of the attacks made on him. Bill developed Alzheimer's and was not active in the resurgence after the early 1980s. Southern Baptists owe a tremendous debt to Bill and his faithful wife Betty.

Dr. and Mrs. Fred Powell. Fred and Donna led in Missouri from the very beginning of the conservative movement. He served as pastor of a great soul-winning church in Excelsior Springs. When Charles Stanley was elected SBC president, he needed a right-hand man, so Fred left his church to join the staff of First Baptist in Atlanta to help Charles. Fred's long, laborious hours, with Donna at his side, allowed the convention activities to flow smoothly, both while at First Baptist Church of Atlanta and later when he served so well as chairman of the SBC Committee on Order of Business. Now back in Missouri, he is working to support Midwestern Seminary. During the fall of 1998, Donna went to heaven. She is sorely missed.

Prayer warriors. Countless, nameless persons labored in effectual, fervent prayer for the SBC and its testimony for Christ. Without their prayer effort, nothing would have been successful. To these faithful prayer warriors we all owe a deep debt of gratitude. To one in particular, I pay tribute. Richard Hall was a youth evangelist when stricken with polio. He still uses a respirator and supports God's people in prayer. John Milton wrote, "They also serve who only stand and wait."

Dr. and Mrs. Jim Richards. Jim first served as pastor in northern Louisiana and then went to Southminster Baptist Church in Baton Rouge. I have met no one in the convention who is a better organizer, a more astute analyst, or a more dedicated detail person than is Jim Richards. He has the amazing ability not only to deal with minutia but also never to lose track of the broad picture. He became a director of missions in Arkansas and has served as chairman of the Committee on Order of Business of the SBC. No one has been more kind and more helpful to me personally than Jim and his wonderful wife, June.

Rev. and Mrs. Mike Routt. Mike has pastored churches in Kentucky. He is a person who has worked diligently and labored effectively. He took care of many details in leading in Kentucky. Mike has stood and led in an area where he has had little assistance. He has done very well.

Congressman and Mrs. Albert Lee Smith. Albert Lee and Eunie Smith were lay leaders who gave unreservedly of their substance and themselves in fighting the battle against forces which would compromise the gospel. Albert Lee was a congressman from the Birmingham area and served on the Baptist Joint Committee on Public Affairs. Eunie has led in Eagle Forum as well as in Southern Baptist matters. They were always available, always dedicated, and have paid a heavy price for their involvement. Albert Lee was killed in a tragic fall in August 1997. Eunie continues her service for the Lord, and Albert Lee is deeply missed.

Rev. and Mrs. Robert Tenery. Robert was pastor of Burkmont Baptist Church in Morganton, North Carolina, where he was an early laborer in the cause. He and his wife Dean spent countless hours contacting people, making them aware of the problems, encouraging messengers to attend the SBC meetings, and generally supporting the conservative movement. The demands of the convention struggle were so great and Robert gave of himself so unreservedly that it resulted in the loss of his church. He now serves as chaplain in a boys' home in North Carolina. The conservative movement could not have succeeded without Robert and Dean Tenery.

Dr. and Mrs. Ron Wilson. Ron and Alice fought many battles, not only in the state of California but with his being an FMB trustee. It was Ron's keen analysis of the situation that caused tremendous changes at the FMB. When an effort was made to draw the attention of FMB members away from the real issues, Ron was always perceptive in identifying problems and communicating to other members of the trustee board. The IMB would not be the same today without the contribution of Ron Wilson.

Mr. and Mrs. Don Workman. Don and Skeet are lay persons from Lubbock, Texas, who have worked tirelessly for Christian principles and for conservative causes. Skeet served well as a trustee on the Christian Life Commission (now the Ethics and Religious Liberty Commission). They both have given their lives to promote the gospel of the Lord Jesus Christ and the principles in which most Southern Baptists believe.

Small-church and bivocational pastors. The backbone of the conservative movement was this group who acted as faithful servants of the Lord. These pastors had nothing personally to gain but gave of all they had because of their deep convictions. I know of some who would drive to SBC meetings, eating peanut butter sandwiches the entire trip and sleeping in their cars. These could afford neither meals in restaurants nor hotel rooms. Their dedication provided the margin of victory. Their praise will not be on this earth but before the throne of grace.

To this list, many more could be added, but these are examples of individuals who, humanly speaking, have caused the conservative resurgence to be sucessful.

Only eternity will reveal the number of people who have come to know Jesus Christ as personal Savior because of their self-sacrificing, tireless work, and the effective manner in which they have led. To this roll call of saints many names could be added, and the omissions of others from this list does not mean that they are less appreciated. However, these are the first ones who come to my mind as I review the conservative resurgence in the SBC.

I listed spouses with the individuals mentioned. This is because a husband and a wife are one. Nancy spent many, many hours on this manuscript, correcting spelling, grammar, and punctuation. She is a true expert and the most wondeful wife any man ever had. Nancy and my children, Jean, Anne, and Paul, could not have supported me any better than they did. They were willing to accept my absences from home when they really needed me. They also believed fervently in the cause and suffered for it financially and in loss of family vacation time and family fun.

This loss they suffered cheerfully, and they were always ready to help. Had it not been for them, their attitude, and their support, I could not have been involved to the extent that I was. I am sure that the others who were involved would say the same of their families. While waiting, the spouses and children prayed and supported. They are the true heroes of the conservative resurgence.

CHAPTER 31

$\mathcal{T}$HE FUTURE OF THE CONVENTION

The course of the Southern Baptist Convention is now firmly set. The Cooperative Baptist Fellowship (CBF), the liberal break-off group, claims to have support from approximately sixteen hundred of the more than forty thousand churches in the Southern Baptist Convention. Even if these sixteen hundred churches fully supported the CBF, that would not indicate real strength. This would represent just more than five percent of Southern Baptist churches. However, I do not believe that the CBF report of sixteen hundred churches is an accurate figure. I have pastor friends whose churches are listed as CBF-supporting churches merely because one member of the church designates money to the CBF and the church forwards that member's money to the CBF. I wish the CBF would forthrightly reveal which churches are supporting its organization and how many of these churches actually give to the CBF out of their budget rather than by designated gifts. I imagine that it would be less than a third of the churches claimed. The CBF income has plateaued for the last two years, and it has taken money out of its reserve funds to support its operations.

I believe the reason the CBF has not split from the Southern Baptist Convention is that most of its leaders realize that, at the present time, they cannot take their churches with them. After a national CBF gathering in Atlanta, I asked Lee Roberts, a Georgia member of the SBC Executive Committee and a person who tirelessly worked for the conservative cause, how many of those CBF pastors who were at the meeting he thought would go home and actually be able to take their churches out of the SBC. His perceptive answer was, "About one third as many as get fired for trying."

During the next few years we shall see liberal pastors try to propagandize their congregations. They will hope to blacken the reputation of conservatives and destroy the reputation of the Southern Baptist Convention among their people so that their churches will be willing to withdraw from the SBC. In some areas liberal leadership is using "denominational study" committees and "intentional interim" programs to this end. Most of these committees never hear from any but liberal speakers, have only liberal books distributed for reading, or hear only liberal accounts of what has happened. This type of propagandizing is unfair and wrong. I doubt that this ploy works in many places, but it will in some.

Obviously a slight splintering will occur because some of the CBF leadership has determined that it can no longer continue to work with institutions that are based on the fact that the Bible is completely true. I am sorry that they hold this position, but if their theology is so different from that which the overwhelming majority of Southern Baptists hold, I can understand their deciding to leave. The very fact that they believe they must withdraw from the convention which they once controlled shows the intensity of the problem that existed in the SBC and the reason for our acting to alleviate the problem.

When some churches split from the convention—and I do think the question is *when, not if*—I predict that the number of churches actually ceasing to be Southern Baptist will be somewhere between two hundred to five hundred. I feel sad that they can no longer support the convention, but we should recognize that at the rate that the SBC is growing, the loss will be made up in a very short time.

Over the years, the liberals had worked to create the denominational hierarchy. They had made the Cooperative Program a sacred cow. When the sacred cow they created was no longer used to support institutions about which they were enthusiastic, they started the process of butchering and barbecuing this sacred cow. This was very confusing to many of their people and caused the CBF real problems in trying to reeducate its followers. At conventions in the late 1980s the liberals used campaign buttons and lapel stickers that said, "Save the Cooperative Program." After our victory was secure, one of my conservative friends wondered if we could buy these stickers from them since this was our group's desire and no longer theirs.

The liberals were faced with a dilemma: how could they create their own convention? To wean their people from the Cooperative Program, they are making the CBF an option within church budgets and state Cooperative Programs. This was successfully done in Virginia, North Carolina, and Texas. It was attempted on a national basis, but an action at the SBC meeting in Orlando instructing the Executive Committee to refuse to forward gifts from the CBF to Southern Baptist Convention agencies created a real problem for liberals.

At the time I failed to understand the significance. I did not realize how dramatic its results would be. Only when the liberals in their publications, writings, and speeches decried the resolution so vigorously did I realize that their strategy had been frustrated. No longer could they say, "Give to the Southern Baptist agencies through the CBF just like you have been giving through the

Cooperative Program." This hurt their reeducation process and caused them to reappraise their strategies.

Through numerous ways the liberals have sought to disintegrate the Southern Baptist Convention. For example, an association in Texas, led by its director of missions, attempted to amend its bylaws, eliminating any reference to the Baptist General Convention of Texas or the Southern Baptist Convention. This way the association could more easily be directed away from Southern and Texas Baptists if and when it wanted to do so. However, alert pastors recognized this danger. When the director of missions refused to back down, the motion to change the bylaws, which required a two-thirds affirmative vote, received an 80

Dr. Paige Patterson, Judge Paul Pressler and his son-in-law Les Csorba at reception following Presidential Election at Southern Baptist Convention in June, 1998 in Salt Lake City, Utah

percent negative vote. Other associations may also have attempted similar tactics.

Some changes are appearing in Virginia and North Carolina. In 1995 in North Carolina, a conservative was elected president of the state convention for the first time in many years. In 1996 he was reelected by more than 60 percent of the vote. In 1997 another conservative was elected. He was reelected in 1998. More and more of Southeastern Seminary's 1900 students are going into the churches of the state and helping them return to basic biblical orthodoxy. This resulted in the election of a conservative president in North Carolina several years earlier than I had anticipated.

The same type of thing will occur in Virginia but at a slower pace. In Virginia the liberal group controlling the Baptist General Association of Virginia (BGAV) passed a constitutional amendment providing that only those monies given for the state convention operation could be counted as gifts used for allocation of messengers to the state convention. To my knowledge no other state convention had previously done this. It disturbed conservatives greatly. One of the reasons the amendment was enacted was that when the Virginia convention created an alternate pattern of giving to allow funds to be channeled to the Cooperative Baptist Fellowship and away from the Southern Baptist Convention, many churches started giving directly to the Executive Committee in Nashville or designating a very large percentage to the Southern Baptist Convention.

The net effect of the liberals' tampering with the Cooperative Program in Virginia was to cause more money to go to the Southern Baptist Convention and less money to go to the state convention. After the reallocation-of-messengers motion was passed, conservatives in Virginia set up a separate state convention, the Southern Baptist Conservatives of Virginia (SBCV), which now has more than 10 percent of the SBC churches in the state affiliated with it. Some people believe that the liberals in the BGAV have gone so far that the convention is irretrievable.

On the other hand, when one recognizes the fact that churches are becoming more conservative in Virginia and more conservative pastors are coming into the state, a good case can be made for conservatives' trying to take back the BGAV in a few years. The pressure of the diversion of funds to the Southern Baptist Conservatives of Virginia already is moving some actions of the BGAV's state office to the right. If the BGAV (and possibly the Texas convention) is lost, these will be the only state conventions to leave. If the Baptist General Association of Virginia does align with the CBF and leave the Southern Baptist Convention, probably many independent Baptist churches as well as many which have not yet left the old Virginia convention will join the new conservative SBCV, and it will become the dominant Baptist voice in Virginia.

Another liberal model is Texas. After the liberals, with the help of Baylor alumni, came into control of the Texas convention, they successfully attempted two things. First, they said all contributions, whether to the CBF, to the Southern Baptist Convention or any other Baptist cause approved by the state Executive Committee, could be considered as Cooperative Program gifts. This gave a shield to those pastors who were trying to woo their members away from the Southern Baptist Convention because they would look good in the Cooperative Program-giving category, however they gave.

The next year, the BGCT followed up this action by decreasing by two percentage points the percent of the CP sent to the national convention. Thus, approximately two out of three dollars Texas Baptists give to the Cooperative Program stays in the state. Only 17.5 cents out of every dollar given undesignated to the Cooperative Program in Texas goes to international missions. Many conservative churches have now started sending some or all of their contributions directly to the SBC Executive Committee in Nashville. They do this because they do not want to have their contributions divided in such a way with the state convention.

It could be that the liberals in Texas have taken on too much. They could face the same result as in Virginia. When the BGCT starts changing the Cooperative Program, some conservative churches will follow by adjusting their giving accordingly. Of course, the liberals in Texas claim that their purpose is not to hurt the Southern Baptist Convention but to build more churches in Texas. If this had been their real intent, I wonder why they didn't work more closely with conservative churches to bring them into their plans, to develop a program which would be all-inclusive, and to create a mutual feeling of trust rather than just forcing the changes on conservatives at the state convention.

Although Texas Baptists are conservative, the liberals have been able to accomplish some of their goals through a troika of support. This has been Baylor University and its alumni association, Russell Dilday's direction of Southwestern Seminary and its alumni association, and the Baptist General Convention of Texas leadership with certain liberal pastors. With the departure of Russell Dilday from Southwestern, the liberals have lost one of the legs of their stool. If Baylor becomes less interested in the BGCT because the school is now independent of the Texas convention, Baylor will cease to be a factor. The state Baptist office cannot with a few liberal pastors maintain control of the convention by itself.

The BGCT hired Dick Maples from the pastorate of First Baptist Church of Bryan to direct a department of church relations. Before he was elevated to this position, liberals circulated on tape a message he preached that was highly critical of conservatives and that contained a number of inaccuracies. Obviously, hiring Maples after such an attack on conservatives did not indicate that the state office had hired him to work with all Texas Baptists. His attitude, as reflected in his message, and the reactions of the many whom he attacked, made this impossible. Thus, one needs to look for the real reason behind his employment.

Purportedly, he was to work with pastors and with churches. His office has developed an "intentional interim" program. It has sought to work with pastorless churches to provide them with "assistance" in how to go about calling a pastor. Some reports indicate that the program has an anticonservative bias. If conservatives had created such an office, liberals would scream that this had violated the autonomy of the local church.

The Baptist General Convention of Texas (BGCT) has taken other steps which concern me. At its Austin meeting in November 1997, the BGCT adopted a program which provided for the printing of some Sunday School literature, the support of non-Southern Baptist theological education, and the sending of its own missionaries. Many people consider this a move toward an independent denomination. Also at the Austin meeting, an amendment was passed changing the manner in which messengers to the BGCT are allocated.

Until then, messengers were allocated on a church-membership basis only. The change adds a requirement of a financial gift to the state convention. A church must contribute $1,000 to the BGCT for each messenger over four. If a church has 2,151 members and it contributes $21,000 to the Texas convention, it can have the maximum number of 25 messengers. Without a contribution, it is no longer allowed more than four messengers. A messenger from a church in Waco which was not a conservative church referred to this provision as a "poll tax." The "poll tax" was approved by a vote of 73 percent to 27 percent at the 1997 Austin convention. The vote required 66.7 percent. It had to be approved again at the Houston meeting of the BGCT in 1998.

It is interesting that at times the liberals have claimed that they have been "disenfranchised" nationally. This implies that we took away their right to vote. Of course, this is not correct. Nowhere have conservatives changed the voting eligibility. The liberals lost in the elections. They did not lose the right to vote. Only in Virginia and Texas has the eligibility to vote been changed. This was done by liberals to disenfranchise conservatives. How loose the liberals are with words when they claim that we tried to "disfranchise" them! We didn't; they did!

I had hopes the "poll tax" could be defeated in Houston, but a small group of conservatives instead put their time and effort into starting a new convention rather than saving the old one. In the 1998 convention, the vote was 3,342 (70.73%) for and 1,383 (29.27%) against. If we had had 290 more votes, we would have defeated the "poll tax." A change of 193 votes would also have defeated it. The conservatives were not recognized at the microphones, and therefore an adequate presentation of the opposition was not voiced. We came so near but yet so far. So many seemed not really to care. This is a tragedy. The enormous resources of the BGCT can now be used to kick start a new liberal convention. I worry that the next step will be to end the geographical limitations on membership in the Texas convention so that liberal churches throughout the country can join. The BGCT could then change its name, and a new liberal denomination would be established using its assets. What the CBF could not do, the taking of the assets of the BGCT would accomplish. To me this is the last major threat of a meaningful split in the SBC.

I find it remarkable that through all this, the liberals were unable to destroy the Cooperative Program as they had hoped. They anticipated reducing contributions to the SBC by 20 percent or more and through its pocketbook bring the convention to its knees. Instead, although in three successive years small losses occurred, these averaged less than 1 percent for each year or less than 3 percent for the three years combined. The losses stopped in 1993, and since then, every year has shown an increase in Cooperative Program giving. The 1998 calendar year showed a growth of 8.16% in Cooperative Program (CP) gifts over 1997. The first three months on the 1998–1999 CP year (October, November, and December) show a growth of 12.37% over the same three months in the year of 1997–1998. Total CP and mission offering gifts now total almost $500,000,000 each year, including the amounts retained in the states. The CP offerings which go to the national work of the SBC together with the special mission offerings now total well over $300,000,000 per year. The CBF offerings, on the other hand, have plateaued between $14,000,000 and $15,000,000. The economic havoc that was threatened by the liberal movement has failed.

The liberals also attempted to disrupt by taking away state institutions. When the conservative movement began, Southern Baptists had more than fifty colleges. The state convention in which each was located owned each institution. Perhaps it is a misnomer to say that Southern Baptists had more than fifty colleges, because having a college in name does not mean that it was a Baptist institution in substance. These colleges varied from very liberal to solidly conservative.

We have now lost Stetson in Florida, Mercer in Georgia, Richmond in Virginia, Wake Forest in North Carolina, Baylor in Texas, Furman in South Carolina, and several others. These institutions now elect their own trustees. I believe that most of the actions removing these institutions from the state conventions were illegal and improper under the bylaws of the state conventions, under their own charters and bylaws, and under the laws of the states in which they operate. Be that as it may, their actions are now complete, and conservatives have neither the will to fight over those institutions nor the determination to do the things that are needed to bring these institutions back to being thoroughly Christian. Liberals dominated many already, and withdrawal from the state conventions was merely a final step in the process. Therefore, in about ten or fifteen cases out of more than fifty colleges the state conventions owned, liberals have succeeded. They might succeed in others, particularly in North Carolina.

However, in many colleges, the movement has been in the right direction. Some institutions that did not pay any attention to their theological moorings and to the spiritual leanings of the people whom they hired on the faculty have now become very sensitive to these matters. A much larger number of students now attend schools that are Southern Baptist in more than name only. These students are receiving the right type of Christian education. How many institutions will return to the fold is a matter that has not yet been determined. However, so far, the only loss by Southern Baptists to the liberals has been a few colleges.

My heart breaks for every student who goes to an institution founded by God-fearing, Bible-believing Southern Baptists where that student's faith is destroyed by apostate teachers who mock and ridicule the faith of the founders. It is tragic to think of every unsaved young person who attends an institution

Nancy and Paul Pressler and their seven grandchildren at family ranch, Hazy Hills, in Dripping Springs, Texas, December 1998

Baptists began who might never hear the gospel of redemption or a believer who could have been useful to the kingdom of God whose ministry will be ineffective for Christ and His gospel because his biblical faith has been destroyed. However, when compared with the tremendous disintegration that could have occurred in our Southern Baptist Convention institutions, this loss does not seem to be quite so great.

None of our national institutions has been lost. Each of the seminaries is returning to its theological moorings. In the case of Southeastern, the liberals decided that if they could not control it, they would try to destroy it. Liberals originally theorized that if Southeastern ever had a conservative president, the institution would die. This has been shown to be erroneous. Southeastern Seminary is now stronger than it has ever been. Its student enrollment of nineteen hundred is by far its highest in history. As one who went on its campus during the heyday of liberalism and saw the type of student it had then contrasted with the type of student it has now, all I can say is, "Praise the Lord!" Today's students are interested in soul-winning, building churches, and telling the good news that Jesus saves. Such is becoming the norm in our other seminaries as well. I praise God for the godly leadership He has raised up to lead each of our six seminaries.

The liberals' answer to this has been to try to create new seminaries. Richmond, Mercer, Wake Forest, Baylor, and other universities have tried to establish their own divinity schools or seminaries. They have done this without impacting the enrollment at our Southern Baptist seminaries. I wonder how many churches will be interested in calling persons who have attended the liberal, non-Southern Baptist seminaries. I feel sorry for those students whose professors or pastors have so prejudiced them against our Southern Baptist seminaries that they have opted for one of these liberal schools. I believe that attending one of them will limit these students' effectiveness and ministry opportunities. These seminaries will probably give no adequate presentation of a conservative position. They will also probably fail to train these students in soul-winning and witnessing. The remarkable thing is that so few students are in the liberal seminaries compared to the number of students who now attend our Southern Baptist seminaries.

As the Southern Baptist Convention has returned to its moorings, I find it interesting to view the state conventions. Each year most state Baptist conventions become more conservative than they were in the previous year. The state executive secretaries who are now being elected are individuals who are, by and large, theological conservatives. The state newspaper editors, in many places, are still liberals, but even some of them have stopped propagandizing as vehemently as they once did for the liberal cause. Their circulation numbers have shrunk so much that the liberals in these posts no longer have the platform they once had.

The storm has passed, and the Southern Baptist Convention has weathered the tumult. We shall move into the twenty-first century stronger than ever. God has blessed, God has provided, and all the indications are positive. The number of baptisms annually is gradually increasing. Contributions, the number of church starts, and missionary appointments are growing. The CBF has relegated itself to the position of a little puppy dog snapping at the heels of a great convention.

Bible-believing individuals build great churches. Conservatives win people to a saving knowledge of Jesus Christ. God uses conservatives to instill holy zeal in the hearts and lives of their people. God can bless and use the Southern Baptist Convention to help bring about a revival in the nation. The only lasting hope for any institution is that constant renewal and constant revival occur. The building stones are in place, doctrinal integrity has been restored, and the SBC is poised on the brink of great revival. If it occurs, it will not only shake almost sixteen million Southern Baptists with our more than forty thousand churches but will also greatly affect the entirety of our nation. Praise God, the hill has been occupied. It was a hill on which to die, because the positive results will be so tremendously good for so long, affecting people for eternity.

Any look at the Southern Baptist Convention struggle would be incomplete without observing what has occurred and is occurring in other major American denominations.

The present Roman Catholic pope, John Paul II, is more conservative than were some of his predecessors. He has changed the liberal leadership of the Jesuits and has appointed so many cardinals that his successor most likely will be a conservative. Roman Catholics face many problems, but these are foreign to the experience of most Southern Baptists. That denomination continues to grow in the United States because of immigration and a high Roman Catholic birth rate.

In 1965, the United Methodist denomination had a membership of 11,067,497. In 1997, the membership was 8,538,662. This is a loss of 2,528,835 members, or 22.85 percent. What has happened? Liberals took over in the United Methodist seminaries. Few people would deny that the predominant position of the leadership of the United Methodist denomination today is a denial of the inerrancy of Scripture. The denomination has a vocal and growing constituency advocating ordination of homosexuals. However, conservative forces within Methodism seek to reverse the direction of the denomination. I pray for them. God has greatly used Methodists in the past and can do so again.

Some United Methodists anticipate that conservatives must ultimately be forced to leave. It is thought that about one-third of the denomination would join a conservative exodus. Those who would exit are situated primarily in the South and Southeast.

In 1965 the Presbyterian denomination was divided between two main bodies, the United Presbyterian Church (Northern) and the Presbyterian Church, U.S. (Southern). That year the total membership of the two bodies was 4,254,460. By 1997 the membership of the combined group, the Presbyterian Church (U.S.A.), was 3,669,489. This was a loss of 584,971 members, or 13.75 percent. Liberal control of Presbyterians' denominational seminaries has devastated its effectiveness as a denomination.

Nevertheless, some reason for hope exists. An outstanding group called the Presbyterian Lay Committee has been functioning for many years with the purpose of restoring the Presbyterian denomination to its former doctrinal integrity and greatness. I know some of its leaders and spoke to its board of directors' meeting more than ten years ago. Only recently has it begun to see real success. In 1996 and 1997, Amendment B to the constitution of the Presbyterian Church U.S.A. was voted on and adopted by a margin of 57 percent to 43 percent of the presbyteries. It provided for ordination only of those clergy who pledged to fidelity within the covenant of marriage between a man and a woman.

Howls of anguish greeted the adoption of this most basic statement of Christian morality. An immediate move was made for its repeal. The vote for the repeal effort lost by a two-to-one margin, a gain of approximately 10 percent for conservatives. Presbyterian laypersons seemed to be awakening. The liberals have gone too far, and some possibility now exists for restoration. It cannot occur, though, unless a seminary is begun or recaptured which will provide a firm biblical basis to train ministers to proclaim the gospel.

The Episcopal Church had 3,429,153 members in 1965. In 1997, it had 2,536,550 members—a decline of 892,603 members, or 26.02 percent. Some of its bishops are openly prohomosexual. A renewal group is under way, and many churches are cutting or withholding their contributions to the national organization. Their battle will be intense.

Among U.S. Lutherans, the Lutheran Church-Missouri Synod reversed the liberal direction of its seminaries before the Southern Baptist conservative movement began. In 1965, Missouri Synod Lutherans had 2,692,889 members. In 1997, they had 2,594,555 members. This is a loss of only 98,334 members, or 3.65 percent. The more liberal group, the Evangelical Lutheran Church in America, together with groups later merged into it, had 5,684,298 members in 1965. In 1997, it had 5,190,489 members, for a loss of 493,809 members, or 8.69 percent.

In 1965, Southern Baptists had a membership of 10,770,573. In 1997, we had a membership of 15,663,296. This is a gain of 4,892,723 members, or

45.43 percent. Before the conservative resurgence began, liberalism had been confined to our educational institutions and only a few churches. Thus, liberalism never reached the influence among us in the churches which would have halted our growth.

The lesson is clear: groups which have stayed faithful to God's Word have grown, and those who have become liberal have lost membership.

I pray that the victory of conservatives in the Southern Baptist Convention will encourage our Bible-believing brethren in other groups and will help them restore their denominations. In most, if not all cases, the conservatives in these denominations started too late. Also, their ecclesiology is not as democratic as is the congregational form of government of Southern Baptists. Those who cannot restore their denominations will probably have no choice but to leave.

Many people complained that the conservative movement was disruptive for Southern Baptists. Regrettably, to a certain extent, that was true. However, the moral and theological issues have been resolved for us as a denomination, and probably we shall see only a small split because of it. If we had failed to deal with the issues, far greater disruption would have occurred, with a larger split. Because the other denominations failed to control the liberal invasions of their denominations in its earlier stages, their conflict and disruption will be great, with far greater detrimental effects to the cause of our Lord Jesus Christ.

Members (Loss) or Gain

	1965	1997	(Loss or Gain)	Percentage
Episcopal Church	3,429,153	2,536,550	(892,603)	(26.02%)
Evangelical Lutheran Church in America (1)	5,684,298	5,190,489	(493,809)	(8.69%)
Lutheran Church— Missouri Synod	2,692,889	2,594,555	(98,334)	(3.65%)
Presbyterian Church (USA) (1)	4,254,460	3,669,489	(584,971)	(13.75%)
Southern Baptist Convention	10,770,573	15,663,296	4,892,723	45.43%
United Methodist Church (1)	11,067,497	8,538,662	(2,528,835)	(22.85%)

(Note (1) 1965 statistics include total for groups merged into present body.)

Grave problems still confront Southern Baptists, however. One is the bureaucracy of the convention. I once wondered how local, independent, Bible-believing churches in the first century developed into the Roman Catholic Church. After observing the manner in which the bureaucracy grew in the Southern Baptist Convention in a very short time, I no longer wonder. The main danger of a bureaucracy is that it becomes an end in itself and not a means to effectuate the principles for which it was founded. History shows us that a bureaucracy, whether political, religious, or business, ends up seeking additional perks for itself and additional favors for those in the bureaucracy. It becomes loaded with individuals whose only qualification is that they have been loyal to the system and, therefore, are rewarded by being placed in the bureaucracy when they fail elsewhere.

The "good ol' boy" system evidently started years ago. Liberals developed under this system, because the liberals were careful not to voice their extreme positions publicly (with a few exceptions) and were careful to pay their dues to the system. Such a system must not be allowed to develop under conservative leadership. We must always seek the very best individuals to lead and to serve in our agencies. We must guard against a reinstallation of a "good ol' boy" system under which anything could occur as long as it didn't harm the bureaucracy.

I fear bureaucratic control and domination. I had nothing to do with the restructuring proposal which the SBC adopted at the 1994 annual meeting in Orlando. In fact, I learned about it only when it was being announced to the convention as a whole. However, I am very enthusiastic about it, because I think it is a realistic attempt to reduce the bureaucracy and to minimize what could have a stifling effect on the presentation of the gospel.

Another great danger to the convention's future is that some people who now might dominate in convention leadership were unwilling to pay the price to lead the convention to be restored to its conservative principles when it was risky to do so. These might seek to lead out of a desire for prominence, personal perks, and privileges, rather than because they are willing to give of themselves so that the original biblical convictions of Southern Baptists might be maintained.

I have heard people say (and others have reported such remarks to me) that certain individuals should be disqualified from service and leadership because they have too many bruises from having fought in the battle. When a person is disqualified for service because that person gave unreservedly to win the victory, we have reached a point of self-destruction. Those who have paid the price should not be excluded because they were willing to sacrifice themselves.

In any great movement are individuals who sit back and watch to see which way the battle will go. When they see which side will prevail, they attach themselves to that side. These people disturb me, because they seem to be self-serving individuals who are more interested in their own advancement than they are in basic principles. They are more concerned with their own future than they are with the cause itself. The possibility of their ascending to leadership worries me.

If they attach themselves to the biblical cause because they perceived it would win, they could at another time sell out the principles which they have come to espouse because they see another "winning" cause. Some people have said that a good leader is one who finds out the direction the people are going and then gets in front of the movement. To me, that is not the mark of a good leader; it is the mark of a poor leader. This type of person leads in order to advance himself or herself and does not lead in order to advance principles. Any movement, particularly a religious one, is in danger when such people attach themselves to the cause.

Those who were unwilling to risk certainly have a place in the convention leadership, but they should not be dominant and certainly should not lead to the exclusion of those who have paid the price and have stood in a principled manner the entire time. Leadership should emerge from people who are principled, who adhere to sound doctrine, who are more committed to the cause than to their own personal advancement, and who are willing to follow the Holy Spirit's leading in promoting sound doctrine regardless of the personal cost. The permanency of the movement will be determined by whether principled leadership continues or whether self-serving individuals take over and build a stifling bureaucracy.

We find that people whom we thought were on the other side are now loudly proclaiming that they were "with us all the time."

The Southern Baptist Convention will continue. It will continue its growth; it will continue its strength; and it will continue winning people to Jesus Christ. Whether it continues in as vibrant a manner as it should will be determined by how dedicated to principle and not to self-promotion the future leaders will be. I pray that God will give us principled leadership.

In an outstanding address to an Executive Committee meeting in Nashville on February 17, 1997, SBC President Tom Elliff summarized his concerns for Southern Baptists. He stated our needs as follows:

1. "A need to certify his or her experience with Christ."
2. The "stranglehold of debt" that is "preoccupying us."
3. The need "to crucify our egos."

These are all grave concerns. Theology is never an end in itself. It is a means to a vital relationship with our Lord Jesus Christ. As we believe and know His Word, we grow closer to Him and develop as believers. The theological issue has been addressed. Now we must see the effects that the victory brings in producing godly lives which glorify the Lord and will attract others to our Savior. If we fail here, all will have been in vain.

The debt issue can be a spiritual issue also. Do we ever overbuild our churches so that a pastor or congregation can boast about what was built? Poor business practices by believers keep others from trusting our Lord. How can we preach sacrifice and give a pittance to our great mission programs because we have so overloaded ourselves with debt?

Perhaps the focus on the egos of Christians highlights the most devastating problem which few have found the courage to address. Believers should die to self. However, sometimes it seems that the need by some for self-promotion motivates rather than a brokenness over the fate of those who are eternally lost. A true Christian leader is best seen when he or she is hidden behind the cross. No one who really wants to be president should ever be elected president of the Southern Baptist Convention. It is a God-given responsibility of service, not an ego trip for recognition. We are all merely sinners saved by grace. If we constantly fail to recognize this, we are doomed to fail as a people. God has called us to be servants, not self-promoters. We need servant leadership for the Southern Baptist Convention.

The battle is over, but we will feel the effects and ramifications of it for many years. How effective it will be on a long-term basis will be determined by whether we follow principled individuals who are willing to risk all and charge a hill on which they are willing to die. Our leaders must be servants of God, not servants of their own ambitions.

Being a lay person, I return to my original pursuits and plan to enjoy my retirement. Those who are called of God to be leaders in the denomination, whether in the pastorate, in our institutions, or as lay leaders, will lead. I shall watch them and pray for them.

The future for Southern Baptists is bright. I praise God for what He has done to bring change in the convention. This could never have originated from individuals. The odds were too great. The victory had to be of God.

The citadel of liberalism was charged and the hill on which to die was captured, but not without great cost. God has given the victory in an amazing way. I praise Him for it. I pray that His people will preserve this victory to His glory until He comes again.

CHAPTER 32

$\mathscr{A}$ LOOK TO THE FUTURE

After the SBC meeting in Dallas in 1985, the conservatives obviously were on a winning course. The liberals had put everything into their effort and came up wanting. However, they were not completely convinced that it was over. They marshaled their forces for additional SBC meetings, particularly in San Antonio in 1988 and New Orleans in 1990. After these two were lost, even they knew the battle had ended.

Now that the conservative direction in the SBC is assured, I finally have an opportunity to take a lower profile. When the victory was won, I was emotionally and physically exhausted. My relationship with God was impacted because I had placed too much confidence in the integrity of some individuals. In many ways I had not been able to separate the perfection of the gospel from the imperfection of its being worked out in the lives of some believers. Even more than that, the fallen nature and innate sinfulness of all people has been painfully impressed on me.

A passage of poetry I learned in school was Alfred, Lord Tennyson's "Morte de Arthur." In it King Arthur gives a wonderful soliloquy as he prepares to die. Talking about God, he says,

> I found Him in the shining of the stars,
> I mark'd Him in the flowering of His fields,
> But in His ways with men I find Him not.
> I waged His wars, and now I pass and die.

King Arthur then concludes, realizing that God alone is true regardless of his experiences with individuals and says, "Nay—God my Christ–I pass but shall not die."

Every believer should have his or her primary comfort from the Word of God, realizing that it alone is entirely true. However, the words of imperfect individuals sometimes express our hope well. Another poem that I learned early in life was John Greenleaf Whittier's "The Eternal Goodness." One verse of it says,

Yet in the maddening maze of things
And tossed by storm and flood;
To one fixed stake my spirit clings;
I know that God is good.

I can identify with Tennyson and Whittier. Since human institutions and individuals are fallible, my hope must be in Almighty God and not in His creation. I have always known this in my mind, but to translate it into the experience of my heart and my emotions has been difficult. I needed several years after the convention controversy was over for God to work in me to bring back the joy of my salvation and the victory of my experience with Him. I never doubted the Truth. I just needed to experience it more fully and completely. I am doing better now.

I believe in a real, personal devil. Satan's desire is to destroy all those who oppose his realm. Satan is not any more interested in me than in any other believer who, although falteringly, tries to do what God wants that person to do. I have felt myself subject to satanic attack, and this has been extremely difficult.

Along with the emotional trauma, I also had physical problems. I had put all my energy into the battle and had not taken care of my body. I ate nervously as a reaction to fatigue and emotional distress. At the end of the battle I found myself overweight with very high cholesterol and triglycerides. My knees had deteriorated to the point that the leg bones were emerging from the knee sockets and causing a great deal of pain.

The convention struggle also took a professional toll on me. Before my involvement in the SBC controversy, I got along with almost everyone. I knew many excellent reporters in Houston, such as Kay Bailey (now Kay Bailey Hutchinson, a United States Senator from Texas), Nene Foxhall, Kay Moore, and many others. They covered the courthouse, and I made it my practice to sit down with them any time they wanted and explain what was occurring in my court or elsewhere in the courthouse. I found particularly in those three reporters a genuine desire to get things straight and to report things accurately.

When I entered the convention controversy, I sometimes found the opposite to be true. I was exactly the same judge as before, but a few of the people with whom I worked at the courthouse and some attorneys could no longer affirm me as a judge because of my standing for those principles in which I believed, which were not related to my performance as a judge. This bothered me. I believe a person should be judged on his or her performance and not on unrelated matters. In spite of these attacks, I still was very pleased with my professional activity and performance.

Although my involvement in the convention did make me some enemies in the legal profession, I was not opposed for reelection after the controversy began. I considered this to be the grace of God. Several years after the controversy began, on two occasions, individuals approached me and asked that I run for the Texas Supreme Court. These individuals offered their help and had the connections and the resources to generate a great deal of statewide support. I believed that with their support and that of those whom I knew around the state, I would have had better than a 50/50 chance to be elected to the Texas Supreme Court.

The first time they approached, I reluctantly turned them down. I told them that the battle was not yet won in the Southern Baptist Convention and that I needed to stay the course and see that victory accomplished. It was a difficult decision, prayerfully made. I recognized that if I turned down an opportunity such as this, these persons probably would not return. However, they did return two years later and again offered to support me—as before, with no strings attached. All they wanted was for me to continue the same conduct that I had on the trial and appellate bench and to adhere to the same principles of strict interpretation and judicial restraint which characterized my judicial philosophy. For the same reason, I turned them down for the second time. God had called me to work in the convention. If I had exited at that time, it would have hurt the effort.

Thus, I closed the door on my professional career advancement. I have been on the ballot twelve times—six in the Democratic primary and six as the Democratic nominee. I never lost an election. After my last election, I switched my party affiliation and became an active Republican. I believe that the Democratic Party has abandoned the moral position which previously had given it credibility.

I had advanced as far as I could in the judiciary because I had turned down my opportunities for promotion. I decided that I would retire in 1990 when I had twenty years of service, as I would then receive my full retirement benefits. However, the voters of Texas elected Ann Richards to the governor's office. I could not resign before her election because it would have cost me too much in my retirement package. I could not retire after her election and give her an opportunity to appoint an ultraliberal who could have influenced the Texas judiciary. In fact, there was one particular individual whom I feared the governor might appoint who would have been disastrous. Therefore I served three more years and did not run for reelection in 1992. My retirement became effective as of January 1, 1993.

Upon retirement I issued the following press release:

For immediate release
June 10, 1991
Judge Paul Pressler Announces Retirement from the Court
Paul Pressler, Justice of the Fourteenth Court of Appeals, issued the following statement on June 10, 1991:

"When I filed for reelection almost six years ago, my wife and I prayerfully determined that this would be my last term. After a total of twenty-five years in office in the legislature and on the bench at the end of this term, I am ready to spend more time with my family and follow other pursuits. I shall not be a candidate for reelection next year.

"I feel fulfilled in seeing the accomplishment of goals which I have sought. Their completion allows me the freedom to change direction while I am at an age where I can vigorously devote time and energy to various other interests.

"I am grateful to Governor Preston Smith and Governor Dolph Briscoe, both of whom appointed me to judicial office, and to the voters who have elected me six times: four at-large from Harris County and two from the Fourteenth Appellate Judicial District. Holding government office is a responsibility and challenge. I am grateful for the opportunities of service which I have had."

Judge Pressler, a Republican, is also now serving on President Bush's Drug Advisory Council, is Chairman of the Board of KHCB, Christian radio station, a Deacon and Sunday School teacher at First Baptist Church of Houston, on the EFICOM Board of the National Religious Broadcasters and active in a number of other professional, educational, religious and charitable organizations. He has served as Vice-Chairman of the Executive Committee of the Southern Baptist Convention, President of the Council for National Policy, and Chairman of the Board of International Students, Inc.

I considered serving as a visiting judge—a role in Texas where retired judges fill in when the need arises. It was an option that was open to me, but I rejected it because of two basic reasons. If I were a visiting judge, I could not raise any money for charitable organizations. Serving as a trustee of the International Mission Board and working with many Christian groups, I wanted to be able to raise funds. Also, as a visiting judge, I could not engage in political activity. I wanted to support candidates who believe in the principles in which I believe. I am pleased that I have successfully worked diligently to defeat some individuals whom I felt needed to be defeated and have participated in electing others who are serving well.

I had greatly neglected my family. By the time of my retirement, my son had been gravely ill for sixteen years, and Nancy had borne a tremendous burden helping him and the girls. My parents were extremely upset with my involvement in the convention. From their perspective, I had thrown away my life and destroyed the goals and ambitions they had for me.

Six years later, my triglycerides and cholesterol are back to normal, my knees are working satisfactorily again, my weight has been reduced somewhat, and I am determined to continue to make progress toward a healthy weight. I have been engaged in building a good legal practice with a firm I founded with three younger Christian attorneys (Frank, Woodfil, Lucas and Pressler), doing mediations, and handling estates. I enjoy these activities very much. Life does exist beyond my activity in the Southern Baptist Convention. My ancestors usually have lived to be more than ninety years of age, and I hope that I have another twenty-five to thirty years left. God has restored to me "the years that the locust hath eaten" (Joel 2:25). Personally, I am grateful.

I always knew that when the victory was won, I should step aside from convention leadership. If I did not, I could be subject to attacks by persons saying that I had participated in order to exercise control. If I withdrew when the victory was won, no one could levy that charge at me with any credibility. As far as SBC activities are concerned in the future, my desire is merely to answer calls of those who desire specific information and be available to counsel with those who need me. Nothing will be done on my own initiative. My desire is to distance myself from convention activities except to finish my term as IMB trustee in the year 2000 and after that, just attend SBC annual meetings. I shall continue to teach my Sunday School class, engage in mission trips, and do what I can to spread the gospel and win people to Jesus Christ. Those are things God has placed a burden on my heart to do.

I plan to spend more time with my family and with our seven wonderful grandchildren, born between 1990 and 1997. We have a great opportunity to be involved in their lives. Regretably our son's condition has not abated. He needs me. Nancy and I are so grateful for our three children and for our two sons-in-law, all of whom are strong Christians active in Southern Baptist churches. We anticipate quality time with each of them.

I also look forward to time with friends, some of whom have been long-neglected. The propaganda by the liberal media has caused many people to wonder whether I have lost my mind and why I became an "extremist." Now I can take time to show them that I am the same person whom they had previously known and that what I was trying to do was to stand for those essential principles of basic Christianity.

Some of the greatest experiences of my life occurred while I worked with the SBC conservative movement. Many wonderful friendships were forged, and God visited us many times as we prayed and worked together. I experienced something that few people are privileged to do. Those in leadership of the conservative movement were some of the most godly and wonderful people I have ever known. They did not participate in this to advance their own careers. In fact, many thought that their involvement in the controversy would end their ministry as a Southern Baptist. They were as surprised as anyone to observe the tremendous victory God gave through the conservative movement. I was privileged to know the people who charged the hill and were willing to die professionally—reputation wise and in every other way, because they believed so intensely in the cause.

Some people have claimed that I would try to profit financially from the SBC controversy. The financial toll on me and my family has been high, but again, it was worth it. I know that if I write this book and market it, taking even a small profit myself from the book, many would be quick to say, "Yes, we see now that what he wanted to do was get into a position to write a book so he could make money off of it." Certainly, such was not my desire, and I could not with good conscience make such a profit. Nancy and I have given the proceeds from this book to charity so that they will be used to glorify our Lord Jesus Christ and further His kingdom. This is our strong desire.

The SBC controversy was a hill on which to die. Many did die—if not physically, in other ways. It was a hill that had to be won, and won it was. I am grateful for those who will lead in the future. I am grateful for the many, many young people who will not be damaged in our Southern Baptist institutions by liberal teachers but instead will go forth with hearts aflame for God. I am grateful for the increased mission activity. I praise God, for only He could have brought about the present result.

I am delighted to put my involvement behind me and to leave the hill which has now been recovered from those others who had captured it.

*R*EPORT TO SECOND BAPTIST'S DEACONS, AUGUST, 1964

Second Baptist Church
6400 Woodway
Houston, Texas
Dear Sir:

As a member of your committee, appointed during the summer of 1963, I have carefully studied, to the extent that it has been possible to do so, the six seminaries supported by the Southern Baptist Convention and the schools and colleges within the State of Texas maintained by funds of the Baptist General Convention of Texas. Based upon the newspaper clippings collected, the various articles reviewed, personal contacts with students, professors and administrative officials of certain of these schools, and other information carefully accumulated, I wish to report as follows:

I. Propriety of the Study. Baptists should constantly study their educational institutions in order to determine if they are accomplishing that task which is committed to them. Only by our understanding them and knowing both their strong points and their weaknesses can we be equipped to be of assistance to them. True support by intelligent people must be based upon adequate knowledge.

Baptists have always believed in the priesthood of the believer. This great doctrine of our faith implies responsibilities as well as privileges. Based upon a mutual faith in Christ, individual believers associate themselves together in order to perform tasks which cannot be done by individuals working alone. A New Testament Church is a God created institution in which all believers should participate. Although not specifically set forth in Scripture, conventions and associations of churches are right and proper because they provide the machinery through which tasks can be accomplished for the Lord which could not be performed otherwise. Nevertheless, our position as believer priests necessitates that we do not abrogate to others the responsibilities which are given to us by the Lord. Included within these responsibilities is that of maintaining the soundness of doctrine and the clarity of Gospel witness in those institutions which we support. If we believed that the Scripture taught an ecclesiastical form of church government with authority placed in the hands of a small group of people, it might be considered presumptuous for us to inquire into those things which are being taught in our denominational institutions. We would be required to leave this inquiry in the hands of those who by virtue of their position are considered to be more responsible to God. Such, however, is repugnant to Baptist thought. Rather, upon each individual believer is placed the responsibility of insuring that his witness and the witness of those institutions and organizations which he supports is that which the Lord would have.

As members of a local New Testament Church, we must intelligently direct the mission gifts of our church so that the financial resources of our church might be most effectively used for Christ. Since we are, in effect, those who pay the bills of our educational institutions, we have a right to know what it is that our money is being used to propagate and how effectively it is accomplishing its purpose.

II. The Center of our Faith. Baptists have traditionally been called a people of the Book. We have repeatedly stated that we do not wish to subscribe to creeds because no creed which does not contain the whole of the New Testament would be adequate for Baptists. We affirm this belief. We believe that all doctrine must stand or fall as it is judged by Scripture. At the same time, we recognize that there must be a latitude for interpretation of Scripture. Baptists have always recognized this. However, the right to interpret Scripture is not a license to explain away its clear teachings. Interpreting Scripture means taking that which is in Scripture and trying to understand what the Scripture is saying. A doctrine which is clearly taught in Scripture (such as the deity of Christ, His Virgin Birth, His substitutionary atonement, and similar doctrines) are ones that should not be questioned because no ground for latitude is given in the clear, forthright teaching of Scripture on these matters. Other doctrines (such as the second coming of Christ, the happenings of the last days upon earth and similar items) are not set forth with such clarity in Scripture that only one interpretation of such doctrine is possible. Upon these doctrines upon which conscientious, intelligent individuals can validly differ when taking the Scripture at face value and trying to understand what it says, we cannot insist upon conformity. We must, however, insist that our basic foundation of belief in the Scripture as God's inerrant Word be upheld in the teaching in our educational institutions. Such a belief is one that has always been held by Baptists. If the bedrock of Scripture is eroded away, we have no basis for believing anything. To open the door for a minor doctrine which is inconsistent with Scripture today, is to open the door for greater variance from Scripture in the future. If our educational institutions are not adhering to the great doctrine of an inerrant Scripture as the foundation of our faith, they are sowing seed which can undermine all doctrines held by Baptists.

III. Definition of Terms: In recent years individuals who have not believed the Gospel have attempted to read new meaning into old terms. The neo-orthodox school of theology frequently uses Biblical terminology to mean things which are quite different from that which has traditionally been believed by Christians. For instance, some in this school of theology will say they believe in the "resurrection of Jesus Christ." When their statement is discussed with them, they will say that they do not believe in a bodily resurrection but that by the phrase "resurrection of Jesus Christ" they mean that "the spirit of Jesus lives on." Again some liberals will refer to the "divinity of Christ," a term which to most listeners is synonymous with the term "deity of Christ." However, upon careful questioning they will admit that in their thinking "divinity" and "deity" are quite different. They will say that they believe in the "divinity of Christ" because they believe that all men are divine but that they do not believe in the deity of Christ because that implies that Christ was God.

In the use of the term "inspiration of Scripture" we have had the same perversion. The word "inspiration" literally means "God breathed." For a long time it was known what a person meant when he said that he believed that the Scriptures were "inspired." Now many people will use the word "inspiration" to mean something quite different. We have heard people say that they believe Scripture was inspired in the same way that Beethoven was inspired when he wrote his music, or Dante was inspired when he wrote his Divine Comedy, or great scientists are inspired when they make their discoveries. Such is not the traditional meaning of the term "inspiration of Scripture." In many Baptist statements, we have been more specific and used concrete terms which should be subject to no variance of interpretation as to what is being intended by the use of such terms. For instance, in the statement of faith adopted by the Southern Baptist Convention in 1925, it is stated that we believe Scripture to be "truth without any mixture of error, for its matter." In a resolution adopted by the San Francisco Southern Baptist convention in 1962, it was stated that the Convention believed in "the entire Bible as the authoritative, authentic, infallible Word of God," and in a subsequent resolution it was stated that Southern Baptist seminaries were urged to remove those who held "theological views which would undermine such faith in the historical accuracy and doctrinal integrity of the Bible." In the statement of faith adopted at the Southern Baptist Convention in Kansas City in 1963, it was stated again that we believe the Holy

Bible to contain "truth, without any mixture of error, for its matter." Our own church constitution states that we believe the Bible to be "the inspired, infallible, and inerrant Word of God." The terms used in these resolutions are clear and unambiguous. If Scripture is said to be without any mixture of error, that means it is without any error of any type. If we say that we believe the Bible to be the inerrant Word of God, that means that we believe it to be completely without error. The position of our Southern Baptist Convention has been clear and unequivocal on this matter over a long period of time.

IV. Academic Freedom. The phrase academic freedom has frequently been used as a shield for teaching diverse viewpoints. Many today would have us swear unswerving allegiance to such a term without fully understanding and appreciating its significance. Academic freedom must be coupled with academic responsibility. Along with academic freedom there must exist another freedom, a freedom of individuals to create educational institutions which will stand for the principles in which they believe. If we say that academic freedom must be unlimited, we are saying that individuals do not have the right to create educational institutions which will adhere to the beliefs and convictions which they hold. Certainly in state institutions open-mindedness and nonpartisanship is demanded when tax moneys are taken from all the citizens of a community and the educational institutions are supported by such funds. However, we should imagine that few, if any, would feel that academic freedom would require that a professor advocating free love be given a pulpit on a Baptist campus, or would allow a Jesuit priest the right to use the religion department of a Southern Baptist institution as a point from which to propagate his doctrine, or would demand that a communist have a right to promulgate his atheistic and materialistic convictions in the religion or economics departments of a Baptist institution. All of us must recognize that there are limits to academic freedom in Baptist institutions in order for there to be any purpose for maintaining these institutions. The question is not whether there should be academic freedom but rather where the limit should be placed upon academic freedom. It is our feeling that a reasonable minimum standard of belief to be held by those teaching in our institutions should be a complete and total allegiance to the Bible as the inerrant Word of God. That if such is not adhered to by our educational institutions, Baptist educational institutions have no reason for existence and should neither be created nor supported by our Baptist people.

On the subject of academic freedom in its December 12, 1962 issue the Texas Baptist Standard editorially commented as follows:

> Academic freedom is precious, but it involves the student just as much as the teacher. When he selects a Baptist School he goes there expecting that the

faith in which he was reared will be respected and not ridiculed. His forebearers established the school for two purposes—the preparation of their children and the propagation of their faith. Any teacher who uses his pedagogical rights to weaken the faith of an inquisitive student is simply out of place on a Christian campus.

V. Our Seminaries.

Background Information. For a long time many Southern Baptists did not view with great interest that which was transpiring in their seminaries. They were grateful to have six well-financed schools with adequate plants and what appeared to be devoted professors teaching in these schools. We were aware that a large portion of our Cooperative Program funds went to support these educational institutions and were content that it be so. Shattering this air of complacency about our seminaries was a book written by Dr. Ralph Elliott, a professor at Midwestern Baptist Seminary, entitled "the Message of Genesis." This book was published in 1961 by the Broadman Press, which is owned by the Sunday School Board of the Southern Baptist Convention. Immediately after its publication, many Southern Baptists became alarmed not only about this particular book, but about the condition in our seminaries which it seemed to reflect. In this book statements are made by Dr. Elliott which cannot be reconciled with a belief that Scripture is "truth without any mixture of error." For instance, Dr. Elliott states with approval the theory that Melchizedek was a priest of Baal when the Scriptures say in Hebrews 7:1 that he was a "priest of the most high God." Dr. Elliott states that he isn't sure that a person named Abraham ever lived, but that if he did live, then certainly all of the activities ascribed to him in the Bible could not have been performed by one man. Elliott says he believes in the general historicity of the accounts of the patriarchs "although it is impossible to deny the fact that sometimes the material may have been legendized just a bit and perhaps heightened as a means of intensifying the dominant characteristics in the patriarch's life." In his book Elliott stated, "We must learn to think of the stories of Genesis, the creation, the fall, Noah's ark, the tower of Babel in the same way as we think of the parables of Jesus; they are profoundly symbolical (although not allegorical) stories, which aren't to be taken as literally true (like the words of the textbook of geology)."

Dr. Elliott wrote an article defending his book which was quoted in the September 7, 1962, issue of the Illinois Baptist, the Southern Baptist publication in the State of Illinois. In this he does not retract his statements. This defense itself shows that he doubts the complete integrity of Scripture and does not hold to a belief that Scripture is truth without any mixture of error.

After the controversy had begun, the Trustees of Midwestern Seminary gave a vote of confidence to Dr. Elliott. The Board of Trustees stated, as reported in the Illinois Baptist of January 10, 1962, that "we do affirm our confidence in him as a consecrated Christian, a promising scholar and teacher, a loyal servant of Southern Baptists, and a dedicated and warm evangelistic preacher of the Gospel." The controversy concerning Ralph Elliott was not stilled by this action of the Midwestern Baptist Seminary Board of Trustees. Various statements were issued by those in leadership positions within the Convention.

Dr. K. Owen White, Pastor of First Baptist Church in Houston, Texas, commenting on "the Message of Genesis" stated,

> The book from which I have quoted is liberalism, pure and simple . . . The book in question is poison. This sort of rationalistic criticism can lead only to further confusion, unbelief, deterioration and ultimate disintegration as a great New Testament denomination.

In dealing with the question the Illinois Baptist in an editorial entitled "the Breakthrough" in the spring of 1962 stated,

> The breakthrough in the matter of academic freedom has apparently been made. Some have heralded the action of the Midwestern Seminary Trustees as a step to freedom. The action of the Sunday School board encouraging Broadman Press to continue 'to publish views which represent more than one point of view' will certainly be counted as another step towards freedom by those who have felt that the Baptist faith and practice need regearing for the space age . . . But freedom must have some limits or it becomes license. We are of the opinion that sooner or later the Southern Baptist Convention will have to deal with the problem of how far this freedom extends.

In an article by McGary Ford, Jr., Pastor of Fairview Church, Amarillo, Texas, in the Baptist Standard of May 30, 1962, it is stated, "We are all disturbed by the developing resentment and distrust of our schools and professors and the apparent distrust of the usefulness of our seminaries . . ." Then he summarized by saying, "We cannot stand idly by and allow the Bible to be attacked in our own schools by men who receive their livelihood from Baptists."

The matter came before the San Francisco Southern Baptist Convention in 1962 although efforts were made by the apologists for Elliott to keep the matter from coming to the floor. They worked for the creation of a committee to study Baptist beliefs in the hope that creation of such a committee would cause a discussion of the Elliott controversy itself to be delayed. It could not be delayed because of the feelings of the majority of the messengers to the Convention. Dr.

K. Owen White presented the resolutions of the group opposed to Elliott to the Convention. No opposition was voiced to the resolution which reaffirmed our faith in "the entire Bible as the authoritative, authentic, infallible Work of God." The Convention then went on to resolve as follows:

> "That we express our abiding and unchanging objection to the dissemi-
> nation of theological views in any of our seminaries which would undermine
> such faith in the historical accuracy and doctrinal integrity of the Bible, and
> that we courteously request the trustees and administrative officers of our insti-
> tutions and other agencies to take such steps as shall be necessary to remedy at
> once those situations where such views now threaten our historic position.

The second resolution was passed over the opposition of those who sup-ported Elliott. Everyone at the Convention, those in support and those in oppo-sition, clearly understood that the intent and the purpose of the resolution was to have Dr. Elliott and those who believed as he did dismissed from positions in our seminaries.

At the San Francisco Convention, new Trustees were elected to fill the expir-ing terms of those on the Board of Midwestern Baptist Seminary. The Midwestern Seminary Board did not meet immediately. Finally, at a meeting held in late October, 1962, the Trustees of Midwestern Baptist Seminary voted 22 to 7 to dismiss Ralph Elliott and issued a ten point statement. Both Elliott and the Trustees were said to be agreed on all but one point of this statement. The point of disagreement was whether Elliott's book should be republished. The fourth point of this statement was to "affirm our belief in the inspiration of the Bible and all parts thereof. The method of inspiration is not to be thought of as a test for Baptist fellowship." This statement uses the very loose term "inspiration of the Bible" and does not follow the wording of the Southern Baptist Convention in its statement of faith referring to the Bible as being "truth without any mixture of error" nor does it use the terms "inerrancy or infallibil-ity of Scripture." A "straw man" is raised by the statement that "the method of inspiration is not to be thought of as a test for Baptist fellowship." The contro-versy did not concern the method of inspiration, but rather concerned the fin-ished product of revelation B not how we got our Bible, but rather what the Canon of Scripture is. Elliott was dismissed because he stated that he could not accede to the request of the Trustees that his book not be republished. Therefore, it was upon this minor issue and not on the issue of theology that Elliott was dismissed.

Dr. J. Marse Grant writing in the Biblical Recorder, the North Carolina Southern Baptist publication, stated as follows,

If Dr. Elliott was dismissed because he wrote the book, this should have been given as the reason for his dismissal— and not the technical point of republication rights . . . The spirit of the San Francisco Convention was unmistakable.

Dr. E. S. James writing editorially on Elliott's dismissal in the Texas Baptist Standard stated,

The Standard believes it would have been much better if the Trustees could have agreed to base their decisions on the man's theology.

Elliott's dismissal did not settle the matter at Midwestern Seminary. The Trustees have since issued statements approving the seminary policies and lauding its administration. However, discontent continued within the faculty. Dr. Heber F. Peacock resigned as Chairman of the New Testament Department at Midwestern Baptist Seminary. He aligned himself with Elliott's theological position and said that his resignation was due to "a situation which does not offer an opportunity to speak the truth." He was not asked to resign and evidently could have remained as far as the administration of the school was concerned. It should be noted that Peacock is one who has held other positions of teaching responsibility in our Southern Baptist Convention. He was head of the religion department at Baylor University in Waco, Texas, and once taught at Southern Baptist Theological Seminary in Louisville, Kentucky.

Some Southern Baptists in Kansas City organized a group known as "Baptists for Freedom" in November, 1962. This group continues to exist, issue publications and work within the Southern Baptist framework. Its viewpoint can be seen by a remark in a communication to one of the members of our committee by Mr. Robert T. Latham, Chairman of the group, believing him also to be a supporter of Elliott, where he stated,

Having lived in Houston for a period and having married a Houston girl, thereby being acquainted with the perspective of the area, I can hope for you that the atmosphere is less restricting than during the days of my sojourn there.

After the resignation of Peacock at Midwestern, Jack L. Gritz writing in the Baptist Messenger, the official publication of Oklahoma Southern Baptists, stated,

At San Francisco last June a vast majority of Southern Baptists assembled in annual convention emphatically declared that such an approach to the Scripture (Elliott's approach) is entirely unacceptable to them and called on the Trustees of their institutions and agencies to take steps at once to correct the situation wherever necessary. (Incidentally, only Midwestern Seminary has issued any statement concerning an effort to comply with the Convention's instructions. Other seminaries and agencies are yet to be heard from.) Probably there are other professors at Midwestern Seminary who are so upset over the dismissal of Elliott that they can no longer serve as effective members of the faculty. Possibly others share the Elliott viewpoint towards the Scripture. In Christian integrity they should resign their positions and not force the Trustees to force them out."

So far there have been no more resignations and the Trustees have taken no action whatsoever to force any such people out of teaching positions in our seminaries.

Elliott's book was published by the Broadman Press which is under the supervision and control of the Sunday School Board of the Southern Baptist Convention. The Sunday School Board met and passed a resolution which in part said,

> The elected Sunday School Board further encourages Broadman Press to continue to publish books which will represent more than one point of view and which will undergird faith and contribute to the Christian growth and development of those who read them.

Commenting on this, the Texas Baptist Standard editorially said,

> We believe the Sunday School Board ignored a potential opportunity to strengthen the faith of all Baptists in its own operations. What a boon it would have been to all Baptist work if the board which governs Broadman Press had simply said: We want books published which will express different views on what the Scriptures say and mean, but we want each of them to acknowledge that the Scriptures mean what they say.

In a further comment on the publishing policy of the Sunday School Board, the Baptist Standard on January 23, 1963, editorially stated as follows:

> The Standard may be alone in the contention, and it may be an old-fashioned idea; but we hold that any book produced by an evangelical press and sold through its bookstores should be of such nature and content that any Bible believer can buy it without fear that it will insult his faith or intelligence. There are two sides to this freedom we hold dear. Each of us should be free to read whatever he chooses, but each of us should be free to believe that when the book is published and promoted by his denomination it will strengthen rather

than weaken the faith of the youngest or weakest saint among us. This is not censoring. It is just plain common sense.

In August, 1962, some 36 religion teachers in Southern Baptist Colleges and Seminaries attending a meeting in Ridgecrest, North Carolina, issued a statement attacking the failure of the Sunday School Board to republish Elliott's book. They made no statement as to whether they believed in the authority of Scripture and made no effort to remove the doubt which had been casted upon our theological and educational institutions by the Elliott controversy. The Baptist Standard on November 7, 1962, stated editorially,

> Why in the world should a group of Bible teachers in Baptist schools think that the most important thing they could resolve about was the responsibility of a Baptist agency to publish a book that flatly denies some plain affirmations of the Bible? We can understand quite well that they were seeking to defend their version of academic freedom. They have the right to do this. Since they thought fit to bring up the matter of the controversial book and since they, too, are Bible teachers, why did they not use the occasion to tell the world whether or not they agree with Elliott's premise? They did not have to bring the question into the public eye, but they did. They did of their own accord, and when they did they obligated themselves to declare their position on the book's contents.

> We have known no time when a session of Bible teachers had such a good opportunity to answer current criticisms of Baptist schools and banish fears from the hearts of many by simply stating their disapproval of the book. If they agree with Elliott, they should not hide it and if they don't agree with him, they ought to say so."

We have yet to see any resolution or statement which would banish the fears which many of us have held concerning our Baptist educational institutions because of Elliott's book.

There has been a large volume of articles and statements concerning the Elliott controversy. To be noted among them was an article appearing in the February 20, 1963 issue of the Baptist Standard by C. E. Colton, Pastor of Royal Haven Baptist Church in Dallas. In this he stated,

> If the time should ever come that we as Baptists have any marked degree of difference in our concept of the Bible as the inspired, infallible, and reliable word of God, the historical basis of our unity will have been shattered; and we are doomed for disintegration. I am perfectly willing for the Bible itself to be

its own fence for Baptists so long as we recognize it as the inspired, infallible word of God.

The Illinois Baptist in the spring of 1962 reviewing the statement of faith adopted by Southern Baptists and Elliott's book said as follows:

> If Dr. Elliott is correct, the Bible is in error and worse, contains planned exaggeration." But Dr. Elliott is really not the issue, nor is his book, controversial as it is. The issue is whether or not a Baptist seminary—Midwestern or any other—can appropriate to itself the right to teach young preachers as truth theories that contradict Baptist's stated doctrinal position—and continue to be supported as a Southern Baptist institution.

Writing in the December 19, 1962, edition of the Baptist Standard, Dr. W. R. White, Chancellor of Baylor University, stated as follows:

> The trustworthiness of the Holy Bible as our rule of faith and practice is indispensably vital to the integrity of our community of faith . . . There are many irregularities that can be absorbed by a great body like Southern Baptists. However, when the taproot is being attacked, however mildly at first, then it is a time to be alarmed, particularly if it is being done by those who are training our leaders.

In an article on Southern Baptists and Genesis in the Baptist Standard of August 14, 1963, Dr. O. Carroll Karkalits, supervisor of research for Petro-Tex Chemical Corporation in Houston, Texas, after reviewing Elliott's book says,

> It is common practice to at least refer to all literature presenting all sides of a question about which there is a difference of opinion. It seems odd that Dr. Elliott failed to mention any of these well known conservatives. Are their points demonstrably incorrect? Is there evidence?

In commenting on the firing of Ralph Elliott, Ora Spaid, Religion Editor of the Louisville Courier-Journal in the November 5, 1962, edition stated,

> Dr. Millard J. Berquist, President of the Seminary, had said repeatedly when the furor over Elliott's book broke out that he would stand by Elliott because, "If they get him, they'll have to get me." But Berquist finally relented and agreed to Elliott's dismissal.

Dr. C. R. Daley, editor of the Western Recorder, Kentucky Baptist weekly, stated,

They (Trustees of Midwestern) must know by now that Elliott is not a glaring example of heresy among the host of safely orthodox teachers in our seminaries. If he is a heretic, then he is one of many and indeed is not at the head of the line. Professors in all our seminaries know that Elliott is in the same stream of thinking with most of them, and is more in the center of the stream than some of them.

Elliott does not deserve a medal for extreme views compared with his fol-low Southern Baptist teachers. If he deserves a medal, it is for his courage in writing a book in which he honestly expresses his views. Some teachers who would share his approach to the Bible, though not necessarily his conclusions, feel his only mistake was to write down his conclusions at this time.

In an article on the Southern Baptist situation in the religion Section of Time Magazine, November 9, 1962, it was said:

The faculty and students of Southeastern Baptist Theological Seminary in Wake Forest, N.C., said President Sydnor L. Stealey, were 'deeply disturbed by the news (of Elliott's dismissal) and very sympathetic toward Dr. Elliott.' A fac-ulty member at Louisville's Southern Baptist Seminary reported the faculty 'almost one hundred percent' in sympathy with Dr. Elliott's views.

Writing on Dr. Elliott's dismissal in the November 14, 1962, issue of the Baptist Standard of Texas, Dr. E. S. James editorially commented,

"The Standard believes it would have been much better if the Trustees could have agreed to base their decision on the man's theology. This paper holds that his flat denial of many plain statements in the Bible and his sym-bolic interpretation of other passages is not in keeping with the Baptist concept of revelation. He has a right to hold that position, but the Trustees had the right to decide whether or not he or anybody else is to be allowed to teach it in a Baptist school . . . The time has come for people in responsible positions to stop saying they believe the Bible as the Word of God and then turn right around and say some of its thoughts and messages are borrowed from pagans. This does not apply to Professor Elliott any more than it does to a large num-ber of others, but he published his views and lost his job. Some others would probably lose theirs if they should put them on the line as Elliott did. There is no doubt that it was Elliott's theology that caused his dismissal. It would have been better if the Trustees could have agreed to say so."

In commenting on the Elliott dismissal Christianity Today, leading interdenominational Christian publication, in its April 26, 1963 issue stated,

> Some conservatives feel the Trustees evaded the real theological issues of the case and looked for another ground on which to dismiss the controversial Elliott, who is said to be no more conservative than others on the same faculty who have adopted more radical critical views but have not put them in print. The same is said of some professors at Southern and Southeastern Seminaries, the New Testament Department of the latter having been charged in some quarters as being strongly Bultmannian.

The controversy has not been stilled. Shortly before the Kansas City Southern Baptist Convention in 1963 a group of 200 laymen of the Missouri Baptist Convention prepared a petition criticizing Midwestern Baptist Seminary for continued liberalism. These laymen called for the firing of all administrators and teachers at the Seminary who "give encouragement to the liberal viewpoint."

Another outgrowth of the controversy was the election of Dr. K. Owen White as the 32nd President of the Southern Baptist Convention. Dr. White was elected primarily because of his leadership of the fight against liberal theology in the Southern Baptist Convention at the previous meeting of the Convention. Dr. White has spoken extensively on the subject of inspiration of the Scripture. Dr. White stated,

> Dr. Elliott was not picked on. It is not a case of making an example of one man— he wrote the book. This is not an isolated case. There has been a growing liberalism in our schools for the last fifteen years at least.

He further stated,

> Certainly there must be a place for academic freedom but the professor must remember he bears a certain responsibility to the denomination supporting him. Academic freedom does not mean freedom to believe and teach anything you choose to believe and teach when it is in open conflict with the vital doctrines of the denomination which you serve.

In this statement he concluded:

> If we part from our conservative position which has marked us through the years, we will lose our impact which has marked us as a great evangelical denomination.

Conclusion. Although much time has elapsed since the start of the Elliott controversy, we still have not seen any clear and unequivocal statement by the

Trustees or faculty members of any Southern Baptist school which is in conformity with the instructions of the San Francisco Convention of 1962. If it were possible for such statements to have been made, it is not understood why they have not been forthcoming. So much heartache, so much confusion, so much distrust could have been dispelled by such statements. It does not seem possible that these statements would not have been forthcoming unless there was something going on in these institutions which their leadership wished to hide.

The Missouri Synod Lutheran Church recently was confronted with a similar situation when Dr. Martin H. Scharlemann, professor of New Testament Interpretation at Concordia Theological Seminary in St. Louis, Missouri, was accused of not believing in the inerrancy of Scripture. Immediately, Dr. Scharlemann issued a statement saying that he believed the Scriptures to be "utterly truthful, infallible, and completely without error." He stated that he regretted that because of inadequate statements in some of his articles he had given the wrong impression. This action on the part of the accused professor forestalled any action by the Missouri Synod and his statement was accepted.

Southern Baptist seminary leaders have not shown the same courtesy. Is it because they cannot truthfully make such statements or is there some vanity of academic freedom which has prohibited them from doing so? Southern Baptists have a right to know. Our fears have not been dispelled. No effort has been made. No reports have been given in conformity with the resolutions of the 1962 Convention. Most of the conferences and discussions with the leaders of Southern Baptist Seminaries held my members of your Committee were unrewarding and unsatisfying.

VI. Result of Theological Controversy. Recently our Southern Baptist Seminaries have lost in enrollment. In 1961 there was a total of 3,541 theological students enrolled in our six seminaries, a loss of 225 over the 3,766 enrolled in 1956 in the five seminaries which then existed. The following reflects the total ministerial enrollment in all of our schools by school year;

1956-57	10,594	1959-60	8,233
1957-58	9,976	1960-61	8,392
1958-59	9,063	1961-62	8,111

Thus there was a drop of 2,483 students or 23% over a six year period. The worst part of this drop came in those enrolled in our colleges where the loss was more than one-third.

In Texas, baptisms have steadily decreased from a high of 69,944 in 1955 to 58,192 in 1962. Most other state conventions report similar declines. The Texas Baptist Sunday Schools increased in enrollment by 79,400 in 1954. The growth in Sunday School enrollment in 1962 was 3,700. The decline in the number of additions to our Sunday Schools continued steadily from 1954 to 1962. Giving has not kept pace with the cost of living index and the growth of membership.

Something is tragically wrong in the Southern Baptist Convention. We must recognize this fact and face up to it. As Billy Graham stated at the Texas Baptist World Evangelism Conference in Dallas a short time ago.

> Southern Baptists statistics are declining. I am convinced the two greatest causes of the decline are a lack of men and women filled with the Holy Spirit and a lack of faith in the Bible as the infallible Word of God.

The doubt cast upon the authority of Scripture by professors in our seminaries is a cancer which is eating out the life of our denomination. It is not known whether it is too late to adequately eradicate this infection which has spread in such a way that it is detrimentally affecting the whole of our Convention. Positive action must be taken in the immediate future if we are to save our Convention from becoming a useless and lifeless group which, although having the form of religion, does not have the power that God seeks to give through His Holy Spirit.

We cannot ascribe these changes and these declines merely to cultural and sociological patterns. God is able to work in any climate and His Holy Spirit can adequately undertake in any circumstance when men are willing to be used by Him. The responsibility for action lies with us as believer priests—ones who are called of God to accomplish His purposes.

Very little time remains in which effective action can be taken. Elliott's supporters hope to train a new generation of preachers who are in agreement with their theological position. They are content to let the opposition pass all the resolutions they wish as long as nothing is done to disturb their positions in our seminaries. We cannot fail in our responsibility to act.

Yours very truly,

Paul Pressler

APPENDIX B

$\mathcal{D}$ELINEATION OF
POSSIBLE PROBLEMS

Paul Pressler
282 Bryn Mawr Circle
Houston, Texas 77024

September 3, 1985

Dr. David Simpson
P.O. Box 24189
Indianapolis, Indiana 46224

Dear Dr. Simpson,

In September of 1984, Dr. E. Harmon Moore, former Executive Secretary of the Indiana Baptist Convention, requested that I set forth specific examples of possible areas of theological problems in our Southern Baptist Institutions. This was done by Rev. David Lucas and printed in the *Indiana Baptist* of May 21, 1985. Dr. Moore was not satisfied with a response from Bro. Lucas and requested that I further delineate such information personally.

I have delayed for many reasons including the following:

1) I have tried on occasions to get together with the leadership of certain of our agencies to present such information to them personally, but they have refused to meet. I feel that it is best to deal directly with the institutions involved;

2) I hoped that these matters would have been taken care of within the system by the various agencies rather than have them printed in a publication without allowing each person involved to have an opportunity to respond to the matter privately prior to its being published.

3) I would prefer that possible examples of problem areas be handled through the Peace Committee rather than publicly when the institutions refuse

to deal with such problems themselves. However, the continued instance of such a distinguished leader of Southern Baptists as Dr. Moore requires a response. Because of his demand, and only because of it, is this information sent to you as Editor.

4) There are so many possible problems, I could at best list only a portion of them regardless of how long I researched.

In reviewing these I would caution every reader to observe the following:

1) These are quotations taken from various writings and statements. In order to appreciate fully what is being said, the reader should go to the full context and study these quotations in the light of the entire presentation;

2) It should be noted that with one exception, and that being one person's giving examples of his experiences in seminary, the accounts given are from published articles or taped speeches; Not used are numerous oral reports and complaints which are frequently brought to the attention of those who have expressed their concern;

3) The items set forth are not accusations against individuals that they are liberal but are a setting forth of areas which should be examined by all Southern Baptists, and particularly the administrators of our various agencies, to see if problems do actually exist;

4) These areas of investigation are freely available to all individuals who wish to do research;

5) The *Broadman Bible Commentary* would be a fertile field for developing other references similar to these, but the ones that are given here from such Commentary are merely representative of that which a person reading *Broadman Bible Commentary* could find;

6) The ones making the statements, their employment and the forum given for the promotion of these ideas should be noted along with the fact that certain quotations are published by agencies of our Southern Baptist Convention;

7) A few examples are used from institutions of State Baptist Conventions. These are because of the interchange between teachers and students in these institutions.

8) The underlining in certain quotations is mine and not the authors. The underlining is for emphasis.

The following items are for examination and investigation by Southern Baptists and particularly those who are hired by all Southern Baptists to make sure that our institutions are responsive to their constituency.

Sincerely yours in Christ,
Paul Pressler

"'Dynamic' Theory of inspiration, 'is not dependent on a mystical, inexplicable, *and unverifiable inerrancy in every word of scripture or on the concept that inspiration can allow no error of fact or substance.*'" (p. 7)

"There is a rather general consensus among scholars that editors collated written material, produced out of the sources described above and gave it permanent form. Trustworthy biblical study shows that the Pentateuch existed essentially in its present form by 400 B.C." (p. 10)

"Its authority is not in inerrancy of word and phrase or perfect consistency of all numbers and events or perfect understanding of God by his chosen servants." (p. 11)

From "The Book of the Christian Faith", an article in the *Broadman Bible Commentary*, Volume 1, published by a division of the Sunday School Board of the Southern Baptist Convention and written by Clifford J. Allen, former Editorial Secretary of the Sunday School Board and General Editor of the *Broadman Bible Commentary*.

* * * * *

"While some person may continue to hold that 'the historic Christian belief in Biblical infallibility and inerrancy is the only valid starting point and framework for a theology of revelation,' such contentions should be heard with a smile and incorporated in the bylaws of the Flat Earth Society. But always we should respect the integrity of a person in an argument or debate, though his position may indeed be quite ridiculous."

"Many who promote infallibility of the Bible are simply dishonest. They know better through education and reading but find it advantageous to exploit the uninformed whom they say they have been 'called' to serve and save. They parlay this false doctrine into success, fame and large churches. Such moral dereliction is far too common in many modern public religious activities. . . . To this type of deceit there is no response except contempt and rejection."

From "Revolt Against the Faithful" published in 1970 by Lippincott by Robert S. Alley, a professor at the University of Richmond, a Virginia Baptist Institution.

* * * * *

"Jesus never really claimed to be God or to be related to Him."

"I see Jesus as really a Jew. I don't imagine for a minute that he would have had the audacity to claim the deity for himself. I think passages where he talks about the Son of God are later additions—what the Church said about Him."

Statement by the same Dr. Robert S. Alley to an atheist meeting at the First Unitarian Church in Richmond, VA, on December 6, 1977 as reported in the *Richmond News Leader* and in a Baptist Press release of December 14, 1977.

* * * * *

"Do you feel that the Baylor religion faculty's view of God and the Bible reflects that of the average Southern Baptist?

Yes: 22.9 No: 77.1

Do you feel that the religion professors at Baylor are concerned about your spiritual well-being?

Yes: 57.6 No: 42.4

Do you feel that the religion professors present the Bible as:

a)the inspired, inerrant word of God 20.6

b)the inspired word of God, but with some human error 62.9

c)a historical account of Biblical times with little application to the people of today 16.5"

From a survey of Baylor University Students taken in April 1984 by a student for a course at Baylor University.

* * * * *

"Only willful ignorance or intellectual dishonesty can account for the claim that the Bible is inerrant and infallible. To qualify this absurd claim by adding 'with respect to the autographs (original manuscripts)' is a bit of sophistry, a specious attempt to justify a patent error."....

"No truth-loving, God-respecting, Christ-honoring believer should be guilty of such heresy. To invest the Bible with the qualities of inerrancy and infallibility is to idolatrize it, to transform it into a false god."

"We are not bound by the letter of scripture, but by the spirit. Even words spoken by Jesus in Aramaic in the thirties of the first century and preserved in writing in Greek, 35 to 50 years later, do not necessarily wield compelling or authentic authority over us today. The locus of scriptural authority is not the words themselves. It is Jesus Christ as THE Word of God who is the authority for us to be and to do"....

Statement by Robert G. Bratcher at a 1981 Christian Life Commission Seminar. Although he was fired as a result of such statements by the American Bible Society, he was later hired by Southeastern Baptist Theological Seminary to teach as a member of their summer school faculty.

* * * * *

"In the first place, Adam like original man in other Near Eastern texts, is a representative man, all of mankind poured into one individual. . . The guidance comes from literary texts outside the Bible that illuminate the meaning of the Biblical account." (p. 47)

From "Archeology and the Bible", an article in the *Broadman Bible Commentary*, Volume I, published by the Sunday School Board of the Southern

Baptist Convention. By Joseph A. Callaway, senior professor of Old Testament at Southern Baptist Theological Seminary.

* * * * *

"Careful and comparative studies of the language and text of Genesis indicate that in its present form it was written probably sometime after the period of David and Solomon." (p. 9)

"The question of the authorship of the book is more difficult. Traditionally is has been called 'The Second Book of Moses,' but there is no ancient authority for that tradition. Also, in considering the problem, we need to recognize that many of Israel's traditions were probably preserved orally for long periods before they were finally committed to writing. To the modern mind, so used to things of value being put in writing to preserve their accuracy, oral tradition seems quite risky. In the ancient world (as well as in contemporary nomadic societies) such procedures preserved the records with great accuracy. Various parts of the records were likely preserved by different groups. For example, the Levites might have kept records of materials that were of particular importance to them, while other groups preserved their materials of significance.

Moses actually wrote some Exodus material (note Ex. 17:14, 24:4 - 7; 24:37). And it is obvious that much more of the material came directly from Moses for many events are recorded of which no one else could have known. These materials also would have been preserved in both oral and written form by various circles within Israel. Somewhere along the way, perhaps at a time of national crisis, these materials were combined and committed to writing." (p.10-11)

From *Laymen's Bible Book Commentary* on Exodus, Volume 2 published by the Broadman Press, a division of the Sunday School Board of the Southern Baptist Convention and written by Dr. Robert L. Cate, Professor of Old Testament Interpretation at Golden Gate Baptist Theological Seminary.

* * * * *

"Dr. Ken Chafin: Down in Houston you could ask Hy Schachtel, retired rabbi, and Hy and I work together, we are close together, if I say does Hy know God, I think Hy knows God.

Phil Donahue: And Hy is going to enjoy his own reward with you in the everlasting world prepared for us?

Dr. Ken Chafin: I believe that, and it is probably because of what God has done in Christ." (p. 5 of transcript)

. . . .

"Phil Donahue: Are you now or have you ever been an evolutionist?

Dr. Ken Chafin: I think that the evolutionary process is the best scientific position that we have.

Phil Donahue: That's a very courageous statement for you to make, it occurs to me.

Dr. Ken Chafin: I am not a scientist.

Phil Donahue: I understand that, sir, but my guess is that would be something that would make, even those who might believe it within the community of Southern Baptists, choke on their own words.

Dr. Ken Chafin: When I look at those first eleven chapters of Genesis and the creation story, I don't see there a scientific description of how the world came to be, I see a religious description, who made it and why?" (p. 10 of transcript)

. . . .

Audience: I am not a Christian but I live by all the ethical rules. I don't harm anybody, I do all the wonderful things that we should do as citizens of this world. Am I doomed? Do you think I will go to heaven?

Judge Paul Pressler: The Scripture says very clearly that all have sinned and come short of the glory of God. I'm a sinner, everyone in this room is a sinner, and the question is, have we taken God's solution to the sin problem?

Dr. Ken Chafin: Jesus said . . .

Judge Paul Pressler: I would be very glad to talk to you afterward.

Dr. Ken Chafin: . . . to love God and to love your neighbor as yourself and that sums it all up." (p.13 of transcript)

Statements by Dr. Kenneth Chafin, professor at Southern Baptist Theological Seminary, made on the *Phil Donahue* program on June 17, 1985.

* * * * *

"The disparity between Genesis and Darwin, if it comes down to it, has really decided for all of us in Darwin's favor," (p. 67).

"And one cannot begin to understand . . . <u>provable inadequacies of Scripture</u> and historically, or its peculiar richness and power to move men to worship and to repentance unless he takes this purpose seriously." (p. 70)

"<u>But to the question, 'Are we bound by the Bible?' we must also answer no</u>, for within the dialogue of faith are other sources of insight which we must hear. Our theology is not exclusively biblical theology, even if we formally hold to an exclusive biblical authority, because we continually measure, test and select from biblical insights in the light of the belief of the church and in the light of our own experience." (p. 81)

From *Shaping Your Faith* published by Word Books and written by C.W. Christian, who is currently teaching in the Baylor University Religion Department.

* * * * *

"On the basis of this and many other conflicting accounts alone, many serious students of the Bible have rejected the dictation theory and all of its claims to literal infallibility and inerrancy. I join them in this rejection, but for reasons deeper than errors in Scripture.

This is why it borders on the heretical to speak of the Bible as the final authority in all matters religious. Again and again the Almighty is pleased to take the Bible and transform its testimony into luminous encounter, but such an event is always of his initiative and through his power. The book then becomes his word to us in an intensely personal way.

This is why the mistakes and errors and conflicting opinions of the biblical record do not invalidate it for me but rather testify to its authenticity. If God had chosen to drop down out of the sky with instant truth as a way of saving us, then we could expect an inerrant and infallible book. But he has not chosen to do so!" (p. 28-29)

By Dr. John R. Claypool from *Is the Bible a Human Book?*, edited by Joseph Green and Wayne Ward and published in 1970 by Broadman Press, a division of the Sunday School Board of the Southern Baptist Convention.

* * * * *

"Folk who have no particular religious interest are turning to courses in Transcendental Meditation, Alpha Training, Yoga, and the many related forms of spirituality. I myself have participated in some of these courses for the double purpose of trying to understand more fully what is happening today in our culture, and also for whatever practical techniques I can learn that will help me to get in touch with this Mystery, Who is at once in us, out ahead of us, up above us, and all about us."

By Dr. John Claypool from an article entitled "Getting in Touch with Power", published in February 1982, page 48 in *The Student*, which is published by The Sunday School Board of the Southern Baptist Convention.

* * * * *

"What is the nature of the error of which the Bible message is completely free? We have said that the truth which constitutes the biblical message is religious or spiritual truth. By a like token, we may now say that the error from which biblical truth is completely free is spiritual error."

"When we talk about truth without any mixture of error, we are talking about the kind of truth that has to do with man's relationship to God."

From page 4 of the February 1971 *Outreach*, a magazine published by the Sunday School Board of the Southern Baptist Convention and from an article entitled "Truth Without any Mixture of Error" written by Dr. Howard P. Colson, editorial secretary of the Sunday School Board.

* * * * *

"The institutions have become unrelated and unresponsive to the grass roots feelings. Doctrinally or inerrancy wise, the poison that Pressler and Patterson claim is biblical criticism. That's what they are after... When the seminaries started teaching biblical criticism and started talking about the documentary hypothesis and other conclusions that some who study that reach, that's when the poison started. When I came to this seminary I can remember only one professor who stood up strongly for the Mosaic authorship of the pentateuch... The seminaries have been moving in that direction. They have been going to the Continent and bringing back that stuff. That's the direction of the seminaries.

If you want the Mosaic authorship of the pentateuch and the historicity of the first eleven chapters of Genesis and Job and Jonah as historical figures, go to Mid-America Seminary. You get it there.

I may be saying something about this seminary (Southern) that is unfair, but I agree with the way it is going."

. . . .

"Can there be a Southern Baptist institution of learning where there is a balanced presentation and where the professors do not tend to influence students in a given direction? I doubt that."

Statements by Dr. C.R. Daley, former editor of the *Western Recorder*, the Kentucky State Baptist Paper, and a graduate of Southern Seminary, made July 20, 1984 to a class at Southern Baptist Theological Seminary.

* * * * *

"Whether the Bible is inerrant is of little concern to the Southern Baptist in the pew . . . . The Bible never misleads us in its message but maybe in technicalities.

Statement from the *Denver Post* by Dr. Russell Dilday, President of Southwestern Baptist Theological Seminary as reported on page 56 of the book *SBC...House on the Sand*.

* * * * *

"Two mistaken impressions have interfered with our understanding of the Book of Job. The first of these is that the "satan" mentioned in chapters 1 and 3 is the devil of the New Testament, evil personified.

. . . .

There was among them one who is called, not by a personal name, but by his duty, hassatan -- literally "the satan" or "the one who accuses."

. . . .

He was a kind of heavenly inspector of believers whose job was to expose the hypocrites.

. . . .

He was God's servant, not his enemy. (See Job 1:6)

<u>There is in the Old Testament no concept of an empire of evil opposed to</u>
<u>God, God was in charge, and "the one who accuses" was His loyal servant.</u>

From pages 6 and 7 of the July 7, 1985 *Adult Bible Study* Volume 15, Number 4, published by the Sunday School Board of the Southern Baptist Convention. The lesson was written by Dr. John I. Durham, Professor of Hebrew and Old Testament at Southeastern Baptist Theological Seminary.

* * * * *

"As trustees we have reviewed carefully the events regarding the *Adult Bible Study* interpretation of Job, especially July 7. We join with the administration in expressing our concern and regret for the errors included in this lesson," the amendment says.

Statement by the Trustees of the Sunday School Board reported in an article by Linda Lawson in a Baptist Press release dated 8/5/85.

"However, a more complete review of the entire lesson shows the manuscript by Durham is not unlike what appears in print. However, the Sunday School Board is accountable and responsible for final editing of all manuscripts."

Statement by Dr. Lloyd Elder, President of the Sunday School Board

* * * * *

Perhaps some plagues are duplicate accounts of differently transmitted traditions. For example, the Yahwist's rendering of the plagues involving the flies (8:20-32, number 4) and the cattle 9:107, number 5) is possibly duplicated by the Priestly account of the plagues involving the gnats (8:16-19, number 3) and the boils (9:8-12, number 6). While dogmatism is inappropriate on the question of duplications, one can be assured that the present ten-plague literary construction found in the text is an artificial one. (p. 476)

"When the J source and the Miriam couplet (Ex. 15:21) are juxtaposed, a probable event unfolds. The Hebrews fleeing Egypt were pursued by the Egyptians using chariots. When the Hebrews confronted a shallow body of water, a strong east wind blew back the water in a reedy, shallow area, permitting the Hebrews to cross. When the Egyptians sought to follow, their chariots were too heavy and bogged down. As the horses attempted to pull free, some of the Egyptians were thrown into the shallow water and mud. In the confusion some Egyptians died." page 478

From "The Plagues and the Crossing of the Sea," *Review and Expositor* 74 (Fall 1977) by Dr. Frank Eakin, Jr. Professor of Religion at the University of Richmond in Richmond, Virginia. The *Review and Expositor* is "A Baptist

Theological Journal" published by the Faculty of Southern Seminary in Louisville.

* * * * *

"In other words, one must come to the place that he sees the parabolic and symbolic nature of much of the Old Testament Scriptures. Genesis is to be understood in this light. It is not science. In the material attributed to J and P, the early writers were in no way trying to give a scientific or literal explanation. These stories are what Alan Richardson called parables - 'parables of nature and man in order to convey deep religious insight.'" (p. 15)

"The particular problem of chapter 5 is the longevity of the antediluvians. Various theories have been suggested, and it is impossible to be absolutely definite about any approach. It is difficult to believe that they actually lived as long as stated.

. . . . In all probability, the Priestly writer simply exaggerated the ages in order to show the glory of an ancient civilization. Mesopotamian and Babylonian stories leading to the depiction of the Flood and have a similar ten antediluvians with exceedingly long ages, often thousands of years older than any of the men mentioned in Genesis 5. The long ages of P are then an exaggerated literary medium for the purpose of expressing the view that sin brings degeneration" (pp. 58-59)

"Perhaps before any detailed statement of evidence has been presented, it already has been surmised that the present writer maintains the historicity of the patriarchal narratives, although it is impossible to deny the fact that sometimes the material may have been 'legendized' just a bit and perhaps heightened as a means of intensifying the dominant characteristics in the patriarch's life. But where heightening has occurred, it is perhaps more valuable than historical fact in that it reveals the soul and pulse of a people who are certain that they live and move under the domination of God." (p. 79)

"Apparently, Abram first went to Melchizedek, a comrad who had joined him in battle, to divide some of the spoils. That some religious understanding was involved did not appear until Melchizedek introduced it. El Elyon means 'highest God.' In the Ras Shamra text Baal is referred to as the Al'iyan (highest God), and he is also called the 'possessor of all things,' a phrase used here in verse 19. This recognizes Baal as the supreme deity in the Canaanite pantheon. It would appear, then, that in verse 19, Melchizedek was blessing Abram by the Baal, whom Melchizedek considered to be the highest god of the city state at Salem. Thus, Melchizedek was extending blessings for, and receiving, tithes in behalf of his El Elyon, to be equated with Baal. Out of courtesy, Abram did not object to giving Melchizedek and his god what Melchizedek deemed to be his share of the booty, but that was as far as he was willing to go." (pp. 115C116)

From *The Message of Genesis* published by Broadman Press, a division of the Sunday School Board of the Southern Baptist Convention and written by Dr. Ralph H. Elliott, who was then a professor at Midwestern Baptist Theological Seminary. In 1962 the trustees of Midwestern dismissed Dr. Elliott for insubordination because of his refusal to agree not to publish his book through another publisher.

* * * * *

The *Illinois Baptist* in the Spring of 1962 reviewing the statement of faith adopted by Southern Baptists and Elliott's book said as follows:

> If Dr. Elliott is correct, the Bible is in error and worse, contains planned exaggeration.

and

> But Dr. Elliott is really not the issue, nor is his book, controversial as it is. The issue is whether or not a Baptist seminary —Midwestern or any other — can appropriate to itself the right to teach young preachers as truth theories that contradict Baptist's stated doctrinal position —and continue to be supported as a Southern Baptist institution.

Dr. C.R. Daley, Editor of the *Western Recorder*, Kentucky Baptist weekly, stated:

> They (Trustees of Midwestern) must know by now that Elliott is not a glaring example of heresy among the host of safely orthodox teachers in our seminaries. If he is a heretic, then he is one of many and indeed is not at the head of the line. Professors in all our seminaries know that Elliott is in the same stream of thinking with most of them, and is more in the center of the stream than some of them.

> Elliott does not deserve a medal for extreme views compared with his fellow Southern Baptist teachers. If he deserves a medal, it is for his courage in writing a book in which he honestly expresses his views. Some teachers who would share his approach to the Bible, though not necessarily his conclusions, feel his only mistake was to write down his conclusions at this time.

* * * * *

In an article on the Southern Baptist situation in the Religion Section of *Time* magazine, November 9, 1962, it was said:

"The faculty and students of Southeastern Baptist Theological Seminary in Wake Forest, N.C., said President Sydnor L. Stealey, were 'deeply disturbed by the news (of Elliott's dismissal) and very sympathetic toward Dr. Elliott.' A faculty member at Louisville's Southern Baptist Seminary reported the faculty 'almost one hundred percent' in sympathy with Dr. Elliott's views."

Writing on Dr. Elliott's dismissal in the November 14, 1962, issue of the *Baptist Standard* of Texas, Dr. E.S. James editorially commented:

> The *Standard* believes it would have been much better if the Trustees could have agreed to base their decision on the man's theology. This paper holds that his flat denial of many plain statements in the Bible and his symbolic interpretation of other passages is not in keeping with the Baptist concept of revelation. He has a right to hold that position, but the Trustees had the right to decide whether or not he or anybody else is to be allowed to teach it in a Baptist school. . . The time has come for people in responsible positions to stop saying they believe the Bible as the Word of God and then turn right around and say some of its thoughts and messages are borrowed from pagans. This does not apply to professor Elliott any more than it does to a large number of others, but he published his views and lost his job. Some others would probably lose theirs if they should put them on the line as Elliott did. There is no doubt that it was Elliott's theology that caused his dismissal. It would have been better if the Trustees could have agreed to say so.

In commenting on the Elliott dismissal *Christianity Today,* in its April 26, 1963, issue stated:

> Some conservatives feel the Trustees evaded the real theological issues of the case and looked for another ground on which to dismiss the controversial Elliott, who is said to be more conservative than others on the same faculty who have adopted more radical critical views but have not put them in print. The same is said of some professors at Southern and Southeastern Seminaries, the New Testament Department of the latter having been charged in some quarters as being strongly Bultmannian.

* * * * *

"The Bible is not a revelation of God, it is a record of that revelation."

"Scientific and historical statements reflect the knowledge that men had of the world in that day; <u>such statements may be in error.</u>"

"The Bible, expresses God's authority, but . . . . it is authoritative only when God actually speaks to us through it." (p. 14)

From an article "Revelation and the Bible" in the January 21, 1985, issue of the *California Southern Baptist* by Dr. Fred L. Fisher, Professor of New Testament at Golden Gate Theological Seminary.

* * * * *

"Daniel presents many historical problems. In fact, the number of historical inaccuracies has led Walter Harrelson to suspect the author to have misrepresented deliberately the historical events and notices in order to provide his readers with a subtle indication that he was actually writing in a much later period with a quite different historical enemy of God's people in mind. Whether or not the errors are intentional, they illustrate that the author writes later than the events and recasts materials in light of his own purpose to inspire men of faith to endure temptation and hardship."

From page 497 of the Second Edition of *People of the Covenant*, published by The Ronald Press Company, New York and coauthored by Henry Jackson Flanders, Jr., currently teacher and former Chairman of the Religion Department at Baylor University, and Robert Wilson Capps and David Anthony Smith, both of whom are identified as teachers in the Religion Department of Furman University at the time of the publication.

This book has been a required textbook at a number of Southern Baptist Colleges and is still widely used.

* * * * *

"The simplest explanation of the problem is that the Genesis writer used an old story that explained why serpents crawl on their bellies to teach the role of the demonic in the fall of man." (p. 129)

From *The Broadman Bible Commentary* Vol. I on *Genesis* published by Broadman Press, a division of the Southern Baptist Sunday School Board and written by Dr. Clyde Francisco, deceased, a former Professor at Southern Baptist Theological Seminary, and Golden Gate Baptist Theological Seminary.

* * * * *

"I do believe that the Bible is the Word of God. I do not use the word infallible because the Bible is written by men. I would ask you to check very closely the statement 'truth without any mixture of error.' The statement says that truth is not mixed with error but it does not say that the Bible is not mixed with error. I could cite many, many instances where a literal, absolute, blind acceptance of the Bible without an understanding of human nature leads to all types of contradictions. . . . I do not believe in the plenary verbal inspiration of the Bible . .

I do not believe that Adam and Eve were one man and one woman. I believe that the terms Adam and Eve represented mankind and womankind. There are volumes and volumes of Biblical scholarship which documents this theory many years back. One of the most simple and basic answers to refute the belief that Adam and Eve were one man and one woman is the simple question 'Where did Cain get his wife?' If Adam was one man and Eve was one woman and they had two sons named Cain and Abel, who were the parents of the woman that Cain married?"

From a letter written by Jack U. Harwell, editor of the *Christian Index*, the Georgia State Baptist Paper to Mr. Joe Dunaway of Rome, Georgia, dated December 31 , 1974, as quoted in the *The Battle for the Bible* on page 95 by Dr. Harold Lindsell, published by Zondervan in 1976.

* * * * *

"I must say at the outset that I do not accept all of the Bible as literally true. (I do not believe, for example, that God ever ordered the slaughter of one's enemies.)

Modern Christians having experienced freedom in individual interpretations of the Scripture need not fear that biblical authority will be diluted by this freedom. Such fear is the chief cause of the irrational and unhistoric position of a few literalists who claim "verbal inerrancy" of the writings. On its face this is antibiblical—for it tends to make an idol of printed pages. Bibliolatry is as dangerous as any other form of idolatry.

Our faith is fragile if we let these fears shake our cherished Baptist belief that no organizational or official position may impose a rigid view upon individual believers."

By Dr. Brooks Hays, layman and former President of the Southern Baptist Convention from a chapter entitled "What the Bible Means to Me" from a book *Is the Bible a Human Book* ? published by Broadman Press, a division of the Sunday School Board of the Southern Baptist Convention, in 1970.

* * * * *

"A number of modern scholars have discounted the healing narratives and miracle stories, ascribing them to primitive mythology and early Christian embellishment. Some embellishment undoubtedly occurred. Moreover, the primitive world view and science of Jesus' day would have given a different cast to healings and other phenomena than the modern world view and science would." (p. 66)

"Indeed, it is difficult to avoid the conclusion that Jesus expected the return of the Son of Man and the consummation to occur within his own lifetime (Mark 13:30). His "error" was due to prophetic foreshortening. So urgent was his sense of mission, it seemed as if God had to consummate his kingdom immediately." (p. 76)

"Indeed, Jesus' sayings circulated as independent pericopae over a thirty to fifty year period before being collected, the churches still expecting his return. A delay of Christ's return, or Parousia, finally forced the writing down of his words but not before they had undergone considerable reshaping. What was written down, therefore, represented the mind of the early Church much more than the mind of Jesus himself. When sifted, it leaves little that one can confidently attribute to Jesus himself. (p. 78)

"The meaning of the Last Supper has been debated by scholars, and Jesus may not have commanded its repetition, as suggested by Paul." (1 Cor. 11:24, 25). (p. 96)

From *Jesus Christ*, published by Consortium and written by Dr. E. Glenn Hinson, a professor at Southern Baptist Theological Seminary.

* * * * *

"Today, it would appear, the covenant and thus the mission of the church could be defined with a greater measure of tolerance. This would not necessitate an abandonment of monotheism nor of the conviction that some sort of special revelation occurred through Israel and Christ and the church. It might necessitate, however, the acknowledgement that the one God has disclosed himself in particular ways through other cultures and religions besides these." p. 287

From *The Evangelization of the Roman Empire* by Dr. E. Glenn Hinson, Professor of Church History at Southern Seminary in Louisville, published by University Press in 1981.

* * * * *

"It is assumed herein that Deuteronomy arose in incipient form during the time of Moses, and continued within the worship center(s) as a living, growing body of oral tradition, interspersed with written legal materials, until the work of the final redactor in perhaps the sixth or seventh centuries B.C. How much material may be legitimately ascribed to Moses remains questionable."

From "Deuteronomy and the Teaching Church" an article in the *Review and Expositor* of the Fall of 1964. The magazine is "a Baptist Theological Journal" published by the Faculty of Southern Baptist Theological Seminary. The article was written by Dr. Roy Honeycutt, President of Southern Baptist Theological Seminary.

* * * * *

"It is impossible to be more specific about the particular nature of the angel of the Lord than to suggest that Elijah was so impressed with the personal, dynamic quality of the word which came to him from the Lord that he spoke of it in individual terms. Few people today would press the literal concept of physical beings who travel from heaven to earth and back again." (p. 227)

. . . .

"This narrative and those associated with Elisha have probably come to us through the hands of the sons of the prophets who treasured memories of the actions of Elijah and Elisha. In the process of oral transmission it seems likely that successive prophets transformed the original historical nucleus of various stories by the addition of materials somewhat akin to the character of stories associated with the saints at certain stages of Christian history." (p. 228)

. . . .

"Whether one interprets the stories literally or as wonder stories in the category of saga and legend, the narrative suggests that Elisha did in fact restore the life of the child. That this is most likely a wonder story in the category of saga and legend is most probable; even so, that the story should be weakened by rationalistic explanations is to miss the point of the redactor's purpose." (p. 238)

. . . .

"Gray suggests that the historical event or factual basis resting behind the miracle of the floating axe head 'may be that Elisha with a long pole or stick probed about the spot indicated (an important point in the text) until he succeeded either in inserting the stick into the socket, or, having located the hard object on the muddy bottom, moved it until the man was able to recover it' (Gray, p. 460)

This proposed reconstruction is helpful not only for understanding this single event, but as an example of the manner in which historical events were elaborated across successive generations until the narrative becomes a combination of saga and legend, inextricably interwoven." (p. 242)

From the *Broadman Bible Commentary* Vol. III on *2 Kings* published by Broadman Press, a division of the Sunday School Board of the Southern Baptist Convention and authored by Dr. Roy Honeycutt, now President of Southern Baptist Theological Seminary in Louisville, KY.

* * * * *

"It is also possible that the experience of Moses was a vision, an inner experience, in which the details were drawn from the thought patterns common to his generation: thought patterns that embraced a literal angel of the Lord and a literal flame of fire. The latter appears to be the best alternative for the present writer." (p. 312)

"On the other hand, transmission within the worshipping community has so overruled the original historical nucleus that the reconstruction of the precise historical details is now exceedingly difficult. (p. 333)

"In the context of the Moses-Pharaoh struggle, a fatal pestilence struck the Egyptian children and effected the release of the Hebrews. Through years of transmission within Israel the memory of the <u>event</u> was so <u>shaped</u> that only the first-born of both man and beast was involved. (p. 347)

"In all probability the tabernacle should be traced to the period the twelve-tribe federation at Shechem, and probably nearer the period immediately prior to the monarchy, if not the era of David himself." (p. 448)

From The *Broadman Bible Commentary* Vol. I on *Exodus* published by Broadman Press, a division of the Sunday School Board of the Southern Baptist Convention and authored by Dr. Roy Honeycutt, now President of Southern Baptist Theological Seminary.

* * * * *

"To apply the concept of infallibility to the Bible may do justice to the fact that it was inspired by a perfect God, but it does not do justice to the fact that this revelation was apprehended and written down by imperfect men. If the human writers were limited, as they themselves claimed, then their limitations belong also to a balanced doctrine of Scripture... Some contend that a recognition of the human imperfections of the biblical writers leads to a 'low' view of inspiration that is defective or even heretical in comparison with a 'high' view which sees the entire process as infallible. Quite to the contrary, <u>I would insist that the Bible is far more miraculous if it conveys the ultimate truth of God by means of ordinary men. The infallible text [i.e. infallible originals or autographs] is a theory, not a reality . . . .</u>

. . . .

<u>Distinguishing between the human and the divine in the Bible may be a tedious process, but it is absolutely essential if the fundamental difference between God as perfect and man as imperfect is to be maintained.</u> . . . . We are now in a position to answer the specific question with which we began. The cumulative force of the evidence is overwhelming: <u>No, it is not wise to call the Bible 'infallible.'</u> That term is subject to too many problems to become a controlling concept in our witness to Scripture."

From "Shall We Call the Bible Infallible?" in *The Baptist Program* of December 1970, by Dr. William Hull, a former Dean of the School of Theology at Southern Seminary in Louisville and currently the pastor of the First Baptist Church in Shreveport, Louisiana. *The Baptist Program* is published by the Executive Committee of the Southern Baptist Convention.

Dr. Hull was selected to deliver the Southern Baptist Convention Sermon in June 1982.

* * * * *

"Men today do not ordinarily hold this view of God as simply willing right and wrong, and so they cannot believe that vicarious punishment is either meaningful or moral. No illustration can be given, so far as I can tell, which makes vicarious punishment morally credible to men today. The stories of one soldier punished for another, a child punished for his brother, a man punished for his friend, may be morally praiseworthy from the point of view of the substitute, but they never are acceptable from the point of view of the punisher. It always seems morally outrageous that any judge would require a substitute. However noble the substitutes act might be, the judge's act seems despicable." p. 61

"But when Jesus said that it was necessary for him to suffer many things at the hands of the leaders, I think he meant that it was historically inevitable that he would, and that the disciples were not to be alarmed about this as it too had been taken into account by God.

Another kind of necessity about Christ's death was the necessity of his obedience.... In short, it was morally necessary for him to follow his vocation from God and this took him to the cross. Thus, the cross was necessary in terms of history and in terms of Jesus' vocation.

But that is not what some theologians have meant when they have referred to the necessity of Jesus sacrifice. They have meant that there is a logical necessity to the cross. They have meant that this was the only route open to God if he intended to save men. That is, in fact, the precise theme of Anselm's book, *Why God Became Man,* as we saw in chapter 3.

Anselm's effort and others like it, however, are misguided because <u>we simply do not know that this was the only way God could have saved men.</u> (pp. 133-134)

From *The Death of Christ* published by Broadman Press in 1978, a division of the Sunday School Board of the Southern Baptist Convention, and written by Dr. Fisher Humphries, presently a professor at New Orleans Baptist Theological Seminary.

* * * * *

"Most of the Old Testament references to such angels are found in the narrative portions of the Pentateuch, or the apocryphal material of Ezekiel, Zechariah, and Daniel. Apparently the angels were not classified as either evil or good but simply were viewed as God's obedient servants, even when testing or chastising human beings.

However, during the Exile and the Post-exilic age, the doctrine of angels changed radically. The dualistic (good god and evil god) and astrological influences of the Zorastrians (SOHR-uh-WAS-tree-uhn; a Persian religion) brought about the concept of a struggle for sovereignty both in the heavens and on the earth. Even the angels were divided into two camps; the good (led by Michael), and the evil (led by Satan). Thus the concept of Satan was transformed from that of public prosecutor for God into chief adversary of God." (pages 26-27)

From an article entitled "Lucifer" in the Fall 1984 *Biblical Illustrator* by Dr. Harry B. Hunt, Jr., assistant professor of Old Testament at Southwestern Baptist Theological Seminary.

* * * * *

"The Bible contains world-knowledge and God-knowledge. World-knowledge is knowledge of the world which man acquires through his own discoveries, memories, and records. This world-knowledge reflects the limits of biblical man's scientific understanding of the world at the time he wrote. But such limited, inadequate scientific knowledge does not belong to the revealed knowledge of God which is the main theme and purpose of the Bible. God-knowledge is knowledge of God which he alone gives in the mystery and wonder of revelation and inspiration. This treasure we have in earthen vessels that the glory might belong unto God, says the apostle Paul (2 Cor. 4:7). This earthen vessel—the language of the writer and the limitations of his world-knowledge—is not to be confused with the divine message of revelation itself. The human inadequacies in the limited 'scientific' knowledge of the biblical writers can and must be corrected by later discoveries. The limited scientific knowledge is one of the most human elements in the Bible. To correct the limited science of the biblical writers leaves untouched the essential story of the Bible.... Many Bible students recognize that there are two accounts of creation in Genesis. The first, from 1 :1 to 2:4a, appears to have been written later than the second, which is from 2:4b to 2:25. The older account in Genesis 2 is more primitive and childlike in its concepts and picturizations of God. Here man is created before any other living creatures . . . . But the stories were not given as a scientific account of creation as such. If one tries to take those accounts as literal scientific truth he does violence to the real intent of the Bible itself. If one attempts this, which account is to be taken as scientifically accurate, Genesis 1 or 2? The order is exactly opposite in each. Both cannot be scientifically accurate at the same time. Why then did God give one story which contradicts the true scientific account—if we could tell which one is? . . . It is a drastic mistake to make the limited science of the biblical writer part of the revelation of himself which God is giving. If one does this, later scientific discoveries will undermine trust in the Bible as a book of truth." pp. 94-97

From "The Bible and Human Science" in *Is The Bible A Human Book?* by Dr. John Lewis and edited by Joseph Green and Wayne Ward, published by Broadman Press, a division of the Sunday School Board of the Southern Baptist Convention, in 1970. John Lewis is Pastor of First Baptist Church in Raleigh,

North Carolina. Editor Joseph Green is the former editor of *Bible Study Books* with Broadman Press, and Editor Wayne Ward is Professor of Christian Theology at Southern Seminary.

* * * * *

"Some of these misconceptions were minor and relatively harmless. Others had a tendency to distort the nature of God himself and were, therefore, not so harmless. One of these ancient concepts which, in my judgement, falls in the latter category is propitiation. Since it is closely tied in with that which we commemorate on Good Friday, it is appropriate that we focus upon this term and its effects upon Christian theology." (p. 1)

. . . .

"The view of Jesus' death as a propitiation of God leaves us in the spectator's bleachers applauding a job well done and untouched by the whole process. This leaves a lot to be desired, to put it mildly." (p. 3)

. . . .

"What I'm saying is that Jesus' death on the cross did not make God either willing or able to forgive--It was the highest expression of that willingness and ability. To make Jesus' death a propitiator sacrifice to satisfy some abstract quality in God called 'justice' or 'righteousness ' or 'Holiness' is a first cousin to blasphemy, in my judgment." (p. 7)

. . . .

"Again I say to you that God as revealed in Jesus Christ has never wanted or needed propitiatory sacrifice. What He does want is penitent hearts that He can so fill with His love that that love will overflow upon every life that touches ours. Jesus' death on the cross is the reflection of a love that knows no bounds—which does not shrink back even from the death itself—in order to win those He loves. (p.9)

Chapel address in the spring of 1983 at Georgetown College, Elizabethtown, Kentucky. By Dr. Joel Lunceford, professor of Greek and Old Testament.

* * * * *

"I argue that Satan as a separate being or spiritual reality does not exist. My own feeling is that God exists in the universe and that he is the only spirit that does exist. Evil in the universe is a result of personal choices we make as individuals, not a result of demonic forces. . . My own conclusion is that all of these occult beliefs are human inventions or creations based either on fear or trickery."

From "Students Find Occult Bewitching." March 7, 1974. Quoting Dr. David Moore, Chairman of the Department of Religion at William Jewell

College in Liberty, Missouri, by reporter Virginia Stollings of the *Kansas City Star.*

* * * * *

"At the heart of Patterson's theory is the presumption that the first two chapters of the Bible are not scientific statements but religious and political tracts.

Patterson compared what he said were the Bible's two creation stories to the wartime speeches of Winston Churchill that rallied support for the Allies. 'Both Churchill's speeches and the Genesis stories,= he said, 'were superb examples of political rhetoric, not historic fact.'"

From the *Houston Chronicle,* page 8, section 1 on Wednesday, February 4, 1982 referring to remarks by Dr. Bob Patterson, presently teacher in the Baylor University Religion Department, made at Texas a Christian Life Commission Seminar at Southwestern Seminary.

* * * * *

"She said that unlike fundamentalist scriptural interpretations, which rely on the English translation of ancient writings, she and many other pastors have been trained in Baptist seminaries to seek the actual meaning of words in the context of the culture in which they were written...

Thus, the taboo against women that goes back to prehistoric tribal religions carried over into the life of the ancient Hebrews and was written into their patriarchal religion...

'The Hebrews were deathly afraid of blood. That's why they had so many blood sacrifices,' she said."

Interview in the *Richmond Times Dispatch,* June 1984 with Dr. Ann P. Rosser, Graduate of Southeastern Seminary, who taught at Southeastern Seminary in the spring of 1984. She is co-Pastor of a church in the Richmond, Virginia area with her husband.

* * * * *

"This does not mean we use phrases like inerrancy, for from the point of view of secular historical recording it is not inerrant. Furthermore, theologically it is not inerrant; otherwise it would not be history."

"It is of value, for example, to know that Isaiah and Deutero-Isaiah were two distinct prophets belonging to different times and associated with very different movements of Hebrew history."

From an article entitled "Theological Emphasis of the Last Three Decades" printed in the Spring 1981 issues of the *Review and Expositor,* the Theological Journal published by the Faculty of Southern Baptist Theological Seminary and written by Dr. Eric Rust, professor emeritus at Southern Baptist Theological Seminary.

* * * * *

"The Garden. Well, was there a Garden? Now if I listen to what the scientist tells me, I can't say yea or nay. I mean, this is, there may have been a Garden. But, after all, as my young hopeful said the other day—well, about two years ago—when I told her about Noah, 'Well, that means that the story of the Garden is parable, too, Daddy.' I said, 'Yes.' She said, 'Well, that explains where Cain got his wife from.' Now, really, I mean if there was only one Adam created and Eve was made out of his rib, well, heaven help us, ever counted your ribs to find out? I mean seriously, I mean . . . You see, take it literally, and you land yourself, you make yourself a laughing stock for intelligent people."

By Dr. Eric Rust, Professor Emeritus of Christian Philosophy at Southern Seminary. From "The Challenge of Modern Science," a recorded address to a pastors' conference at the University of Richmond in 1959.

* * * * *

"I do not measure up. I do not hold to an inerrant view of the Bible."

. . . .

"In fact for years we have been divided on inerrancy. We just did not know it."

Presidential address by Dr. Cecil Sherman to the North Carolina Baptist Convention as quoted in the *Biblical Recorder.*

* * * * *

"Sherman said the call for 'parity' by current SBC President Jimmy Draper, wouldn't be parity. It would be war. Those things (widely divergent theological and doctrinal interpretations) don't live well together. For example, three fundamentalists and three nonfundementalist at Southern Seminary would not make for a happy institution."

Statement by Dr. Cecil Sherman, pastor of First Baptist Church, Asheville, North Carolina, quoted from *The Religious Herald,* the state paper for Virginia, December 9, 1982.

* * * * *

"A teacher who might also be led by Scripture not to believe in the Virgin Birth should not be fired." "It (the Virgin Birth) is in two Gospels, but not in two others," he added. "Did Mark and John make a mistake by forgetting to list it? If the Virgin Birth is desperately important, (Mark and John) must have erred."

Statement by Dr. Cecil Sherman, quoted in *Christianity Today,* August 5, 1983.

* * * * *

"Women: The gospel is liberation.

Female Liturgist: We don't have to stay in our place.

Women: The gospel frees us from the law.

Female Liturgist: Jesus broke the law and tradition in his treatment of women.

Women: Jesus was a feminist!

Male Liturgist: When you are free, then we are free. We need to be free from ourselves.

We need to discard our "masculine role" and discover who we really are.

Male: The gospel is liberation.

Male Liturgist: We are free to share our responsibilities.

Male: The gospel frees us from the law.

Male Liturgist: Jesus challenged the status quo.

Male: Jesus calls us to full humanity.

All: We reject the notion that one sex should build bridges and the other keep the home.

We reject the idea of "proper roles," for roles belong to the realm of law, and freedom belongs to the gospel.

We believe the words of the New Testament that in God's time and place there is no male and female no mankind or womankind, but simply humanhood, simply God's people.

We can and will be more human.

We will find ways of being men and women together."

From a litany used in the Seminary chapel worship service at Southeastern Seminary on March 17, 1983.

* * * * *

"It is a great pleasure and honor for me to introduce a friend, Mr. Samuel Dorr, today. Mr. Dorr is the cofounder and President of Dignity-Integrity, the Louisville Chapter. Dignity-Integrity is a Christian support group mainly based in the Roman Catholic and Episcopal community for homosexuals and their friends. Dignity-Integrity is also a good way of describing Sam Dorr as I know him. He is a faithful, loyal and committed church person, a perceptive and sensitive teacher and a loving Christian brother. I hope we can hear him in that spirit today."

Mr. Dorr says later: "Homosexuality is my sexual orientation. What I do with that is preference....

"I am a gay Christian.

"It (my homosexuality) is a pilgrimage. I am still on that road and I hope it will never end."....

"We do not encourage celibacy as opposed to another lifestyle or another option of sexual expression or non-expression. . . . .

"Homosexuals are assaulted in that they cannot express their feelings publicly as do heterosexuals."...

"I do not condemn someone who seeks more than one homosexual partner."...

"I am not a Biblical literalist so I would not say that God thinks homosexuality is wrong."

The introduction is by a young lady identified only as Paula, a student at Southern Baptist Theological Seminary in Louisville introducing the speaker at the official meeting of the Ethics Club of the Seminary.

* * * * *

Changing Views of Southern Seminary Students

	Diploma Students	First Year	Final Year	Ph.D.–Th.M. Students
I know God really exists: I have no doubts about it.	100%	74%	65%	63%
Jesus is the Divine Son of God: I have no doubts about it.	100%	87%	63%	63%
I believe the miracles happened as the Bible said they did.	96%	61%	40%	37%
Jesus was born of a virgin: completely true.	96%	66%	33%	32%
Belief in Jesus Christ as Savior: absolutely necessary	100%	85%	60%	59%
	(p. 52–54)	(p. 60–61)	(p. 63–64)	(p. 70–71)

From a Masters of Theology Thesis by Southern Baptist Theological Seminary student, Noel Wesley Hollyfield, Jr., in July 1976 and approved on August 26, 1976 by G. Willis Bennett, Chairman, E. Glenn Hinson, and Henlee Barnette, professors at Southern Baptist Theological Seminary.

* * * * *

"And as you read the Old Testament it is one account after another of this kind of sin and this kind of interpretation of what was happening as God's way of striking back. To ascribe such terrible things to God was itself another evidence of how sin had obscured man's understanding of himself. Man was so sinful that he could not see that he was a son of God, nor could he understand what the Father was truly like." (p.20)

"One way to deal with this kind of crisis is to remember that doctrine is never fixed once and for all. It is always changing, though perhaps not within the time-span of your intellectual crisis or even within your lifetime. But over the long haul, doctrine does and will continue to change. This means that a person might be able to stay in a church during a time when many of the expressed beliefs are contrary to what he believes. He can do that honestly because he knows that those beliefs can be changed. And more, he can have a part in encouraging the change. . . . Then there is another point to be made. In your brief life you cannot be responsible for the whole theology of the church. If you can accept this kind of reasoning it will make it possible for you to repeat statements of faith with some clear conscience. It is not in dishonesty that you do this kind of thing. It is an admission that at the doctrinal level we cannot have every statement or belief agree in every detail with what we believe. (p. 31)

"If I had to state the major goals that a person might set for himself in being a disciple in our world, I would list these:

1. To work for peace wherever there is war
2. To work at distributing the wealth of the world
3. To work at assuring civil liberties to all people
4. To work at a healthy balance in the use of the environment
5. To work toward a moral climate that matches the dignity of man.

Do you think these goals are directed toward major world problems that God is interested in seeing solved?" (p. 72)

From *Being a Disciple*, published by Broadman Press and written by Dr. Temp Sparkman, now a professor at Midwestern Baptist Theological Seminary.

* * * * *

"The cross has saving value as Christ enables us to die to self that we might live to God. Substitution is a serviceable term for the death of Jesus if properly employed. To transfer to it all that belongs to the word in current usage is to obscure the New Testament doctrine. In modern sports, a player may be taken from the game and be replaced by a "substitute". But Jesus never becomes our substitute in that sense." (p. 145)

"William J. Wolfe has well observed: God did not punish Christ. It is monstrous to picture the Father deliberately inflicting punishment on his beloved obedient Son as a scapegoat." (p. 15)

From *New Testament Theology* by Dr. Frank Stagg, a professor emeritus at Southern Baptist Theological Seminary, published in 1962 by Broadman Press, a division of the Sunday School Board of the Southern Baptist Convention.

* * * * *

"To follow Jesus Christ, you have no option but to be a humanist."

From an article on Page 1 of the February 24, 1982 *Fort Worth Star-Telegram* quoting Dr. Frank Stagg, a professor emeritus at Southern Baptist Theological Seminary.

* * * * *

"In discussions with his audience, which had a woman-to-man ratio of more than two to one, Steely was asked to comment on I Timothy 2:11-15. Steely said he would have to say to the writer: 'Paul, your logic doesn't persuade me.'

The teacher said Paul 'does the same thing in I Corinthians, and, of all things, calls on the Law (as justification) which in Galatians, he asks us to forget.'

'Such logic is not true to his (Paul's) teaching the gospel.'

'It seems bold, bodacious even, to take issue with the apostle,' admitted Steely, but quickly took gentle issue with a conferee who referred to Paul's writing as 'wrong.'

'I would never use the language 'wrong.' referring to scripture,' said Steely. 'He is just not coming through with the pure, undiluted strain of the gospel. Paul was not perfect. One reason Paul is my hero is that he was. fallible. There is none perfect but our Lord Himself.'

Steely said there are 'hard sayings' in scripture (about the role of women) and 'we cannot pretend they do not exist,' but observed that some of these words of Paul 'are in direct conflict with Paul's own words ... and in conflict with what I think is his (Paul's) overall conception of the gospel.'"

From page 11 of an article in the *Religious Herald* (Virginia State Baptist Paper) of March 28, 1985 reporting remarks of Dr .John E. Steely, Professor of historical theology at Southeastern Baptist Theological Seminary for 29 years. The meeting was held March 11, 1985 in Norfolk, Virginia and sponsored by the Virginia Department of Christian Life Concerns.

* * * * *

"Careful and comparative studies of the language and text of Genesis indicate that in its present form it was written probably sometime after the period of David and Solomon." (p.9)

From *Layman's Bible Book Commentary: Genesis*, Vol. 1 published by Broadman Press, a division of the Sunday School Board of the Southern Baptist Convention and written by Dr. Sherrill G. Stevens

* * * * *

"A careful reading of the hymn in its entirety (vv. 1-18) leads us to believe that its final composition may have belonged to later times. Its verses or lines may have grown with the years. For instance, while the hymn was given soon after the crossing of the Red Sea, verses 13-16 recount how God protected Israel during the days of her sojourn in the wilderness.

In verse 17, the worshiper remembers the Temple and the worship of God in Jerusalem during the time of Solomon. Much like a ballad, the song would have covered many years. In its entirety, the song praises God for his goodness to Israel." (p. 51).

"However, such a characteristic was not an essential feature. For instance, Revelation was written by John. He wrote in the last decade of the first century. Daniel, however, may be an assumed name, although there are some who think that Daniel was the actual author." (p. 61)

From the July, August, September, 1979, Convention Uniform Series, *Young Adult Sunday School Quarterly*, Volume 21, Number 4 of the Sunday School Board of the Southern Baptist Convention.

* * * * *

"When Paul wrote his personal letter to Philemon or his letter to one of the churches, he obviously was not trying to be a learned theologian. He wrote in the heat of his feelings and used language to make a point and to move to action, not as an attempt to set forth a reasoned system of thought. Therefore, what he says in one passage may not coincide exactly with what he says somewhere else. Whole theological systems have been founded on passages which were treated as accurate, theological formulations, when the writer would have been horrified to see his words so used and abused." (p. 10)

"The validity of the biblical message does not depend upon the accuracy of the world view or scientific concepts of the men who wrote God's message. Rather, the Bible brings a spiritual message which must be judged on the basis of spiritual reality—not scientific accuracy." (p. 11)

From *How to Study Your Bible*, copyright 1979 by the Sunday School Board of the Southern Baptist Convention.

* * * * *

The survey indicates that 90% of the students drink and 8% acknowledged they have a drinking problem. 64% said that within a three-month period they had driven while drinking too much and 30% confessed to having missed at least one class due to a hangover in that same time span.

The results of a survey of students at Wake Forest University as reported in the *Southern Baptist Advocate* of April, 1984.

* * * * *

"'Biblical inerrancy is not what we think is important,' said Dr. Wayne E. Ward, a professor of Christian theology at Louisville's Southern Seminary who admitted that none of his colleagues would likely hold to the inerrancy of the Bible."

From an article from the *Dallas Times Herald* written by Bruce Buursma, Staff Writer in May or June 1979.

* * * * *

"CASE #1: One professor taught that "Paul, the Apostle, was an 'egomaniac' and many of his writings should be discounted due to his particular 'personality' problem." For example, in class he mocked Paul (with a gleam of ridicule in his eyes and an emotional quiver in his voice), "Can't you hear him, 'I, Paul, am an old man...I am the chief of sinners.'" Then, he flatly stated, "Paul did not really believe that any more than I believe I'm the chief of sinners."

CASE #2: In another class, I listened day after day and week after week to a professor in seminary ridicule those who believed in the Biblical View of Creation. He stated clearly, "Evolution is not a theory. It is a fact!" As he puffed away on his pipe, striking an intellectual pose, he laughed at evangelists by name-including "hell-fire preachers like Billy Graham"—and called the evangelical magazine "Christianity Today" a "periodical so out of date it should be called Christianity Yesterday."

CASE #3: On another occasion, the professor declared before us all, "I'm sick of all this bloody religion! We sing these ridiculous songs like 'The blood, the blood, nothing but the blood.' I wish we could get every church in the SBC to tear them out of our hymnbooks." Not only did I stand and publicly disagree with the professor, but I went directly to the office of the president to complain about what had happened and to communicate my feelings that "we were paying good money (God's money from our churches) to sit as students under unbelief and a mockery of the blood of Christ." Even as a student 15 years ago I knew that Biblical authority had been blatantly denied.

CASE #4: Another professor, when pinned down by questioning, believed and taught the Bartian view of universalism (or universal salvation) that "when Christ entered the world he came to save the whole world; therefore, the whole world will be saved, whether or not they profess to be 'believers.'"

CASE #5: I was shocked in class when a professor clearly communicated that he did not believe that "Lazarus was really dead in John 11. He had only fainted." He went on to explain that he doubted other Biblical "miracles" and said, "They must be understood in light of an existential and spiritual message of truth to the individual, whether or not the actual events are true."

CASE #6: I could enumerate many more illustrations of doubt or denial of Biblical truth in Southern Baptist institutions supported by the prayers and finances of godly people throughout the Convention. For example, there is the denial of the virgin birth. A professor friend told me that "80% of the Academy of New Testament Professors do not believe in the virgin birth."

Statements of his personal experience at Southern Baptist Theological Seminary from 1966 to 1970 by Rev. Jim Wilson, pastor of Delaney Street Baptist Church of Orlando, Florida, as recorded in the *Southern Baptist Advocate* of May 1983.

VOTES FOR PRESIDENT OF THE SOUTHERN BAPTIST CONVENTION

1979-1998

Houston 1979

Adrian Rogers	6,129	51.36%
Robert Naylor	2,791	23.39%
Bill Self	1,673	14.02%
Abner McCall	643	5.39
Doug Watterson	474	3.97
Ed Price	223	1.87

St. Louis 1980

Bailey Smith	5,739	51.67%
Frank Pollard	2,382	23.45%
James Pleitz	1,516	13.65%
Richard Jackson	1,089	9.81%
Stan Boone	213	1.92%
Jimmy Stroud	167	1.50%

Los Angeles 1981

Bailey Smith	6,934	60.4%
Abner McCall	4,524	39.30%

New Orleans 1982

Jimmy Draper	8,081	46.03%
Duke McCall	6,124	34.88%
Perry Sanders	1,725	9.83%
John Sullivan	1,625	9.26%

(Run-off)
Jimmy Draper	8,331	56.97%
Duke McCall	6,292	43.03%

Pittsburgh 1983
Jimmy Draper	Unopposed

Kansas City 1984
Charles Stanley	7,692	52.18%
Grady Cothen	3,874	26.28%
John Sullivan	3,174	21.53%

Dallas 1985
Charles Stanley	24,453	55.3%
Winfred Moore	19,795	44.7%

Atlanta 1986
Adrian Rogers	21,201	54.22%
Winfred Moore	17,898	45.78%

St. Louis 1987
	1987	
Adrian Rogers	13,980	59.97%
Richard Jackson	9,331	40.03%

San Antonio 1988
Jerry Vines	15,804	50.53%
Richard Jackson	15,112	48.32%
James Craig	276	.88%
Anis Shorrash	82	.21%

Las Vegas 1989
Jerry Vines	10,754	56.58%
Daniel Vestal	8,248	43.39%

New Orleans 1990
Morris Chapman	21,471	57.68%
Daniel Vestal	15,753	42.32%

Atlanta 1991
    Morris Chapman   Unopposed

Indianapolis 1992
    Edwin Young   9,981   62.05%
    Jess Moody   3,485   21.66%
    Nelson Price   2,619   16.28%

Houston 1993
    Edwin Young   Unopposed

Orlando 1994
    Jim Henry   9,876   55.18%
    Fred Wolfe   8,023   44.82%

Atlanta 1995
    Jim Henry   Unopposed

New Orleans 1996
    Tom Elliff   Unopposed

Dallas 1997
    Tom Elliff   Unopposed

Salt Lake City 1998
    Paige Patterson   Unopposed

INDEX*

*This index list does not contain Pressler family members or relatives.